Chocolate
the definitive guide

SARA JAYNE-STANES

grub Street

Grub Street • London

To Richard, a very serious chocolate lover indeed, without whose patient munching this book would never have known no end.

Published by
Grub Street
4 Rainham Close
London SW11 6SS

Email food@grubstreet.co.uk
www.grubstreet.co.uk

British Library Cataloguing in Publication Data

Jayne-Stanes, Sara
Chocolate: the definitive guide
1. Chocolate 2. Cookery (Chocolate)
1. Title
641.3'374

ISBN 1-904943-12-8

Food Photography by Marc Stanes
Illustrations by Bee Willey

Printed and bound in India by Replika Press Pvt Ltd.

Author's Note
It is customary for the seeds or beans to be known as cacao, and they will be referred to as such in this book. However when they reach the factory and are processed they become cocoa and chocolate.

The publisher wishes to thank El Rey for kind permission to reproduce photographs from their archive; Pauline Bewick RA for the permission to reproduce the picture on page 81 (Venus Nipples) and Peter Williams and Wedgwood for the china used for photography.

CONTENTS ·

ACKNOWLEDGEMENTS

My mother, Lilian for unwavering belief in my literary abilities. Richard, my husband, for loving patience and support and eating himself near to death by chocolate! Marie-Pierre Moine, friend, author and food writer - for recipe testing, advice, time translating and interpreting and holding hands. Anne Dolamore of Grub Street, friend and publisher, for encouragement. Teresa Chris, friend and agent - for listening. Michel Roux MOF, Chef Proprietor of The Waterside Inn, for support and inspiration. Professor John Huber, Senior Lecturer, Thames Valley University Academy, for listening and endless advice. Dervila O'Grady, friend and colleague - for support over and above the line of duty.

Carole Bloom, US friend and food writer, for her support and encouragement and writing about chocolate in the States for this book. Robin Dand, formerly with the International Cocoa Organisation - for advice, endless conversations about cocoa and chocolate and substantiating 'Futures'. Brian J. Turner, Chef and television personality, Prop. Turner's and Chairman of the Academy of Culinary Arts. Claire Clark MOGB, Head Pastry Chef at Claridges for support and recipe testing, nothing was ever too much trouble. Ernst Bachmann, Pastry Chef Prop. Bachmann's Patisserie. Martin Dockett, Pastry Chef Proprietor, La Glacerie for expert advice and recipes. Graham Dunton, Pastry Chef, Dohler. Ian Ironside Pastry Chef, Gleneagles. Robert Mey, Pastry Chef Retired, Hyatt Carlton.

Michael Nadell, Pastry Chef Prop. Nadell Pâtisserie. Yolande Stanley, Pastry Chef and Lecturer, Thames Valley University. Frances Bissell, Matthew Fort and Gary Rhodes for generosity of praise. Roman Beldowsky, friend for endless translating from 'Mexican' and Spanish texts. Michael Aldridge, Director Food Services, Eurostar and Dagmar Woodward, General Manager, Inter-Continental Paris for invaluable help with Parisian chocolate. John Kealey, for expert help and advice with correcting and proofing the manuscript. Cath Kerry, Australian chef and food writer, for writing about chocolate in Australia for this book. Cherry Ripe, Australian food writer and author - for information on chocolate in Australia. Dr Peter Rogers, for authenticating, although not necessarily agreeing with, some of my research. Henrietta Green, friend, journalist and broadcaster - for endless column inches about my chocolate and for support. Toby King, Ritter Courivaud for the advice and the Cacao Barry Chocolate. Jean Louis Lagneau, *chocolatier* par excellence. Cacao Barry Chocolate - for advice, lessons and recommendations about the best chocolate shops in Paris. Ana Lara Aguilar and Lupita Ayella of the Mexican Ministry of Tourism, for masterminding my research trip to Mexico. Cathy Matos, of Cathy Matos Mexican Tours, for help on a trip to Mexico and the flights. Glynn Christian, author and food writer and friend, without whom this book would not have happened in the first place. John Bednall, Managing Director, Restaurant Show for Chocolates New York. Sarah Foden, Librarian, Cadbury Limited. John Newman OBE, Director and Secretary BCCCA.

Ivan Day, academic and passionate food historian - for information on 17th and 18th century chocolate confectionery. Marguerite Patten OBE - for advice on chocolate during World War 2. Robin Weir, food writer and historian. Elisabeth Luard, artist, food writer and friend. Edward Wohlmuth of Barry Callebaut - for copious advice and authenticating Chocolate Defs. Paul Halliwell and Beverly Dunkley of Barry Callebaut - for information and chocolate. David Lyell of Town and Country Fine Foods for obtaining images from El Rey. Bunny Rush and Andrew Nott of Express and Clotted Cream Dairy Company for ingredients. Roz Denny, for support and testing of a dozen recipes. Nicola Porter, The Chocolate Society. Terry Farris for recipe testing. Sanjeev Ramchandani of Keylink for chocolate etc for recipes testing. Dr. Basil Bartley, for specialist advice on the origins of chocolate and the genetics of the bean. Anton Mosimann for unlimited access to his library at the Mosimann Academy. Joe Hyam for advice and historical recipes, Guy Salter for Laurent Perrier, Olivier de Loisy and Isabelle Calleja for the Chocolaterie de l'Opéra. Alice Wooledge Salmon with help and advice on my Paris trip. Guy Parker for posing so naturally for the ice cream shot. Sarah Crouchman, Head Pastry Chef, Churchill Inter-Continental, for the superb preparation of the dishes for the photographs which were taken by Marc Stanes.

Thank you all.

FOREWORD

During 20 years of conversations with Sara Jayne, the subject somehow always has come around to chocolate. Then when it was not enough to look, learn and talk about chocolate, in 1983 she started making chocolates. Chocolate truffles to be precise and they were, and still are the best truffles I have eaten anywhere in the world. They are sensual and seductive with tastes exploding - they are *Sara à la bouche*.

Her next project was this book. I knew it would be a masterpiece but it is more. This definitive book contains everything I have always wanted to read about chocolate, from its history to wonderful luscious recipes from her friends and chefs. Sara's words talk to you, they are as edible as the chocolate that she writes about.

To summarise what must have taken years to write, I will just say that in my opinion, this unique book is the most important reference on chocolate in the world today.

MICHEL ANDRÉ ROUX • MOF

INTRODUCTION

Chocolate is unique. The main secret of its exquisite pleasure is that it is the only substance to melt at blood temperature, gently exploding into a warm, sensual liquid, filling your mouth with an incomparable, hedonistic feeling that is so good that you just want to go on and on savouring it. That's chocolate ecstasy, and this glorious and deeply satisfying experience has earned chocolate a role in everything from seduction to health to politics, religion and slavery. Of course, we're talking really 'proper' chocolate here - the intensely dark sort of chocolate, that floods the tastebuds with overtones of spice, fruit and cocoa - not the over-sugary, commercial chocolate, on which the majority of us chocolate lovers have been weaned and 'tastewashed' since birth. Sugar merely kills the taste.

I eat food for pleasure, as well as to live. I feel about food like some people feel about skiing, mountaineering or other adrenaline-exciting pursuits. I am an absolute purist when it comes to chocolate - suffering for my beliefs and happily resisting anything but the real thing, paying little or no heed to the cost. It was not always so. I vividly recall my young schooldays when an aunt would come and take me out for the afternoon. It was always some boring trip (or so I naively thought at the time) - a visit to the zoo, or a museum, or Harrods, but always, always adequately compensated by a visit to the Chocolate House in Regent Street (long gone, sadly). Here I would revel in the largest, gooiest chocolate eclair and a hot chocolate drink. This was life! The steaming brown liquid would arrive in a tall glass heaped with clouds of the palest butteriest whipped cream, just beginning to melt and mingle with the chocolate, and finished with the obligatory dark cocoa powder and a chocolate flake.

And then, during my final year at school, when at last I was deemed old and wise enough to travel the hour and a half from home every day, I would eke out my 2/6d (12½p) weekly pocket money at 6d per day, wantonly spent on chocolate 'feasts'. In those days, you could buy a Mars Bar and a Bounty and a Milky Way, all for 6d (2½p). I cherished and savoured every mouthful in an attempt to make my rations last the length of the journey. School friends might use the time for study or homework, but I would just sit on the top of the bus (it was always on top of the bus - you could see the world go by better that way) oblivious to life outside while I bit into the ethereal cocoa confections - Caramelo, Wagon Wheels, Aero, Mars Bar, Toblerone, Crunchie, Caramac, Flake, Walnut Whirls, Fruit & Nut, Bournville Plain - whatever. Black Magic was a treat at Christmas. I drew the line at Milk Tray but loved Kit Kat. I never shared - that would have been inconceivable!

The meaning of the world calorie was not in my personal dictionary, and alas, although not surprisingly, all this surreptitious chocolate consumption took its toll and by my late teens I was a podgy example of over-indulgence. I gave it up in an effort to achieve a more fashionable figure. After a few weeks I did not miss it one scrap and strangely enough, withdrawal symptoms were never a problem.

Fifteen years or so later, when not a morsel of cocoa had passed my lips, I met the Académie Culinaire, that elite association of Head Chefs, Pastry Chefs and Restaurant Managers, passionate about food standards, cooking and service and education - now the Academy of Culinary Arts. At the same time I had a boyfriend who could never get enough chocolate and he persuaded me to make some chocolate petits fours for a dinner party. Two of our guests had just opened a specialist food shop locally and asked me to make some to sell, which I did. To my utter amazement, they took off. Thanks to the talents and teaching of some of the members of the Academy, like Michel Roux, Professor John Huber, Ian Ironside, Michael Nadell, Martin Dockett, Claire Clark, and others, I learned what real chocolate was about. Now I am joyfully re-acquainted with chocolate again but this time to the real stuff - pure 70% cocoa solids or thereabouts - chocolate which gives me a sensory 'hit' every time I eat it. The sophisticated elegance of Valrhona, Cacao Barry, Chocolaterie de l'Opéra and Lindt.

As a chocolate maker I am often asked to describe my own favourite chocolate and chocolate confectionery. You can understand that fifteen years' professional experience has inevitably influenced my appreciation of chocolate. I have become passionate about fine, serious chocolate, made with a good quality bean and a modest amount of sugar. It is one of the world's greatest natural ingredients and like a fine wine, in which the better the grape, the *terroir* and the love invested, the better the wine, so it is the same for chocolate. For its quality and character, chocolate very much depends on the variety of the cacao bean, its geographical source, the way it has been cultivated and finally the methods employed to make the bean into chocolate.

And so, you may ask, what is my definition of a perfect chocolate confection? It's got to be hand-made - I know all about economies of scale but I don't think a machine has yet been invented or perfected that can touch a man's passion or skilled and practised hand. The centre should be enrobed with a thin coating of 60% - 70% couverture made from a *criollo* bean grown somewhere in Central or South America - possibly Mexico or Venezuela. There should be the sight of a glossy finish. And the smell of the chocolate. It should have the perfume of a lush, full and fruity dark richness with intense cocoa-y overtones and a balance of spicy acidity. The bite should be crisp and clean through its chocolate coat, which after all is only the means to hold its 'soul' - yielding to the charms of the filling such as a truffle which should be light and creamy in texture and intensely chocolatey in flavour. The combination of flavours should be clean and distinct with a long clearly defined aftertaste. I know that some swear by

chocolates straight from the fridge while others believe that this is sacrilege and chocolate must be enjoyed at room temperature. I'm one of the former. Holding a bite of cool chocolate on the tongue soon brings it to a contrasting body heat - the temperature in the mouth at which it gently explodes. If it's cloying, syrupy and sticks to the roof of your mouth it's nothing short of an impostor.

I found a soul mate, Jeanne Bourin, the French writer and chocolate lover, who admits in *The Book of Chocolate* the splendid rationalisation of chocolate and all its glories: "I came into this world with a relish for life and its gifts, and chocolate happens to be one of the most tempting that one can possibly imagine.

Moreover, is it not our fate in this world to wrestle incessantly, endlessly, with temptation? When it is not gluttony that torments me, it is the vanity which incites me to diet in order to lose the surplus pounds brought on by my first indulgence. Torn between the desire to give myself up to the temptation of chocolate and that of losing weight, I experience ups and downs in which rigour and gustatory pleasure alternate. However, I must admit that, as the years pass, rigour seems to me to be increasingly distasteful and also in the long run, pointless!"

Barely a handful of books have been written about the complex subject of chocolate as opposed to collections of chocolate recipes. Maybe it's because chocolate doesn't fit in the template of the historian or simply because of the centuries' old puritanical perception that food and drink are not subjects which literature should foster or champion. Apart from Michael and Sophie Coe, most authors have not tackled the whole story - the history, geography, social and religious elements. I hope I have gone some way to address this and why the world's favourite food is the world's favourite food. It deserves all the praise it gets and more.

The book is the result of several years of research, visiting chocolate - producing countries, factories, shops and talking to anyone and everyone who has any interest in chocolate at all. I want you to share my experiences and hope you enjoy reading it as much as I enjoyed writing it. This book is about cacao, cocoa and chocolate - enjoy it.

SARA JAYNE-STANES • 1999

Pod to Palate

Botanists have yet to establish with certainty where the cacao plant had its first evolutionary birthplace. The genus *Theobroma* from which the species *Theobroma cacao* comes, is supposed to have originated millions of years ago in South America, to the east of the Andes. The Ice Age of two million years ago caused the Amazonian forests to expand, contract and fragment. This had the effect of further diversifying the forest flora which needed to adapt to its new habitat and could be an explanation for the original amalgam of the genus *Theobroma* from the *Sterculiaceae* family and the sub-speciation in *T. cacao*.

The fact that still more indigenous varieties of the cacao plant existed in the area where the Colombian and Ecuadorian Andes meet the Orinoco and the Amazonian jungle in South America, has led several authorities to believe that this was the original area from which this plant eventually developed from its genus some 4,000 or 5,000 years ago.

It is further believed that, as part of the natural process, the cacao plant spread northwards, due to various natural phenomena, such as pollination by insects, the wind and the weather. The strongest and most resistant varieties succeeded in crossing the Isthmus of Panama, and acclimatizing themselves with relative ease in their new happy surroundings to the north west of Venezuela and as far as the central regions of present day Costa Rica, Guatemala, Belize and the southern most part of Mexico, in Central America.

Theobroma has been divided into twenty-two species of which *T. cacao* is the most widely known: the other species cultivated are *T. bicolor* which is used for a drink called *pataxte*, and is grown on a very small scale in areas of Southern Mexico down to Bolivia; *T. grandiflora*, grown in the north east of Brazil and also used in the preparation of a drink; and *T. speciosum*, found in the upper Amazonia. As with others of this species, cacao is cauliflorous, meaning its pods grow directly on the tree; a pattern common to wild trees of the lower storey growing under the rain forest canopy.

Cacao can only grow at tropical temperatures and when sheltered from the wind and unstressed by drought. To shade or not to shade? That is the question. Some farmers favour growing another crop such as bananas, which are taller and fuller in foliage than cacao, so as a result the cacao trees will use less water and therefore less nutrients - otherwise irrigation is vital (not always easy), as are added artificial nutrients. As a hobby, enthusiasts have grown the tree under glass in England; it requires a warmer temperature than either tea or coffee, and only after infinite care can the tree be persuaded to flower and fruit.

However, the bean is very fragile and its germination time is limited to 3 months. The trees stubbornly refuse to flourish outside a band 20° North and 20° South of the Equator, and at a mean temperature of 20° - 36°C and need at least 1250 mm of rainfall per annum.

Having said all this, just to confuse us all, historians continue

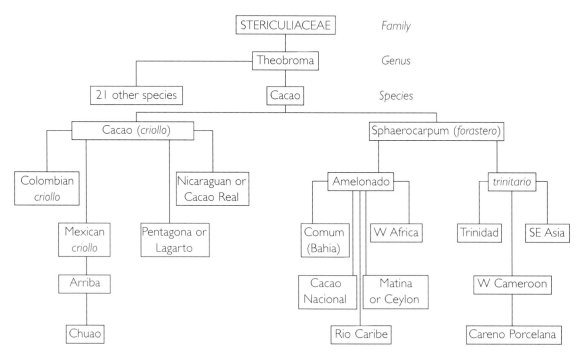

Family tree of *Theobroma cacao*

to question the geographical origins of cacao, and another widely held opinion is that it is more likely that South America has always had and retained its own indigenous variety of cacao, *forastero*, while Central America quite naturally sported its own species of *criollo*.

Although there are many different varieties of cacao beans, the three which are most widely used, are the *criollo*, the *forestero* and the *trinitario*. Each of these has a number of its own hybrids which vary again according to the vagaries of the different countries in which they are grown. Hence a Venezuelan *criollo* will be quite different from a *criollo* from Ecuador. It is important to bear this in mind as the contents of the chart above are accordingly affected by this observation.

CRIOLLO, meaning 'native' or 'of local origin' and probably originally from Central America, now represents only about 5% of the world's production. A few types are grown in the north east corner of South America in Venezuela and in smaller quantities in both Southern Mexico and in the state of Tabasco, Belize, Guatemala, Jamaica, Ceylon and Madagascar. The pods when ripe are soft and red and contain about 30 beans which are white or at their darkest,

pale purple. They are very high quality, very aromatic and distinct and substantially lacking in bitterness - although this depends upon where the tree is raised. The *criollo* is high in cocoa butter and is used in the best quality chocolate but rarely alone because it is so scarce and therefore very expensive. It is finicky to grow and doesn't like adapting to different climates. It is one of the world's finest aromatic beans.

FORASTERO, meaning 'foreigner' or 'stranger', was most probably originally from the Amazon Basin. An important expansion of cacao cultivation in the Eighteenth century came with the introduction of the Amelonado type from the Amazon Basin in Brazil, to the state of Bahia in the same country. It is considered ordinary everyday cocoa for everyday chocolate and represents 80% of the world's cocoa. When ripe, the pods are green and still hard and contain an average of 30-40 pale to deep purple seeds. It has slightly bitter flavour and is sometimes called in coffee terms "cocoa's *Robusta* beans". The exception is the Nacional variety of *forastero* grown in Ecuador which is often compared to a *criollo*.

TRINITARIO was developed on Trinidad as a hybrid of the other two as a result of the near total destruction of the *criollo* plantations by either disease or more likely a hurricane known as the 'blast' of 1727. Seeds for new plantings were brought from Venezuela and crossed with the *forastero*. Resulting hybrids have characteristics of both *forastero* and *criollo*. The pods are mostly hard and of variable colour as are the beans, between 30 and 40 of them, although white seeds rarely occur. Unlike its 'parents', *trinitario* has never been found in the wild. It makes fine chocolate and represents about 10-15% of the world's cocoa. Its blends are fine and rich in fats.

A novel school of thought currently exists that the term *forastero* is a nonsense. A few eminent men in their field hold this theory. Dr. Basil Bartley, a cocoa geneticist for over 50 years, is one.

Dr. Bartley has doubts about the lineage of the "so called *forastero*. One thing is clear about the Amazon cacao populations, and that is that there cannot be any general name applied to them. So that to lump them all together and call them a variety named *forastero* is absurd. Each population-cum-variety is an entity by itself (a *criollo* in its native location) and each should receive a specific name; the grouping under Amazon/Orinoco only indicating the general origin. The practice of lumping all of the Amazon cacaos together creates the general impression that the quality of every Amazonian variety is inferior to that of the *criollo* types".

My interpretation of this is to emphasize that *forastero*, when literally translated, means 'stranger' or 'foreigner' and most of the Amazonian indigenous beans are classed as the *forastero* type. If we are to believe that cacao originated from both South America and Central America then truly the word *forastero* for beans from that area is a contradiction - for how can an indigenous, native seed be a 'foreigner'. This would then lead us to suppose that all cacao seeds are directly or indirectly related to the *criollo* (native) family, which makes sense. However, as I said, this seems to be a new line of thought and one which perhaps is too extensive to discuss here.

There is nothing quite like seeing for yourself the beauty and fascination of the cocoa plantations and if you can stand the heat it is a worthwhile treat for it's a truly exhilarating experience, although there is a very healthy specimen at Kew Gardens, just outside south west London, for anyone who can't make the journey to the tropics.

Let me share with you my own adventures from a recent trip to Mexico. It was in Ciudad Hidalgo, just outside Tapachula, on the borders of Mexico and Guatemala in cacao-growing country that I made my first much contemplated visit to a cacao plantation. The temperature was a humid 40°C.

The owner of the Ciudad Hidalgo plantation, Hernando de la Torre, and his family has been producing cacao for over 100 years. The farm produces over 800 tonnes of cacao beans annually, mainly *criollo*, which de la Torre sells to the rest of the cocoa-growing world mainly for cultivation but some also goes to North America and Europe for chocolate.

Cocoa's cultivation requires tropical climates, altitudes below 300 metres and an annual mean temperature of 24°C. In its wild state, the cocoa tree is naturally tall - sometimes reaching as much as 15 metres - and 'rangy', but under cultivation it is not encouraged to grow to more than 5-8 metres and becomes commercially viable when it matures to 4-5 years. Its top production is achieved from 10 - 15 years of age and with adequate care, the cocoa tree can yield abundantly until it is 50 years of age or more.

The leaves of the tree reminded me very much of the edible English Chestnut tree - only much bigger. Some of them stretched a foot in length and four inches across and, as we moved further into the undergrowth, I could see the sun piercing the thick parasol, which sheltered us from the torture of the heat. My feet sank into the cushion of fallen leaves and bark, which covered the ground like a soft quilt. I could smell the chocolate. Although I already knew how they grew, it was a surprise to see for myself how the pods spring directly from the trunks and the lower branches, where we could see the tiny white buds - about the size of a grain of rice - pushing their way into life. In more mature trees, the buds had turned into delicate little waxy white flowers, like lilies, not more than a few centimetres in width and height which then 'fruit' into the seed pods. A tree can produce six thousand blossoms a year but, on average only one fruit develops for every 100 flowers. The pods, between 15-25cms long, grow into shapes like rugby balls or large lemons with furrows from end to end, or even stumpy irregular cucumbers according to the botanic variety. The peak of the crop happens during October to December and then again, although less prolifically, the trees bear from May to July. (It varies in different parts of the world.) The pods are green or gold, turning yellow, sometimes purple, to brown, and they may be compared to Chinese lanterns hanging in the woods. You would never know from the appearance of the pod that the contents are edible, any more than you would perhaps surmise that tea leaves could be used to produce a refreshing drink. The experienced farmer can tell by the colour and a dull sound on tapping when they are ready to harvest. Each tree produces fruit for only about 0.5 to 2 kg of beans per year and so it is important not to damage the stem while gathering, as this will jeopardise the next crop.

The pods are often low enough to be picked by hand or cut with a cutlass. The canopy almost eliminates the back-breaking work of weeding as nothing grows in the shade. The leaves covering the ground decay to provide fertilizer and a breeding ground for the tiny insects that help to pollinate the cocoa flowers. It seems an almost perfect ecosystem as well as a cool refuge from the mid-day heat.

As if to read my mind, our planter-host took a machete from the scabbard which hung by his side and with one deft cut he severed a pod from the tree. Then with another slash he cut the thick, almost woody rind and broke open the pod. Normally, all the pods would be harvested in this way and collected in a pile and after about 3-4 days when enough have been gathered to make it worthwhile, they are cracked open with the machete and the seeds or beans are extracted by hand.

Now I could see inside the pod, which contained between 30-40 beans, which are formed like a giant corn on the cob. The inside of the pod and its mass of beans are covered in a gleaming white pulp, juicy, like melting snow. The beans are a pale, amethyst colour. I could smell ripe melon and lychees and the temptation to taste was overwhelming - so I pulled out a bean and put it in my mouth. The taste of the bean with its sweet white pulpy liquid is very edible at first, like condensed milk mixed with something between a grape and, indeed, a melon, but it oxidises very quickly and becomes bitter.

The beans are covered with leaves and left in the sun to ferment for three to six days, depending on the variety. The temperature climbs to about 60°C, which helps to shape the flavour by getting rid of the pulp, which in the heat softens and drains off, also softening the bitterness of the fresh seeds.

With regular stirring by hand, the beans are aerated for uniform fermentation, which is important to destroy the embryo thus preventing any germination and so preserving the seeds. This also causes a chemical reaction, which will develop the colour and, most importantly, the flavour. They are then spread out to dry and raked regularly for about 2 weeks to ensure even drying which brings the humidity right down from over 80% to about 6-7%. 1 kilo of cacao loses 20% of its weight after drying. Then the beans are ready to sell and start their travels around the world to be processed into cocoa and chocolate. The process by which today's chocolate is made is a highly refined version of the methods practised by the women of Tuxtla Chico, some of whom I was thrilled to meet.

Tuxtla Chico is a village close to the Cuidad Hidalgo plantation where many of the inhabitants are descendants of the Aztecs and probably the Maya long before them. Here the women make chocolate, entirely by hand, from recipes estimated to be more than 3,000 years old. None of them have ever tasted 'European or American' chocolate. Like the locals from Oaxaca, the strength of the family unit is vital to the lives and livelihoods of these families, but unlike some of the Oaxacans, who are suspicious of strangers and cameras which they fear will expose their souls, we were welcomed unselfconsciously into their homes. In one of them, we were treated to the whole chocolate performance - and what a performance it was. We watched absorbed as an aged, lined grandmother, her middle-aged daughter, Angela Berez, and grand-daughter, turned cocoa beans into chocolate, employing nothing but their hands, a stone rolling pin and a traditional concave stone, about 60cm x 40cm, called a *metate*, now worn to an even deeper curve punished by many years of use.

The de-husked beans, which have been roasted in a domestic iron stove, are heaped on to the *metate* and then crushed to a coarse paste with the 'pin'. The paste is then rolled repeatedly with the pin until it oozes glossy, ebony-coloured fresh chocolate liquid. Finally, some 50% weight of raw sugar is added (sugar is not part of the original ancient recipes, that would have been honey and/or spices or nuts, such as cinnamon or almonds - still also used today). Now, working with about 1 kilo of the cocoa and the sugar mixture, the grandmother's experienced leathery hands mould it into an homogenous ball. She then repeats this exercise while Angela, seated at a wooden table ingrained with years of chocolate, divides one of the balls in half and rolls it by hand into a 60-cm diameter sausage.

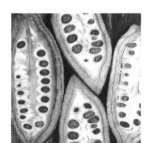

When it's perfectly symmetrical, Angela breaks off 25-cm thick discs and drops them into an enamel bowl, half-filled with cold water. They are left overnight to cool and set so they are ready for sale in the market the following day.

Here in Tuxtla Chico, the locally grown beans cost only about 10 pesos (£1) per kilo. The sugar is 4 pesos and the price of the chocolate sold in the market is about 20 pesos per kilo. These village women make an average of 20 kilos of chocolate twice a week (40 kilos per week) and spend 3 days in the market. I could not have anticipated the particular emotion that this modest practice might arouse, but watching the women in Tuxtla Chico hand-making chocolate, the sole source of income for a number of poor families who live in the tropical cacao-growing areas, proved a surprisingly humbling experience. I imagined their Maya ancestors, centuries before them, using the same methods and techniques.

The next morning, we met Angela Berez again selling her chocolate in Tapachula market. The market was scorchingly hot and swarming with people - shoppers, stall-holders, beggars, flies, cats and dogs and every conceivable product you can imagine, clothes, shoes, cameras, papers, meat, chickens, fish, fruit, vegetables, cold food, hot food, toys, games, all rubbing shoulders. The odours of the market at mid-day were pungent and despite the fascination, I was not unhappy to leave it all behind - but not, of course, before I had bought a kilo of the chocolate we had seen Angela making the previous evening. This is a meaty chocolate both in flavour and grainy texture.

Mexico, whilst once dominating the world's cocoa supply, is now almost insignificant in terms of the world's cocoa production, representing less than 2%. The main competition is from West Africa - the Côte d'Ivoire and Ghana; Latin America - mostly Brazil; and from South East Asia - Malaysia and Indonesia.

Probably two thirds of the world's cocoa comes from trees grown on smallholdings. While it is certainly true that in Brazil and Malaysia, for example, cocoa cultivation extends to large areas of land where cocoa tree upon cocoa tree stretches far into the horizon, in many of the cocoa-growing countries such as Mexico, Belize, Guatemala, and Ghana, for example, the notion of acres and acres of trees, like commercial fruit orchards, is a long way from reality.

It is the care that small farmers take with fermentation and drying that produces the world's best cocoas and much superior to the cocoas grown on mass-produced plantations where the individual care and variety in the type of beans are often sacrificed to monocultural uniformity.

A good example of this is in Ghana, the world's second largest cocoa producer, where cocoa farmers own small amounts of land on which cocoa grows side by side with other tropical fellows like bananas, yams and plantains. Intercropping is one of the keys to their success.

There is growing recognition that small farmers not only provide better quality but are more efficient producers as well. One of their advantages lies in the use of the land to provide for the rest of a family's nutritional needs. They are less dependent on the cash economy for their basic survival. Cocoa is both social security for old age and the only inheritance many families will ever see.

Cocoa farming is a serious business in Ghana and the Ghana Cocoa Marketing Board, which controls all Ghanaian cocoa, has extensive powers. It decides what price should be paid to the farmers and only it may export the cocoa. Importantly, the Board retains control over the quality of the cocoa bought and subsequently exported. Such strict quality controls have meant that the cocoa industry considers Ghana cocoa to be the best of the world's bulk cocoas. However, many of the major chocolate manufacturers are willing to reduce the cocoa content in their product and replace cocoa butter with a cheaper fat substitute. So one wonders just how important quality is in global cocoa production.

While there are some 500,000 to 600,000 farmers there are also over a million caretakers - caretakers are employed by the farmers as 'custodians' of their farms, who watch over them from dawn to dusk. In a country of 19 million people this makes cocoa by far the largest contributor to people's livelihoods. However, a large proportion of Ghana's cocoa farmers are in their sixties or seventies. It is hard to get young people to take up farming and stay in the village. A situation is evolving where it is the caretakers who do the actual work while the owners are absentee city dwellers. Nevertheless, it is only just over 150 years since the bean found its way from Brazil radically to change the horizons of West Africa.

Over recent years cacao-producing countries have considered the merits of processing beans at source and exporting the intermediate products, i.e. the cocoa liquor, butter and powder. At the moment some 30% of all processing does already take place at source and the debate is whether this should increase. While on the surface this seems eminently sensible, there are underlying problems.

North America and Europe consume most of the cocoa products and this is where the chocolate factories are located. These highly mechanised factories are geared for processing cacao beans from start to finish and could not cater for butter or liquor in solid form - the only way that these origin processors could deliver the product. For example one factory in the Netherlands can deliver 120 cocoa powders which comprise different colours, aromas, fat contents, degree of alkalisation and the addition of lecithin stabilisers. Most powders in origin countries could not hope to match these variations with the same degree of accuracy and consistency, if only for the technical reason that they generally have access only to one type of locally grown cocoa bean, while the processors of Europe and North America have a vast range of beans from across the cacao-growing world.

Health regulations in Europe and North America also present extra difficulties. It is harder to make products with low bacteriological counts in hot damp conditions than in temperate climates. Factories in origin countries have to take so much greater care in their production processes and this increases the cost of production.

As the labour costs in origin countries are vastly lower than in Europe and North America it makes economic sense to run factories in producing countries that are labour intensive and not capital intensive - which cocoa processing factories are. For example in 1990 the average hourly wage costs of manufacturing in Western Germany were over US$ 20, the United States just below $ 15. In Malaysia the hourly rate was just under US$1 - if you think this is extortion then take a close look at Indonesia; it's half that! Unfortunately cocoa processing is capital-intensive and origin processors have to import most of the costly equipment that needs only a few skilled people to operate; hence the ability of the industrialised countries to compete successfully.

Chocolate Timeline

5000 BC. The beginnings of agriculture on the coast of the Gulf of Mexico and the Altiplano Central. Varieties of cacao are thought to have begun their migration across Central and South America.

3000-500 BC. The Olmec civilisation emerges, probably the first to cultivate the cacao bean, which hitherto had grown wild across South America. Olmecs are at their most prodigious in about 1500 BC. The age of ceremonial centres: Cuicuilco and La Venta.

0. Cacao is cultivated by the Maya, from Guatemala, in the lowlands south of Yucatán and El Petan and the first stages of the cultivation of cocoa in that region begins. The emergence and development of centres of civilisation in Itzapa, Teotihuacán and Monte Alban.

150 AD. The classical age begins with the zenith of Teotih-uacán. Cacao is already being used in religious ceremonies.

400. The ceremonial burial of the Blue River Vase with its remains of the cocoa drink; first concrete evidence of cocoa's use in funeral rites.

500. The apogee of Monte Alban. Cultivation begins in Veracruz and Tajin.

600. The Maya well established in the Yucatán Peninsula. The use of cacao beans as money becomes accepted through-out the region.

700. The decline of the Teotihuacán civilisation. The Itzaes invade the Maya lowlands. The climax of the classical Maya civilisation: Tikel, Uaxactun, Copan and Palenque.

900. The god Quetzalcoatl reigns over the Toltecs and is subsequently deified, to be worshipped by the Aztecs as the god of chocolate. Mexican mythology believes that Quetzalcoatl came to earth on the beam of the Morning Star with a cacao tree from Paradise and gave it to the people. They learn how to roast and grind cacao seeds and to make a nourishing thick paste which can be dissolved in water. They add spices and call this drink 'xoco-atl' (bitter-water) and believe that it brings knowledge and good judgement.

1000-1400. The post classical age begins in the Altiplano (the central high plain), Tula and Xochicalco and cacao becomes known in that area. The dominance of the Itzaes in Yucatán: Chichén Itzá. The development of the Mixtec civilisation. Cultivation of the cacao extends to Oaxaca and Veracruz.

1200. Aztecs reign supreme in the Altiplano and Mesoamerica. They demand tribute from those they have subjugated - including the Maya.

1486. The conquest of Soconusco and the spreading interest in cacao by the Mexicans. The Iztaes gain control of cocoa trade in Central America, Yucatán and the Caribbean.

1500. Supremacy of the Aztecs.

1502. Christopher Columbus lands on the island of Guanaja, off the coast of Honduras and receives a gift of cacao beans - which he fails to take seriously.

1519. Hernán Cortés lands on the coast of present day Mexico and embarks on his famous conquest of the Aztec Empire. Cortés meets the flamboyant, cacao-loving Emperor Motecuhzoma (Montezuma II) and Cortés and his men are introduced to the drink of *xoco-atl*.

1521. The glorious Aztec city of Tenochtitlan falls to the Spanish conquistadors and so ends the public political existence of the Aztecs as we have come to know them. Montezuma is stoned and fatally wounded by his own people; he dies shortly afterwards, disenchanted with his failure to overcome the Spanish invaders. With him dies the Aztec royal lineage.

1522. Cortés establishes a cacao plantation in the name of Spain, in the lands he conquered from the Aztecs, where "henceforth 'money' will be cultivated".

1528. Cortés brings back to Charles V of Spain a boat load of spoils from the New World including cacao beans and utensils for making chocolate.

1560. *Criollo* is transported from Venezuela to the island of Celebes (now Sulawesi), in Indonesia, where plantations are established.

1569. Controversy starts within the church after Pope Pius V declares that drinking chocolate does not break Lenten fasting, as he personally finds it so unpleasant that it could not possibly cause any moral undoing.

1575. Girolamo Benzoni, Milanese traveller, publishes his *History of the New World,* complaining that "chocolate seemed more a drink for the pigs than a drink for humanity" - but eventually warms to some of its charms.

1589. Cocoa beans begin to arrive regularly in Spain and the first workshops for making chocolate are established.

Flanders (present day Belgium and the Netherlands), then under Spanish rule, discovers chocolate.

1591. Juan de Cárdenas writes the first medical work dealing with the effects of chocolate on health.

1606. Francesco d'Antonio Carletti returning from Spain is thought to be one of the many Italian travellers to have introduced drinking chocolate to Italy.

1609. *Libro en cual se trata del chocolate* appears in Mexico. It is the first book devoted entirely to the subject of chocolate.

1615. Louis XIII marries Anne of Austria, daughter of Philip III of Spain; she introduces chocolate to the French court.

1640. Chocolate arrives in Austria via Italy. Monastic communities spread its use throughout the Holy Roman Empire - notably in Germany.

1648. Thomas Gage, English Dominican monk publishes *A New Survey of the West Indies*, which includes many references to cocoa and chocolate.

1650. The first cacao plantations set up in the West Indies.

1657. The first British 'factory/shop' selling chocolate is set up by a Frenchman in Queen's Head Alley, Bishopsgate Street, London.

1659. David Chaillou, the first chocolate maker in France, is granted the Royal Warrant from Louis XIV.

1660. Louis XIV's marriage to Maria Teresa daughter of Philip IV, encourages the court's taste for chocolate. Charles II taxes chocolate for the first time in Britain.

1662. Cardinal Brancaccio hands down the judgement of Solomon: "*Liquidum non frangit jejunum*". In other words: "Liquid (in the form of chocolate) does not break the fast."

1670. Helmsman Pedro Bravolos Camerinos decides that he has had enough of Christian voyages of exploration and settles in the Philippines where he spends the rest of his life planting cacao, thus laying the foundation for one of the great plantations of that time.

1671. Praline is discovered by accident when a clumsy kitchen boy drops a bowlful of almonds on the floor. The angry chef tries to box his ears and in the process, spills a bowlful of hot burnt sugar over the almonds. Maréchal Plessis-Praslin, a duke who is renowned as a gourmet, is waiting for his dessert. "What now?", thinks his personal chef and, in desperation, serves the marshal with the almonds covered with a coating of cooled sugar. The guest is delighted with the new dessert and promptly gives his name to the new sweet - not, however, the full name but simply 'Praslin'. Since then this sweet has undergone many changes including the development of the modern term 'Praline' from the original.

1674. The London shop Coffee Mill (now Berry's the Wine Merchants in St. James's) and Tobacco Roll offers solid eating chocolate in the form of pastilles for the first time.

1677. Brazil creates first cacao plantations in State of Para.

1679. France acquires plantation in West Indies and the first cocoa beans soon arrive in Europe.

1681. The French revenue appropriates its monopoly on the cacao trade.

1687. Sir Hans Sloane first encounters the drink on his sea voyage to Jamaica. Sloane later discovers the potency of adding milk to the chocolate drink, which he introduces to England. First chocolate shop opens in Bayonne, France.

1690. First known recipe for chocolate included in an English dictionary of food written and published by William Salmon in London.

1692. Louis XV levies a tax on cocoa to help finance his war effort. Bianco opens the first Chocolate House in St. James's, now White's Club.

1697. Heinrich Escher, the mayor of Zurich, visits Brussels where he drinks chocolate and returns to his home town with the tidings of the new sweet drink.

1704. The whim to restrain foreign imports encourages Frederick Ist of Prussia to impose a tax on chocolate in Germany. French café proprietor Pierre Masson publishes a book called *La Parfait Limonader, ou le manière de preparer de chocolat*, containing a recipe for drinking chocolate.

1711. Emperor Charles VI transfers his court from Madrid to Vienna, so chocolate moves in via the Danube.

1720. The reputation of the coffee houses of Florence and Venice for offering chocolate is spreading far beyond their borders. Italian *chocolatiers* are well versed in the art of making chocolate and are welcome in France, Germany and Switzerland.

1725. Mary Tuke starts the family grocer's shop in Walmergate, York - later to become Rowntree.

1727. The Blast - either a cyclone or disease or both - devastates the cacao plantations of the West Indies - Jamaica, Trinidad and Martinique.

1728. Churchman (later to become Joseph Fry in 1761) invents the water-mill-powered steam engine to produce a finer smoother chocolate. At the same time he is granted letters of patent by King George II.

1732. Dubuisson invents a tall horizontal table for grinding cacao, which improves working conditions in chocolate factories. But there is indifference among chocolate manufacturers for 'mechanisation'.

1740. Chocolate remains a costly commodity; unscrupulous manufacturers across Europe attempt to increase their profits by selling adulterated chocolate.

1746. Cacao is introduced to Bahia, a state of Brazil, by the French.

1750. Switzerland discovers chocolate thanks to Italian chocolate makers selling their products in Swiss markets.

1751-1772. 28 volumes of the great *Encyclopedia* published by Denis Diderot and Jean d'Alembert. This contains a notable and now often used illustration, circa 1763, of a French chocolate factory, using a chocolate table and a crude method of pressing cocoa butter - an invention later credited to Van Houten.

1753. Cocoa is given its official Latin Botanical name of *Theobroma Cacao Linneaus* by Carl von Linné (name means Food of the Gods).

1755. North America, in those days not the land of the plenty, at last learns of chocolate.

1761. Joseph Fry purchases the firm and patent from Walter Churchman.

1765. John Hannon sets up chocolate factory with Dr. Baker in Massachusetts.

1766. Lombard of France, claiming to be '*la plus ancienne chocolaterie de France*', starts business. Joseph Fry invents the first crude tablet of eating chocolate.

1767. Bayldon and Berry, later to become Terry's of York, set up shop in York, England.

1770. Pelletier opens the first 'industrial' chocolate factory in France: the *Compagnie Française des Chocolats et des Thés*.

1778. Doret invents a hydraulic machine for grinding cocoa paste and mixing it with sugar. The first chocolate-based pâtisserie, Schioccolati Torte is made in Austria - forerunner of the Sacher Torte.

1779-1780. Debauve is appointed *chocolatier* to the French Queen. Machine-made chocolate is produced in Barcelona.

1790. Joseph Storrs Fry (son of the founder) introduces the steam engine made by James Watt, to power the machines to grind the cacao beans.

1792. The Swiss Josty Brothers open a chocolate factory in Berlin, Germany.

1795. Fry's invention is patented.

1796. Majani chocolate is founded in Italy.

1800. Debauve et Gallais, King Louis XIV's chemists, set up shop in Paris. They become *chocolatiers* to the King.

1804. In his *Almanac Gourmand*, Grimod de La Reynière mentions four Parisian *chocolatiers* worthy of praise including Debauve.

1807-1808. The Continental Block disrupts imports of cacao and sugar. Cocoa and chocolate become prohibitively expensive and adulteration proliferates.

1810. Venezuela's leading position in the production of chocolate is established. A survey shows that it produces half the world's requirements. The Spanish consume one-third of the entire cacao production. The first Swiss chocolate factory is set up in a former mill near Vevey. The founder, François-Louis Cailler, had learnt of the secrets of chocolate making during a trip to Italy.

1815. Van Houten sets up his chocolate factory in the Netherlands.

1819. Pelletier equips his French factory with steam-driven equipment.

1822. The first commercial cacao plantations are established in Brazil and within the space of a few decades become the leading producers on the world's cocoa markets. Also the first Trans-Atlantic crossing by a ship with an auxiliary steam engine.

1824. John Cadbury starts his chocolate business from the humble origins of a Birmingham shop. First seeds of Brazilian cacao planted in Sao Thomé by the Portuguese.

1825. Jean-Anthelme Brillat-Savarin's *La Physiologie du goût* (*Philosopher in the Kitchen*) is published, praising the virtues of chocolate. The Menier chocolate factory opens on the Marne at Noisel in France. In the Netherlands, Coenraad Van Houten invents the world's first chocolate press and his technique for extracting cocoa butter.

1826. Suchard opens a chocolate factory at Serriers in Switzerland. Italian born and trained Guiseppe Maestrani starts production in Switzerland. Pierre-Paul Caffarel starts production in Turin, Italy.

1828. Van Houten patents the first alkalised cocoa powder.

1830. Advances are made in the technique of moulding. At his factory in Lausanne, Charles-Amédée Köhler mixes hazelnuts with chocolate for the first time.

1832. Franz Sacher invents the famous Sacher Torte.

1836. Spanish and German colonists begin to grow cacao commercially in Bahia, Brazil. Cailler opens a second chocolate factory in Vevey, Switzerland which he later sells to Daniel Peter, the inventor of milk chocolate.

1842. Charles Barry leaves his homeland of Wales and sets up the Barry chocolate factory at Meulan, France.

1845. Sprüngli-Lindt opens first factory.

1847. In England, Fry's make history again by inventing a way to mix cocoa butter with chocolate liquor and sugar to produce the world's first bars of eating chocolate. The Poulain hand-made chocolate factory is established at Blois, France.

1849. George and Richard Cadbury introduce their first chocolate bar.

1850. Cacao is transplanted from Sao Thomé to Fernando Pó (now Bioko).

1851. Great Paris Exhibition.

1853. Demand for cocoa and chocolate flourishes in Britain after the relaxation of the impossible duties imposed since the mid Seventeenth century. A tax of 1p per pound is levied, making it cheap and accessible at last. Cocoa is cultivated on the West African Island of Fernando Pó.

1857. In England, Albert Jarman Caley opens a chemist's shop in Norwich. In Belgium, Jean Neuhaus (originally a Swiss chemist) sets up his company, later to become Côte d'Or.

1860. In France, Napoleon lifts the tax from chocolate.

1861. The Italian chocolate maker Caffarel creates the gianduja, hazelnut chocolate (pronounced 'jondooya').

1862. Henry Isaac Rowntree acquires a tea and cocoa business from another Quaker, William Tuke in York. Domingo Ghirardelli establishes his confectionery business in San Francisco, California.

1866. Cadbury's market the first 'Cocoa Essence' as pure and unadulterated, using the Van Houten method, i.e. no additives. Excessive amounts of cocoa butter have up to now, made chocolate a greasy heavy drink to which many forms of adulteration - some good and some bad - have been introduced to make it more digestible.

1870. Charles Neuhaus opens the Côte d'Or chocolate company in Belgium.

1874. Menier builds a factory near Paris.

1875. After eight years of experiment, Swiss Daniel Peter puts the first milk chocolate on the market using evaporated milk powder from his friend Henri Nestlé. The Prince of Wales encourages Madame Charbonnel, Parisian chocolate maker, to start a chocolate shop in London with Mrs. Walker.

Fry's introduce the Chocolate Cream Bar - which still reigns today as Fry's Peppermint Cream - nearly 150 years later.

1879. Cadbury's buy the Bournbrook Estate to create their model factory and village for their employees. First commercial cultivation of cacao in Accra. Tettie Quarshie, via one of his apprentice workers, brings cacao from Fernando Pó to the Gold Coast (now Ghana).

1880. Rudolphe Lindt discovers how to make the smoothest, chocolate by 'conching' - and adding extra cocoa butter. It is the result of a mistake after one of Lindt's employees forgets to turn off the machine one night. Cacao is introduced to Nigeria.

1884. Poulain includes a free metal figurine and coloured print in each tin of his chocolate powder.

1886. Albert Jarman Caley launches his drinking chocolate business - later to become one of Britain's largest and most successful.

1887. Rowntree introduce Elect Cocoa to compete with

Cadbury's Essence.

1891. First 80 lbs. of cacao exported from the Gold Coast.

1893. Milton Hershey devotes himself to chocolate. Stollwerk Chocolate Company Germany create a thirty thousand pound chocolate statue of 'Germania' within a thirty-eight foot tall Renaissance temple at the World's Columbian Exhibition in Chicago. The Van Houten Company creates a full-scale Sixteenth century Dutch town hall in chocolate at the same exhibition.

1896. *Cocoa - All About It*, is published by Richard Cadbury, writing under the pen name Historicus. Le Cordon Bleu Ecole de Cuisine holds its first class in Paris. Chocolate consumption in England reaches 36 million lbs.

1900. Spain, formerly the classic land of chocolate, falls far behind. Germany takes the lead in consumption per head followed by the United States, France and Great Britain. In just a decade or two another country will be playing first violin in the orchestra of the chocolate nations - Switzerland. The reputation of Swiss chocolate is bolstered by an unbroken series of medals at international exhibitions. Lindt sells his secret formula for fondant chocolate to Sprüngli for 1,500,000 francs. The partnership Lindt & Sprüngli begins. Jean Tobler starts his chocolate factory, soon to produce the famous Toblerone in a shape based on the Swiss Alps. Milton Snavely Hershey sells his caramel factory for one million dollars and devotes himself to chocolate, and later to a model town called 'Hersheyville'.

1905. Cadbury's Dairy Milk is launched.

1907. The Hershey 'Kiss' is invented. Buitoni launches their Baci. These are creamy chocolates filled with roasted hazelnuts. The word *baci* means kisses in Italian.

1908. Max Felchln begins chocolate production in Switzerland.

1909. Cadbury (and other cocoa and chocolate manufacturers across Europe) veto cacao from Portuguese West Africa due to the intransigence of Portugal on the abolition of slavery. Cadbury encourage the plantations of cacao in Ghana with seeds from the trees of the islands of Fernando Pó, which were originally sourced from Aztec trees four centuries before.

1910. Cacao production begins in the Ivory Coast (Côte d'Ivoire). Leonidas is founded in Belgium.

1911. The Callebaut factory opens in Belgium. The Dutch company, De Zaan, is founded. Frank and Ethel Mars found Mars Inc in Washington.

1912. The Belgian chocolate factory Neuhaus invents both the praline chocolate and the ballotin box to put them in.

1913. Jules Séchaud, Swiss *chocolatier*, makes the first filled chocolates.

1914. Banania a drink made from cocoa powder, sugar and banana flour, is launched in France.

1915. British and European cocoa manufacturers develop the first CBS (cocoa butter substitute) to replace the cacao stocks lost due to the import and export problems of the First World War.

1917. First devastation of the cacao plantations in Ecuador, due to Monila Pod Rot.

1919. Cadbury Brothers buy J.S. Fry & Sons. First of the Fanny Farmer chain of confectionery shops opens in New York.

1920. Frank Mars creates the Mars Business in Minnesota.

1921. Cadbury's launch Fruit and Nut.

1922. Witches Broom was second disaster to hit cacao in Ecuador. La Chocolaterie de Vivarais - later to become Valrhona - begins in the Rhône, France.

1923. Frank Mars invents the Milky Way in America.

1925. The New York Cocoa Exchange is created.

1929. El Rey, the chocolate company, founded in Venezuela. The Belgian Drap Company establishes Godiva chocolates.

1930. Mr. Benson and Colonel Dickson start Bendicks in

London soon to create the famous Bendicks Bittermints. Cadbury-Fry launch Fry's Crunchy and Cadbury's Whole Nut.

1932. Forrest Mars, son of Frank, sets up the British arm of the Mars Company in Slough. The Mars Bar is born and soon becomes one of the world's consistently top-selling chocolate and caramel bars. John Mackintosh buys the Caley chocolate manufacturing company.

1933. Black Magic chocolates are launched after extensive market research including 'one very superior garden party.'

1935. Rowntree launch Aero chocolate - to compete with CDM - but with a secret process which creates lots of tiny air bubbles.

1936. Mars launch 'Energy Balls', now called Maltesers - tiny pieces of Horlicks-flavoured centres, exploded in a vacuum and coated in chocolate. Rowntree launch Quality Street, named after a play by JM Barrie.

1937. Rowntree's famous Kit Kat, Rolo and Smarties begin their long lives.

1938. Cadbury's Roses are introduced.

1940. US Army asks Hershey to develop a chocolate that could survive tropical climates in a soldier's pocket and sustain him when there was no other food, based on the old Aztec notion that a soldier could march all day with only chocolate to sustain him. After Pearl Harbor 500,000 'D' Field rations were produced every 24 hours.

1941. Confectionery and chocolate rationing are introduced in Britain to combat World War 2 shortages - particularly of sugar.

1942. The Caley Factory in Norwich is destroyed as part of the Baedeker bombing, in retaliation for the Dresden and Cologne bombings.

1948. Marc Cluizel establishes his chocolate factory in Normandy, France. It later becomes Michel Cluizel in honour of the first employee, his son.

1950. La Chocolaterie de Vivarais becomes the Valrhona company in the Valley of the Rhône in France.

1952. World War 2 rationing ends in Britain after 12 years.

1955. The Bernachon family establish their artisan chocolate shop in Lyon, France.

1964. The American company, W.R.Grace, buys the Dutch De Zaan cocoa company.

1969. Cadbury Group merges with Schweppes.

1968. Antonio Escriba opens his confectionery and pastry shop in Barcelona.

1969. Rowntree merges with John Mackintosh of Nova Scotia, Canada.

1970. Suchard and Tobler merge to become one of the largest chocolate companies at the time.

1973. El Rey in Caracas begins to export its quality chocolate and cocoa.

1975. Robert Linxe opens La Maison du Chocolat in Paris.

1977. The Dutch company, The Nederland Group, buys Chocovic of Barcelona, Spain.

1980. The Club des Croqueurs de Chocolat is founded in Paris by Claude Lebey, Nicolas de Rabaudy and Jean-Paul Aron.

1983. Chantal Coady opens Rococo in the King's Road, London.

1988. Nestlé buys Rowntree. Cadbury Schweppes buys Poulain of France. In Italy, Andrea Slitti creates her own unique line of chocolates.

1990. Chocolate Society founded in Britain by Nicola and Alan Porter.

1992. Jo Fairley and Craig Sams start Green & Black organic chocolate. In France, Michel Azouz initiates the Grande Fête du Chocolat held on the second Saturday in October each year.

1993. Sylvie Douce inaugurates the Salon du chocolat held every October/November in Paris. First Eurochocolate Festival in Perugia.

1994. La Chocolaterie de l'Opéra is started by Olivier de Loisy, formerly Managing Director of Valrhona. The European chocolate harmonisation war hots up - Europe's pure chocolate is threatened by impending legislation designed to allow all European countries to add 5% vegetable fat to their chocolate - in line with the United Kingdom, Ireland and Denmark. Passionate loyalty to their chocolate by the French, German and Dutch prevents a quick decision - the fight goes on. The Chocolate Club is launched in Britain.

1995. Caley's Marching Chocolate re-emerges after 40 years.

1996. Cacao Barry and Callebaut merge to become Barry Callebaut. Robert Steinberg and John Scharffenberger begin production of Scharffen Berger chocolate using Old World techniques.

1998. First Chocolate Show in New York (November). First International Festival of Chocolate at the Royal Horticultural Halls, London (November/December).

2000 and beyond The future of chocolate looks exciting, the market for real quality, hand-made chocolate is growing, so chocolate comes full circle and the beans, the source and the husbandry feature in its journey throughout the next century.

March 2000. The European Parliament finally resolved the issue of harmonisation and in the future, to enable British milk chocolate to be exported, it must be called 'family' milk chocolate and the ingredients must be clearly stated on the label. (Plain and white chocolate are unaffected). In addition, we purists lost the vegetable fat fight, the addition of which will be legalised across Europe, again provided that it is clearly labelled and that the vegetable fat is a 'cocoa butter equivalent'. The lesson here is to know your label and to read it.

2001. Gerard Coleman and Anne-Francoise Weyns start l'Artisan du chocolat in London.

2003. Pierre Marcolini opens his London Shop together with David Colic and Deborah O'Neil. Various online chocolate sites appear including seventypercent.com. First London Chocolate Week.

2004. The Academy of Chocolate is formed in London between a group of chocolate lovers, chaired by the author of this book, including as Patron Michel Roux; Chantal Coady; Gerard Coleman; David Colic; Martin Christy; William Curley; Chloe Doutre Roussel; Michael Edey (responsible for London Chocolate Week); and Sarah Jane Evans. The purpose is to encourage chocolate lovers to 'look beyond the label'. Tastings, workshops, awards, a schools' programme are all planned.

The past twenty years has seen a significant increase in production from South East Asia.

The History of Chocolate and The Great Chocolate Makers

IN THE BEGINNING…

As befits its image, chocolate, or rather cocoa, has a long and colourful history. Its official Latin botanical name *Theobroma Cacao Linnaeus*, was given to it in the Eighteenth century by the Swedish botanist, Carl von Linné. This turned out to be a triumph of perception on his part, as this was long before 'theobromine' was known and isolated as one of the cocoa bean's most significant ingredients and one which is considered to have the most stimulating effect.

However, the logical reason for this 'celestial' name was to reflect cocoa's place in the world of the Olmec, Maya, Toltec and Aztec gods.

Received wisdom has it that the history of chocolate is a hotch potch of conflicting evidence depending upon your source of information. Sometimes it's muddled, sometimes it's negative and contradictory. With apologies to those of you who thrive on controversy, and, bearing in mind Voltaire's observation in *Jeannot et Colin* "all our ancient history, as one of our wits remarked, is no more than accepted fiction", I have taken the middle road.

One thing is crystal clear, and that is we do not really know when cacao, (pronounced ka-kow or ka-ka-u) - as it is called by all the countries around the Equator that grow it, and cocoa by the colder climates of the English-speaking world, where it is mainly eaten and drunk - was first discovered. We do know for certain that man's love affair with the cacao plant began in the southern regions of the cultural area known as Mesoamerica, which today covers the Mexican States of Michoacan, Veracruz, the State of Mexico, Morelos, Guerrero, Pueblo, Oaxaca, Tabasco, Campeche, Yucatán, Chiapas, and Quintana Roo, and the territories of Guatemala, Belize, Honduras, El Salvador, Nicaragua and Costa Rica. It was chiefly in this massive landscape, which joins North and South America - and possibly even as far as Ecuador - that the plant was cultivated and where, over the centuries, its numerous uses were recognised and espoused.

The early natives of Central America discovered only a handful of the possible beneficial uses of this plant, since they already had a tremendous range of other botanical species to satisfy their basic needs. They used the fleshy part of the cocoa bean for food and to brew an alcoholic drink, and the outer shell to prepare a medicinal potion.

The **Olmec** culture, the mother of the Mesoamerican civilisation, flourished along the coasts of Tabasco around Veracruz from about 1500 BC until its decline in about 400 BC. Their influence gradually spread through the highlands of Mexico, the Valley of Mexico, known as Anáhuac, Oaxaca, and westwards to Guerrero.

They traded extensively across Central America, importing obsidian for blades and dart points from as far away as Guatemala, where Olmec relief carvings in the rock have been revealed, often showing warriors brandishing clubs.

After 900 BC the heart of the Olmec culture shifted from San Lorenzo to the island of La Venta. Magnificent jade ornaments and concave mirrors of iron ore found at La Venta would have been used by priests to focus the sun's rays to start fires - a sure sign of their supernatural powers. At some time during this Middle Formative Period (900 to 300 BC), the Olmec established trading posts as far away as Pueblo and the Valley of Mexico.

Unfortunately, no tangible evidence exists to tell us that cocoa was widely used, although there are certain writers who have mentioned the probability that the Olmec indulged in its power as a ceremonial drink. As Sophie and Michael Coe point out in their absorbingly detailed account of *The True History of Chocolate*, "the environment favoured by the *Theobroma Cacao* and the Olmec alike - the humid tropical rainforest - is about the most unsuitable imaginable for archaeological preservation, and unless a Great Olmec stone monument turns up with an indisputable hieroglyph - which is the style of writing at that time and for many centuries after - of a cacao tree or pod, we are left with historical linguists rather than archaeology as our only source of evidence".

As the power of the Olmecs faded the centres of civilisation in the central highlands grew, and by the First century AD the largest city in pre-Columbian Mexico had developed at Teotihuacán (not to be confused with Tenochtitlan described later) in the Valley of Mexico. Teotihuacán dominated Mexico for the first six centuries AD trading with Monte Albán (near Oaxaca) and with the Maya kingdoms that had grown up in southwestern Mexico and others as far south as the Valley of Guatemala. The capital city covered some 21 sq.km. with blocks of apartment houses, markets and many small factories, temples supported by platforms and palaces smothered in a tapestry of murals.

Teotihuacán relied on the surrounding countryside for its food and raw materials. The inhabitants settled in some of these areas and further dominated others as many miles away as the Yucatán peninsula and Guatemala. The peoples from Teotihuacán were close to the Maya and the two shared a number of cultural characteristics. Historians and archaeologists are not at all sure what caused the decline of Teotihuacán but it was totally deserted around 750 AD.

Nevertheless, it is the Teotihuacán civilisation that influenced later Mexican peoples including the Toltecs and the Aztecs.

While Rome was busy refurbishing the Mediterranean region, the **Maya** were building a remarkable civilisation in Central America. The heart of the Maya kingdom was in present day Guatemala, where they constructed architectural masterpieces around 600 BC - known as the Early Classic Period. They did not build great cities like Teotihuacán, which thrived in Mexico during this period, but their temple sites also included large plazas, courts for ball games and stone carvings. Thatched roof temples stood at the top. These temples and others like them were reminiscent of the massive stone architecture of the Egyptian pyramids and were (and still are) the most distinctive hallmarks of Maya culture. There are even today a number of these sites around Mexico, which have been preserved. The most famous of these is the overwhelming Palenque, which is well worth a pilgrimage to wonder at the sheer manpower which must have been employed in its construction, in the very beautiful and almost inaccessible jungle - especially if you like hot food and lots of *mole* (the traditional chilli/chocolate sauce for which there is a recipe included in this book).

The Maya originated a system of writing, which they used to record astronomy, religion and history. Adapting some of their temples as observatories, they developed a calendar that was the most accurate the world had known until the introduction of the Gregorian calendar in 1582. They also developed the concept of zero, unheard of in Roman numerology.

The Maya commemorated their sovereigns with *stelae* (upright stone slabs or pillars). Typically these slabs pictured the image of a ruler along with hieroglyphs identifying him and describing his lineage and achievements. Paintings show seated rulers, often garbed in lavish costumes made from painted textiles and feathers, holding court with lesser mortals. Many Maya craftsmen were skilled at working jade into jewellery, ornaments and pendants.

Cocoa played a significant part in the complex rituals of the Maya. The fleshy part of the cocoa bean represented the heart, and the drink made from it was recognised as its blood, both necessary elements in maintaining the equilibrium of the cosmos.

According to Mesoamerican belief, as the sun set it had to confront the jaguar of the night so it could reappear again the following morning. The pink colours of the sky at dusk and at sunrise were the blood the sun lost in its struggle against the night. As the sun needed blood to survive, it was essential that this lost blood was replaced by man's, namely the drink made from their precious cocoa bean. Inevitably, cocoa and chocolate were often employed as objects of sacrifice and offering.

As it was so closely connected to religious imperatives, it was intrinsic to the Mesoamerican psyche that a number of ceremonies were celebrated with the very best beans offered to the gods of agriculture. These were particularly important at both sowing and again at harvest time, which was celebrated round a pole from which youths slid down in the fashion of 'fliers'. This elaborate ritual is still performed today and has become a tourist attraction in parts of Mexico.

Again, like the Toltecs and the Aztecs, the Maya believed that cocoa, the food of the gods, was from divine sources. But to the Maya, the discoverer of cocoa and of cotton was the god Hunhapu, while to the Toltecs and Aztecs it was Quetzalcoatl; and it was Xmucane, another of the god-creators, who invented nine different kinds of drink to make men strong and fearless. Of these, three were made from cocoa and maize.

The Maya regularly squandered ceremonial gifts on their gods, such as cocoa and resin, although these were strictly controlled by the immensely powerful priests who guarded it under lock and key. Cocoa featured specifically at the parties at the end of the dry seasons when there was desperate need for rain. Beans were buried in the four-corners of the region to tempt all the provider gods to send down the 'heavens'. Cocoa was also offered to pacify 'El Mam', the god of the 'ill-omened' days, the final days of the year.

During the ritual rinsing of the body or vessels during the ceremony of *Calputzihil* or re-birth, which was a kind of bar mitzvah or initiation into adulthood, water was mixed with ground cocoa and used to consecrate the youth or youths.

The feast of the cocoa merchants during the month of *muan* or April represented profound holy importance to honour their patrons and protectors El Chuah, Chac and Hobnil. El Chuah, god of merchants, was also by extension, the patron god of cocoa probably because merchants often traded cocoa beans for other commodities such as cloth, jade and ceremonial feathers and used the beans as currency. The celebration was held in a cocoa grove where a sheep, stained the colour of the (cacao) fruit, was sacrificed. Spotted cocoa-brown hairless dogs (called Aztec dogs today and still very much around) were regularly sacrificed in the name of cocoa. At the end of the celebration, as the smell of burning incense still pervaded the air, gifts of cocoa were given to those present.

During the 10th century, for reasons never quite fathomed (like the fall of Teotihuacán), the Maya abandoned most of their temple complexes and returned to simpler forms of life. Their world may have been disrupted by invasions from Central Mexico by the Toltec among others. (During the 10th century the Toltecs took over the old Maya centre at Chichén Itzá in Yucatán). Other thoughts on the Maya decline include crop failures, overpopulation, epidemics, and natural disasters. Extraordinarily, for such an advanced and sophisticated peoples, within a few decades the jungles had absorbed most of the Mayan centres - which makes a trip to Palenque even more valuable.

The oldest archaeological remains which produce any evidence of cocoa of any absolute certainty is a vase which was found in grave No. 19 of the Blue River, a Mayan city situated near the present day borders of Belize, Mexico and Guatemala, and dated 5th century AD. The remains of a drink prepared from cocoa were found inside this polychrome vase, and on its outside there were two phonetic symbols, meaning *kakaw*, or cocoa. These traces were part of the elaborate burial of a priest, indicating that, even at that time, cocoa was considered an aristocratic drink, which held important, symbolic and religious significance.

From that date, archaeological treasures become more and more abundant; and in subsequent periods, traces of the use of the cocoa plant can be found in Guanacaste, Costa

Rica, and Tikal in the Yucatán Peninsula. Moreover, we know that three aristocratic families of this city shared the same surname of *kakaw*. These findings indicate that the domestic cocoa consumption of the elite reached its peak between the 2nd and the 4th centuries, the middle of the so-called Classical era.

It is now widely acknowledged by Mesoamerican experts that it is the Maya who were responsible for establishing the lore of chocolate and how to use it; and under their influence, its acclimatisation and cultivation across an immense land mass as far as the coasts of Tabasco and the south of Campeche (in Mexico), down to Belize and the Gulf of Honduras.

We also owe to them its adjective *kaj*, meaning bitter, and the noun *kab* (juice without added sweetness); which indicates strongly that the resulting beverage, therefore, must have been somewhat bitter. Nahuatl, a local language added the suffix *atl* (water) to these words which comes out as *kajkab-atl* or *cacahwatl*. In addition, the word CHOCOLATE whose use began after the Spanish conquest also has a hybrid origin: *chukow* meaning hot, from the Mayan language, and *atl*, from the Nahuatl. It would seem that the Maya, unlike the Aztecs after them, liked their chocolate hot. In other parts of Mesoamerica, as we have seen, the Nahuatl language pronounced bitter as *xoco* - pronounced *whoco*. They also used *atl* as water, which again would have been pronounced *whoco-atl*. The Maya language, moreover, contained several words relating to different strains of cocoa and their different preparations, thus demonstrating that, before the Spanish conquest, the Maya were fully aware of it and its many uses.

However, while on the subject and just to confuse the issue over origination of the name of chocolate, other later explorers like Thomas Gage reported that the word comes from 'chocolate-chocolate-chocolate' - supposedly the sound that the water makes when the chocolate is stirred into it with a molinet - also called a *molinillo* - a wooden spatula ribbed with a series of wings carved out of the stem - until it bubbles and rises to a foam. Pictures of ancient Mesoamericans are often depicted with a woman pouring a

liquid from a height. Frankly, it looks a painfully ridiculous piece of protocol - until you understand the point of it - the original 'cappuccino'!

There is also a school of thought that the transformation of the name to 'chocolate' happened when a printer's error in France turned *xoco-atl* into *chocolaté*. The accent was removed by an English printer and completely abandoned by France - hence it is now known as chocolate in the English speaking world and *chocolat* in the French…

It was also the Maya who were the first to use the cocoa bean as money, successfully exploiting its use as coins throughout the rest of Mesoamerica, the coasts of the Caribbean, and the north of the South American continent.

Although, almost exclusive to the rich aristocrats, there was the odd occasion when cocoa was allowed for social purposes. Among the Maya, ground cocoa was drunk to celebrate civil festivities; and was an indispensable part of a bride's dowry. Before the bridegroom performed the 'bended-knee ritual' of proposal to his bride, he had to first get his request sanctioned by her parents and to demonstrate his sincerity he offered them over 350 cocoa beans - which was a lot of money. At events such as christenings and weddings, everyone might enjoy cocoa in small cups. Any cocoa leftovers were normally given to the women who had ground and prepared it.

Towards the end of the 7th century AD, a group of merchant peoples, who migrated from Chakanputún or Xicalango, the coastal region known as the Laguna de Terminos, in the Gulf of Mexico, began to explore and to settle in the East and the West coasts of Yucatán, and eventually dominated the whole of the peninsula, the lower Petén region, and the Caribbean coasts of Honduras and Belize. These people, known as the Putún or Itzaes, were distinct from the other Maya communities because uniquely, they were also in touch with the peoples of the high rise plateaux of Central Mexico. They also used the cocoa bean as currency.

At the time that the Itzaes were infiltrating the Maya nations, the use of the cocoa bean as a means of exchange dominated to such an extent that between the 7th and 9th centuries AD, it had replaced green Jade stone 'coins'. Consequently, it became the sole means of currency across an extensive geographic area. When they had finally achieved complete control of their empire, the Itzaes discovered that this included several areas of production of cacao in Tabasco, Campeche, Petén and the South Belize. This gave them very firm control over their 'Royal Mint' cocoa production in Central America.

Some time later, other parts of Mesoamerica took the cocoa bean to their hearts, not only as coinage, but also for its gastronomic and ceremonial uses. Commercial cultivation took off in many of these places, such as Xoconocho (Soconusco) in Chiapas on the Pacific coastal plain, where, since the 11th century AD, the cocoa bean had existed as the chief means of exchange.

The Itzaes continued to weald their power until the 16th century - although over a much diminished geographical area.

The Toltecs were the indigenous peoples who migrated from the north of what is now Mexico, after the decline of Teotihuacán, and in the 10th century AD established a military state at Tula, about 64km north of today's Mexico City. Their army dominated neighbouring societies and the race itself was considered sophisticated and erudite with an astonishing range of talents including metal smelting, stonework, distilling, and astronomy. Not surprisingly, their architecture reflects Olmec, Mayan and Teotihuacán influences. The ruins of Tula, sometimes called Tollán, include three pyramid temples, the largest one of which is surmounted by columns 4.6m high in the form of ornate human figures, and is thought to be dedicated to Quetzalcoatl, (*Ket zal-co-atl*), the Toltec and Aztec god and legendary ruler of Mexico, and is usually depicted as the Plumed, or Feathered, Serpent. The sight is so astonishing that, just like Palenque, you are likely to stare in awe and wonder.

Quetzalcoatl is a Nahuatl (one of the most widely spoken local dialects) name. In the 10th century AD the Toltecs transformed what had been a god of soil fertility, once worshipped in Teotihuacán (before the 7th century), into a kingdom under Quetzalcoatl who was described as 'light skinned and bearded' which was unknown among the tanned natives. Mexican mythology continued to believe in the rather charming, if not quirky, story about Quetzalcoatl coming to earth via the beam of the Morning Star, Venus, with which he became associated and, as luck would have it, he brought a cacao tree with him from Paradise cultivating it in his holy garden at Tula and which he then gave to the people. They soon learnt how to roast and grind the seeds (or beans) of the cacao pod to make a nourishing thick gruel. They dissolved this in water and added spices and called this drink '*xoco-atl*' (bitter-water) and swore by it in the belief that it brought knowledge and wisdom. But Quetzalcoatl was forced to get drunk through the cunning deceitful tricks of the sorcerer Tezcatlipoca, the god of the night sky and ruler of the opposing deity in the dualistic Toltec religions, and had to flee to the East - but not before turning his cocoa plants into mesquite scrub bushes - a common sight in Mexico's untamed countryside even today.

The Aztecs later made him a symbol of death and resurrection and a patron 'saint' of priests. In the religion of the Toltecs, the legend of Quetzalcoatl's exile is symbolic of a move away from agricultural ceremonies to the customs of human sacrifice (also adopted by the Aztecs).

The Aztecs moved south and eventually developed the deserted Mayan city of Chichén Itzá (in the Yucatán Peninsula) as their capital and an important religious centre. The Toltec Empire declined in the 12th century AD when the Chichimecs, and other indigenous peoples, plundered the central valley and eventually ransacked Tula. The Maya people they had conquered earlier subsequently consumed the Toltecs in the south. By the 13th century, the fall of Tula and the Toltec Empire made way for the rise of the Aztecs.

THE AZTECS - people of the Fifth Sun

The Aztecs were sovereign across Central and Southern Mexico from the 13th to the 16th century and are best known for having established an elaborate and extensive empire, which was eventually destroyed, for the most part, by the Spanish invaders.

The name 'Aztec' comes from a mythical homeland in the north called Azatlán; the Aztecs also used to call themselves the Mexica (from which the name Mexico is derived).

After the fall of the Toltec Empire, waves of immigrant Aztecs poured into Mexico's central plain and penetrated the lakes in the valley of Mexico in the 16th century. They were regarded as nothing more than Chichimecan barbarians but their goal was the riches of the peoples and one of the symbols of the culture they found was cacao. Their priests urged them to "conquer, win and subjugate for yourselves … so that you yourselves acquire and enjoy the fine emeralds … the fine cacao come from afar … and many other things that fire pleasure and enjoyment …" Once the Aztecs had become the major power in the valley and had won their prized goals, they adopted cacao as the symbol to remind themselves that they had finally thrown off their Chichimecan origins.

As late arrivals, the Aztecs had, at first, been forced to occupy the swamps on the western side of the lake. Powerful neighbours who demanded 'tribute' - a form of taxation - from them surrounded them, and their only piece of dry land was a tiny island surrounded by marshes.

That the Aztecs were able from this unpromising start to build a powerful empire within two centuries was due in part to their belief in a certain legend. According to this legend, they would establish a great civilisation in a marshy area where they would see a cactus growing out of a rock, and perched on the cactus would be an eagle eating a snake. The priests said they saw this when they arrived in the swamp. Today as a reflection of this tradition, the eagle, cactus and serpent appear on all Mexican paper money and on the Mexican flag.

The shallow bed of Lake Texcoco was transformed by the Aztecs into *chinampas* - highly productive gardens formed by building islands with the mud dug up from the bottom of the lake. Causeways and bridges connected the islands with the mainland; canals throughout the city provided transport for people and goods.

As a result of its position and high degree of almost military organisation, by 1325 the city of Tenochtitlán (pronounced *Ten-osh-tit-lan*) was thriving. When the Spanish, led by Hernán Cortés began their conquest in 1519, it was possibly the largest and most beautiful city in the world, similar in concept to Venice. Today the central plaza of Mexico City lies over the main Aztec ceremonial centre of Templo Mayor where recent excavations unearthed some of the most spectacular and exciting archaeological discoveries of the late Twentieth century.

The Aztecs used pictographic writing that was inscribed on paper or animal hides. In execution and concept these 'codices' are of extremely high quality. Unfortunately, although barely a few survived the destruction of the Aztec libraries by the Spanish and their missionaries during the 16th century, they can be found in libraries and museums around the world. The Bodleian Library at Oxford has one of the best examples called the 'Codex Mendocino' sometimes known as the 'Mendoza'.

The Aztecs also used the calendar system that was developed earlier by the Maya. This system consisted of 365 days divided into 18 months of 20 days to which were added 5 'hollow days' which were considered very bad luck indeed.

Great markets flourished in nearly every street and, it is said, attracted up to 60,000 people daily from the suburbs and the countryside.

Like the Maya, a host of gods ruled over the Aztecs, who without fail made daily regular offerings of cocoa and roses to, *Tlaloques*, *Huitzilopochtli*, *Xiuhtecuhtli* and *Yacatecuhtli*, the gods of rain, of fire, of war and of trade, respectively. Also, like the Maya, cocoa occupied an important if not essential place, attaching the mythical origin of their lands to the god Quetzalcoatl, the Toltec god and legendary ruler of Mexico, who (or which) had also been slavishly worshipped by the Toltecs and earlier civilisations before them. Quetzalcoatl, as we have seen, was described as light-skinned and bearded, and according to prophecy, would eventually come 'home' from his exile. So, when the Spanish conqueror Hernán Cortés appeared in 1519, the Aztec king Montezuma II was easily persuaded that Cortés was, indeed, the resurrected god.

During the religious festivities of the merchants, on the day of *ce quiahuilt* (1st of the month), huge quantities of cocoa and *xoco-atl* which had been in preparation for weeks ahead, were consumed; and in the celebrations of *panqueetzaliztli* and *nahuiehecatl* (4th of the month of the wind) the merchants made their offerings of cacao, roses and tortoiseshell covers and distributed them among their guests. Merchants, naturally, by virtue of their profession, had access to large quantities of cocoa beans.

As you can see, cocoa was everywhere - even taken to the grave as part of the funeral rites of the major nobles, at the coronation celebrations of a new lord, or at the conquest of new territories. And cocoa was always one of the principle gifts exchanged with the enemy before hostilities erupted.

According to Aztec traditions and others before them, there had been other worlds called 'Suns'. Each had been created by the gods and then destroyed by human beings. The Aztecs, and the rest of mankind, including us, live in the Fifth Sun, which was mythically born in the great ancient city of Teotihuacán. But one day even this sun - and therefore life itself - was doomed to be obliterated, this time by monstrous earthquakes. Only by strictly observing their religious duties could they hope to ensure the continuation of their world, and the only way to make certain that the sun would make its appearance each morning was to keep it continually supplied with human blood.

So, human sacrifices were integral to the Aztec way of life. For warriors the ultimate honour was to die in battle or to volunteer for sacrifice as a major ritual. Death meant moving on to another even more glorious life - so what was a little sacrifice. Prisoners were often used for less important ceremonies. Victims were forced to climb the steps of the pyramid, where priests would then stretch them across a convex stone and, while they remained perfectly still, rip their hearts out with a knife. (It is alleged that they were fed cocoa to make them feel better about it…) It may at first seem abhorrent and primitive to us but not so much when you consider it as a matter of their immensely strong beliefs and culture. It was for these reasons, quite justified in the Aztec mind, that their reputation as barbarians sacrificing thousands has remained relatively unchallenged throughout history. However, in *The True History of Chocolate*, the Coes are at pains to point out that they believe that the "number

of victims who died under the knife was grossly exaggerated by the Spanish, probably to justify their own reprehensible actions during and after the invasion of Mexico; at most a few thousand prisoners may have lost their lives each year - compared to the tens of thousands claimed in Spanish accounts". And if you think about it, to the Aztecs the status of sacrifice would have been much less of an honour had it been such a common everyday practice. However, there is a very sympathetic streak in me that hopes that those who did die enduring such savagery for their honourable beliefs eventually found sanctity in the 'after-life'.

In spite of the Aztecs' extensive knowledge of the cocoa plant, they could not grow their own cocoa trees because of their unsuitable geography and climate and so had to rely on their cocoa beans from tribute and trade. In much later times (15th century AD), when their expanded empire established a regular trade with the coastal regions, their passionate interest in cocoa spurred them on to conquer the far distant territories of the coast of Vera Cruz and Soconusco in Chiapas. Several Mexican emperors actually succeeded in cultivating the cocoa plantations nearer the high rise plateau of Altiplano. It was their efforts that brought cocoa to Oaxtepec and in Alahuiztan and Guerrero respectively.

Mirroring the Maya, the Aztecs ate and drank the fruit of the cocoa plant, in a wide variety of forms, ranging from the most natural and simple, to the most complex and sophisticated. In the first place, the fleshy part of the cocoa bean was consumed like any other fruit, as were the leaves and the kernels. The latter could be eaten either raw or dried, although the former was the more usual. The Aztecs' favourite method of preparing cocoa was to grind it dry and mix it with maize, which would result in a powdery paste called *cacahuapinolli*.

Nevertheless, the most significant gastronomic use of cocoa was the cold, refreshing slightly bitter drink made from finely ground cocoa beans dissolved in cold water. Quite probably this recipe was the forerunner of our own chocolate which goes way back to the time before the domestication of cocoa to the 1st or 2nd century BC. The basic preparation of this beverage was very important, but from this sprang a number of different variations. Bernardino de Sahagán (an honourable Franciscan priest and traveller who returned to Mexico during the mid 16th century and learnt the Nahuatl language to get to know and understand the people), author of the *General History of the Things of New World*, wrote one of the most imaginative descriptions of the way it was made:

"They opened it (the cocoa pod) first in this way: then the beans are (roughly) ground or broken up; the second time around they are a little more finely ground; and the third time, ground to a very fine powder; they then mix that with grain of maize and cook and rinse them well, and thus 'cooked' and mixed, they add water in a glass, and if they add only a small quantity of water, it goes to make marvellous cocoa, and if they add a large quantity of water, there is no foam, and in order to prepare it well, one should keep to the following: in order to be known that it is filtered after the filtering it rises until it overflows, and together with this rises the foam, which is then strained away, and at other times it's made very thick and it's mixed with water after being ground, and he who knows how to make it well, sells the cocoa well made and delicious, such that only nobles drink it, either white and foaming or brown, or red and fine, without much dregs, and the bad cocoa has a lot of dregs and a lot of water, thus not making any foam, but only a few bubbles". (*Sic*)

And Bernal Diaz, one of Cortés' fellow Spaniards, wrote "…when drinking it one has to open the mouth wide because, on account of the foam, it is necessary to give it sufficient room to strain itself away, and enter the mouth, little by little". He went on: "From the beans, we are told, the aristocrats and the chiefs, prepare a certain drink … which they hold in high regard, and only the most important among them make use of it, and those that can, do so, because the common people do not make use of it, nor can they savour such a drink in their gullet or palate, because it is no more than making oneself deliberately poor by swallowing one's money, or throwing it away where it is best."

It seems that cocoa was enjoyed both dissolved in water and with or without maize. It was also quite normal to add great quantities of herbs, fruit and flowers. Honey was the main means of sweetening and vanilla the commonest aromatising agent. Colourings were also used, lime for instance, and *achiote* which turned the cocoa a red colour. Red peppers, grains of the *pochotl* tree, chillies, or rose water were added and many other different local herbs and flavours, and exotic flowers such as the *mecaxochitl* (string flower), *xochinacaztli* (flowery ear), *eloxachiquihuitl* (Magnolia), *tecamaxochitl* and *chichihualxochitl* (varieties of chillies) and many others.

It is also very likely that cacao was mixed with a local plant like the 'coca' which would have given it its invigorating properties which created the legend of chocolate as an addictive stimulant.

Because of its high calorie content, *xoco-atl* was used to boost lost energy or as a fortifier before a hard day's work. On the eve of a battle cocoa was served to the soldiers to give them strength and as a complement to their rations. It was also given to those that suffered hallucinations, called *nancatl*, to reinforce their courage.

"This beverage" Cortés is reputed to have said, "is the healthiest and most substantial of those known in this part of the world, because when he who drinks but one cupful of it, although he may have to perform a hard day's work, may go through the day without eating anything else".

To avoid having to grind the cocoa beans every time, they made a kind of cocoa and maize cake by using a little water and allowing the mixture to thicken until it solidified. This cake would last for a week and when it was needed for a drink, pieces were broken off and dissolved in water. This is very much how the natives of Central America still make it today.

Less common was to make this drink hot, or at least lukewarm, as the Maya had preferred, which was at that time called 'cooked cocoa' and was considered to be a great delicacy. The fat was extracted from the beans, then the ground mixture placed in a vessel, some water added and heated on a low fire. After a few minutes, when the cocoa fat had risen to the surface, it was strained away with a small wooden spoon. This mass was then squeezed in a willow cloth, and the end result was cocoa fat that was almost completely pure. This was then dried for some hours and once it had set it was used for the drink exclusive to only the most important people; and even they had to follow a strict routine:

"When the Indian chiefs or the nobles drink the cooked cocoa, they do it little by little, and only the chief swallows more than one or two draughts at a time, and if anybody takes more than that, in the presence of the chief, they're considered extremely vicious and ill mannered."

Fernando de Oviedo, 16th century New World traveller, who tells us that "Having ground the cocoa and boiled it, with a little water, one can make excellent oil for stewing and for eating, and for many other things", also described another use for this cacao butter. Could this be the forerunner of our current vogue for confits - stewing in goose fat, I wonder?

Before the Spanish conquest, Mesoamericans relied on numerous prescriptions that included cocoa, recommended for a wide range of ailments. It was given to consumptive and emaciated wretches, with hope for their recovery; and it was also used to treat some liver disorders, "dissolved together in water with ground bones of their (the Aztecs) giant ancestors exhumed in the mountain, it was used as a cure for diarrhoea and dysentery; mixed with chile peppers it was considered effective against certain gastro-intestinal disorders, with *achiote* it helped to control fevers and abnormal 'expectations'. On the other hand, its use was not recommended for illnesses of the throat or the coughs, or when the patient has spots on his neck or on his legs or feet".

Oil of cocoa (cocoa butter) was used until very recent times to heal wounds and scratches, and as Fernando de Oviedo says: "It's a holy thing for many ills, pains and sores … and for wounds it was quite excellent, and it acts favourably on any pain or ill, spots to swellings or tumours".

The fat of cocoa also has cosmetic applications; among the natives of Central America it was customary to smear it on their faces mixed with *achiote* to produce a bright red colour as "he who is the most bedaubed is the handsomest", and at the same time it gave them some protection against the sun. As well as a suntan lotion is could also be used for burns; and for greasing spears and polishing metals.

Clearly, cocoa formed a part of almost every aspect of the life of the diverse societies of which Mesoamerica was composed; it was a nutritious and self-sufficient foodstuff, an article of great economic importance, a coveted symbol of social position, an effective medicine and a means of communication with their gods. Because of all this, it significantly attracted the notice of the Spanish conquerors, and later on, the entire world.

But it was only the Aztec nobility and those who had distinguished themselves at war who had the right to drink cocoa - and in the spirit of their forebears and their male dominated civilisation their women were allowed only to take it on special occasions; the majority of the people were permitted to enjoy it only during certain ceremonies, and the penalty was death if they dared to drink without a licence. Consequently, cocoa was known as *yollotlieztli* - the price of blood and heart. This cocoa exclusivity gave immense social superiority to the elite over the rest; nevertheless, the Aztec nobles had to fight hard to win the principle of access to this commodity. Few foodstuffs were so highly valued as cocoa, and perhaps none was quite so difficult to obtain. All the chronicles agree that the "foodstuff that is held in higher esteem than all the others is the *xoco-atl*."

The nobles found a source of energy in cocoa without making them drunk, in contrast to the fermented *Octli* made from the pulp of the agave which only the elders were permitted to drink freely. Drunkenness was punishable by death among the puritanical Aztecs. Cocoa, therefore, was enthusiastically encouraged as a digestive at great banquets where it was always accompanied by much pomp and circumstance.

…"when they had finished eating" (Bernardino de Sahagán points out) "cocoa was served in little cups, and which are all different, some painted with various kinds of pictures, and their lids are very rich, as are their gold and tortoiseshell spoons to stir their cocoa with; other sorts of cups are painted black, as are also their stands, which are made of tiger or deer skins, where they can sit, or place their gourds of cups".

Cocoa was regarded as a source of noble inspiration. The plantations themselves were like gardens full of the rain forest tree with its exquisite tiny orchid-like flowers. It is said that *Motecuhzoma Ilhuicamina* (Montezuma I - the Heavenly Shooter) sent representatives to Soconusco, the most fertile part of south west Mexico where cocoa thrived, to bring back cocoa plants for his garden where he insisted they were planted for his solace and motivation.

The exquisite cocoa flower and its delicate perfume have also inspired Nahuatl writers as a symbol of beauty. Cocoa in its different manifestations is often symbolised as the human ideal of happiness - as a Nahuatl poet informs us:

"I drink my cocoa
And I rejoice,
My heart is content,
My heart is happy"

There are still recipes that have obviously been preserved since the days before the Spanish conquest, and which without a doubt, are descended directly from the cocoa drink of native ancestors. Today, the *tejate* of Oaxaca and the *pozol* from Chiapas seem to be the beverages that are most like the original cocoa except that now sugar is added to balance the natural bitterness of the beans.

Today's chocolate lovers the whole world over owe an immense amount to its gastronomic development by the Mesoamerican peoples and to its new uses introduced by the Spanish. After the Spanish conquest, cocoa and chocolate were eventually to be enjoyed by all classes of society in New Spain and to become one of the most sought after drinks and delicacies in the world.

SPANISH CONQUEST

Since the 2nd century AD, when the Roman Empire traded with Han Dynasty China, luxury goods travelled along the 'silk road', a land route stretching from Europe to the borders of China (Marco Polo's Chinese travels took place in the 1270s); but by the 14th century, political change had made the silk road so hazardous that Europeans began to search seriously for alternative routes by sea.

But by 1492 no one had found another way to China. Enter the legendary **Christopher Columbus** (1451-1506)

who proposed a revolutionary idea of sailing west across the Atlantic Ocean on the assumption that he could sail right round the world and eventually arrive at China. At that time nobody in Europe knew of the existence of the American continent which lay in his path.

When Columbus was, at last, able to rejoice at the sight of land it was, in fact, San Salvador in the Caribbean; but he thought that he had found China - or the Indies as the Far East was then known. Hence, from that day on, the name for the Central and South Americans has become known as 'Indian'.

On his fourth and final voyage from Cadiz to the New World, Columbus landed at the Caribbean Island of Guanaja (Gwun-a-ha), off the coast of Honduras in 1502. He wrote in the ship's log "a large native boat with 25 oarsmen came to meet us with their chief … they presented us with gifts such as fabrics, fine copper … and 'almonds' which they used as money and with which they prepare a drink". Despite this encounter with 'almonds' - as cocoa beans became known since the Spanish did not have a word for cocoa - there seems little evidence that he liked it. (Today the beans are still known as almonds in many languages). And even if he did appreciate it, it was obviously not enough to record it as any significant part of his conquest. He took some of the 'almonds' back to his patron, Ferdinand II of Aragon, who had financed his expedition, and there the matter rested. Columbus died four years later - little knowing of the destiny of the great bean. The discovery of chocolate would have to wait for the conquest of the Aztec Empire by the Spanish explorer **Hernán Cortés**, nearly two decades later. Columbus had succeeded in exploring most of the massive stretch of east coast between Honduras and Brazil but the coast of Mexico remained virtually virgin until 1517 when Cortés landed on the coast of Veracruz.

By this time, Aztec culture and civilisation had become significantly advanced, and little existed that had originated from the post-Toltec period.

When Cortés arrived in 1519, Montezuma II was ruling with much ceremonial pomp according to the customs of the time which demanded that his allies of mutual conquests prove their affection with massive tribute. Cacao was prominent in various forms as a beverage, medicine and money, and was sent to his court in the north from the far south of the country, which was the source of its natural habitat.

The following illustrates a typical consignment of tribute from afar:

20 chests of ground chocolate
80 loads of red chocolate
800 Xicaras (drinking vessels for chocolate)
200 loads of chocolate
20 bags of gold dust
20 Lip jewels of clear amber, decorated with gold, etc.

The units of measure were based on multiples of 20: a *tlzonti* = 400 beans; a *xiquipilli* = 20 *tlzontis*; a load = 3 *xiquipillis*, or 24,000 beans. One could thus estimate a load at about 48 - 50 pounds. One of Montezuma's warehouses contained 40,000 loads of cocoa beans, which, based on the above calculations, was a supply of some 2,000,000 lbs.

In his book *Cocoa - all about it*, Historicus (pen name for Richard Cadbury at the turn of the 20th century) quotes Oviedo, noting that in Nicaragua: "A rabbit = 30 beans, whereas 100 beans would buy a good slave". A slightly clearer idea of worth can be calculated from the values related by Thomas Candish who, during a voyage begun in 1586 relates that 150 cacao beans were then "as good as a Real of Plate or about 6 pence". Even forgetting the changing purchasing power of money, this was a high price considering 385 years of inflation since that time. Small wonder that Oviedo writes that, in Nicaragua, "none but the rich and noble could afford to drink it (xoco-atl) as it was literally 'drinking' money".

To use as coins, the cocoa beans were washed and left to dry in the sun. Once hardened they were immensely valuable and, as we have seen, were used for trading throughout Meso-america. Only maize has ever been able to overshadow its social and cultural importance.

The value of the cacao bean encouraged an inevitable underworld of counterfeiting. The extraordinary lengths to which the counterfeiters went is described by Sahagán: "…

cacao beans are placed in [hot] ashes, toasted full in the fire; he counterfeits by making fresh cacao beans whitish; he stirs them into [hot] ashes and then treats them with chalk, and wet chalky earth; then he stirs them into wet earth. With amaranth dough, wax, and avocado pits - broken into pieces, which are then shaped like cacao beans - he counterfeits cacao; he covers this over with cacao bean hulls and places this in the cacao bean shells. The whitish fresh cacao beans he intermixes and mingles, introduces, ruins with the shrunken, the chilli-like seed, the broken, the hollow, the tiny. Indeed he castes, he throws in with them wild cacao beans (*Theobroma bicolor*) to deceive…"

The Aztecs, and probably others before and after, were so skilled at counterfeiting deception that they put their talents to playing with the gold and silver coinage of the Spanish invaders. By the early 16th century this practice had reached such a peak that the Spanish Viceroy of New Spain, Antonio de Mendoza, tried, with no success whatsoever, to outlaw the deception.

Probably the most crucial moment in the history of chocolate occurred in **Montezuma** II's court during the years of the Spanish conquest in 1520 and the height of the Aztec civilisation. The Emperor greeted Hernán Cortés with a golden goblet of a dark, frothy brew called *xoco-atl*. The Spanish thought that the cold, ground cocoa bean drink was bitter and grainy, but they were soon to learn that the Aztecs worshipped it as an aphrodisiac. Bernal Díaz del Castillo, one of the Spanish conquistadors, wrote in his book *The True History of the Conquest of Mexico* "sometimes they brought him [Montezuma] in cups of pure gold a drink made from the cocoa plant which they said he took before visiting his wives. I saw them bring in a good fifty large jugs of this chocolate, all frothed up, of which he would drink a little. The guards and attendants being served similar jars - to the number of 2,000 at least. They always served it with great reverence".

The Spanish were bemused to find that this stimulant and tonic, the strict prerogative of the Aztec elite, was of course also money - "nothing more than the beans from a domesticated tree known locally as *cacau*, but more valuable than gold".

In fact, Cortés had plenty of opportunities to try *xoco-atl* before he had his historic encounter with the Emperor. At that time, as we have seen, cocoa was cultivated in several regions mainly in Colima, Chiapas, Guerrero, Morelos, Yucatán, and Tabasco; and it was in Tabasco where Cortés first tried the beverage made of cacao and corn. By the time he arrived at Tenochtitlan, (now Mexico City), the Aztec Empire capital, unlike Columbus, Cortés had discovered a taste and some affection for *xoco-atl*.

Cortés landed on the coast of Tabasco with eleven ships and 700 men. They were greeted by some of Montezuma's envoys that had been sent to find out the purpose of the 'new' men. The Aztecs stood back in total amazement phased by their first ever sight of not only horses and the wheel for transport but cannon-fire. A local slave, Doña or Lady Marina, whom, it is now widely believed became Cortés' mistress, was given to him to be his guide and interpreter.

It was Marina, so history says, who told Cortés of the legend of Quetzalcoatl, (the fair skinned bearded god who was expected to return after years in exile to save his people from extinction) and realising the spoils that were to be had, armed with this story and his obvious military threat to the Aztecs, he set off to the capital Tenochtitlan. To prevent his men deserting, he set fire to all the ships. It took many months to reach the city. Indeed, Montezuma at first, most certainly believing that Cortés and his army were the Aztec saviours sent by the gods to save their world, was ready to welcome them with open arms. However, Montezuma, on hearing of some brutal habits of the new men, realized they were mortal, and could die just like they could, had second thoughts and tried - but failed - to stop them by offering them vast amounts of bounty including gold and money (cocoa beans). But this had the opposite effect of exciting temptation and all attempts to arrest the progress of Cortés and his men were useless, and once they had established themselves in the city, Cortés put Montezuma under 'house arrest' and used him to try to control the Aztec Empire.

Here were two charismatic men, both fervently believing in the holy rites of their own separate God and idols. Can you imagine the impacts of these two opposing beliefs,

Catholic conqueror and Pagan protector - so different, yet so similar.

Extraordinary as it may seem, despite an unpromising beginning, Cortés and Montezuma established an almost amiable respect for each other's inherited powers - although history to this day is divided over whether this was because Montezuma continued to believe to his death that Cortés was the resurrected god or whether Montezuma was 'set up'.

Thus, friends or not, Cortés had a job to do which was to take the Aztec city and its people in the name of Spain.

Finding the Aztecs a worthy foe and difficult to defeat, Cortés was keen to reach a peaceful conclusion and attempted to talk the Aztecs into a settlement. Montezuma wanted to believe the Spaniards' assurances, he hated the violence and death of his people. However, Montezuma's court and his armies were less convinced.

Eventually, Cortés coaxed Montezuma out of his palace prison, still attended in all his former glory by servants and loyal courtiers, to speak to his people and to persuade them that the Spanish wanted a peaceful resolution. Reluctant but hopeful, Montezuma addressed the Aztec people; but even as he spoke one of them hurled a large stone, which concussed him. Although it was not life threatening, Montezuma's spirit was shattered and a few weeks later he died - most probably because he simply lost the will to live, aching with remorse to have failed his country and subjects. Despite Montezuma's absolute refusal to accept The Last Rites of Communion, remaining a 'heathen' to his last breath, he actually requested that his sons and daughters should be brought up by Cortés and in the Catholic faith. Montezuma died in the arms of his own nobles and with him died the royal line of the Aztecs.

Cortés was clearly moved by the death of his friend and the "news was further received with real grief by every cavalier and soldier in the army who had access to his person; for we loved him as a father - no wonder seeing how good he was".

Montezuma's death incited the Aztecs to even further rioting and by the July of 1521, they had forced the Spanish out of the city. It was many months before the Spanish were strong enough to try to recapture it. After a siege lasting 75 days, the capital fell. It was, effectively, the end of the Aztec civilisation - although breakaway groups lived scattered around the area for many more years. When the Spanish had razed Tenochtitlan - and most of the other Aztec forts, they rebuilt on the ruins and renamed the capital Mexico City.

Even after the conquest, the Spanish continued their wave of slaughter - in the name of religion - and those Aztecs who did not die under the Spanish artillery died from smallpox and other European diseases against which they had no resistance. The few nobles who survived refused to stoop to the manual work of the labourers and common farmers - (many of whom had been 'cannon fodder' as is universally common in wars) so the Spanish imported slaves from Africa to work on the farms and the cocoa plantations. This was the beginning of the slave trade and the interbreeding of the Central and South Americans. There are very few pure pre-Hispanic races today, but nevertheless, they do exist.

Many of the Spanish colonists were still far from convinced by the Aztec habit of drinking chocolate. But when they had used up their wine stores and grown bored with water, they found ways of improving on the Aztec recipe. Some enterprising nuns from Oaxaca had the idea of sweetening it with cane sugar (which was cultivated in the Spanish colonies of the Caribbean), vanilla and orange flower water. Now even Benzoni, who had thought it tasted like pigswill had to accept that chocolate had become more than acceptable. "It is bitter in taste, but quenches the thirst and refreshes the body".

CHOCOLATE'S JOURNEY TO EUROPE

Although the Spanish invasion of Mexico began a new chapter in the story of chocolate, there is some dispute over *xoco-atl*'s route back to Spain. It was probably Cortés although there is not a word about cocoa in the detailed records of the first treasures which he shipped home - but then you would hardly expect Cortés to rush home to his king pronouncing 'Sire, sire, look what I have found for you…' - landing a fistful of cocoa beans at his feet. After all, cacao was still a relatively new discovery for the Spanish, and

Mexico had surrendered many more instantly recognisable and important and valuable treasures like gold, obsidian, other precious metals - and chilli, and, as we have seen, most of them continued to think of chocolate as pigswill!

The first actual documentary evidence for the initial appearance of chocolate in Spain (and therefore Europe) concerns the Maya, who are usually lost in the past as far as our story is concerned. The **Kekchi Maya** of Guatemala lived in the beautiful Alta Verapaz. The Spaniards called it Verapaz, 'True Peace', because this is where the benefactor Dominicans led by Bartolomé de Las Casas had won over the rebellious Kekchi by understanding and kindness rather than violence. In 1544, the Dominican friars took a delegation of Kekchi Maya nobles to visit Prince Philip of Spain, presumably to thank him for his magnanimity (a virtue which he seldom displayed after he became Philip II).

The Kekchi visitors arrived in their native costumes which prompted the Prince to express concern at the unsuitability of their clothes for Spain's cold winter climate. Among the presents they brought him were, most precious (to them), 2000 quetzal feathers from the resplendent bird that was, and still is, found in their forests; clay vessels, lacquered gourds, plant products such as various chillies, beans, sarsaparilla, maize, *liquidambar* (a plant from the witch hazel family) and *copal* (resin) incense. To the court they also bought vessels of beaten chocolate.

Of course, we must not overlook the fact that there was much to-ing and fro-ing across the Atlantic from the New World to Spain by armies, civilians and the clergy to whom the responsibility may also reasonably be attributed.

Whatever route cocoa followed to Spain, despite the initial contempt shown by the conquistadors for its bitterness, its spell was cast and it soon became irresistible - especially to the Spanish Government that seized on its popularity and taxed it to the point that chocolate was, once again, the lot of the privileged few. Understandably though, cocoa beans were in short supply, and the first business to make chocolate, supplied by regular imports, was not established until 1580.

During the Sixteenth and early Seventeenth century Spain was a trendsetter. Europeans flocked to the Spanish court to see what was fashionable - and they found chocolate. If Spain had made any efforts at all to keep it to herself, its secret escaped through the unhappy political alliance in 1615 of Anne of Austria, daughter of Philip II of Spain to Louis XIII. Louis was nine when his father, Henry IV was assassinated in 1610 and his mother Marie of Medici, became Regent. She was determined to reverse her husband's policy of warring with Spain and instead arranged to cement the relationship between the two countries through the double dynastic nuptials. Louis and Anne were both only 14 when they married despite strong opposition from the French Protestants and the nobility. Thus Anne took the knowledge of chocolate across the Pyrenees to France and the French court.

The court adored chocolate for its unique taste but mostly because they considered it blessed with many virtues, including mood enhancers for some, while mixed with different ingredients, others experienced astonishing curative properties, stimulants, and some even aphrodisiac powers.

When the Spanish princess, Maria Teresa married Louis XIV in 1660, her passion for chocolate inspired her to give it to Louis as a wedding present packed in an expensive ornate chest. She also took her maid, La Molina, with her to France who was solely responsible for preparing the royal chocolate. At that time 'decent' women were not supposed to drink chocolate in public. Maria Teresa is reputed to have said that "my loves are only my chocolate and my king" - probably the order of preference in her affections reflected the fragile relationship between her and her husband, who was a womaniser and preferred the niece of Cardinal Mazarin, Madame de Maintenon. Despite Maintenon's reputation as a rigid puritan, history alleges that she and Louis were lovers while the king was married to Maria Teresa.

Louis XIV became one of the most prominent kings in Europe - as well as one of the great gourmands of his time. Everything was done to excess. His banquets and balls became legendary throughout Europe for their exorbitant superabundance. He created a fashion for other kings to follow which created challenge upon challenge for all the other European monarchs to aspire to be the gastronomic 'superstars' through their entertainment.

After Maria Teresa died, the King secretly married Madame de Maintenon who tried, without much success, to discourage him from some of his previous extravagances when chocolate would have been regularly served at all public functions as well as a major part of the court's daily imbibings. But his court was hooked.

Sieur **David Chaillou** of Toulouse was one of the first great Parisian chocolate makers to the Court of France. A patent was granted to him in 1659 first by the chocolate-mad Cardinal Mazarin who succeeded Cardinal Richelieu (and who may have been among the first to have introduced chocolate to France as a medicine and cure for his ailing spleen), and then by the king, Louis XIV.

Madame de Sévigné, whose letters to her daughter, Madame de Grignan, are a wonderful source of French court gossip, traces the fluctuating fashions of chocolate at Louis XIV's court: "And now, my dear child, I must tell you that chocolate no longer holds the place in my esteem that it used to do … those who used to praise chocolate, now speak ill of it … it flatters you for a time but presently lights up a fever that continues, and at length carries you to the grave … let me entreat you to no longer be an advocate for it, for it is no longer in fashion with the genteel part of the world" (15th April 1671). However, the lady was obviously addicted to its charms, and had a change of heart for on 28th October in the same year she wrote again "I have in mind to be friends again with chocolate…"

Her daughter ignored her mother's oscillating chocolate fondness and continued to indulge regularly herself. Eventually she gave birth to a 'black, feverish' child who was blamed on the chocolate - and once again, her mother despised it.

Be that as it may, and Chaillou's customers may well have been the rich aristocracy to whom the habit of taking chocolate had become a sign of one's wealth and success, in real terms this was a small market, and it was the fervour of the travelling monks that was responsible for bringing chocolate to a wider public in France in about 1660. It is curious therefore, to notice the controversy that at one time raged among the religious fraternity about where and when it was lawful to take chocolate in Lent - and whether or not it was to be regarded as a food or a drink. Although the clergy did not revere chocolate with quite the same religious intensity as the Mexicans, they certainly thought it important enough to control its uses.

A RELIGIOUS CONUNDRUM

A succession of Popes in the Sixteenth and Seventeenth centuries agreed that cocoa was so disagreeable that it could not possibly be responsible for the cardinal sin of self-indulgence - so it was alright to drink it as it "does not break the Lenten fast". As a consequence, the 'exquisite' beverage became more acceptable to the supreme Church of Rome which, in turn, meant that the question of the fast took on a new urgency. However, it took until 1662 for Cardinal Brancaccio to issue the official 'Judgement of Solomon' which proclaimed that "*Liquidum non frangit jejunum*". In other words: "Liquid (in the form of chocolate) does not break the fast." But the eating of chocolate was a very different matter and clearly one had to wait until Easter at the end of Lent to indulge.

The chocolate habit was just as ecclesiastically vexed in Colonial Mexico. In 1650, the Society of Jesus in the New Spain (to which Mexico was referred) published an act forbidding the use of chocolate; but this was soon rescinded when it proved impossible to enforce, and when many of their students left the schools 'in anarchy' because of it.

Thomas Gage (1600 - 1656) whom Elisabeth Luard quotes in her book *The Princess and the Pheasant*, was the "reprobate son of the English Catholic Gage family of Firle in Sussex, traveller, epicure and seventeenth century supergrass, and rogue in the mould of his contemporary the Vicar of Bray … disinherited by his father after a quarrel with his Jesuit schoolmasters, he served as a Spanish Dominican friar for sixteen years of his adult life. As such he travelled to the New World as a missionary monk with the Dons, the first

Englishman to do so. Appropriately for a young man of his culinary interest, Brother Thomas joined the expedition to New Hispania by stowing away in a biscuit barrel about a galleon in the Spanish port of Sanlúcar de Barrameda. Once in Mexico he developed a passion for chocolate which featured regularly in his topographical writings" … and as we have seen is one of those credited with 'inventing' one of the more spurious origins of the name of chocolate (choco-choco-choco).

Gage, who ended up anti-Catholic and anti-Spanish, wrote the famous *An English-American, His Travail by Land and Sea, or a New Survey of the West Indies*, which is full of cocoa and chocolate related anecdotes. In fact, it is from him that we get much of our Maya and Aztec history including the tale of very upper class white ladies of San Cristobel de las Casas. The ladies claimed weak stomachs and were therefore unable to get through mass without "a cup of hot chocolatte and a bit of sweetmeats to strengthen their stomackes" which was brought in by maids - interrupting both mass and sermon and enraging priests and preachers. The bishop thought fit to issue a written warning of excommunication to all who dared to eat or drink in the House of God during divine service. Enraged but unrepentant, the ladies announced that they would no longer attend Mass. Gage and the local Dominican prior did their best to appease the various parties, warning the bishop about threats to his life - but the bishop was unmoved, replying that his life was worth nothing compared to the glory of God and the sanctity of his house. The cathedral was now deserted, as everyone went to Mass in the convents, where chocolate was allowed, making nonsense of the bishop's rantings about excommunication.

Shortly afterwards the bishop became critically ill and took a ghastly eight days to die from drinking poisoned chocolate from a *jícara* (chalice - a favourite means for poison in both hemispheres); but not before asking God to pardon the perpetrators who were alleged to be a lady friend of Gage and one of the bishop's pages (who were apparently lovers). Gage, haunted by the recent fatal events, recounts that he soon feared for his own life when the lady began to make advances and departed in haste. This treacherous poisoning inspired the story, which was soon buzzing throughout Mexico: "Be careful of the chocolate of Chiapas".

It was generally expected that the Spanish colonial nuns and friars would not object to the practice of chocolate drinking, for we discover that two of these cloisters were "talked of far and near, not for their religious practices, but for their skill in preparing drinks which are used in those parts, the one call chocolatte, another *atole*. Chocolatte is (also) made up in boxes and sent not only around Mexico but much of it yearly transported into Spain".

So we see that in Colonial Mesoamerica, as in Catholic Europe, there were ecclesiastical prohibitions to observe - or ignore - particularly affecting the consumption of chocolate during fasts.

A Mexican recipe for *Champurrado* with *Atole* which was popular at the time (*champurrado* is the traditional chocolate drink and *atole* indicates that it is thickened with maize).

"*Atole* made from the treasured cacao bean was reserved only for the noblemen of Montezuma's court, who drank it from the special gold ceremonial cups. The women of the court were served their *atole* flavoured with *chia* (seeds) and topped with chilli". Today, the pretty colonial town of Oaxaca, 500 kms south of Mexico City, is especially famed for its chocolate, which is sold in all of its markets. The recipe comes with the following warning: "It does pay to heed the time proven advice: '*Ni amor recomendazo ni chocalato recalentado*' (Neither rekindle a love affair nor re-heat chocolate)."

Serves 6

115 g/4 oz	*nixtamalia* (maize - you can use cornflour)
55 g/2 oz	*piloncillo* (raw sugar) or honey
1-4 sticks	cinnamon and/or 1 split vanilla pod, seeds scraped
140 g/5 oz	Mexican chocolate (65-70% is fine)
250 ml/8 fl oz	hot water
1 litre/32 fl oz	milk or water

Mix maize with water and leave to stand for 15 minutes. Strain and place in a saucepan with the rest of the water or milk, the *piloncillo*, cinnamon stick/s and the vanilla pod and seeds if using. Cook over a medium heat stirring for 10 minutes. Add the chocolate. Stir for another 15 minutes until chocolate melts. Remove the cinnamon and vanilla. Pour immediately into 6 mugs from a height to work up a froth. (This recipe was given to me by Susanna Palazuelos in Acapulco, one of the stars of Mexico's culinary world).

The Lenten question was still an issue with the Catholic Church a hundred years on. A consensus of opinion on the subject, published in Venice in 1748 states that "… consumers are troubled and afflicted when in Lent they empty chocolate cups. Excited on the one hand by the pungent craving of the throat to moisten it, reproved on the other by breaking their fast, they experience grave remorse of conscience, and with consciences agitated and torn by drinking the sweet beverage, they sin. Under the guidance of these skilful theologians, the remorse aroused by natural and divine light being blunted, Christians drink joyfully. For all agree that he will break his fast that eats any portion of chocolate, which dissolved and well mixed with warm water is not prejudicial to keeping a fast. This is a sufficiently marvellous presupposition. He who eats 4 ozs. of exquisite sturgeon roasted has broken his fast. If he has it dissolved and prepared in an extract of thick broth, he does not sin".

Chocolate was not always as 'holy' as it might seem. In 1701, a ship from South America arrived in Spain with eight large crates marked 'Chocolate for the very reverend Father General of the Company of Jesus'. The customs inspectors of the time were highly suspicious at the incredible weight of the crates, which, when searched revealed gold bars covered in cocoa beans. The Jesuits disclaimed ownership, knowing that all gold was royal property. An agreeable solution was eventually reached: the king took the gold and the monks got the cocoa.

Religious follies apart, from small beginnings, cacao was on its way to becoming an international commodity and Europe's most desirable luxury. This is clearly reflected by the quantity, albeit tiny by today's standards, of cocoa beans supplied to the French market after 1684 when France conquered the Antilles (Cuba and Haiti) and set up their own cocoa plantations in the Caribbean.

By now it was also making its way across Holland, Belgium and Germany. Price lists of apothecaries in these countries show that cocoa was sold as early as 1640. In 1697 the Mayor of Zurich tasted chocolate on a visit to Belgium. He was hooked and took it back to Switzerland.

In 1711, the uncrowned King Charles III, barred from succession to the Spanish throne, returned to Austria as Emperor Charles VI - with the secret of chocolate. The Viennese court loved it.

Throughout the Seventeenth and Eighteenth centuries, cocoa and chocolate were considered to be medicine as much as a food. As many as thirty books, treatises and pamphlets were written on the perceived vices or virtues of chocolate. The debate raged on throughout the Seventeenth and Eighteenth centuries while the wealthy classes continued to drink chocolate just for the sheer pleasure of it.

Silversmiths and porcelain manufacturers, such as Limoges, were commissioned to create elaborate chocolate services. The idea of course, came from Mexico where chocolate drinking from golden goblets had begun. What they produced was as extraordinary as it was costly. Madame de Pompadour (1721-64) was reported to have the most expensive porcelain chocolate service ever created. It was, after all, a way of showing both status and position in the courts. Those who had it flaunted it.

Casanova (1725-98) is another who helped to sanctify chocolate. It is said that he preferred it to champagne: "Regarding chocolate I judge it to be of neutral effect; a cloying product fit for serving maids; yet possessed of value as an endearment, an incentive working not upon the body but upon the mind; it generates in those who relish it, a complacent and yielding disposition. Deprived of chocolate the lover of serving maid is deprived of his persuasive helpmate."

Chocolate was immortalised by Mozart, circa 1790, in his opera *Cosi Fan Tutti*. Mozart used chocolate as a symbol of social comment when the maid, Despina, brings hot chocolate to her mistresses, Fiordiligi and Dorabella. Despina sings of her sadness that she works so hard and yet is allowed no pleasure from chocolate. It has taken her half an hour to pound and prepare and all she can do is smell it … but she has no will power and sings "of chocolate I savour only the aroma. Yes, fine ladies, it is you who will drink it, and I must content myself with looking at it … By Bacchus, I am going to taste it" and she does "Oh, it's so good!"

As we can see, it was not only the Spanish and French who championed chocolate and the cultivation of cacao but other Europeans who had fallen under its spell and also pursued its propagation during their exploratory journeys across the Tropics.

In addition to France's own supply from the Caribbean, the main suppliers to Europe in the late Seventeenth and Eighteenth centuries were Spanish-controlled Ecuador and Venezuela. Spanish colonists found wild *forastero* cacao in Ecuador and pounced on the opportunity to cultivate it. The cacao's lack of quality compared to *criollo* was compensated by its abundance and vigorous growth. In Venezuela, a type of exceptionally tasty *criollo* cacao, known as Caracus, was widely grown. This cacao was exported to Europe and to Mexico where a royal decree against the imports of South American cacao was rescinded to allow free trade within the Spanish territories.

Since chocolate-mad Spain consumed nearly half the world crop, it didn't leave much for anyone else. Unsurprisingly, the chocolate-eating countries, whose indigenous climate and agricultural characteristics made it impossible to grow at home and who were by now totally hooked on the intoxicating beverage of the Aztecs, set about cultivating supplies in the potential cocoa lands of their own colonies. This included Java, Sumatra and Ceylon where the

Dutch cultivated cocoa when their attempts at growing coffee in the Seventeenth century had failed. The Dutch were also responsible for cocoa in Sri Lanka, New Guinea, Samoa, Indonesia, the former New Hebrides, and the Philippines; the Belgians in the Congo; the English expanded in the West Indies, and the Germans in the Cameroon.

CHOCOLATE IN EUROPE - THE INDUSTRIAL YEARS

In France, as you would expect from its culinary tradition of putting taste first, the flavour of chocolate was of indisputable importance. So much so that anything but the hand-made preparation of chocolate was sniffed at.

Not surprisingly then, neither the machine perfected to grind cocoa in 1732 by **Dubuisson**, nor the hydraulic grinding machine to make cacao into chocolate, invented and championed in 1778 by a man called Doret, who was authorised *chocolatier* to King Louis XVI and whose factory was granted the title of *Chocolaterie Royale*, found much credibility across the length and breadth of France.

Despite France's reluctance to embrace technology, in his travels around Europe, Englishman Joseph Townsend in 1786 noted that even Spanish chocolate was mechanised using polished steel rollers each turning independently, powered by a cog and a donkey…

In *The Philosopher in the Kitchen*, a unique collection of gastronomic meditations on cookery and the art of eating at the turn of the Eighteenth century (published in 1825), Jean-Anthelme Brillat-Savarin deplores the 'blasphemy' of factory-made chocolate, preferring the practised skill of a man's hand to perfect its manufacture. "For some time now, machines have existed for making chocolate; we do not believe that this method adds anything to its perfection, but it achieves a great saving of labour, and those who have adopted this method should be able to sell their chocolate cheaper. The contrary, however, seems to be the case…"

Savarin continues: "The grinding and mixing demands no less care, for it is on their absolute perfection that the digestibility of the chocolate partly depends… Those who have never used their hands can have no idea of the difficulties which must be overcome before perfection can be attained in any detail, nor of how much care, skill and experience are needed to produce chocolate which is sweet but not insipid, strong but not bitter, aromatic but not sickly, and this but free from sediment …

"Being ourselves very fond of chocolate, we have run the gamut of nearly all the dealers, and we have now settled upon Monsieur Debauve, of No. 26 Rue des Saints Pères; he is a purveyor of chocolate to the King, and we rejoice to see that the sun's rays have lighted on the worthiest of them all. Such are the qualities of Monsieur Debauve's chocolate; it owes its supremacy to the sound choice of materials, a firm determination to allow nothing inferior to leave his factory, and the keen eye of the proprietor which watches over every detail of the work. There is nothing surprising about that: Monsieur Debauve is a distinguished pharmacist and brings to his chocolate-making all the learning he had acquired for use in a wider sphere."

King Louis XIV's pharmacist **Debauve** and his nephew **Gallais**, also a pharmacist, set up as Messrs. Debauve et Gallais in 1800. Their belief that chocolate's medicinal properties were synonymous with health was unwavering.

The Debauve et Gallais shop still exists today in the rue des Sts. Pères on the Left Bank, listed in the Monuments Historique as a fine example of Louis Quinze architecture in the heart of Paris' chocolate heaven. D & B were famed for creating chocolate without sugar and although the chocolates have considerably changed since Savarin's day, the company still has much archive material to support Debauve's reputation as the most illustrious chocolate maker of the century. Back in 1825, Monsieur Debauve described himself as the "creator of analeptic chocolate prepared with Persian *salep*, *bechique* and pectoral chocolate prepared with tapikoa (unknown in France but successfully used in Britain for the treatment of pulmonary infections in the early stages) from India. Whenever unhappiness, unease of the soul or other afflictions, have made the nervous system fragile, the right diet is beneficial. It should be at the same time tonic, soothing, anti-spasmodic - which explains the popularity of the chocolate pastilles with vanilla, orange flower, almond milk and sugar-free health chocolate". Consequently they offered tonic chocolate, prepared with cachou from Japan; coffee-flavoured chocolate; stomach-improving chocolate for the sick; chocolate with orange flower water for ladies prone to spasms; white chocolate with theobromine and arrowroot from India; Royal chocolates with and without vanilla; Brillat-Savarin's ambergris chocolate; and for amateurs of foreign chocolates, they imported large consignments of chocolate from Cadiz and Bayonne.

Furthermore, Debauve et Gallais listed: 'The King's crunchy with two vanillas', 'the Queen's pastille soothing with almond milk', 'the Ladies' chocolates with orange flower water against spasms', the 'Maiden's chocolate, ganache with barley sugar cream', 'Chocolate for people suffering with coffee'! and 'Tablet for the Sick and Afflicted'.

Although a few of these Seventeenth and Eighteenth century recipes for cooking with chocolate have survived, chocolate was preferred as a drink for some two centuries more - until its mechanical manufacture was simultaneously developed during the Nineteenth century by a number of European entrepreneurs - less precious than the French about mechanisation. Indeed, it was the founder of Fry in 1795 who invented the process of manufacturing chocolate using a steam machine; and a half a century later in 1847, his grandson invented the first eating chocolate. John Cadbury, founder of the great empire, set up a modest shop in the heart of Birmingham in 1824.

Particular acclaim goes to the French, who, once they overcame their initial disregard for mechanisation, became masters in the art of varying the degrees of the fluidity and proportions of cocoa butter they used. Their marketing techniques were also far ahead of the British and, indeed, their eating chocolate was imported by Cadburys in the middle of the Nineteenth century and sold simply as 'French eating chocolate'.

The Europeans seemed more willing to pay the high prices to indulge in the luxury of chocolate - an example of the cultural difference between the British and the Europeans who traditionally spend more on their food than the British. Consequently, the popularity of eating chocolate had more of a head start in Europe, particularly in France where their confectioners had already carved themselves a worldwide reputation for fine chocolates. Chocolat Menier opened a factory in London in 1870 and less than 3 years later had a production rate of 500 tons a year.

In Switzerland meanwhile it was around 1875 when the firm of **Daniel Peter** conceived the concept and discovered how to combine chocolate with milk using his friend Henri Nestlé's slightly earlier invention of powdered milk by evaporation.

Another notable event in chocolate's edible story came as a result of a mishap in 1880 when another Swiss, **Rudolphe Lindt**, discovered how to make the smoothest-melt-in-the-mouth chocolate by 'conching' - and adding extra cocoa butter. This happened when one of Lindt's employees forgot to turn off one of the mixing machines at the end of a day's work in the factory. The following morning, Lindt was amazed to find how much more fluid the chocolate had become. The chocolate world adopted the process, which Lindt named after the machine's paddles, which were shaped like a shell for which the Spanish word is 'la concha'.

With agencies in London, Leeds, Liverpool, Edinburgh and Glasgow, Van Houten in Holland had unrivalled sales of cocoa, while the French cornered the dark chocolate market and Swiss companies such as Peter, Cailler and Kohler were leaders in sales of milk chocolate.

CHOCOLATE TO BRITAIN

England got its taste of chocolate in the mid-Seventeenth century. Apart from satisfying the demands of the rich for drinking chocolate, its stimulating powers were fully appreciated.

It's almost impossible to identify the first single source of Britain's encounter with chocolate and the tempting of the British palate. However, we are certain that its introduction was as a result of the discoveries of the early English explorers, like Thomas Gage and Sir Hans Sloane, of eponymous Sloane Square fame, together with a combination of the travelling monks and a very strong French and Spanish influence.

Knowledge of cocoa must have come during the latter

half of the 16th century via Spanish ships which fell victim to British (and international) sailors and pirates, but there are no factual documents recording these incidents apart from the odd historical comment indicating a total lack of interest. So much so that, in fact, upon discovering a shipload of cocoa beans in 1579, the contemptuous English sailors tipped the lot overboard thinking that these beans were sheep's droppings.

Thomas Gage wrote of this incident: "Our English and Hollanders make little use of it (cacao) when they take a prize at sea, as not knowing the secret virtue and quality of it for the good of the stomach, of whom I have heard the Spaniards say, when we have taken the good prize, a ship laden with cocoa in anger and wrath, we have hurled overboard this good commodity not regarding the worth of it". These beans, no doubt, were worth a fortune in cocoa.

However, we are certain that by 1652 the English were aware of chocolate as James Wadsworth wrote of it as "an Indian drink".

'Twill make an old woman Young and Fresh;
Create New Motions of the Flesh,
And cause them long for you know what
If they but taste of chocolate'.

Another important factor in our story lies with Cromwell's capture of the island of Jamaica from the Spanish in 1655. A healthy crop of cocoa had been established there by the Spanish some years before and soon became England's source. And in 1656 we find amongst various customs and excise duties granted to Charles II by the all-seeing Chancellor of the time: "For every gallon of chocolate, sherbert and tea made and sold, to be paid by the maker thereof..8d".

I think it is important to remind ourselves just what England was like in the turbulent mid-Seventeenth century and a quote from the Coes sums it up brilliantly: "In an age of religious bigotry and personal and public tragedy, the 17th century was, in some respects, the most brilliant in all English history, with significant figures in the arts and sciences, not to forget literature. Unconcerned with the Papal Inquisition which plagued the great Italians of the time such as Galileo, English scientists like Isaac Newton were free to explore the universe and the human body. Newton discovered gravitation and the secrets of the solar system, while William Harvey rethought Galenic medicine with the discovery of the circulation of the blood".

Such was the context in which Englishmen and women first adopted the three great 20th century 'addictions'; tea, coffee and chocolate. Although these drinks originated in three different continents - Asia, Africa and America - and came to England by different routes, they arrived almost simultaneously (coffee preceding by only a few years).

The 'new' drink began to make its mark among the English about the time of the Commonwealth, which was the government established by Parliament and led by Oliver Cromwell after the execution of King Charles I in 1649 and until the Restoration in 1660.

The first publicly recorded news of chocolate seems to have come via a Frenchman. A notice appeared in the *Public Advertiser* of 1657 informing its readers that "In Bishopsgate Street, by Queen's Head Alley, at a Frenchman's house is an excellent West Indian drink called Chocolate to be sold, where you may have it ready at any time, and also unmade at reasonable rates".

These so-called reasonable rates were about 6/8d to 10 shillings per pound, (approximately 34p-50p) - which was three to four weeks wages for the average worker in those days, and although in principle freely available for all, such a high price made chocolate exclusively a rich man's indulgence. The government made sure that it stayed that way, following the Spanish and French examples before them, with high import taxes. To their delighted avarice, chocolate was a guaranteed boost to their revenue. The excessive import duties encouraged regular smuggling for which the guilty could expect at least 12 months in jail. It would be another 150 years before import taxes were reduced and, thanks to both this and the Industrial Revolution, the masses at last could afford it.

It was popular at the court of King Charles II. The day after his return from exile, Samuel Pepys, a civil servant and famous topical chronicler as well as a self confessed lover of chocolate, is often quoted on the drink, for example: "waked in the morning with my head in a sad (condition) taking through last night's drink, which I am sorry for. So rose and went out with Mr. Creede to drink our morning draft, Chocolate to settle my stomach". (April 1661).

In November 1664, Pepys wrote again: "About noon, out with Commissioner Pett, he and I went to a Coffee House and there drank my morning Chocollatte, very good … and slabbering (dribbling) my band (neckband) sent home for another…" Not much prose here but you can almost hear his mouth watering…

Pepys did his fair share of womanising, probably aware of Dr. Henry Stubbes' consideration that chocolate "becomes provacative to lust upon no other account than that it begets good blood".

Henry Stubbes (1632-76) was considered a great master of the chocolate art and one of the most universally respected and referred to authorities. He considered the aphrodisiac qualities of chocolate:

"The use of Chocolate in Venery, and for Supplying the Testicles with a Balsam or a Sap is so ingeniously made out by one of our learned Countrymen already, that I dare not presume to add any thing after so accomplished a Pen; though I am of the Opinion that I might treat of the Subject without any Immodesty or Offence. Gerson, the grave Roman Casuist, has written the Nocturnal Pollution and some have defended Fornication in the Papist Nunneries; hysterical Fits, hypochondriacal Melancholy, Love Passions, consumptive Pinings away, and spermatic fevers being instances of the Necessity hereof, natural instincts pointing out the cure. We cannot but admire the great Prudence of Moses who severely prohibited that thee should be no Whore among the daughters of Israel, yet that most wise Legislator took great care for their timely Marriage, upon these very Accounts the Casuists defend the Protestant Clergy in their Marriages. And Adam is commanded in Paradise to increase and multiply, therefore I hope this little Excursion is pardonable being so adequate to this Treatise of Chocolate: which if Rachel had known, she would not have purchased Mandrakes for Jacob. If the amorous and martial Turk should ever taste it, he would despise his Opium. If the Grecians and Arabians had ever tried it they would have thrown away their Wake-robins and Cuckow-pintles; and I do not doubt but you London Gentlemen, do value it about all you Cullisses and Jellies; your Anchovies, Bononia Sausages, your Cock and Lamb-stones, your Soys, your Ketchups and Caveares, your Cantharides (Spanish fly), and your Whites of Eggs, are not to be compared to our rude Indian; therefore you must be very courteous and favourable to this little pamphlet, which tells you most faithful Observations".

And those who were not privileged to have access to the ear of the king and his court found comfort in the chocolate houses springing up in the smart centres of Mayfair and the City. English aristocracy could rest, have a cup of cocoa, or even purchase a small amount of solid chocolate, which was probably prepared and imported, from Spain or France, to take home to brew for themselves. These Chocolate Houses were the prototypes for London's famous gentlemen's clubs and were open to anyone who was decently dressed and of reasonable manners.

One such was White's Chocolate House which has become even better known, eventually emerging as the highly respectable White's Club, though at one time it too enjoyed its days as a notorious gambling centre. It includes amongst its former members Lord Byron, Edward Gibbon, Robert Walpole, Jonathan Swift and Voltaire (in exile) and, through the centuries many, many more famous and infamous men. It was about the middle of the Seventeenth century when an Italian immigrant, Francesco Bianci (Francis White) started White's Chocolate House in the highly fashionable St. James's in London. Bianci most probably brought the recipe with him from Italy where chocolate had been introduced by a number of Italian explorers, picked up on their global travels. This included the Milanese historian and voyager **Girolamo Benzoni** (1518-70), one of the first Europeans to describe cocoa and chocolate and probably one of the very first to have introduced it to his native country. As we have already seen, Benzoni is quoted as having described the taste of chocolate in the New Americas as "astringent and ungrateful".

Another Italian, the infamous slave trader and explorer, Antonio Carletti, some half a century or so later is also credited with bringing chocolate to London after "inflaming the Italian passion for cocoa". On one of his early Seventeenth century global voyages he had stopped at St. Jonat, which lies on the border between Guatemala and El Salvador, and a zone of very high cocoa production. Carletti tells us that both natives and Spaniards, "and any other nationality that goes there" use chocolate… "once they start it they become so addicted that it is difficult for them not to drink it every morning, or late in the day when it is hot, or when on shipboard, because they carry it in boxes, mixed with spices, or made into tablets which dissolve quickly in water".

Over the years, another chocolate house, the Cocoa Tree, developed into a gaming house and became a gentleman's club in about 1853. It still carried the name in 1932 when it closed it doors for the last time.

The Coffee Mill and Tobacco Roll, were also celebrated late Seventeenth century London coffee houses where you could enjoy chocolate made into cakes and rolls 'in the Spanish style'. You could also appreciate the more usual preparation of chocolate as the drink which Christopher Wilkins, in his book *The Natural History of Chocolate* (17th c), recommends variations of the ingredients according to the constitutions of the consumers: "in cold constitutions, Jamaica pepper, cinnamon, nutmegs, cloves, etc. may be mixed with the cocoa-nut (bean); some add musk and odiferous aromatick oils. In hot consumptive tempers, you may mix almonds, pistachios, etc., sometimes china and arsenic; and sometimes steel and rhubarb may be added for young green ladies". Wilkins also deplored the use of sugar as being "such a corrosive salt and such an hypocritical enemy of the body".

Charles II tried to suppress the intrigues of the chocolate houses, many of which were plots against the monarchy and state, by banning them. Although without success, he did manage to install spies to report back any 'irregularities of intention'.

Chocolate houses continued to be part of the London scene for nearly a century and a half and, as 'drinking houses', they were maintained as alcohol-free zones and so as an alternative to alcohol provided an important focus for broadcasting the topical news. There were no strident, controversial newspapers and free speech was not encouraged.

By the end of the Seventeenth century, the habit of drinking tea, coffee and chocolate matched the consumption of wine, which gave wine merchants something to grumble about. To embrace patriotic fervour, Parliament was asked to ban brandy, rum, tea, coffee and chocolate to encourage liberal sales of gin, whisky and ale. But all attempts at legislation failed.

Drinking chocolate (as opposed to 'eating' chocolate) enjoyed its greatest popularity in the late Seventeenth and early Eighteenth century. At that time, either chocolate or coffee was the normal breakfast drink among the gentry, accompanied by a light meal of wigs (a type of bun), spiced bread or buttered toast. Fifty years later, chocolate for breakfast was rare, for it had been surpassed by tea and to a lesser extent, coffee. The chocolate houses closed down or took on other roles, such as the example of Whites - from cocoa house to gambling centre to the gentleman's club that exists today.

What did it look and taste like? Drinking chocolate was made by scraping or grating chocolate powder from one of the cakes and adding a liquid to make a paste and then adding more liquid. Other recipes of the day called for the addition of egg yolks (as an emulsifier) or fortified wines, such as Port or Madeira and one of the main English innovations was to add both claret and egg yolks which made a sort of wine caudle (custard): "To make chaculato. Take half a pint of claret wine, boil it a little, then scrape some chaculato, very fine, and put into it, and the yolks of two eggs, stir them well together over a slow fire till it be thick, and sweeten with sugar according to your taste".

Sometime later, milk was included, and still a drink, it was thickened with egg or starch (usually arrowroot): "then mill it with a mill for that purpose till it becomes thick and proper for drinking. This mill is a stick with an head at the end full of notches, which you must at the little end hold in your hand

and hastily twirl about". This would have resembled the *molinillo*, a chocolate mill found all over Mexico and in Spain, and seems to have been usefully and widely employed as the forerunner to the balloon whisk because it is often found in recipe instructions of the day.

French recipe books available in Britain at the time give numerous ways of preparing it. A Monsieur Pierre Masson, who ran a café in Paris, published a book in about 1704 called *Le Parfait Limonadier, ou le manière de preparer le chocolat … et autres liqueurs chaudes et froides …* Masson's recipe for chocolate went something like this:"To make four cups of chocolate you need four cups of water. Take a quarter pound of chocolate and chop it finely on a sheet of paper; if you prefer it sweet, then take a quarter pound of sugar and crush it and add it to the chocolate; boil the water in a chocolate pot and plunge the chocolate and the sugar into the chocolate pot and stir it well with the chocolate stick (which would have been the *molinillo*). Place it in front of the fire and when it rises, withdraw it before it boils over and beat it well with the stick to make it froth; as it does pour it into the cups one by one … if you want to make it with milk, take as much milk as you would for water and proceed as above…"

Since the time of the Norman conquests, England has enjoyed many of its confections from early French origin, like Hundreds and Thousands, which the French called *Non Pareil* meaning 'none of the same' or 'unequalled'; 'bonbons' almost literally meaning 'goodies'; 'dragee' meaning 'dredged'! Probably the most significant appropriation of a French word is the English dessert, which comes directly from *desservir* to leave or clear the table.

Ivan Day, the patient and yet deeply passionate contemporary food historian, who lives in the north of England, has specialised in the knowledge of and practical exposition of Seventeenth and Eighteenth century sweets and chocolate.

Ivan tells us that then, England imported its chocolate - i.e. cocoa beans - in a 'raw' state. Chocolate dealers roasted and then pounded them roughly in a mortar with powdered sugar - like icing sugar and which was common then.

This was all much richer than today's drinking chocolate

for at that time no-one had yet worked out how to separate the rich cocoa butter from the cocoa mass - although the Maya had gone some way to crack this one 2,000 years before - and similarly in the West Indies chocolate was heated so that the cocoa butter rose to the top and was skimmed off and used for cosmetic and medicinal purposes. But it was not until the early Nineteenth century that the chocolate factories in England and other European countries developed the industrial processes for defatting cocoa - and what to do with it.

Today's refined chocolate becomes fluid at moderately high temperatures, and when properly tempered it is used for pouring into moulds. Back then however, the raw chocolate would have been refined by warming it in the oven which would have ripened it into a sticky mess; but with the correct amount of sugar, and a good mixing, it was transformed into a malleable paste which could be pressed into moulds.

Soon after chocolate first appeared in England, recipes appeared from France and Spain containing instructions on how to transform it into chocolate cakes and rolls. "Take cacao nuts gently dried in an iron pan, and peel off the husks, powder them very small so as to be sifted; then to every pound so prepared, add of white sugar six ounces, cinnamon half an ounce, one nutmeg, one vanilla (pod) of the best; ambergris or musk each four grains, if for high price for Spanish chocolate, in the English it is left out". All these ingredients to be worked together with an iron roller on an iron plate over gentle heat, and while it is warm it may be made into rolls or cakes or cast in moulds, or what form thou pleasest".

Other early chocolate confectionery known as Nuts of Rouen or Queen's Chocolatas were first sold in London by a dealer called Richard Mortimer. Of South American origin, they were made in Martinique and before that in Nicaragua. Around the 1640s, the French settlers in Martinique sent them to Rouen - and from there they spread across the rest of Europe. Nuts of Rouen are mentioned in a number of early chocolate books such as Henry Stubbes' *The Indian Nectar*. Ivan describes them as "gruesome - they are cocoa beans with strips of cinnamon bark larded through the middle and they were supposedly purely medicinal. They are rolled in sugar paste - like icing - ending up as uneven round shapes with spikes of crusty sugar sticking up like hedgehogs - or sputniks! They were prescribed for medicinal remedies, particularly for the digestion. However, Mortimer couldn't resist advertising them as aphrodisiacs - which was a type of early marketing! Chocolate, like toffee, was accredited with this reputation initially, and enthusiastically spread by the chocolate people.

"Cannelons of 17th century Italian origin" says Ivan "tasted superb. This was a form of chocolate cigarette made from a fine pastry with lots of sugar, egg yolk and butter, rolled up in paper and cooked in the oven. Finally, chocolate was crammed into the hollow centre".

Another favourite recipe of Ivan's is a 1690 English version of the Italian *Sorbetto de Chocolada* "… just 175g/6 oz raw chocolate, 150g/5 oz sugar and 600 ml/1 pint water. Because it's made from raw chocolate and the cocoa butter content is very high, this substitutes for the cream. It is really just a straightforward frozen chocolate drink as they used to make it centuries ago. It started in Naples, then a colony of Spain, and where the Spanish influence was tremendous. They were chocolate-crazy and they knew all about freezing - it's the best ice cream ever!"

English housewives soon copied chocolate almonds, which would be purchased from French confectioners in the 1670s. Flavoured at first with musk and ambergris, and later by orange flower water, the almonds were served for dessert along with crystallised fruits and candies. Chocolate itself was used to flavour other confectionery such as chocolate puffs (little light cakes of sugar and beaten eggs). Chocolate cream was a second course dish for which thick cream, eggs, and melted chocolate were milled together 'that it may go up in a froth'. The more solid part was put into dishes and the froth, which had been reserved on a sieve, laid over it. Later smooth chocolate cream, like tea and coffee creams, became more usual.

The first known recipe for chocolate in an English cookery book was by **William Salmon** in his 1690 edition of *Salmon's Dictionary*. He describes three types of chocolate drink then current: that made with water alone but fortified with a little brandy; that made with milk; and 'wine chocolate' in which "the liquid element was supplied by three quarters of a pint o water and half a pint o choice red port or rather choice sherry". For his recipe Cream of Chocolet (*sic*): he writes: "Make a pint of thin chocolate with spring water, and let it be cold, then beat the yolks of three eggs; mix it with the chocolet, sweeten it with double refined sugar, and strain it, set it over a gentle fire, keep it stirring till it begins to be thick, then pour it into glasses". Strangely, in the 1710 edition of the same book, there is no mention whatsoever of chocolate.

A 1695 recipe for 'chocolate puffs' which resembled mini-meringue mushrooms is recorded in *The True Way of Preserving* and subsequently copied by Elizabeth Raffald in her book *The Experienced English Housekeeper* in 1769. Raffald also tells us how to make chocolate: "Scrape four ounces of chocolate and pour a quart (2 pints) of boiling water upon it, mill it using a chocolate mill, and sweeten it to your taste, give it a boil and let it stand all night, then mill it again very well, boil it two minutes, then mill it and it will leave a froth upon the top of the cups".

Chocolate pastilles were not designed to be sweets at all but moulded in the shape of peach kernels, almonds, cockle shells, cocoa or coffee beans - even grains of wheat. Although made of a mixture of sugar paste with a little chocolate added for flavour, it was like a hard sucking sweet. The first English recipe for chocolate pastilles appeared in a 1718 recipe book written for housewives or housekeepers. Chocolate was available in grocers and coffee shops but continued to be very expensive, however the literate ladies for whom such books were written tended to be quite well off.

In her now famous book of 1747, *The Art of Cookery Made Plain and Easy - By A Lady*, Hannah Glasse offers not a single recipe for chocolate - neither drink nor confectionery - but she does recommend the use of a chocolate mill (similar to a wooden *molinillo*) to whisk syllabubs, implying that, as a general rule, chocolate was not liberally used by the housewife.

However, this is amended in a later book when she says in her recipe Water of Chocolate that (this water) "should be used in the winter and at any time when flowers and fruits are wanting; this is prepared only by grating some chocolate into water, as greatly as the quantity requires and adding a good quarter of a pound of Sugar to Every Quart; afterwards all being well steept and infus'd for some time, and the liquid must be strained in order to be iced or cooled".

Ivan goes on to describe how the confectioners of the time used to make flat chocolates, which were the original chocolate drops - and the genesis of the name. These were made by rolling a series of chocolate balls - then putting them on to a large sheet of paper which was held by two people at opposite corners "who would bounce the malleable chocolate up and down, drop it on to a flat table, then throw them into Hundreds and Thousands" - the original Smarties.

Frederic Nutt who first mentioned this method of fashioning the early chocolate drops in *The Compleat Confectioner* in 1789, learned his confectioner's art from Dominico Negri. Negri immigrated to London to train at a shop called the Pot and Pineapple in Berkeley Square, which later became Gunter and Negri and then the famous Gunter's pastry shop. He went into partnership with a woman called Mrs. Whitton and from a 1769 trade card we can see that they sold, among other things, Neapolitan Diabolinis - which are as popular today as they were when first introduced over 200 years ago. Diabolinis were, in fact, one of the earliest 18th century versions of the chocolate drop. They were literally hand-made - the confectioner first oiled his hands with almond oil, then wrapped an almond or pistachio nut in chocolate. According to Ivan Day, "this is a brute of a task because it collapses - but the solution was to drop it into a bowl of little Hundreds and Thousands (*non pareil*) which stuck to it, thus keeping its shape". Celery or poppie (*sic*) seeds or orchis (iris) root also achieved this effect remarkably well. Candy or sweetmeats evolved from herbs and medicines as a method devised to make the stuff more acceptable. Some of them, of course, were actually very good indeed and many herbs and spices became favourites, like peppermint and ginger. In England, the abundance of sweetmeats sold on barrows would have included chocolate drops, brandy balls, ginger nuts, aniseed balls and boiled sugar pulled over a hook. Sweets were wrapped in old newspapers and pages from discarded books - complete with noxious printing ink.

BRITISH CHOCOLATE PIONEERS

However it was **Sir Hans Sloane**, (1660-1753) whose interest in chocolate led to further developments in its manufacture. Sloane was a distinguished physician and President of the Royal College of Surgeons. He was also an icon of 17th century England and close friend of many other significant historical celebrities of the epoch including Christopher Wren, John Evelyn, Isaac Newton, Handel, and Samuel Pepys. His renowned passion for collecting eventually helped found the British Museum. Furthermore, that exquisite and charming oasis of nature in the middle of Chelsea, the Physic Garden, exists today because of Sir Hans Sloane. A sea voyage served to add his name to the history of chocolate. In 1687 during his travels across the world, he arrived in Jamaica, and discovered cocoa, being greatly impressed with its restorative properties. On his return to England, he was encouraged to publish his account of the voyage. The first of two volumes appeared in 1707 under the title of *The Voyage to the Islands of Madera, Barbados, Nieves, S. Christophers and Jamaica with the natural history of the Herbs and Trees, Four footed beasts, Fishes, Birds, Insects, Reptiles, etc of those islands*. *Theobroma Cacao* was among the many plants which were illustrated. Sloane was one of the first to advertise the food value of chocolate when mixed with milk and made a great success of promoting it as a potion. He sold his recipe to Nicholas Sanders of Solihull, already a chocolate manufacturer, and who in turn passed it to his trade successor. The latter eventually sold the rights to Cadbury Brothers in 1849. For 26 years they successfully marketed the chocolate drink under the title Sir Hans Sloane's Milk Chocolate.

To understand the debate on chocolate and health in Seventeenth and Eighteenth century Europe, you would need to understand the Humour Classification system - hot, cold, dry, moist, fire, water, earth, and air - on which European medicinal practice was founded. The theory had been developed from ancient Greek, Egyptian and Indian ideas by Galen, a second century Roman physician. It was the only 'scientific' approach to medical treatment for centuries.

The four elements of the universe - fire, water, air and earth - were linked to the fluid contents of the body by four qualities - hot and cold, dry and moist. The balance of the four fluids determined character and disposition; Black bile (Melancholy), Phlegm (Phlegmatic), Blood (Sanguine), Yellow bile (Choleric).

Drugs to cure disease could be hot or cold, dry or moist. A cold drug could cure a hot fever. Food and nutrition were also classified in this way. The apothecary's job was to prescribe the herbs to balance the humours and thus bring the patient back to health. This principle is still followed today in Chinese herbal medicine and acupuncture.

There was endless debate about the hot or cold nature of chocolate when it was introduced to Europe. Some believed it to be hot and dry and others cold and moist depending upon the circumstances. The Spanish thought it cold and so liked to add pepper and spices to neutralise its 'morbid' effects.

As you might imagine, such an active principle inevitably attracted its enemies too, for it was considered by many to be an aphrodisiac "an inflamer of passions", which should be prohibited to the monks.

By some it was considered downright dangerous: Dr. Duncan of the Faculty of Montpelier, London (1706) said "coffee, chocolate and tea at the first use only as medicines while they contained unpleasant, but since they were made delicious with sugar, they are become poison … it however, did not deserve it as a passport, that would be stopped at the gate of the House where the Soul dwells…" and the following warning appeared in the *Spectator* (London) on 29th April 1712: "I shall advise my fair readers to be in a particular manner careful how they meddle with romances, chocolates, novels and the like inflamers, which I look upon a very dangerous to be made use of during this great carnival" (May).

Even in those days, the injudicious addition of sugar was considered immoral if not unlawful. A few years earlier, a London doctor had declared "at first coffee, tea and chocolate were used only as medicines while they continued unpleasant, but since they were made delicious with sugar they are become poison".

A notice printed at the Black Boy Inn, by St. Dunstan's Church in Fleet Street, exclaims: "As for the great quantity of sugar which is commonly put in, it may destroy the native and genuine temper of the chocolate, sugar being such a corrosive salt, and such an hypocritical enemy of the body. Simeon Pauli (a learned Dane) thinks sugar to be one cause of our English consumption, and Dr. Willis blames it as one of our universal scurvies; therefore, when chocolate produces any ill effects, they may be often imputed to the great superfluity of its sugar".

In this period too Spanish Fly, (*Cantharides*) a pungent and toxic ground preparation of the green beetle *Lyttavescatoria* was originally used to raise blisters but found to be successful as an aphrodisiac. At one of the Marquis de Sade's Marseille balls, chocolate pastilles containing Spanish Fly found their way into the desserts - the ensuing orgy which developed caused de Sade to flee for his life. His temporary exile in Sardinia was spent womanising and writing letters home to his wife begging for chocolate … (Marquis Donatien de Sade 1740-1814 was the French writer whose sexual perversions gave rise to the word 'sadism').

Given its perceived medicinal properties, it is no surprise that the early English chocolate manufacturers were apothecaries or chemists. Making chocolate is a complex process and requires specialised equipment to heat, measure and blend the ingredients as well as the necessary skills - all of which they already had. As we have seen, chocolate lozenges were sold alongside other semi-medicinal sweets and some pills appear to have been covered in chocolate. Of today's famous chocolate makers, Fry, Terry and indeed, Caley were founded by apothecaries. Others became involved in cocoa throughout the grocery trade. Isaac Rowntree worked in his family's grocery business before branching out into chocolate manufacture, and John Cadbury began by dealing in tea and coffee in his Birmingham shop.

In addition, many of these men were devout Quakers, encouraged to produce an alternative to the devil in alcohol by their strict beliefs. The Quaker religion was founded by George Fox (1624-91). Their principles were based on the proper education of their children, care of the needy, racial and religious tolerance and the treatment of all offenders in a spirit of love rather than punishment. Consequently they refused to take oaths (believing it to be a form of swearing and therefore against the scriptures); preached against war and slavery and often found it necessary to oppose the authority of the church or the state. As pacifists and non-conformists, they eschewed any form of intoxicant, the army and universities, so access to the professions was impossible. Consequently, the energies and talents of Quaker families were directed towards business, and the reformation of the social and industrial society of Victorian Britain. Many Quaker families have made their mark on the British business scene - in addition to Cadbury's and Fry's, Rowntrees and Terry's of York developed confectionery and chocolate businesses; Sampson Lloyd of Birmingham founded Lloyd's Bank; the Hanburys brought tinplate to Wales and the Darbys of Coalbrook were the fathers of the British iron industry.

THE FIRST BRITISH CHOCOLATE FORBEARS

During the 17th century, grinding of the little chocolate that was available was still accomplished solely by hand. The first recorded chocolate manufacturer in England was **Walter Churchman** of Bristol in 1728. He also had premises in St. Paul's Churchyard, London from where he probably supplied some of the fashionable chocolate houses. An enterprising man, he had invested in a water engine, which enabled him to grind his chocolate more finely, and in 1728 he was awarded letters patent by George II. The notice advertising this achievement was published in *Farley's Bristol Newspaper* in June 1731: "His Majesty having been pleased to grant to Walter Churchman Letters Patent for his new invention of making chocolate without fire, to greater perfection in all respects, than will appear on Trial by its immediate dissolving full flavour, smoothness on the palate and intimate union with Liquids and as it is so much finer than any other sort, so it will go much further and be less offensive to weak digestions, being by this method free from grit and gross

particles so much disliked which is referred to the fair and impartial experiment."

FRY'S

The Churchmans were not the only chocolate manufacturers in Bristol. **Dr. Joseph Fry** (1728-87) who was born in Wiltshire, was apprenticed to an apothecary called Dr. Henry Portsmouth of Basingstoke and learnt an immense amount about the medical properties of plants and herbs and the compounding of drugs - which in those days included cocoa. He settled in Bristol as a qualified doctor and apothecary when he was about 20 and soon discovered that he preferred inventive and entrepreneurial pursuits in favour of medicine. He was made a freeman of the city in 1756 and three years later an announcement appeared in the local press stating: "The best sorts of chocolates made and sold wholesale and retail by Joseph Fry, Apothecary in Small Street, Bristol". By this time he had invented a number of recipes for chocolate and moved to larger premises in Narrow Wine Street.

When Charles Churchman died in 1761, Fry leapt at the opportunity to purchase the patent and broadcast the fact very plainly in the local paper; "Churchman's chocolate is now made only by Joseph Fry and John Vaughan jun., the present sole proprietors of the famous water engine at Castle Mills". This was one of the many technological advances that the Fry family were to pioneer over the next two centuries. Competition must have increased for the *Public Advertiser* in 1776 emphasised that the water mill was the only one of its kind in Great Britain.

In those days, progress was a matter of trial and error. Joseph Fry was a great innovator able to adapt the inventions and experience of others for his own business use. Basic chocolate production techniques involved roasting the cocoa beans over an open charcoal fire, hand winnowing and grinding and then crushing on a heated stone slab - still very similar to the methods passed down by the Maya and Aztecs. The cocoa mass was then mixed with flavourings and sugar in copper or tin pins, then shaped into tablets. Eating chocolate was unknown and consumers would make a chocolate drink by placing the tablet in the bottom of a chocolate cup adding hot water or perhaps milk. It was still a relatively coarse and thick drink with quite a lot of obvious cocoa butter but it was nevertheless an enjoyable potion and, of course, one of its principal attractions was that it was exceptionally nourishing and had no equals.

Inadequate supplies of raw materials limited production. The burden of heavy import duties still excluded all but the richest people from buying Fry's Bristol chocolate. In 1771, one pound of Fry's famous chocolate retailed at 7/6d (35p), a sum nearly equivalent to an average agricultural labourer's weekly wage.

Joseph Fry wrote to the Lord's Commissioner of the Treasury in 1776, imploring, unsuccessfully, for a reduction in duty, not only on manufactured chocolate at two shillings and threepence, but on the raw materials as well, at the rate of ten shillings per cwt of cocoa beans. Fry also had to compete with manufacturers who still used a primitive method and adulterated the product. For many manufacturers were adding potato starch, arrowroot and even powdered seashells. Despite early attempts to control the problem, adulteration continued and increased over the centuries, other than the starch which was accepted to balance the excesses of the fatty cocoa butter.

Upon his death in 1787, an obituary appeared in the *Gentleman's Magazine* lauding Fry for:

"The manufacture of chocolate, both in his own name and as a succeeding Patentee to Churchman, was carried by his own skill and a management to a degree of importance, now well known, to over a large part of Great Britain; a manufacture which is likely to remain a very considerable source of profit to his widow and family".

Indeed, Anna Fry, his widow and their son, Joseph Storrs Fry (1767-1835) did take over the business, changing its name to Anna Fry and Son. The business prospered and the first advertisements began to appear, stressing the healthful properties of cocoa.

By the middle of the Nineteenth century, the present system of conventional medicine had displaced the humours classification and medicinal chocolate, sometimes with herbal contents, was sold as a tonic, often taken on an empty stomach for maximum buzz or as an aid to digestion after a meal.

Anna Fry's cocoa was recommended "by the most eminent in preference to every other kind of Breakfast, to such who have tender Habits decayed Health weak Lungs or scorbutic Tendencies, being easy of Digestion, affording a fine and light nourishment, and greatly correcting the sharp Humours in the Constitution".

Directions "To make Cocoa in the Pot" were as follows: "Take an Ounce of Cocoa (which is about a common teacupful) boil it in a Pint and a half of water for ten or fifteen minutes, then keep it near the fire to settle and become fine, after that, decant it off into another Pot for Immediate Use. It is drank as Coffee, sweetened with a fine, moist sugar and a little cream or Milk should be added. It is best not to be made long before it is drunk, lest by that means it will loose part of its flavour. NB this cocoa does not require much boiling; therefore it will go quite as far as any other sort, with a less quantity of water than is commonly directed".

Joseph took the business to another dimension when he moved to Union Street and in (circa) 1790, made history again for the company when he purchased a James Watt steam engine to grind his beans. George III granted a patent in 1795 recognising Joseph Storrs Fry's invention of an improved method for roasting cocoa beans.

After Anna's death in 1803, Joseph Storrs Fry went into partnership with a Doctor Hunt and the business became Fry & Hunt. In 1822 Dr. Hunt retired and Joseph brought his three sons, Joseph (1795-1879), Francis (1803-86), and Richard (1807-78), into the business and the well-known name of J.S. Fry & Sons was adopted.

For many years Fry's produced most of the commercially available chocolate in the UK, although cocoa imports totalled less than 100 tons per year. In the first half of the 19th century, however, competition increased not only from Rowntree of York but also from a new Birmingham company started in 1824 by John Cadbury.

In 1826 *Butter's Medical Directory* referred to J.S. Fry's chocolate lozenge as a "pleasant and nutritious substitute for food when travelling".

Of Joseph Storrs Fry's three sons, Francis, a scientist by profession, was the most dynamic and the business owes a great deal to him for its prosperity.

In Holland in 1825 **Coenraad J Van Houten** created and patented the world's first hydraulic chocolate press, which separated cocoa butter from the cocoa mass, thus extracting and separating approximately ²/₃ of the fat. The remaining 'cake' was considered more digestible and so, for the first time the now familiar article, cocoa was manufactured.

In 1828, Van Houten then introduced another variation based on a secret he had heard about from a Mexican Indian 'doctor', who made chocolate more beneficial for his patients by mixing chocolate with sifted wood ashes. The brew was claimed to be healthier, more readily digestible and was used as a cure or restorative. Van Houten was enough of a chemist to realise that the active component in the ashes was potash, and his process utilised this knowledge to alkalise the cocoa powder. Thus alkalisation - the addition of alkaline salts (potassium or sodium carbonates) potash - was born. A further result of this process was a darker coloured cocoa, which was milder in flavour and easily mixed with water. His process became known as 'Dutching' - hence Dutch chocolat - named after the country of its origin.

It did not take long for other manufacturers to realise that they too could mix the cocoa paste with sugar and a measured quantity of cocoa butter to produce a relatively fine mixture that could be moulded into bars.

Based on the invention of the Van Houten method of pressing cocoa, in 1847 Francis made history yet again for the Fry family by finding a way of producing eating chocolate - some say it was a world first. Be that as it may, it was certainly the first in England. He did this by blending cocoa liquor and sugar to which he added cocoa butter instead of the customary water. The addition of the cocoa butter meant that for the first time it could be poured into a mould - thus introducing the forerunner of chocolate in bars as we would recognise it today - albeit still very rustic and grainy and the flavour was rather harsh in comparison with the wonders yet to come; but to the people of that time, it was 'heaven' and they were enchanted and so the love affair with the world's most popular 'food of the gods' took on a new and more dedicated direction.

Fry & Sons was proud to exhibit its chocolate at the Great Paris Exhibition of 1851. Subsequently, demand for cocoa and chocolate rose, further aided by the relaxation of the towering duties on cocoa in 1853. In the same year, Fry's introduced another innovative product - chocolate-covered cream sticks, the first chocolate confectionery ever to be made on a factory scale.

In 1875, Francis developed Fry's Cream Stick (first introduced in 1853) into Fry's Chocolate Cream Bar. The reason for designing the bar with clear-cut divisions was that the cream is what confectioners call 'short eating'; and the chocolate has the 'crisp snap'. The bar is made so that it can easily be broken: the word 'cream' describes the smoothness factor rather than the ingredients. The recipe for this famous original remains secret even today and the bar has the same delicious taste.

In 1882, J.S. Fry & Sons was the first company to use 'artificial cold', now known as refrigeration, as a means of cooling cast chocolate; and in July 1886, the first penny slot machine, then called chocolate boxes, was installed on Mansion Street station in London to deliver a small lozenge to the travelling public, on which J.S. Fry & Sons seized the opportunity to capitalise.

By 1887 Fry's was by far the largest manufacturer of chocolate and cocoa in the country and at the height of its prosperity, the company even boasted its own cocoa plantation in Trinidad which provided an alternative source to the plantations of West African and 'slave-grown' supplies which they abhorred and boycotted. Their output accounted for nearly a quarter of all the chocolate sold in Britain, with sales totalling more than ¹/₄ million pounds.

A rapidly exploding population and improved living standards contributed to an increase in turnover and profits as did the fact that Fry's had become the sole supplier of cocoa and chocolate to the Royal Navy which was gradually being weaned from its reliance on alcohol - known as 'grog' in the Navy.

A **Captain James Ferguson** is thought to be responsible

for introducing the cocoa bean to the Navy at the end of the 18th century through his regular sea voyages to the West Indies. Admiralty records show that cocoa was first noted in 1784 as a substitute for butter and cheese. $\frac{1}{2}$ lb. cocoa and $1\frac{1}{2}$ lbs. sugar = 1 lb. butter or cheese; although the official introduction of chocolate as a standard ration at 1 oz (one ounce) per man was not recorded until 1825. This was a substitute for the breakfast 'burgoo' or gruel, which was made of oatmeal and water and bread. Later reports from official Admiralty documents of 1868 state that "Directions given to forward a sample of Chocolate made from 70% of cocoa, 15% of arrowroot and 15% dried (*sic*) sugar - sample being approved - directed 12 cakes to be made each cake to be marked into small squares representing each man's allowance".

The British Navy in 1830 consumed more chocolate than the rest of the nation together, and until relatively recently, it was served daily. The Navy believed that cocoa was a nutritious, warming substitute for alcohol and therefore a particularly appropriate 'slurp' for naval duty.

The Army was Britain's second major chocolate consumer. In 1851 the cocoa allowance for each man on the front line was increased to one and a half ounces a day although after the Crimean War this was cut to one ounce. Although cocoa has no part in wars, the supply and demand is certainly affected.

The British chocolate companies of Cadbury, Fry and Rowntree found their strong Quaker beliefs compromised in 1899 when Queen Victoria ordered thousands of tins of chocolate as Christmas presents for every member of the troops on land and sea in the Boer War. This was a message of encouragement for the boys and to make sure they knew that their efforts were appreciated and remembered by their relatives and friends at home. Keen royalists and patriots, the companies made a concession by branding their tins, which were simply decorated with a royal crown and the words: South Africa 1900, and contained a half a pound of chocolate.

One of the 100,000 tins apparently saved the life of Lord Roberts, who was the leader of the British forces in South Africa. He sent it back to Queen Victoria, describing the circumstances in which he had been carrying the tin in his jacket while inspecting the troops on the front line and how it had deflected a bullet that would otherwise have killed him.

According to papers I found while researching at the Imperial War Museum in London, chocolate continued to be an important part of a soldier's diet during the heavy battles of the First World War.

One of the most remarkable features of Fry's at the time was the extensive range of products included in the brochures. 220 different lines were shown in the 1896-97 brochure ranging from penny and two penny novelties to the most complex and beautiful fancy boxes in gilt satin and silks, each retailing at a price several times greater than the weekly average earnings of the girls who packed them.

Five Boys Chocolate was introduced in 1902, featuring 'Desperation', 'Realisation', 'Pacification', 'Expectation', 'Acclamation' and 'Realisation'. The model for the picture on the packet was the photographer's son and the grimace of 'Desperation' on his face was achieved with a rag soaked in ammonia! Five Girls Chocolate was soon introduced to complement Five Boys.

One of the most prized possessions in the company archive is a photograph of Captain Scott's 1910 expedition to the Antarctic showing the explorers making cocoa and it was adapted as a theme in an early Fry's Cocoa advertisement.

"Messrs J.S. Fry & Sons supplied our cocoa, sledging and fancy chocolate, delicious comforts, excellently packed and always in good condition. Crunching those elaborate chocolates brought one nearer to civilisation than anything we experienced sledging" (signed) Captain R.F.Scott.

Fry's Turkish Delight was created in 1914 and no other manufacturer has so successfully achieved such a smooth Turkish Delight flavoured with genuine Attar of Roses and covered with milk chocolate.

In the course of its long history, J.S. Fry & Sons was awarded over 300 Grand Prix Gold medals and diplomas and held Royal Warrants from Queen Victoria, Edward VII, George V and several European monarchs - a formidable achievement.

Immediately after the First World War, J.S. Fry & Sons greatest rival, Cadbury's bought the company in 1919 and the British Cocoa and Chocolate Company was formed. A young member of the Cadbury family, Egbert, known as 'Major Egbert' due to his distinguished war career, joined the Fry side of the business and became a dominant influence until his retirement in 1963.

During the period between the two great wars, the country suffered from the Great Depression and Fry's had to fight hard to maintain its position. A succession of 189 new lines was introduced in a drive to keep up sales. One of them, Crunchie, introduced in 1929, was a real winner and is still one of Britain's top selling brands.

During the war years of 1939-45 when confectionery was rationed to the public at 2 ounces (50g) per week, the company continued to produce high quality chocolate and cocoa for the military services. An air raid emergency service of mobile canteens distributed hot cocoa to shelters and towns in the Southwest immediately following bad air raids. A large section of the factory was taken over by the Ministry of Supply for the use of the Bristol Aeroplane Works.

Orders placed by the government included Vitamised Chocolate which was distributed to children as the countries across Europe and in other war zones were liberated.

After the war, automation crept in and took over from the girls in mob caps who were unknown as 'Fry's Angels'; what had been a family run business became a public company in one of the most competitive business sectors. Product ranges were rationalised and to broaden its interests.

Direct involvement of the Fry family was declining and the last links were severed in 1952 with the death of Cecil R Fry, the great, great grandson of the founder, although the factory maintained its identity as J.S. Fry & Sons Limited, a subsidiary of the Cadbury Group until the 1967 re-organisation of the business.

Today it is a highly sophisticated, 24 hours a day operation, using eleven fully automated plants, with the latest quality control technology. 14 different Cadbury products are turned out here, most of which are best selling household names. These are produced in 100 different packages with many brands made in various sizes to suit the many different chocolate-eating occasions. Different techniques are used to produce the countline bars, so called because they are sold by number not weight, and other products such as mini eggs and covered chocolate nuts.

Moulding: A layer of chocolate is first set in the moulds, the filling is added and the base of the bar is sealed with a layer of chocolate. Caramel and Chocolate Cream are made by this method.

Enrobing: The centres are extruded on to the conveyor in a sheet and the different ingredient layers are built up as appropriate. The sheet is then cut very precisely to size before the bar's area is covered with liquid chocolate. Crunchie, Double Decker and Fuse are examples of brands made this way.

Panning: This technique for making mini-eggs, chocolate covered nuts and Tasters uses large continuously revolving drums. The covering of the chocolate or in the case of mini-eggs, the sugar coating, is gradually built up around the centres over several hours.

The range of Fry's chocolate bars over the years have included such names as Ripple, Little Folk, Punch, Jersey Cream, Valencia, Cartes Coconut Bar as well as its extensive range of Easter Eggs well known during the pre-war eras. The name Fry's can still be seen on two of the original products, which are still popular today - Fry's Chocolate Cream and Fry's Turkish Delight. Around 1,000 people are employed producing in excess of 50,000 tonnes of finished chocolate products every year.

Dr. Joseph Fry could not have envisaged his little shop in Bristol expanding first to take over much of the city's centre, and then to become a massive factory in the nearby countryside and, finally an association with a fellow Quaker family from Birmingham, forming the confectionery division of one of the major international food companies in the world - Cadbury Schweppes.

CADBURY

The fellow Quaker was **John Cadbury** who was also destined to shape the story of chocolate.

One of ten children, John Cadbury (1801-89) was a mere 22 years in 1824 when he opened his shop next to his father's business in Bull Street, a fashionable part of Birmingham. His father was Richard Tapper Cadbury who was a draper and silk merchant and had moved to Birmingham from the West Country in 1794.

Trading in tea and coffee, and what he thought of as a small sideline, chocolate production, were the humble beginnings of the great Cadbury Empire. His operation was so small that he roasted all his own beans and ground them by hand with a mortar and pestle. John Cadbury experimented with a range of cocoas and chocolate drinks, the latter having sugar which were sold in blocks - like the early Mexicans. Customers then scraped a little off into a cup or saucepan and added some hot milk or water.

Young Cadbury had considerable flair for advertising and promotion. His first advertisement in the *Birmingham Gazette* on 1st March 1824 presents his new sideline very succinctly:

"John Cadbury is desirous of introducing to particular notice 'Cocoa Nibs' prepared by himself, an article affording a most nutritious beverage for breakfast."

Customers at John Cadbury's shop were amongst the rich and prosperous families of Birmingham who were the only ones who could afford cocoa and chocolate in those days - chocolate was still a luxury enjoyed by the elite … but surprisingly, the public also took to his product immediately.

In John Cadbury's day the majority of the cocoa beans were imported from South and Central America and the West Indies - while today Cadbury's buy their beans mainly from Ghana and also from Malaysia. He was soon established as one of the leading Birmingham tradesmen. His plate glass window, in place of the usual bottle glass panes, attracted considerable attention, as did the Chinaman dressed in national costume who presided over the counter.

In 1831, a small factory was rented in an old malthouse in Crooked Lane, Birmingham, and John Cadbury became not only a purveyor of drinking chocolate and cocoa but also a manufacturer. The earliest cocoa bean products were balanced by mixing the ground cocoa with potato starch and sago flour to absorb the excess cocoa butter, with other ingredients designed to ensure healthy properties in the drinks. By 1842, John Cadbury was selling sixteen sorts of drinking chocolate and eleven cocoas. The earliest preserved price list from the time shows drinking chocolate in cakes and powders with names such as Churchman's Chocolate, Spanish Chocolate and Fine Brown Chocolate with cocoa in powder, flakes, paste and cocoa nibs including granulated cocoa, Iceland Moss, Pearl and Homeopathic cocoas.

Chocolate for eating was still a novelty at the time. One such product which was on the list was French eating chocolate - which would have been very different from the smooth, almost creamy product which we associate today with French products. In 1835 his brother Benjamin Head joined him and he extended the scope of his factory.

The enterprise prospered and in 1847, a larger factory was rented in Bridge Street, off Broad Street, Birmingham and the family business became Cadbury Brothers. The retail side of the business in Bull Street was passed to a nephew Richard Cadbury Barrow and in 1849 became Barrow Stores which traded in central Birmingham until the mid 1960s.

Taxes on imported cocoa were finally reduced by Gladstone in 1853, a turning point for cocoa and chocolate which brought the products within the reach of a wider section of the population.

Cadbury Brothers received their first Royal Warrant on 4th February 1854 as 'manufacturers of cocoa and chocolate to Queen Victoria'. The company still holds Royal warrants of appointment today.

John Cadbury contributed much to the character of Birmingham's city development. Besides taking part in public life, he was also a champion of the underprivileged, which had influence on the direction of his business enterprise. By providing tea, coffee and cocoa and chocolate as an alternative to alcohol, one of the causes of so much poverty and deprivation amongst working people, he felt that he was helping to alleviate some of the misery.

John Cadbury never really got over the death of his wife, Candia in 1855 and in the same year he suffered an attack of rheumatic fever causing the business to decline, to the extent that the partnership between the brothers was dissolved in 1860. This was probably the most difficult time in the company's history.

John Cadbury's sons, Richard (1834-1899) and George (1839-1922) had joined their father in 1850 and 1856 and took over at 25 and 21 respectively in 1861 when John retired due to his poor health.

Of the dozen or so employees who worked at Bridge Street, half were girls who were earning less than 5s per week and making product of inferior quality. Had today's Trades Descriptions Act been in force, it would have found that added quantities of treacle, starches from flour, potato and sago were such that Cadbury's cocoa represented less than 20% of the total product - but still constituted accepted additions to this particular preparation of cocoa.

Dissatisfied with the quality of cocoa products produced by all manufacturers, including their own, (George Cadbury himself described the drink as merely a "comforting gruel") the brothers took a momentous step in 1866 and following a visit to the Van Houten factory in Holland, they purchased the new cocoa press. Now they were able to produce the much more palatable cocoa powder, named Cocoa Essence - without the need for adulteration. This was really the forerunner of the Cadbury cocoa we know today. Although Fry had been the first to use this process, Cadbury was able to refine, develop and market it to a greater extent than its rivals which had a great bearing on its future prosperity and was to change the whole of the British cocoa business.

This opened new potential as an honest claim for the purity of the product. Consequently, Cadbury's new Cocoa Essence was extensively advertised as "Absolutely Pure - Therefore Best". Trade and medical opinion in the *Lancet* fully endorsed this new untainted product.

At that time, Parliament was intensely concerned about the adulteration of food. The Food and Drink Act was introduced in 1860 and threatened heavy fines for those found to be manufacturing or selling adulterated foodstuffs. However the bill had not been effective in preventing the adulteration of cocoa. Cadbury's 'new pure cocoa' was welcomed as a major breakthrough and resulted in the passing of the Adulteration of Foods Acts in 1872 and 1875. Cadbury received a remarkable amount of publicity during the discussion and sales dramatically increased.

The introduction of the new Cocoa Essence was not the only innovation that improved the Cadbury Brothers' trade. The plentiful supply of cocoa butter remaining after the cocoa was pressed made it possible to produce a wide variety of new kinds of 'eating' chocolate. Refined plain chocolate was made for moulding into blocks or bars and chocolate cremes, which were fruit-flavoured centres covered with chocolate. The quality of the chocolates produced by the company was such that in the 1870s Cadbury began to threaten the monopoly of French producers, which dominated the British market.

The Cadbury fancy chocolates - or assortments as they are now more usually called - were sold in decorated boxes with small pictures that children could cut out to stick in scrapbooks.

Richard Cadbury, who had considerable artistic talents, introduced more ambitious and attractive designs from his own paintings and many of his original designs still exist. Using his own children as models or depicting flowers or scenes from holiday journeys, Richard Cadbury introduced the first British made fancy boxes, which proved to be a marketing coup.

One famous painting for Cadbury's Chocolate Cremes, featuring one of Richard Cadbury's daughters, was described by *The Grocer* in 1869: "Among the pictorial novelties introduced to the trade this season, few, if any, excel the illustration on Messrs. Cadbury's four ounce box of chocolate cremes. It is chaste, yet simple and consists of a blue eyed maiden, some six summers old, neatly dressed in a muslin frock trimmed with lace, nursing a cat. It is designed and drawn by Mr. Richard Cadbury (a member of the firm) and reflects great credit upon him for its artistic excellence. The picture is got up in colours by Messrs. Goodall and Co of London".

Elaborate chocolate boxes were extremely popular with the late Victorians and their popularity continued until their disappearance during the 1939-45 war. Chocolate boxes were designed with after-use very much in mind. Designs extended from superb velvet-covered caskets with bevelled mirrors and silk-lined jewel boxes to pretty boxes with kittens, flowers, landscapes or attractive girls on the top.

By the late 1870s, the flourishing Cadbury business had outgrown the Bridge Street factory. The workforce had risen to 200 and after 32 years, in 1878 the Cadbury Brothers started their search for a new site. Rather than take a factory in the recognised industrial quarter of Birmingham, they decided to go for the country. "If" they said "the country is a good place to live in and play in, why not to work in?" They realised the importance to the public - their customers - that food should be made in clean, healthy premises and that they would need space for future expansion and to create better working conditions.

Because of the popularity of French chocolate and its reputation for quality, a French sounding name - Bournville - was chosen for the site.

Cadbury Brothers, already the first name in cocoa, now set out to make itself pre-eminent in chocolate confectionery. Among the many innovations in the factory was the appointment in 1880 of M. Frederic Kinchelman, a master confectioner from the continent who was engaged to impart the secrets of his craft to Bournville workers. Cadbury was soon making chocolate-covered nougats, pistache, bonbons delicés, pâte d'abricot, caramels, avelines and other specialities together with chocolate of the finest quality. M. Kinchelman was known as 'Frederic' the Frenchman and one of the confectionery rooms was known as 'the Frenchman's' until quite recently. In 1881, amidst much excitement, Cadbury received its first overseas order from a Cadbury representative in Australia.

The 1890s mark the point where British cocoa producers began successfully to hold their own against foreign importers like Van Houten and French chocolate makers,

although the dominance of the Swiss Daniel Peter milk chocolate continued for a while longer. That decade saw the scale of development, production, and marketing reaching a stage where they could expand faster than the available market. Competition would become fierce.

Cadbury's first milk chocolate was made by adding milk powder paste or condensed milk to the dark chocolate mass recipe in 1897, cocoa butter and sugar. By today's standards this chocolate was coarse and dry and was neither sweet nor milky enough for the public taste. The Bournville experts led by George Cadbury Junior set out to meet this challenge. Four years and a considerable amount of money were spent on research, new recipes using fresh milk, and a new plant with production processes which were designed to produce the new chocolate in much larger quantities - not merely a good as but better than the imported milk chocolate. And so, in 1905 Cadbury's Dairy Milk, ready to challenge the Swiss dominance of the milk chocolate market, was introduced - a name intended to be descriptive, but which evolved into one of the most evocative brands in the world - and put Cadbury's in the strongest position of recovery after the Great War. The famous blue and white label was also introduced.

THE COCOA SLAVE TRADE

But while the British public were happily munching their way through their beloved chocolate and cocoa, it was not without its human cost and one which was highly embarrassing for devout Quakers.

Just before the turn of the Twentieth century, although slavery was considered illegal, rumours were rife about the conditions of slave labour in Portuguese West Africa, where, by now, one fifth of the world's total cocoa was produced. It was reported that only by force were workers employed to work on the Islands, and so natives were rounded up in Angola and driven down the coast under conditions of appalling hardship. No worker who reached the islands ever returned home. With many of the chocolate companies boasting benevolent advantages at home, trade with the Portuguese-administered slave plantations on the islands of

Sao Thomé and Principé presented an immense social and moral hypocrisy.

Since 1886, about one third of the Islands' crops had been bought by the British firms of Cadbury, Fry, Rowntree and Terry - all of whom happened to be operated by families of strict Quaker principles whose Samaritan principles were offended by the alien practices of slavery. A century earlier, John Cadbury, (the founder) and later his son George, had both made attempts to abolish slavery. Similarly both Fry and Rowntree had made earnest representations to the governments of the time.

It therefore seemed morally incumbent on the Quaker firms, now relying so heavily on crops from the new cocoa-growing areas where the practice of slavery had reached new heights of inhumanity, to do the same. So it fell to William Cadbury (George's nephew and third generation Cadbury) to investigate these allegations. William Cadbury enjoyed the wholehearted support of Rowntree and Fry and also of Stollwerk and other German companies - not one American company was willing to put itself on the line for obviously self-incriminating reasons (Americans at that time, for the most part, being arch perpetrators of 'Negro' enslavement). From the time of first enquiries in 1901, it took six years to pursue the issue through Lisbon with the Portuguese Government and with the Islands.

Together with Mr. Joseph Burt, a friend and business colleague and the author of an extensive report on the conditions of slavery, and with the full support of the British Foreign Office, Cadbury tried to persuade the Portuguese Government and the plantation owners to improve conditions. Cadbury had to tread carefully, as it was implicit that, since Cadbury and other English firms relied heavily on supplies from slave forces, they themselves were profiting from the misery of others. This was particularly significant in view of the comparatively idyllic lifestyle of the workplace at Bournville, and the importance of its reputation to the sales of Cadburys' chocolate. However, Cadbury got absolutely nowhere with the Portuguese authorities and in 1908 he decided to go to West Africa to investigate for himself. This action alerted the hacks in the press and brought things to a head when the *Standard* (one of the national newspapers of the time) published a damning accusation which read, in part:

"We learn with profound interest from Lisbon that Mr. William Cadbury, the head of the famous firm of cocoa manufacturers, is about to go to Angola, where he will investigate for himself the manner in which 'labourers' are recruited for the plantations of islands which supply Messrs. Cadbury with the raw material for their justly celebrated products… One might have supposed that Messrs. Cadbury would have long ago ascertained the condition and circumstances of those 'labourers' of the West Coast of Africa and the islands adjacent who provide them with that raw material… In his model village and factories of Bournville, the welfare of the work people is studied as closely as the quality of the goods manufactured… The white hands of the Bournville chocolate makers are helped by the unseen hands some thousands of miles away, black and brown hands, toiling in the plantations, or hauling loads through swamps and forest. In the plenitude of his solicitude for his fellow creatures, Mr. Cadbury might have been expected to take some interest in the owners of those same grimed African hands, whose toil also is so essential to the beneficent and lucrative operatives of Bournville".

Messrs. Cadbury had no alternative but to sue for libel. William Cadbury was in the dock for three days during which time a horrified court heard the precise implications of the miseries of slavery. A missionary at the time, Charles A Swan was quoted in William Cadbury's account in his book *Labour in Portuguese West Africa* in 1910: "…The awful mixture of rum bottles, shackles and bleaching bones was enough to make one sick at heart. There was also the emaciated body of a young lad who had been left to die that morning; there he lay with the shackles on his feet and hand, and the stick with which he had helped himself along to his unknown future, till his weary limbs refused to move and the spirit took its flight. My men picked up ninety-two shackles for legs and arms or neck without ever leaving the path to look for them; most of them still contained the sap of the wood. Can any proof more positive exist that the trade is not a thing of the past, as it is constantly affirmed?"

At the end of the lengthy case the jury were out for fifty-five minutes. To an amazed court they awarded for Messrs. Cadbury - with damages of 1/4d - a farthing.

Despite this landmark 'outing' and the sustained efforts of Cadbury and many others, the Portuguese were not moved to make any changes to the practices of the cocoa farmers or to improve the conditions of the slaves. So Cadbury severed relations and ceased trading with the islands in 1908. The policy became official in 1909 and the boycott was joined by most of the other chocolate manufacturers of Europe and eventually from America.

Cadbury's began to source its raw materials from The Gold Coast (now Ghana) in British West Africa where seeds from the Sao Thomé and Principé plantations were transplanted and where cocoa planter Tetteh Quarshie had originally introduced the Amelonado from Fernando Pó in 1879. This has become the ancestor of African cocoa and opened the doors for the spread of cocoa throughout West Africa, the Ivory Coast, Nigeria and the Cameroon.

A few years' later conditions did begin to improve but not before the boycott had spelled disaster for Portuguese West African trade.

It was thus with an easier heart that George Cadbury Junior was to introduce Bournville Cocoa and Bournville Plain chocolate both of which are very similar in original concepts, and which were introduced in 1906 and 1908 respectively.

By 1913, CDM (as Cadbury's Dairy Milk is known) had become the company's best selling line, a position that it has enjoyed ever since. Today, more than 250 million bars of CDM are made every year and sales reach over £100 million in value. While advertising and label design have changed with fashions and considerable strides have been made in refining techniques the recipe is basically the same as it was when it was launched. Milk Tray Assortment was launched in 1915 and its Flake countline in 1920.

Industrial technology made such advances that in the years between the wars, the Bournville factory was rebuilt and equipped for mass production as the hitherto luxury product became well within the financial reach of most people. Several factors led to the reduction in prices of chocolate -

replacing expensive South American Guayaquil cocoa with the cheaper Accra from British West Africa, falling raw material costs, processing efficiency and lower transport costs. Increased production, supported by advertising, resulted in more sales and consequently lower prices.

In 1919 Cadbury Brothers merged with J.S. Fry & Sons of Bristol whose product range complemented that of Cadbury. The Cadbury factory at Somerdale near Bristol is on the site of the original J.S. Fry factory.

George Cadbury died in 1924 and his popularity as one of the most unique, fair and altruistic benefactors of his time was endorsed by the fact that over 16,000 people attended his memorial service.

Cadbury grew from strength to strength with new technology being introduced to make the Cadbury confectionery business one of the most efficient in the world.

The merger of the Cadbury Group with Schweppes in 1969 and the subsequent development of the business have led to Cadbury Schweppes taking the lead in both confectionery and soft drinks markets in the UK and becoming a major force in international trade.

In 1989 Cadbury bought the Trebor Group and Bassett Foods. The sugar confectionery brands were brought together under the overall umbrella of Trebor Bassett Limited with well known names such as Trebor, Bassett, Barrett, Maynard and Sharps joining Pascall and Murray. Sugar confectionery production was moved from Somerdale.

Despite the extraordinary growth in the Cadbury business over the last century, some things don't change, for example, industrial paternalism still reigns at Cadbury today - employees receive a Bible and a single carnation when they get married.

However, the family element no longer dominates and the only member of the Quaker Cadbury family to be involved in the running of the business is Dominic Cadbury, who is Chairman.

Without doubt, Cadbury led the creation of Britain's mass market for chocolate with its coup, the development and introduction of CDM - an appealing but standardised milk chocolate that benefited from the cost and price advantages of large-scale production. It was **Rowntree** however that eventually adopted its marketing methods, product development, branding and advertising for a wealthier market, developing an enviable range of different lines.

ROWNTREE

Rowntree's Quaker heritage is also the central theme of its history - even its production methods and marketing ethics were part of this.

The firm of Rowntree dates from July 1862 when Henry Isaac Rowntree (1838-83) bought his former employers' cocoa, chocolate and chicory business, Tuke and Co.

Sales in 1862 were less than £3,000, a tenth of those of Cadbury and a twentieth of Fry. Rowntree's output was approximately 12cwt, two thirds of which was Tuke's Superior Rock. This was soon renamed Rowntree's Prize Medal Rock Cocoa and made with the traditional technology, which was fine ground, mixed with sugar and sold in cakes. It was of a higher quality than Rowntree's other varieties, which were mixed with some starchy substance. Both types of cocoa never-theless contained the cocoa shell as well as the nib, and when mixed with hot water (as a drink) tended to be fatty.

While the last three decades of the Nineteenth century marked a period of major technological advances in the industry, and the emergence of new concepts such as mass marketing and branding, Rowntree's strict Quaker principles refused to countenance advertising, insisting on selling by reputation alone. Advertising to Joseph Rowntree meant competition, a form of war, with his fellow chocolate companies, which was strictly against his Quaker principles. Cadbury and Fry - fellow Quaker companies - on the other hand, did not share this reluctance, and forged ahead promoting their products. In fact, both Cadbury and Fry's comparatively large sales could only be sustained by advertising, justified in their eyes because it meant greater profits and therefore security for their workers.

Rowntree's failure to appeal to the expanding mass market meant it remained significantly smaller than Fry or Cadbury, despite bringing out new lines and increasing sales at a faster rate. It lacked the financial power to invest in a Van Houten cocoa press, and the chocolate department remained a small outfit run by a mere seven men and two machines, unable to compete with Cadbury's Pure Cocoa Essence.

Rowntree got its break when by happy coincidence a Frenchman, M. Gaget, called on it with a new selection of pastilles. In true Quaker fashion, Rowntree's seized on this as a non-alcoholic alternative to the unprecedented success of recently-introduced liqueur sweets by German chocolate manufacturer Stollwerk. Pastille production was also considerably more economical than investing in Van Houten machinery, requiring only a pot to boil sugar and one man to stir it. Two years later, Rowntree became the first British company to introduce fruit pastilles, sold loose in 4lb wooden boxes.

A period of major expansion followed from 1891-92, building Fruit and Gum Blocks, Cake Moulding Store and Packing Rooms which were directly connected to the North Eastern Railway by a specially-constructed line. This meant that as well as crystallised pastilles, Rowntree's could begin production of clear fruit gums. Further construction from 1896-1898 included facilities for chocolate creams and boxed chocolate assortments.

The increased capacity matched the 1890's growth in demand for cocoa and chocolate products (more than doubling), and Rowntree sales quadrupled. Still, Rowntree failed to develop commercially successful products to compete with the now evidently growing demand for milk chocolate and alkalised cocoa.

In 1916 Rowntree's developed a cocoa butter substitute suitable for higher-grade products. Techniques for extracting cocoa butter from the shell were also improved.

By July 1917, Rowntree was ready to manufacture saccharine in bulk and in just three months saccharine sales became extraordinarily lucrative. By 1919, the fine chemicals department had developed vanillin and theobromine, a commercial alkaloid extracted from the cocoa bean, in addition to a successful technique for extracting citric acid from cane sugar. Rowntree's successes attracted the interest of Cadbury and Fry, who by October 1919 were keen to invest in the experiments and commercial benefits.

Post-war, with improved earnings and a greater mass market for cocoa and confectionery products, Rowntree adopted new advertising styles aimed at children, and through them, parents. Cocoa Nibs became Britain's best known advertising personalities during the 1920s.

Packaged chocolates were the way of the future - by the end of the Twenties, fewer and fewer shops were selling loose chocolates while 2d and 6d tubes and packets of chocolate nuts and raisins were popular.

By 1930 British tastes were forever linked with the taste of Cadbury's Dairy Milk which played a key role in Rowntree's misfortunes and so Rowntree was threatened with bankruptcy and forced to revolutionise its policy at product development and marketing - and revolutionise it did. George Harris was the company's saviour. He had married into the family (Friede, daughter of Frank, Joseph's nephew) and therefore by default, into the business, joining the firm in the Thirties as marketing director. It was during this time that some of Rowntree's most famous products, as we know them today, were added to the company portfolio: Black Magic chocolates (1933); Aero, and Chocolate Crisp (1935) - later to become Kit Kat, which has held its position as the UK's No. 1 confectionery brand for the last 9 years (it is estimated that 47 bars are eaten every second); Quality Street and Dairy Box (1936); Rolo and Smarties (1937). Not surprisingly in 1937, George Harris succeeded Seebohm as chairman. Successful innovations continued including the introduction of Polo Mints in 1948, but in the Fifties George Harris's style became increasingly autocratic, and he was rather unceremoniously ousted as chairman.

Fruit pastilles and Fruit Gums continue to this day as successful lines, while After Eight was introduced in 1962 and Yorkie in 1976.

In 1969, Rowntree and Co Ltd merged with John Mackintosh and Sons Ltd, becoming Rowntree Mackintosh Ltd, adding such famous products as Toffee Crisp and Fox's Glacier Mints to its range. In 1987, the company became Rowntree Plc, and a year later was acquired by Nestlé SA. By 1989, the two companies' interests were sufficiently merged and strengthened for Nestlé shares to be quoted on the London Stock Exchange.

The founder's heritage lives on today in the work of the Joseph Rowntree Foundation which is the UK's largest independent social research and development charity.

Terry's of York is one of Britain's oldest confectionery making companies. In 1767 Bayldon and Berry set up business in York, concentrating on sweets, lozenges, comfits and candied peel. Joseph Terry, an apothecary and a zealous Quaker, joined the company in the early 1800s and by 1812 was in total control. The company, now named Terry's, was among the first companies to make eating chocolate, like Fry, setting the trend for eating rather than drinking it. The firm moved again in 1829 to a larger shop in St. Helen's Square, near Cooney Street, in York, where a restoration of the original shop still exists.

By the middle of the century, the Terry's reputation had become celebrated, both within the domestic and export markets. A new factory was built entirely for the manufacture of chocolate and, in 1867, a price list included 13 different types of chocolate creams, as well as batons, tablets and medallions. Another first for Terry's, aware of the market's possibilities, in the latter part of the 19th century, was the introduction of an assortment of chocolates - in a box - before chocolates had been sold loose. The other chocolate giants soon followed.

All Gold first hit the shops in 1932. As did another of Terry's chocolate delights for which it is probably the best known - the Chocolate Orange. The company lost its independence after World War 11, and in 1982 became part of the large United Biscuit Group. The last member of the Terry family to take a prominent role in the firm was Peter Terry who retired in 1985. In 1993 the company became Terry-Suchard.

Terry's Extra Strong mint lozenges, had their origins in the traditions of the apothecaries, which would have been a medium for medicinal dose of something or another!

CALEY'S OF NORWICH LIMITED

The story of Caley's Marching chocolate is the Sleeping Beauty of the chocolate industry. **Albert Jarman Caley** opened his chemist's shop in London Street, Norwich in 1857 and shortly afterwards, thanks to the combination of an inspirational mind and his knowledge of chemistry, he began to manufacture mineral water and drinks in the cellars of the premises. In 1880, he opened a factory in Chapel Field East, Norwich using water from two deep artesian wells on site for his mineral waters and in 1886, looking for something to occupy the factory during the quiet winter months, he launched into the manufacture of drinking chocolate. This was soon followed by eating chocolate. Alfred Caley retired in 1894, and handed over the very successful business to his son Edward and nephews Frederick and Stuart who diversified into production of Christmas Crackers. By the turn of the century, following Cadbury's lead, it was fashionable to have brightly illustrated lids on packaging and in particular chocolate boxes, and Alfred Munnings, a then penniless artist living in nearby Dedham, was commissioned by one of the Caley's directors to design both the Caley chocolate box lids and the crackers. Many of them are now famous symbols of that era and some early originals can still been seen in the Borthwick Institute/Rowntree Museum at York.

In the early 1900s, the company was sold to the Eastern Africa Trading Company, although the business was still family run, and expanded into new buildings in Norwich. Caley's Marching Chocolate, the high cocoa plain chocolate ration pack for troops created at the turn of the century, became familiar for its comforting khaki-coloured wrapper and the Caley's slogan of 'fighting fatigue and fortifying the nerves'. It was an attractive and positive nutritional proposition and Caley's Marching Chocolate became a firm favourite among the troops during the First World War. It was known as 'Marcho' and considered to provide great sustaining power without the thirst-creating tendency of many other forms of chocolate. This seems a deeply revealing observation at a time when the relationship between the oversweet confectionery that we call chocolate and the fact that excessively sugary substances give one a raging thirst would not have been immediately connected as it would be now. Tens of thousands of soldiers found it of immense benefit on exhausting marches and in the perils of the trenches and after the war the chocolate became a national institution. George VI took a liking to it, and requisitioned it for troop rations during his coronation procession in 1937.

By 1932 Caley's had become a nationwide everyday brand and the company employed over 4,000 people, comparable with Cadbury Fry. The company was wooed and won for a price of £138,000 by the confectioners John Mackintosh, the toffee people. Mackintosh took the company up market. Its 1933 brochure promised a New Caley Programme and the entire re-organisation of the Caley business. "We make bold to say that these changes will be found revolutionary. We claim that the new Caley Chocolates are of a quality and a refinement of texture that is new to chocolate manufacture and with new machinery of which we have the exclusive rights … This machinery and the new methods of production enable us to offer an unexcelled quality at prices that make every line 'competitive' in the most vigorous sense of the word. Every line sets a standard of comparison for value and money". The brochure went on to claim: "… The fame of Caley's Marching Chocolate is such that it is almost superfluous to reiterate here how strongly it has maintained its place. … So excellent and established a line is naturally unaltered so far as the recipe is concerned, but the new method of manufacture to which we have already referred, gives it an added refinement and smoothness which is certain to enhance its already great popularity".

The listed products included Marching Chocolate in 3s/6d and 1/- cartons; Gold Crest Milk Chocolate; Whipped Cream Walnuts (Milk and Plain); Whipped Cream Logs; Whipped Cream Brazils; Coffee Whipped Creams; Chocolate Fruit Salad; Lemon Milk Chocolate Croquettes; Chocolate Liqueurs; Royal Highness Chocolates; Princess Caskets; Chocolate Surprise; Nougatine Bars; 'Bundles' of Neapolitans; among many others. Its customers included the Royal Family, London clubs, embassies and MPs. It was in 1937 that the company first produced the famous Rolos.

Eric Mackintosh, the Chairman of the company, was

friends with the Monheim family owners of the famous Trumpf confectionery business in Aachen, Germany. Together they invented and patented automatic moulding plants, which produced unique bars with six centres each with different fillings. Subsequently, the company produced the Caley Assorted Chocolate Block: six different chocolates in one bar, coffee, praline, gooseberry, caramel, Turkish delight, nougat. This was Caley's last branded product.

During the Second World War in 1942, the factory was devastated by an incendiary bomb, some say it was strategically targeted in deliberate attempt to destroy the supply of Marching Chocolate to the troops! The factory was eventually rebuilt and officially re-opened by the Duchess of Kent in 1956.

At its peak during the 1960's some 2,000 people were employed by Mackintosh although with the merger of Mackintosh and Rowntree in 1969 came mechanisation and the need for a large workforce diminished. By the time Nestlé bought the company in 1988 the workforce totalled less than 1,000 and the famous name of Caley was no more.

During the last few years, with the threat of the closure of the Norwich factory, three Nestlé managers, Terry Long, Roger King and Roger Stevenson with over 80 years experience of the chocolate business between them, bought the Caley name. In October 1997, the three partners re-launched the original Marching Chocolate based on the same pre-war recipe with 70% cocoa and pitched at the British taste for chocolate with a 'rounder' edge. Marching Chocolate is unarguably one of the best commercial chocolates produced in Britain and a worthy match for any European imports. It is packaged in the same original khaki-coloured wrapper but now decorated with a striking image of marching troops. By March 1997, British supermarket chain Tesco had recognised a good thing when they saw it and began to stock the product. Now Tesco's shelves are testament to their conviction and the growing need to fill the chasm at the top end of the British chocolate market. In April 1998, the company launched Caley's Milk Marching Chocolate in similarly distinguished packaging but with a royal blue background. It's a good 'meaty' chocolate with a high level of cocoa solids, more than acceptably balanced with a low level of milk (from a local Norfolk herd, of course) to sugar.

EUROPEAN CHOCOLATE MAKERS

At the beginning of the Nineteenth century, it was customary for apothecaries to grind cacao beans to a paste to make chocolate, which was usually drunk by the aristocratic rich. It was a grainy bitter concoction but adored nonetheless.

Nowadays, chocolate connoisseurs are familiar with a different kind of chocolate - a chocolate that is 'refined' and 'conched' to a degree that makes it so smooth that it is impossible to detect any particles on the tongue. To reach this platform of perfection, it was the enterprising industrialists of the Nineteenth century such as Fry, Van Houten, Cadbury, Lindt, Poulain, Menier, Charles Barry and Charles Callebaut, who invented and nurtured the process of refining our chocolate almost beyond its early Nineteenth century rough facade and brought this delicious commodity within the means of even the most modest incomes.

BARRY CALLEBAUT

The Callebaut chocolate family goes back to 1850 when Charles Callebaut set up a complex under the name 'Gebroeders Callebaut' in Wieze, a few dozen kilometres outside Brussels. It consisted of a brewery, a malt-house, a milling house, a dairy and mineral waters. Chocolate called 'Meurisse' represented only a small part of the business but in 1911 the Callebaut company began to produce its own-name chocolate bars and tablets for the consumer and in 1925 started the couverture production line to supply manufacturers.

In 1930, Callebaut made the first brave steps towards exports; twenty years later the company had grown, so much so that it was supplying manufacturers with chocolate not in its usual form but in warm liquid transported in tankers. This practical cost-saving system has since become widespread. The firm still supplies virtually made-to-order couverture products for hundreds of customers and has numerous 'off the shelf' products for purchasers buying less than 5 tons a year.

In 1981, Callebaut was sold to Interfood (Tobler-Suchard) which, two years later took over the Belgium Suchard NV company. The whole Interfood company was then bought in 1983 by Jacobs Kaffee, creating the Jacobs-Suchard Group.

Jacobs-Suchard bought the Van Houten plants in Belgium, Germany, USA and Canada; then Comet, the most important producer of chocolate drops in Canada was incorporated in the Industrial Chocolate Division.

In 1988, the whole Van Houten-Callebaut Jacobs-Suchard conglomerate was again taken over by the Philip Morris Group. K.J. Jacobs, however, bought back the Callebaut Industrial activities; followed soon afterwards by the the S&A Lesme Group in Britain. This was the foundation of the Callebaut AG Group.

At the heart of the massive present day chocolate works in Wieze, a remote rural part of Belgium, you can still see the original house where the Callebaut family started its tale of chocolate. It is famous for miles around. It is unusual among chocolate producers for the whole 'bean-to-bar' process to be undertaken in one location. However, for Callebaut, 'it all happens here in Wieze' - from the arrival of the beans from the docks - usually kept apart from the principal process for fear of contamination - to the finished product, be it bar to liquid chocolate in tankers.

Before they merged in 1997, both Cacao Barry and Callebaut individually, enjoyed a similarly high reputation across the chocolate world and since their merger, they have become the largest single independent chocolate company in the world. If you love chocolate and have never visited a chocolate factory, then it's a must.

For many years Cacao Barry has been one of the world's leading cocoa processing groups, covering all chocolate-related activities, from processing the cocoa beans to formulating semi-finished products to manufacturing chocolate couvertures.

The Group's roots go back to 1842, when Charles Barry, an English industrialist, established a company trading in foodstuffs in London, and took an immediate interest in cocoa. He moved to France at the time of the industrial revolution and started a production unit there. For a long time Cacao Barry was a traditional chocolate factory, supplying retailers, artisanal bakers, confectioners, and grocers with products such as cocoa powders and chocolate bars for general consumption. At that time, Cacao Barry was very close to the consumer and the Barry brand name was known by the general public.

From 1953 Cacao Barry products were no longer available directly to the public - so were no longer in competition with any of the large manufacturers who had now become Cacao Barry's own customers. However, to preserve the company's knowledge and reputation in the trade, it formed the 'Gastronomy' Department, delivering finished products (blocks of chocolate couverture, bakers' sticks, icing pastes etc) to artisanal bakers and confectioners.

Over the decades both Cacao Barry and Callebaut have made a major contribution to the development of the chocolate industry. They have introduced many innovations, improved the quality of their products and gained an invaluable level of expertise, to the benefit of the industry and of everyone who loves chocolate in all its forms. And so it came to pass in 1997, that the French Barry Group and Belgian Callebaut became Barry Callebaut, one of the world's largest producers of chocolate and chocolate products (after Nestlé). Now the company offers a choice of over 1,000 recipes, both to the industrial biscuit, ice cream and chocolate manufacturers and to master bakers, patissiers and chocolatiers and restaurants throughout the world.

Barry Callebaut is also active in the Fairtrade market with milk and dark chocolate manufactured as Fairtrade products. The underlying principle is to support third world countries by paying more for the raw materials. Under strict guarantees, the extra money finds its way to farmers in these countries. Another exciting development is Callebaut's organic 70% and 56% dark; 34% milk and ivory with 28% cocoa butter. This 'ecological' chocolate is made with at least 95% organic raw materials in which the use of artificial pesticides or fertilizers is strictly forbidden and the control procedures and standards are governed by EU regulations.

Despite the merger, both companies are still producing chocolate under their own names. Between them, they have

17 production facilities across the world, and intend to feature research as part of their programme of innovation. Barry Callebaut operates gourmet chocolate schools in Belgium, Canada, Côte d'Ivoire, France, Italy, Poland, Singapore and the United States. The company's objective is to make the Barry Callebaut Institute the standard for the cocoa and chocolate industry.

Under their single names, both Cacao Barry and Callebaut have recently launched their new 'Origins' chocolates. These are chocolates from either a single bean or from a single area of the cocoa-growing world. For example, Cacao Barry have produced Saint Domingue, a 70% smooth well balanced chocolate from the Dominican Republic which melts like butter on the palate; a 60% Equateur from Ecuador; milk from Papua New Guinea and ivory from Indonesia (see Tasting). They are still producing their old favourites Fleur de cao; Ultime and Lenôtre, for example.

Callebaut on the other hand, produce a 70% from Sao Thomé; 60% from Granada; milk from Java and white from Arriba.

What is so good about origin chocolate is that you can identify the difference between the beans. You can discover flavours never before associated with chocolate that grab the tastebuds such as tobacco; tea; acidity; citrus; nutty; herbaceous or floral overtones; and honey; and others too numerous to mention. This is what the best chocolate is all about. Unfortunately we can't buy Barry Callebaut products directly but you are more than likely to have eaten them as many of the best manufacturers use Barry Callebaut in their own recipes.

On a recent visit to the British factory, I was inspired to see a GMO-free production line among the hundreds of special recipes that are tailor-made by Barry Callebaut for specific customers. This particular GMO-free line is produced for one of Britain's supermarket chains. Unfortunately with the advance of genetically modified foods the majority one of the world's staple ingredients, soya, is a victim of the new technology. Soya is also the ingredient from which lecithin is derived; and lecithin is important in the manufacture of chocolate as it is used to maintain the homogenous fluidity of chocolate and chocolate products which may be low in cocoa butter.

LINDT AND SPRÜNGLI

The story begins in 1845. The confectioner, **David Sprüngli-Schwarz** and his son, Rudolph owned a small confectionery shop in the Marktgasse of Zurich's Old Town. They decided to employ a fashionable new recipe from Italy for manufacturing chocolate in solid form, and using the method already adopted by François-Louis Cailler in Vevey and Philippe Suchard in Neuchâtel. The consequence of their success involved a move to bigger premises at the upper end of Lake Zurich.

In 1859, Sprüngli & Son opened a second and larger confectionery and refreshment room at Zurich's Paradeplatz and in 1870, chocolate production was relocated to larger premises at the "Werdmühle" in Zurich. When Rudolph Sprüngli-Ammann retired in 1892, he had acquired a widespread reputation for the quality of his products and as an expert in his field. He divided the business between his two sons. The younger, David Robert, received the two confectionery stores. The Paradeplatz store, the larger of the two, enjoyed magnificent success.

The elder brother, Johann Rudolph Sprüngli-Schifferli, inherited the chocolate factory from his father. A far-sighted and adventurous entrepreneur, Johann expanded in 1899 and built a new factory in Kilchberg, a nearby town. At the same time he was offered the option of acquiring the small but famous chocolate factory of Rudolphe Lindt in Berne - and Lindt & Sprüngli was born.

Rudolphe Lindt was probably the most famous chocolate-maker of his day. In 1879 he developed the technique of the 'conche' and was the first to produce the chocolate with the wonderfully delicate flavour and melting quality, which we know and love to this day. His 'melting chocolate' soon achieved fame and contributed significantly to the worldwide reputation of Swiss chocolate.

During the first two decades of the Twentieth century, the Swiss chocolate industry enjoyed almost incredible expansion, especially in export markets. Lindt & Sprüngli played a powerful role in this boom which persisted throughout the First World War. In 1915 the company exported some three-quarters of its output to twenty different nations around the world.

The Second World War brought rigid import restrictions on sugar and cocoa and, in 1943, rationing. Even though sales ceased to grow between 1919 and 1946, Lindt & Sprüngli withstood all these critical episodes, because it adhered at all times to maintaining quality: even when consumers could hardly afford it, they still wanted only the best of chocolates.

After the war, demand on the Continent exploded first within the home market and later abroad.

In 1972 the Lindt & Sprüngli Chocolate Process (LSCP), developed by the company itself, was introduced into production. This was the most significant improvement to the manufacturing process since the invention of the conche and not only secured the quality of the product, but also required less energy and space than dozens of conches.

In January 1998, Chocoladefabriken Lindt & Sprüngli AG announced the acquisition of the American Ghirardelli Chocolate Company, based in San Francisco, California and perhaps best known as 'Manufactory at Ghirardelli Square,' a tourist site and store location that has become a must for many of San Francisco's visitors. Besides this store, it has locations in Chicago, Las Vegas, and at Disney World in Florida. It currently generates about 100 million US-Dollars in sales.

Fortunately for us all, Lindt is available in practically every supermarket nationwide and is one of the better of the industrial chocolates - well worth a try if you haven't already.

LA CHOCOLATERIE DE L'OPÉRA

"One never knows where passion will lead" chirps the blurb reassuringly. Adrien Bourgeat did not realise that he would shape the destiny of his heirs when, in 1936, he acquired his first chocolate business. He was followed by his son-in-law and then his grandson, to whom he transmitted his knowledge and passion. They were at the forefront of such developments as the 1980's French innovation of preparing couvertures with a high cocoa content and as artisans, they are always on the look out for original ingredients, interesting flavours or exclusive products.

Perpetuating the family passion, by acquiring Chocolaterie de l'Opéra in 1995, Olivier de Loisy, formerly Managing Director of Valrhona, has been developing a new approach to chocolate. This approach is a 'first', as it offers, at last, the possibility of discovering chocolate in its purest expression.

Chocolaterie de l'Opéra has launched a new concept to create a selection of couvertures: Les Pure Plantations with a single selection of cacao beans, whose origin is guaranteed. To accurately pass on the original taste of every variety of cocoa to the chocolate has required Chocolaterie de l'Opéra to be radically innovative throughout the creative process, made possible by a thorough knowledge of the plantation areas acquired over generations. This enables a choice of cacaos that best reflect the distinctive characteristics of the variety whether in South America, West Africa or South East Asia and is the philosophy and basis of the Les Pure Plantations range… from Venezuela, Brazil, Ivory Coast, Papua New Guinea, Ecuador.

As you would expect from a chocolate company with a name like Opéra many of its products have musical bonds like Diva, Passionato III, Allegro, Soprano, Mezzo', etc., etc.

Chocolaterie de l'Opéra is a company of like minded individuals who concentrate all their knowledge to stay away from the beaten track to create unique chocolate. "If you too do not compromise when it comes to chocolate then its time you discovered Chocolaterie de l'Opéra".

VALRHONA

Valrhona manufactures one of the world's greatest and most venerated chocolates, known for taste experience and available to both professional chocolate makers and chocolate-lovers alike. Valrhona was also one of the first companies to launch a range of grand crus on the basis of the wine grower's maxim that the better the fruit, the better the end product. A grand cru is a single variety bean, or a bean from a single country such as 64% Caraibe made from Caribbean *trinitario* beans; and the famous 70% Guanaja named after the Caribbean Island of Guanaja where

Christopher Columbus landed in 1502 and made from both the florally flavoured *criollo* beans and pungent *trinitario*.

The company was the inspiration of an enterprising pastry chef called Monsieur Guironnet in 1922, and began its life as La Chocolaterie de Vivarais across the Rhône River from Tain Hermitage.

The trademark of Valrhona (from the Valley of the Rhône), was adopted at the beginning of the 1950s.

Since the 1980s Valrhona has launched a variety of different quality products including Guanaja (Valrhona was one of the first chocolate manufacturers to offer a dark bitter chocolate with a 70% cocoa content); Equinoxe; the Coffee Collection; Caraibe; Manjari; Jivara Lactée, as well as inaugurating in 1998 La Coupe du Monde de la Pâtisserie (competition) - which takes place every year. They have been the official sponsor ever since.

To give you an idea of a Valrhona buyer's life, in a two-year period for example, he might review some 80 cocoa plantations in 22 countries including Venezuela, Ecuador, the Caribbean, Sri Lanka, New Guinea, Ghana. "I visit these places regularly" the buyer says "because we work directly with the producers, avoiding the intermediary of a cocoa dealer. My job is to ensure, from the beginning, the maintenance of that unbroken standard of quality which sets Valrhona apart". (Most of the time cocoa is bought from dealers working in the wholesale markets and who are therefore unsure of the exact sources of this raw material. As a consequence, many manufacturers are largely ignorant of the circumstances in which their cocoas have been produced and mix beans from many different varieties of cocoa without regard to their differing qualities, muffling the exquisite characteristics of this noble plant.)

Valrhona continues to care for the beans throughout the factory process, starting with the roasting which is done in small batches. They are then finely ground and meticulously blended. Speed of production is not a consideration and the original artisan methods of production are preserved to develop a chocolate taste superior to any other.

Fortunately Valrhona is widely available and can be bought directly from the Chocolate Society (see Directory). But if you are ever in the area of the Rhône it is worth a visit to the factory shop as nothing compares to chocolates made fresh that same day.

CHOCOLATES EL REY

In the early stages of the South American conquest the Spaniards discovered a particularly fragrant strain of the cacao bean growing wild in the region south of Venezuela's Lake Maracaibo and throughout the tropical lowlands bordering the Caribbean on Venezuela's northern coast. Despite its unwillingness to travel, by the middle of the seventeenth century, this uniquely fragrant cacao bean was sweeping the world and had become Venezuela's main export crop. Venezuela was then producing more than half the world's cocoa requirements - minute in comparison to today's world output, but this was at a time when cacao was the right of the rich and aristocratic.

Since this time cocoa has become widely available and due to their price and limited availability the fabled *Chuao*, *Rio Caribe* and *Porcelana* (also known as *Sur del Lago*) beans have traditionally constituted only a tiny percentage of the cocoa beans that go into a truly premium chocolate. But they make all the difference in the world.

When Jose Rafael Zozaya and his father-in-law Carmela Tuozzo founded Tuozzo Zozaya & Cia in Caracas in 1929, they were still hauling their cocoa beans in by mule and narrow gauge railway. They dedicated themselves to producing some of the very best chocolate in the world and they called it El Rey - The King. This family owned business continued to prosper for the next 45 years and in 1973, they decided it was time to expand and to move the company towards processing cocoa and exporting its high quality derivatives (liquor, butter and powder) to the United States and Japan. Since 1989, El Rey has moved to a formidable position in the global market unifying its three factories under one roof and installing cutting edge equipment to rival the world's finest technology.

But technology can only go so far. Exceptional chocolate begins with the land and the El Rey's cocoa beans still come from small plantations in secluded coastal valleys, the grassy llanos, and the foothills of the Andes where generations of farmers have perfected the art of nurturing these beans. El Rey uses only 100% Venezuelan Cacao, fermented, sun dried and processed with the most advanced technology. "From this marrage of art and science are born premium chocolate couvertures that redefine world standards of excellence". Nibbling on a morsel of any of El Rey's chocolates, ranging from 41% dark milk (toasted caramel), to 58.5%, 61%, 70% and 73.5% extra bitter sweets, is a powerful reminder that chocolate is not a single identity but an abundance of flavours supported by a gentle, mellow softness. Terrific.

GREEN & BLACK

The story of Green & Black goes back to the day when **Jo Fairley** first set eyes on some bars of mahogany organic chocolate on her then boyfriend's desk. The boyfriend - now husband - was Craig Sams, proprietor of Whole Earth Organic and resolute believer in maintaining humanitarian rights of suppliers and producers, and preserving the world's natural resources. The beans had been sent to Craig by one of his West African peanut producers in Togo. Jo Fairley loved the chocolate that the beans produced and seized on the idea of producing Britain's first organic chocolate. The Pelletier factory was the first to produce it. They had to source one of the original machines and made sure that the product was conched for at least three days. It was a simple matter to persuade Craig to market and sell the chocolate through Whole Earth's distribution line. Between them they decided to call the chocolate Green & Black: Green because it reflects the Fairley-Sams high quality organic philosophy, and Black because it is the colour of the chocolate. Altogether a good old fashioned English name.

Shortly after the launch a call from Sainsbury's promised its long term future but at the same time posed a problem of supply. Jo recounts a hair-raising time with the Togo uprising (during the early Nineties Togo Revolution) and a volatile blockade on the ports. Jo, realising that it was impractical to rely on one source, and, remembering acquaintances made on a holiday in Belize in 1990, pursued another supply. The Maya in Belize were, of course, one of the first in cocoa history to have domesticated the cocoa bean over two and a half thousand years ago, and still grow it under the rainforest canopy, interspersing the cocoa trees with the original wild trees to maintain disease resistance.

The Maya civilisation of Southern Belize was built around one great ceremonial centre - Labaatun which flourished deep in the heart of the rain forest over a thousand years ago. In the trading economy of the Mayan world, the cocoa bean was a universal measure of value. Because Labaatun was located in the Maya Mountains, and the cocoa trees thrived in the wild there, it became the centre of the cocoa bean economy - the stock exchange of the Maya world. In the 1920s excavations revealed the importance of Labaatun as the main cocoa trade centre and also unearthed the legendary and fabulous Crystal Skull that has fascinated and bemused archaeologists for decades. Colonists took over the land in the 1850s, logged the forest and established plantations. In the end they failed, and place names like 'Go To Hell Creek' and 'Hellgate' testified to their despair at attempts to tame nature in the region.

The Maya re-established villages in the Maya Mountains, their own homeland, farming in harmony with the seasonal rhythms of soil and climate. Throughout this time the Maya have practised subsistence farming, trading surplus cocoa beans for cash. In the early 1990s, the growers faced ruin through the price-promise initially made, and subsequently broken, by a giant American corporation. Hershey's offered the Maya farmers $1.75 per lb. for their beans, and encouraged them to plant hybrid trees (as opposed to the indigenous) which 'cropped better'. Some of the younger farmers were seduced by Hershey's promises, borrowing money to pay for the young plants and for agrochemicals with which to treat them. Fortunately, most refrained from altering their traditional methods. Their caution was justified because in 1992, Hershey slashed its offer to a mere 55 cents a lb. for the beans. Take it or leave it. Many of the younger Maya farmers lost their land to the banks when the promised price failed to materialise. Many could not even afford to harvest their crops and so left them to rot on the trees, migrating from their villages in search of casual labour.

Many set off to work in neighbouring Guatemala for wages to send money back to their families.

Enter the Maya's champion: Green & Black - at $1.55 per lb. Jo Fairley said "trading direct with the Maya growers organisation (a co-operative of 350 farmers), we offered a unique long term contract, guaranteeing a better price, so they have security of income and an incentive to remain on their land, protecting it from loggers or large companies trying to buy up rainforest land for intensive farming. We take all their production at a price that exceeds the market price for cocoa beans by a favourable margin. This is in line with strict guidelines, conditions and prices established by the Fairtrade Foundation (FtF)".

Green & Black's Maya Gold produced from cocoa grown by the Kekchi Maya was, in fact, the first chocolate product to be awarded the Fairtrade Mark.

However Green & Black's chocolate is more famous for its organic guarantee. A book published in 1993 by the Women's Environmental Network, *Chocolate Unwrapped* by Cat Cox describes the appalling conditions on some of the modern cocoa plantations. The beans farmed for Green & Black however, come from a naturally integrated system of cocoa trees that grow beneath the enormous natural shade of the jungle canopy on which chemicals have never been used. Nature spaces them at about 30 feet apart. The organic *forasteros* without artificial fertilisers take longer to mature; but in the right conditions the end result is better, healthier beans with lots of great flavour.

The crops are certified organic by the Soil Association, who regularly visit the growers to ensure organic standards are fully met.

Encouragingly, the level of Green & Black success, in addition to its numerous awards including the Soil Association's Organic Food Awards, The Caroline Walker Trust Award, and the Booker Tate Award for Small Business - indicates not only Jo Fairley's passion for chocolate but also the growing number of consumers who are concerned about the integrity of their food.

Green & Black chocolate is widely available throughout the UK and most supermarkets stock it.

THE NEW WORLD

North America, a century behind England, had to wait for its chocolate until the invasion of the English and Dutch settlers in the 18th century, when chocolate made its great global circle, returning home to the continent from whence it came. In 1765 thanks to John Hannon, a chocolate maker recently emigrated from Ireland, chocolate manufacturing began when he convinced the apothecary Dr. James Baker of Dorchester, Massachusetts, that it was good for the health and made a good case for the project's financing. They set up in an old mill where the cocoa beans were ground with the aid of water power. The product was advertised with confident assurance: 'Satisfaction or money refunded'. John Hannon died in 1799, lost at sea, but it was not until 1852 that the company became known as The Baker Company and when Dr. James' grandson took over in 1820, it became the Walter Baker Company, notable today for its squares of baking chocolate, the basics of nearly every American brownie. It is better known today as Baker's Chocolate, and is now the chocolate division of the General Foods Corporation.

Over 100 years ago, this firm acquired the right from the Dresden Art Gallery to a painting by the Swiss artist Jean-Étienne Liotard entitled *A Chocolate Server* painted in about 1745, to use as its trademark. Liotard used chocolate as the central theme of several of his paintings but none is more famous that his pastel portrait of a Miss Nandl Baldauf. Nandl was the maid who regularly brought the artist his morning drink of chocolate while he was staying in Vienna on a royal commission to paint the Empress Maria Theresa and her family. Nandl was strikingly pretty and caught the artist's eye. He asked her to pose for him every morning just as she appeared at his door with his chocolate. The picture was called *La Belle Chocolatière* (The Beautiful Chocolate Server), and has become the most popular painting ever to immortalise the chocolate theme. Nandl is carrying a small black lacquer tray with short bracket-feet which supports a Meissen chocolate cup decorated in a Japanese floral 'kakiamon' pattern. The tall narrow cup is held in an elegant metal chocolate frame on a *trembleuse* (popular at the time to stop the precious drink spilling over) and additional pieces of a sweetmeat rest in the shallow scalloped base. The accompanying glass of water was a popular German custom to prepare the mouth in contrast to the hot chocolate. The painting was immediately sold by Liotard to Count Algarotti in Venice in 1745 who wrote of the portrait as "a Holbein in pastel".

Nandl went on to live a fairy tale. For twenty-five years she was the joy of a Viennese nobleman who eventually married her and she became Princess Dietrichstein.

Very little occurred with chocolate in the United States for the next hundred years. The gold rush in California in the mid-Nineteenth century was the impetus for two chocolate pioneers to establish themselves. Domingo Ghirardelli opened his confectionery business in 1862 and Etienne Guittard followed in 1868. Both of these companies are currently large-scale chocolate-manufacturers. In 1893 Milton Hershey, a candy manufacturer from Philadelphia, Pennsylvania, attended the World's Fair in Chicago. He saw a demonstration of German chocolate-making equipment and was so struck by it that he bought it and changed his focus from making caramels to making chocolate. Hershey has been quoted as saying, "caramels are only a fad, chocolate is a permanent thing." In fact, Hershey first invented the chocolate candy bar that Americans love so much today. He became known as 'the Henry Ford of chocolate' because he made chocolate available on a wide scale to the majority of the American population, in the same way Henry Ford did with cars. During the twentieth century chocolate has rapidly become one of the most popular candies in the United States. Milton Hershey is regarded by Carole Bloom, the American food writer and chocolate lover, as the father of American chocolate.

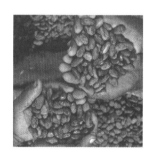

American, English, and European chocolate manufacturers obtain their beans from the same sources. The main difference between American and European chocolates is in how the cacao beans are processed. In general, Americans have become used to eating chocolate that is sweeter than the European variety. Although there are several factors involved in processing the cacao beans into chocolate, in general, chocolate manufacturers in the United States roast the beans quickly at a high temperature, which leaves them needing more sugar to mellow the flavour. European chocolate manufacturers roast their beans longer at a lower temperature. This produces a mellower, richer flavour that needs less sugar. This is true for all types of chocolate: dark, milk, and white. It's clear that Americans like sweet chocolate. Milk chocolate is very popular in the United States, as it is in England and most American chocolate bars are made with milk chocolate. Also, large retailers of boxed chocolate confections, such as See's, Fannie May, and Russell Stover, include a large selection of milk chocolates. Dark chocolate and white chocolate are offered in much smaller quantities.

America is currently experiencing a significant increase in chocolate consumption. Americans consume close to 12 pounds per person annually and that figure is steadily increasing. The boxed chocolate is the fastest growing segment of the confectionery industry in America with over 60 million households purchasing boxed chocolate in 1998.

American tastes have evolved due to both people and food travelling more frequently. As Americans become more exposed to top quality chocolate the demand for it is definitely increasing. Also, many artisan chocolatiers and confectioners are finding a market exists for their products. Some of the top artisan chocolatiers are Richard Donnelly in California, Fran Bigelow of Fran's in Seattle, Washington, and Larry Burdick of L.A. Burdick in Walpole, Massachusetts. In San Francisco, Scharffen Berger, a small pioneer chocolate company, is producing excellent quality chocolate couverture from raw cacao beans. This venture is very unusual because producing chocolate from the bean is a time-consuming and arduous task.

It seems that high quality milk chocolate will be one of the next big trends we will see in the United States, especially for use in desserts and pastries. Overall, Americans are beginning to demand higher quality chocolate.

CHOCOLATE IN THE SOUTHERN HEMISPHERE

Australia does not seem to feature on our chocolate map but in fact, the recent Pacific Rim culture has propelled Australia on to the world's gastronomic stage - and this includes good chocolate. *Haigh's Book of Chocolate* is a fascinating story of Australia's best loved family chocolate factory and plots the history of the Haigh family from 1915 to the present day. It is engagingly written and full of outspoken thoughts about the manufacture and sociology of chocolate including the fact that Cath Kerr, its author, hates the word 'chocoholic' which she considers demeaning. I think she has a good point. Cath Kerr is one of Australia's most prominent working chefs with a strong academic interest in food. She runs the new restaurant at the Art Gallery of South Australia where incidentally she is also a Gallery Guide (or 'docent' as they say in America). She admits that she is "interested in why and how we eat, and in recipes in so far as they show a historical or sociological change or development… The world does not need another recipe book!"

Haigh's continues to make chocolate from beans sourced by contacts in various parts of the world. The company uses particular bean blends for milk and dark chocolate and for its couverture for example.

Cath's favourite recipes use chocolate in savoury dishes as this shows the interesting historical progression of chocolate.

She also touches on the meaning of chocolate as a luxury item, symbol of love and affection and of course as a consequence, on the fear of chocolate and of food in general in our society today. I also like the thought that chocolate was seen as a Catholic indulgence while coffee was a Protestant stimulant to thinking and mental activity.

Another fine chocolate maker recommended by Cath is Kennedy & Wilson.

Peter Wilson (ex-wine-maker at Yarra Yering vineyard) and Julie Kennedy have been making a small range of carefully blended, hand-crafted chocolate now for only two years. They are available, in beautifully simple ink-illustrated boxes, from very select food stores. They make chocolate with (not filled chocolates) specified cocoa content such as milk and dark chocolate thins, bitter-sweet cat's tongues and a cinnamon chocolate.

Rather than buying pre-blended couverture, they tested cocoa liquors from 15 countries from Ghana to Madagascar and now select, blend and finish their own chocolate. Their grinding and conching process goes very close to the edge. It is such that the final chocolate is incredibly smooth and velvety, any smoother and it would disappear.

It's a very small production but has quickly become very prestigious. So far they are not too interested in filled chocolates although they are working on a small range for the future. Their interest is in the chocolate itself rather than the confections that can come from it. They apply their wine palate to the blending of the cocoa liquor.

Outside of the mass production of Cadbury's and Nestlé, there are small chocolate makers in each state who make fine chocolate confections but all using imported couverture, generally Callebaut. Swiss Glory in Adelaide, for example, makes an excellent range of chocolates in the European truffle/ganache style.

CHOCOLATE YESTERDAY, TODAY AND TOMORROW

Like much of the diet of the Western World, the slow but insidious decline in the quality of our chocolate began during and after the Second World War. It was the scarcity of raw materials during World War II, particularly cocoa beans and sugar, that was to blame for the drastic cuts in development and manufacture. Rationing of the nation's food supplies was introduced in 1940, although cholcolate and confectionery were spared until July 1941, and lasted until 1952. Post-war shortages consigned many popular confectionery lines to temporary obscurity. Indeed, many were never seen by the public again. In addition, according to Robin Weir, to the chagrin of the manufacturers, rather than create a huge market when rationing was lifted, manufacturers found that "the perverse consumer did not go mad on the excesses as expected but rather as a matter of habit from the previous austerity of 12 years, stuck to his allotted rations".

Today, most British chocolate is little more than flavoured confectionery - an ignoble product compared with the chocolate of our European neighbours - despite the fact that, as we have seen, the British are one of the 'greediest' nations of chocolate eaters, guzzling their way through approximately 170 g or 6 oz per week!

Britain's living legend and much-respected doyenne of 20th century British food, Marguerite Patten OBE, remembers well the draconian sweet rationing of the War. The value of the coupons started at a miserable 2 ounces (55 g) sweets per person per week and rose during the rationing period to 6.5 ounces (190 g) - and there were no exceptions for children. Marguerite set about her task as cookery-angel of mercy, creating a number of recipes for the hard-pressed housewife, which included chocolate cakes as well as all aspects of the British diet, which might have been victim to shortages of rationing, even creating a recipe for mock chocolate.

The war diet prompted a number of true entrepreneurial initiatives, one of the most unusual advertisements for confectionery, which emphasised the value of chocolate in the diet, appearing in the *News Chronicle* of 1945: 'Two good reasons for Mars Bars - they add extra value to the Wartime Diet and they save sugar and stretch the sweet ration'. A recipe was included for **MARS POTATO BUNS**: 1 Mars Bar; 2 oz fat; 1 oz dried egg; 1 level tsp grated raw potato; 1 oz dried fruit (optional); 4 oz flour; $\frac{1}{2}$ tsp baking powder; $\frac{1}{2}$ tsp salt; 1 tbsp water. Cut up Mars Bar and melt slowly in the water. Rub fat finely into the flour. Sift in dried egg, baking powder and salt; stir in potato and dried fruit and melted Mars Bar to form a stiff dough. Place in small rocky heaps on a greased baking sheet and bake in the hot oven (425°F) for ten to fifteen minutes.

Many more recipes appeared in magazines and Ministry propaganda with substitutes for shortages of sugar, butter and real chocolate. Newspaper readers sent in their chocolate offering like the ones below:

CHOCOLATE BUTTER: 1 tsp marg; 2 tbsp choc or 1 dstp cocoa; 2 tbsp caster; black coffee or milk; a few drops vanilla (optional).

Cream the marg and sugar. Add cocoa. Mix with enough black coffee (or milk mixed with vanilla) to make mixture pliable for spreading.

CHOCOLATE SPREAD (uncooked): 1$\frac{1}{2}$ tsp cocoa; 1 oz sugar; 1 oz marg; 1 tsp coffee essence.

Cream together marg and sugar 'til light and fluffy. Work in the cocoa. Last of all stir in the coffee essence and beat again.

CHOCOLATE SPREAD (cooked): 1 teacupful milk; 1 tbsp cocoa; small lump marg; 1 tbsp custard powder; 1 tbsp sugar.

Mix together custard powder, sugar and cocoa with a very little milk. Put marg in saucepan with the rest of the milk and when boiling pour on to cocoa mixture and return to pan. Boil 'til thick stirring all the time.

STEAMED CHOCOLATE PUDDING for 4-6. 3 oz marg; 5 level tbsp golden syrup; 1 egg; 4 oz self raising flour; 1 oz cocoa; 5 tbsp milk; 2 tbsp blackcurrant jam.

Grease 1$\frac{1}{2}$ pint pud basin. Cream together marg and syrup. Beat in eggs (mixture might curdle). Sift together flour, cocoa; fold in creamed mixture alternately with milk to soft dropping consistency. Place jam in the bottom of the basin and chocolate mixture on top. Cover with greaseproof paper, tie with string and steam over boiling water for 1$\frac{1}{2}$ to 2 hours. Turn out and serve with a plain sauce.

Many of the artisans who had been the feature of the pre-war food industry were unable to get back to manufacture because of labour losses due to the hostilities and post-war shortages. Even four years after the end of the War the Ministry of Food declared that no increase in the supply quotas of cocoa bean or sugar would be made.

As a consequence a number of Britain's favourite and most respected chocolate and confectionery manufacturers were prepared to make a number of lower quality products if they could satisfy the volume of demand. Hungry for respite from the austerity of war, and forgetting the joys of the quality, which had been commonplace, people accepted less and eventually expected less… and were not disappointed.

A few companies like Fortnum & Mason, Charbonnel et Walker, Bendicks, and Harrods, for example, who, before the War had promoted sales of hand-made chocolate, continued to produce exquisite chocolates. But they too eventually succumbed to the march of modern machinery, if not entirely, then at least in part.

The Belgian chocolate manufacturers, many of whom were from Brussels which still today boasts literally hundreds of artisan chocolate makers, were however benefiting from a strong marketing campaign to promote their 'continental'-style chocolate, and succeeding in impressing the nation's chocolate tastes.

Otherwise we feasted indiscriminately on mass produced chocolate bars, a fact which was noted by American food writer Catherine Calvert in 1982 in the American magazine *Town and Country*: "Oh the Brits do love their chocs. Walk into any newsagents and be dazzled by the heights to which Cadbury raises its humble chocolate bar, such as the Flake, which shatters into shards of pure chocolate which rain upon the plate, to listen for the crackle of wrapping paper in the theater (*sic*) as dowagers arch a finger to pick out the perfect bonbon with which to sweeten the last act, or watch what arrives with the coffee after the nicest dinners…"

But wait…, that was in 1982. Since then chocolate affairs have been improving in leaps and bounds for the growing number of people who are exhilarated by really fine chocolate. Thanks to the inspiration and energies of people like Nicola and Alan Porter of the Chocolate Society, Chantal Coady of Rococo, Jo Fairley of Green & Black, Gerard Ronay - not to mention Professor John Huber, Michel Roux and other skilled artisans whom the media have not yet discovered, now there seems to be an exciting 'real' chocolate renaissance. British food writer and trailblazer, Henrietta Green, waves the chocolate flag in her quest for better British foods and is instrumental in making sure that fine chocolate gets a place in her books and in the food festivals she regularly organises.

We used to have to make our pilgrimages to the chocolate houses of Paris, Brussels or Zurich for decent chocolates. There, every street seems to flaunt its own spectacularly ravishing chocolate shop; but now we are beginning to see the same attractive shops making an appearance in London. Every good restaurant has a chocolate pudding on its dessert menu. London saw its first International Festival of Chocolate at the Horticultural Halls in Victoria in 1998. As I write there are more festivals, exhibitions and salons then ever before. In the space of twelve months alone, the Chelsea Physic Garden in London celebrated cocoa in honour of one of its patrons, Sir Hans Sloane, who invented milk chocolate (as a drink) in the Seventeenth century; the History of Cocoa and Chocolate has been immortalised at the Castle Museum in York, Cadbury World at Bournville is great fun and informative for both adults and children as well worth seeing; and the great botanical gardens at Kew commemorated the cocoa plant in its own Exhibition of Chocolate.

WELL, WHAT NOW?

200 years ago most of the world's supplies of cocoa came from Venezuela and Central and South America, before nature even gave a thought to the possibilities of an African home for the precious tree. Now, in the blinking of an eye, more than two thirds of the world's cocoa is grown in the Ivory Coast and Ghana.

However, in the face of the industry's current habit, of manufacturing chocolate by blending a variety of different cocoas to ensure a uniform standard and flavour, a number of good chocolate manufacturers have woken up to the concept of a new range of products, based on the traditional recipes for chocolate made with a single origin variety bean. A thorough knowledge of the plantation areas acquired over generations inspires the right choice of cacaos that best reflect the distinctive characteristics of the variety, whether from Venezuela, Bolivia, Brazil or Ecuador in South America, the Ivory Coast or Ghana in West Africa or Papua New Guinea or Indonesia in South East Asia.

Some of us just can't get enough chocolate. So let's have more salons, festival and artisan chocolate shops and chocolate sensitive supermarkets. Chocolate is looking good. Here's to the future. Go on … indulge yourself!

From Bean to Bar

Nothing prepares you for the sight of the manufacturing process as well as the experience I enjoyed in Oaxaca in Mexico a couple of years ago. Oaxaca is one of Mexico's gems, a pretty, colourful Hispanic town lying in a valley between the towering Sierra Madre de Sur and the Puebla Oaxacan range of mountains. Its population is around 700,000.

It was viciously hot and that afternoon, in the peak of the heat, about 28°C, we stopped at a chocolate shop called La Guelaguetza. *Guelaguetza* means gift or mutual offering, which is rather appropriate for chocolate. The shop's owner was Maria Teresa Nunez de Gomez, an elegant, sophisticated lady with a deep olive complexion. Her thick black hair was immaculately sleeked back behind her head and tied with a wide black bow. She had huge brown eyes and a smile to match. The spotlessly clean shop specialised in all things chocolate - but chocolate for the traditional Mexican drink rather than for eating - although it is exceedingly edible.

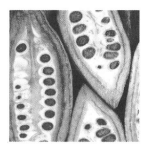

There were a couple of tables and chairs at which to rest while enjoying the drink, and sacks of cocoa beans everywhere. A huge bowl of beans was perched on the counter next to another of cinnamon, one of almonds, and another of sugar and some really smart old-fashioned iron and brass balance scales. There was a black cat lurking somewhere in the background - the way that only cats do!

La Guelaguetza house recipe is on 2 to 1 of chocolate and sugar respectively - but customers' own preferences can be very easily accommodated.

Maria Teresa weighed the cacao beans together with a few cinnamon sticks and a handful of almonds. Because Maria Teresa wasn't the sort of person to get her hands dirty, she handed the ingredients to an assistant, who took them to the side of the shop where three giant, solid cast-iron 'mincing' machines stood ready for action. These are the old-fashioned machines, which grind and pulverise the cacao bean to a paste and then a thick 'saucy' liquid. First, the beans are tipped into the funnel at the top and then, by a series of cogs and rollers driven by an electric belt, they are transformed into chocolate liquor. The thick liquid dark brown cocoa, a combination of cocoa butter and nibs, or kernels, oozes from a spout at the base of the machine like chocolate sauce and is caught by a large tin basin, which contains a specific weight of sugar. The two are thoroughly amalgamated by hand in a slow swirling motion until the mixture becomes a thick crunchy paste. Maria Teresa explained that the sugar isn't added at the initial stage with the cocoa beans because the heat caused by the friction of the rollers would caramelise it.

While the chocolate is still warm and pliable, Maria Teresa skilfully filled plastic moulds to produce finger length flat-bottomed conical sticks. Even in the heat, it soon sets.

She made us a jug of steaming hot chocolate by adding boiling water to some finely broken sticks. She took a *molinillo* - a wooden spatula ribbed with a series of wings carved out of the stem - and whirled it backwards and forwards between the palms of her hands in a rubbing motion. The spinning chocolate 'swizzle' stick whisked the chocolate and water together to candyfloss froth. Maria Teresa poured the liquid into two cups, which she offered to us. Not used to steaming chocolate in such high and humid temperatures I think we drank more out of curiosity than real desire, but the drink was actually delicious and chocolatey. Despite our language differences, she was clearly delighted with our reaction and she loaded us up with boxes of La Guelaguetza chocolate to take away - and a present of the jug and the 'whisk'.

From this rather crude, elementary practice of making chocolate, I at last understood the basic principles of the highly sophisticated technical performance which every bean goes through before it gets to you.

You'll be amazed at its journey, as it is totally transformed from a humble rainforest bean to a bar of glorious chocolate.

When I began to research this book, there were a few questions I wanted to know. Firstly, why do chocolate manufacturers buy through the Commodities Market rather than directly from the growers? I turned to my now friend and mentor Robin Dand, a well respected and acknowledged expert on cocoa markets and who has explored the subject in his book *The International Cocoa Trade*.

Robin explained that chocolate factories, as a rule, do not own plantations therefore they must buy their cocoa from outside, i.e. the sellers. Although it would seem logical for the two parties to deal directly with each other, in fact, this does not happen to any great extent - although, in some cases, the situation is changing.

There are a number of reasons for the middle-man. Firstly, the manufacturer's (buyers') requirements might not coincide with the plantation's (sellers') needs to export. Similarly, he (the manufacturer) might not find an exporter who wants to sell on the same day. As a result a service industry, the Commodities Market, consisting of dealers and brokers, has developed. These intermediaries also help to keep the price of cocoa stable.

The second reason is that buyers can often find another source offering the same cocoa cheaper than the exporters.

The third reason is that it is the factories' function to make chocolate. Consequently they do not want to get involved in trading the beans when they can get others to do it for them.

As the trade in cocoa increased at the end of the Nineteenth century, so did the risks to the manufacturers of running out of the type of beans they needed. For example, the chocolate manufacturers could either buy cocoa in, say, January for delivery in say, June, or wait the six months and then attempt to buy the cocoa on the spot market. Manufacturers who delayed until they needed the beans ran a two-fold risk. Firstly, the required variety of cocoa might not be available in six months time. Secondly, the spot price in June could be higher than the forward price of six months earlier. On the other hand, buying forward might help safeguard the supply of raw material to the factory, the first risk, but in no way ensures a good price.

So now much wiser as to the nature of the cocoa trade I set off on yet another trip to see every stage in this cocoa-to-chocolate process which took me to Meulan, a suburb of Paris, and the home of Cacao Barry, one of the world's finest chocolates.

As the train drew into the station, the pervasive all-consuming smell of pure chocolate drenched the air. The factory appeared on the horizon as a large unprepossessing square concrete block - but this was merely a disguise for its inner workings. Before we venture inside one of the world's largest and best chocolate houses, imagine one wall of the building in which there are three massive outlet or input valves. Hooked up to these valves were three appropriately sized tankers, one providing pure cocoa mass (or liquor), one cocoa butter - (both of which had been processed from freshly imported beans in another factory on another site to prevent cross contamination from the importing countries) - and a third with sugar. All three ingredients are used as required according to specific recipes.

Once inside, my expectations of men and women in white coats and chefs hats with vats of chocolate being stirred and coaxed into pure chocolate blocks were bitterly disappointed. There were, indeed, vats - some 20 metres high and 20 metres in circumference, each containing couverture in a state of 'conchment', which is the term applied to the mixing of the chocolate - but they were sealed as a modern day gesture towards the EC propensity to comply with the rules of health and hygiene. But there was one last uncovered vat, which from a gangway, I could peer down inside to watch the giant paddles conching (stirring) the chocolate - another few weeks and I would have missed it. At the epicentre of all this activity was a glass panelled box with a lone technician staring intently at a bank of computers. Here computers dictate and maintain the action and temperatures, which are so vital to the process. If the temperature should fluctuate by a mere decimal point, not only does the computer flash a warning signal - but it puts it right.

This was state-of-the-art chocolate making at its 21st century apogee.

Once the beans arrive at the processing factories the actual process depends upon which type of chocolate you want, be it plain, bitter, milk, or ivory, then a recipe specifies the amount of chocolate liquor (beans ground to a liquid - also known as 'solids' or 'mass') and sugar with or without milk solids. 70% bitter chocolate contains 70% cocoa solids and 30% sugar with some flavouring like vanilla added.

STORING: The beans are stored in sacks, huge silos or warehouses, which are strictly controlled for hygiene, temperature and air humidity levels. There is a universal move to phase out sacks in favour of a more economical mighty container method. Samples are taken to check the quality of the beans.

CLEANING: The process begins by cleaning to get rid of any foreign bodies - such as string, twigs, metal, remains of shells, broken or caked beans, bits of earth, dust and sand which are removed by screening and suction.

PRE-DRYING: The cleaned cocoa beans are tipped on to a vibrating belt heated by infra-red strips to obtain what is called the 'pop effect': i.e. the 6-8% moisture in the beans is reduced to 4-6% by the heat and the shells become more brittle, making the separation of nib - the inner seed of the bean after the shell has been removed - and shell easier during shelling.

BLENDING: Beans are blended with varieties from different countries according to each manufacturer's recipe.

KIBBLING/SHELLING: This operation consists of separating the shell from the nib. The pre-dried cocoa beans are sent to the breaker, a sort of mechanical mill, and are broken into large particles. These are then tipped on to a cascade of sieves, known as 'tarares' or 'winnowers', with decreasing mesh sizes. On each sieve, the seed coat, germ and shell are sucked out by air and amassed on one side. Compressed and granulated they will be used as fertiliser or in cattle feed. Once this operation is completed, only the all-important cocoa nib remains which then goes on for roasting.

ROASTING: Like coffee, cocoa only develops its real colour and flavour when roasted. The roaster is a rotating cylinder with double casing and the air circulated inside is heated by a burner, which transfers its heat to the nibs inside. The nibs are roasted at a temperature of between 120°C to 140°C. They lose up to 10% of their original weight. The degree and length of roasting time depends upon the origin of the beans and the type of cocoa or chocolate required. The 'chef' controlling roasting should be able to judge when the cocoa has reached the favoured colour - this is crucial or the taste and quality may be compromised or even ruined. The hot nibs are then poured into a cooler (a sealed tank ventilated with cold air) before being sent for grinding.

GRINDING/REFINING: The nibs are now ground to become a liquid paste, also called cocoa mass, and/or liquor and later referred to as solids. At this stage the chocolate contains approximately 55% cocoa butter.

Now the cocoa liquor will be divided into different routes, according to whether the mass is to be manufactured into chocolate, or to be pressed to produce cocoa butter (some of which may be re-added according to the recipe for chocolate) or cocoa cake, from which cocoa powder will be made.

Now comes the actual manufacturing process of the chocolate, a mixture of cocoa liquor, sugar cocoa butter and sometimes milk. The percentage of each depends upon the variety and type of chocolate.

ROUTE ONE

MIXING: The cocoa mass is mixed with other raw material such as sugar and/or milk products, in a mixer with granite millstones until it becomes a smooth homogenous paste called a 'dough'.

REFINING: The dough is refined through 5 revolving steel rollers which reduces all the solid particles to 20 microns or less for top quality chocolate. That the more minuscule the particle the better the mouthfeel of the chocolate. Your tongue should only anticipate and recognise chocolate as a smooth, silky experience - an exceedingly desirable distinction.

The mixture which comes off the top of the fifth roller is in powder or flake form.

CONCHING: This operation is essential for finesse and smoothness as it homogenises the chocolate and develops its flavour. The friction of the paddles, which are formed like a giant mixer, creates heat, which melts all components, and so it becomes liquid. More cocoa butter may be added now - depending on the recipe.

The conching time should be long enough to drive off the unwanted volatile oils and bitterness, but not too long to also get rid of some of the more complex chocolate flavours comprising over 400 flavour compounds.

When I started in the chocolate world, the longer the conch the better the chocolate - and when I say longer I mean 4-5 days. However, with the wonders of modern technology this prolonged process has been reduced to a matter of 8 - 28 hours. But still many elite and prestigious chocolate houses boast the longer 4-5 day conch for their grand crus products.

TEMPERING: Once conching is over, the chocolate has to be tempered in order to pass from a liquid to a solid state so it goes through a temperature cycle, very precisely calculated to encourage fine, stable crystallisation of the cocoa butter and its homogenous dispersal throughout the chocolate. Stored in tanks at 40°C, the chocolate enters a tempering machine, i.e. a cylinder with a dual casing, which cools it to 27°/28°C then reheats it to 29°/30°C for milk chocolate and to 31°/32°C for plain chocolate. This is known as the crystallisation curve.

The liquid chocolate is either transported to it destination in huge tankers or it goes on to:

MOULDING: Chocolate is now moulded into the familiar blocks or pistolles that we buy.

CHOCOLATE MANUFACTURING (see below)

DARK		MILK	WHITE
mix		mix	mix
Cocoa liquor +		Cocoa liquor +	
*Cocoa butter +	(*In certain recipes)	*Cocoa butter +	Cocoa butter +
Sugar		Sugar +	Sugar +
		Milk solids	Milk solids
GRINDING		GRINDING	GRINDING
CONCHING		CONCHING	CONCHING
		STORAGE	TEMPERING
			MOULDING
LIQUID CHOCOLATE			SOLID CHOCOLATE

ROUTE TWO FOR LIQUOR

PRESSING: After grinding, the cocoa liquor is pressurised at 350-530 bars (kg/cms) in mighty hydraulic presses with wire mesh screens. This high pressure screening enables separation of the liquid part - the cocoa butter which is then deodorised and moulded into cakes and blocks. The solid part known as cocoa cake, appears in the shape of a pancake, the fat content of which varies from 10% (reduced flat cake) to 24% (fatty cake).

COCOA CAKE: Crushed into a fine power. Then alkalised - also known as 'Dutching' after Van Houten who invented it at the beginning of the 19th century. Alkalisation changes the pH of the cocoa, mellows the flavour, and, most importantly, darkens the colour. (Discovered by the Aztec 'medicine men' who used to use it as a stomach remedy by adding wood ashes from the fire to chocolate to make it more digestible).

COCOA BUTTER: Is deodorised and refined for use in white chocolate.

PACKING: The cocoa powder is bagged in 25 kg bags, then palleted and stored to await its fate.

Chocolate is the combination of the roasted ground kernel of the cacao bean, the principle part of which is cocoa butter, which is the fat released when the bean is ground, and sugar. Chocolate may also contain lecithin, a natural emulsifier, and flavours such as vanilla, and in the case of milk chocolate, milk solids.

A really good chocolate, often referred to as plain, bitter, bittersweet, or dark couverture, made with a quality bean and a modest amount of sugar, is one of the world's greatest natural ingredients, and, like a fine wine, the better the grape and the love invested, the better the wine, so it is the same for chocolate. For its quality and character, chocolate very much depends on the variety of the cacao bean, its geographical source, the way it has been cultivated and the methods employed to make the bean into chocolate. Thus a high cocoa content alone is not the answer to a good chocolate - necessarily. The answer lies in the bean.

Hand-made, incidentally, is misleading because a hand-made chocolate can be so called as long as it is hand finished. The majority of manufacturers would go out of business if they relied on mass production of chocolates by human hand. There are many superb machines which take the back-ache away from the chocolatier including simple enrobing machines which spray a 'curtain' of tempered chocolate over the centres as they pass through on a conveyor belt.

Dark chocolate is defined by the characteristics of the cocoa content (usually marked as cocoa solids) which can be as much as 99% and as little as 30%. Just because it has a high cocoa content does not always mean that it is going to be a great chocolate. The techniques, style and recipe of the chocolate maker and the variety and blends of the beans are the vital components in rendering a chocolate good or a bad. The remainder principally constitutes sugar. Like many other flavourings, such as salt, a little enhances the flavour, while a lot merely kills the taste - it also destroys the natural mouthfeel of the chocolate, which is one of its most significant qualities. Cocoa butter has the unique property of melting at body temperature, which dissolves into a warm liquid in the mouth.

I have my own chocolate preferences, which vary from 64%-73% - much more than that and it tends to be mouth puckering. Every chocolate aficionado will agree, however, that the bean, the vital ingredient, must be of the finest quality.

Cocoa butter is an expensive product and very popular in the pharmaceutical industry as an unparalleled base for cosmetic and skin preparations as it rarely goes rancid and is a unique protection against sun and weather. (The Central American Indians used cocoa butter as an antiseptic, a skin cream and also to grease their weapons of war!) It remains stable until it touches the skin where it melts and spreads luxuriously at body temperature. Its popularity and value to the cosmetics industry is one of the reasons why chocolate manufacturers are tempted to follow the British habit of replacing 5% of the cocoa butter with vegetable fat.

COUVERTURE, (plain, bitter, and bittersweet) which literally translated from the French name, by which it is universally known, means 'covering'. However, just to confuse us all, covering chocolate in this country is not the same thing at all as I describe below. Couverture should be made from at least a minimum 46% cocoa solids - and I emphasise that this is the minimum legal necessity. Most quality chocolate which I use and for which Cacao Barry, Amedei, Valrhona, Chocolaterie de l'Opéra or Lindt, for example, gain their reputations, are made from 60%-70% (or occasionally more), cocoa solids and only 40% - 30% sugar. The higher the mass and the lower the sugar content, the better the chocolate because a modest amount of sugar enhances the flavour, softening the bitterness and bringing out the true depth and flavour of the chocolate. Some couvertures have vanilla added - an excellent and very traditional partner - other couvertures do not. Hopefully, all chocolate of this quality will contain a natural vanilla, but some more commercial chocolate may contain an artificial vanillin. You can easily detect the synthetic aftertaste.

The complex nature of couverture chocolate is a suspension of sugar and cocoa particles in cocoa butter (fats from the cocoa beans). The sugar and cocoa particles remain solid at normal temperatures, but cocoa butter is an intricate fat structure, so this type of chocolate requires tempering. This is the heating and cooling process used to bring the material to a melted, amalgamated and crystalline state. The different components it contains have different setting points. Tempering encourages and amalgamates those fats to form crystals, which will ensure a high gloss. If the temperatures are too high, the various fats will separate and the chocolate will either not set or will set badly with white fat streaks on the surface; or if the temperature is too low, then a tell-tale white sugar bloom will be evident. Both these faults may also happen when chocolate has been stored badly in fluctuating temperatures. Occasionally, the chocolate may have a grey streaky fat 'bloom' on it. This could be that it has been tempered incorrectly or stored badly and some particles of cocoa butter have risen to the surface because of fluctuating temperatures. It doesn't always signify that it is stale (although it could be) and does not necessarily affect the taste. The recommended storage temperature for chocolate is between 16 - 18°C with minimum humidity.

The more significant white powdery appearance is a light film of sugar bloom usually caused by the chocolates coming into contact with water or condensation. This happens if the chocolates are unprotected in the fridge and/or when they are 'shocked' at meeting the air outside the fridge at a warmer temperature. The moisture will dissolve the sugar on the surface of the chocolate. When the water evaporates afterwards, the sugar re-crystallises into rough, irregular crystals on the surface. This may cause the 'bite' to be dry and powdery and may spoil some of the appearance and therefore the pleasure. Both of these effects can happen very quickly during and after the production process. It is mainly instinct, but also experience which will tell you if you should be tempted to bite any further.

Properly tempered couverture will set and form a hard protective surface with a good gloss and a brittle snap when you break or bite into it. Good-tempered chocolate also tends to have a longer shelf life with minimal bloom.

You can, of course, use couverture in all your recipes. I do. I think it infinitely preferable. Use a cheaper, inferior cooking quality chocolate in a recipe and you are probably adding some more hidden fats and the end result is simply not as pleasurable.

CHOCOLATE PASTE (known as 'block') is pure chocolate or cocoa mass to which no sugar has been added. It is not for eating neat although is very edible, but is used in pastry work and when you want a real smacking chocolate taste. Confusingly it is sometimes known as Baking or Baker's Chocolate. Just to confuse the issue further, what we describe as Baker's chocolate here in Europe, means quite the opposite in America where Baking or Bakers chocolate (after Walter Baker, one the pioneers of American chocolate) means couverture chocolate.

COMPOUND or **COOKING CHOCOLATE** - again confusingly sometimes known as Baker's or Baking Chocolate or 'Pâte à Glacer' - is also widely commercially used for cooking and cake decorations. It usually contains little or no cocoa butter which is replaced with a hydrogenated (chemical) or fractionated (natural) fat and lecithin stabiliser. (Large amounts of cheap and plentiful vegetable oils, such as soya bean and cottonseed, are converted to soft solids like margarine or lard by a process of hydrogenation. To remove any unpleasant smell or offensive taste so that they can be used for cooking, the oils are hydrogenated by heating to a temperature of about 200° C [392° F] and mixed with fine particles of nickel as a catalyst while under 3 to 4 atmospheres [units of pressure] of hydrogen. These artificially produced fat products are used extensively in foods.)

It does not, therefore, need tempering and, depending upon the manufacture, can be used for covering but it will not have the same qualities as tempered couverture and I cannot stress emphatically enough that it is, in fact, a cheap substitute. Strictly speaking, we should never refer to flavoured coating or compounds as chocolate.

COMMERCIAL CHOCOLATE: Most of the chocolate we eat in Britain, often referred to as the 'UK type', is legally permitted to contain up to 5% vegetable fat of a type that is considered compatible with cocoa butter. The fat does not need to be specified but is usually from nuts, Illipe or perhaps palm oil. This type of chocolate is almost certain to have a very high sugar content, in the region of 55% +, which means that the cocoa solids content will be no more than 30%.

The trouble with this type of chocolate is that it does not have the brittle snap and clean bite and tends to leave a nasty aftertaste and a clingy sensation on the palate. It is of course infinitely more cost effective and profitable for the manufacturers who promote it as having a higher melting point and therefore longer shelf life.

MILK CHOCOLATE: couverture should be made from at least 31% cocoa solids - but by law eating chocolate needs only either a) 20% as reflected in most of our British products - and 20% milk solids and the rest is sugar; or b) 25% cocoa solids and 14% milk solids, which is favoured by the Continent. The taste will vary according to production methods and also to the way the milk is treated before it is added. In Europe, most of the manufacturers use a condensed milk similar to that invented by Nestlé and used by Peter in the first milk chocolate products. In the more commercial chocolate countries like America and the UK,

we use dried milk powder, often caramelised and known as 'crumb', which gives the UK milk chocolate its familiar caramel flavour. 95% of the chocolate sold in Great Britain is milk and Cadbury has the largest share of that market. I know that there are millions who will disagree with this, but I think that unlike the continental milk chocolate, which has a well-defined cocoa flavour and smooth finish, we are used to a cloyingly sweet product with an unclean aftertaste and barely any hint of cocoa.

WHITE CHOCOLATE is often dismissed by chocolate aficionados as not real chocolate. I disagree. Cocoa butter is one of the main ingredients of the cocoa bean and therefore merely because white chocolate does not contain cocoa powder is hardly a reason to reject it. However, it is a matter of personal taste and as a product on its own it does have many merits.

White chocolate (couverture) is a combination of not less than 20% cocoa butter and maybe sometimes up to 45%, not less than 14% milk solids, and sugar which accounts for the rest of the product. It is flavoured with vanilla although many producers add other flavours such as orange. White chocolate is also the basis for the blue, yellow, pink and other colour chocolates - which is fun. You can buy this from Ritter Courivaud, Town & County and Keylink (see Directory).

Some experts are of the opinion that the best dark chocolate comes from France and Belgium, milk from Switzerland and white from Holland - this is not to be taken too literally but I think that there is some truth in this.

ORGANIC: Organic chocolate is produced from cocoa beans which are grown without pesticides, chemicals or artificial fertilisers. On the back of every Green & Black's Organic Chocolate you will find the company's pledge "Dark Chocolate has more cocoa mass (solids) and less sugar than you will find in other dark chocolate - and it's organic too. Your support for organic growers helps to make the world a better place". Although most organic chocolate tends to have a stronger chocolatey flavour, this has nothing to do with the fact that the cocoa is grown organically because, again, it is the variety of the bean, where and how it is grown that makes the difference. Duchy Originals, which is the company established in 1990 to encourage more sustainable methods of farming and food production, is also using an organic chocolate for most of its dark chocolate products which commit the company to the same principles.

What organic nearly always implies, nevertheless, is the admirably committed and ethical mission philosophy of the producer to use organic beans. The producer has taken the time and trouble to source pesticide-free beans which will also tend to make a higher class of chocolate. One of the down sides of organically-produced chocolate is that its producers tend to think organic means worthy and this tends to come out in the end products. This is a personal opinion and not based on any technical accuracy whatsoever, but it is also an experience, which is shared by a number of chocolate friends. Another reason given is that organic chocolate relies on beans bred primarily for their resistance to pests and disease rather than for taste, and therefore the chocolate does not always compare as well with its conventionally-produced cousin. However, when I suggested this to the exuberant Jo Fairley, owner and creator of Green & Black's multi-prizewinning organic chocolate, she dismissed this as manufacturers' propaganda. To be truly organic of course, the production process must also be chemical free… and manufacturers have to set up a dedicated organic line.

CHOCOLATE AND ITS FUTURE

As the price of cocoa rose after 1973, so the cocoa content in chocolate went down as manufacturers tried to avoid passing price increases on to customers in order to keep up sales. They found ways to use less cocoa: Firstly, by promoting confectionery with filled cheaper centres which meant fewer solid chocolate bars. Secondly, by using a proportion of other cheaper vegetable fats instead of cocoa butter.

Even when the cocoa prices fell it took time for the ingredients ratio to improve as, having altered their recipes, the manufacturers were not inclined to return to higher cocoa quantities. Although in the 1990s, cocoa prices were at their lowest ever, the ingredient ratios have never returned to their previous levels. The change in chocolate-eating habits as a result of the 1970s constraints meant that people have adapted to eating more filled centres, especially cereal centres, and improvements in processing worked against the return to a high proportion of cocoa to chocolate.

Manufacturers continually look for cheaper methods of production. Apart from processing improvements, the obvious way is to substitute expensive ingredients with cheaper alternatives. With chocolate, this means finding cheaper fat to replace cocoa butter - called cocoa butter equivalents (CBEs).

In the UK, as in Denmark and Ireland, we have traditionally added 5% vegetable fat to our chocolate (some countries are legally allowed to add even more). Manufacturers say that this is what we want. Well, it is certainly what we have grown used to. In addition it is claimed that vegetable fat has keeping qualities that cocoa butter does not. Debatable. In any event, in 1973, when UK, Ireland and Denmark were among the first to join the EEC, Legal Exemption was granted to permit these three to continue using vegetable fat in their industrial chocolate recipes without breaching European law. All was well, until one by one new member states, also producing chocolate with vegetable fat, began to join the EC and found themselves prevented from doing so since the 1973 exemption did not extend to them. The current proposals are designed to harmonise the law across Europe; and obviously there are a number of countries in favour of 'No Vegetable Fat in Products Called Chocolate' (this is the title of their slogan). On the other hand, a number propose that all the EC member states should be allowed to produce chocolate with added vegetable fat and still call it chocolate.

Politically it makes sense to bring all the EC countries into line. However the current position, modified in the early Nineties, allows for 7 EC member states to use vegetable fat, while 8 member states cannot.

The 5% vegetable fat/chocolate issue, currently under review by the EC, is pressing for European harmonisation, i.e. to allow every European country to add 5% vegetable fat to the current legal minimum 30% cocoa solids contained in plain chocolate - milk and white chocolate are also affected in different proportions.

The situation is far from resolved. CAOBISCO who represent the chocolate confectionery manufacturers, such a Cadbury, etc., is fiercely in favour of harmonisation. The cocoa campaign, representing many smaller independent chocolate makers across Europe, is equally fiercely against the motion.

The British are far from alone in this chocolate chaos. Popular Australian journalist, Cherry Ripe, writes from there that "locally made products at the moment must contain a minimum of 15 per cent cocoa solids". But, would you believe, new regulations proposed by the Food Authority (ANZFA) threaten to remove even these modest compositional standards. Cherry goes on "According to the latest issue of the consumer magazine *Consuming Interest*, buying a chocolate bar would become a lottery and allow cheap imitation confectionery to pass itself off as chocolate… Chocolate manufacturers are up in arms. The Food Authority is saying that many food standards need to be streamlined because they might impede innovation, and it only wants to retain food standards for health and safety reasons. But the current Food Standards on chocolate provides a simple assurance to consumers that when they purchase a product labelled as chocolate they can be confident that it substantially derives from the cocoa bean. Consumers might start looking for imports from France or Belgium which comply with rigorous international compositional standards. At present few Australian bars of chocolate are sufficiently labelled to be able to tell what is in the chocolate unlike the German Milka or Swiss Lindt which explicitly state that they contain a minimum of 30% cocoa solids".

But on a happier note chocolate at last seems to have been given a clean bill of health. Many of us feel guilty about eating chocolate - it's a hangover from our youth. We shouldn't. It is true that chocolate does contain fat and sugar, but I am a great believer in my old Granny's adage that 'a little of what you fancy does you good!' Good quality chocolate - around 70% cocoa solids - contains a host of naturally occurring chemicals including theobromine, phenylethylamine and caffeine and others, all of which are known to be reproduced by the brain when excited by, for example, the passion of a love affair. Indeed, recently, researchers in America have found that some of these chemicals are similar to those contained in cannabis…

Chocolate was blamed for migraine, making us fat, spots and acne and constipation. However, we've come full circle and scientific research has since completely exonerated chocolate of these accusations. Further research indicates that dark chocolate, rich in cocoa solids, lowers cholesterol levels and contributes to the prevention of cardiovascular disease. The higher the cocoa solids the better, as the fibrous part of the bean has also recently been found to contain the same powerful anti-oxidants found in grape skins and therefore red wine which are considered to have anti-ageing effects - among other exquisitely desirable blessings.

Oxidisation of these low-density lipoproteins is known to be linked to furring of the arteries, which can lead to heart attacks. A 41 gram piece of chocolate contains about 230 milligrams of polyphenols compared with 210 in red wine which help to protect the arteries. However, like any fat, it contains 9 calories per gram so go carefully, especially on the milk and white chocolate which contain high proportions of dairy products and are irredeemably fat saturated. According to a report in The Times 1996, "Cocoa fat contains both saturated and mono-unsaturated fat, but it seems that as one of them is fatty stearic acid it may not raise the blood cholesterol level. When stearic acid is acted upon by an enzyme in the body, it is partly converted to oleic acid, which is a beneficial mono-unsaturated fatty acid found in olive oil. In addition, chocolate contains significant levels of a flavonoid compound polyphenol which prevents oxidisation of a specific type of combined fat and protein complex in the blood". On the bad side, all chocolate contains high proportions of sucrose, and lactose in milk, which scientists view with suspicion as it seems they may increase the levels of triglyceride, another fat circulating in the blood, by stimulating its production in the liver. Apparently cocoa powder protects your teeth from tooth decay by preventing the sugar from damaging the enamel.

PRODUCTION OF COCOA BEANS BY COUNTRY

	1988/9	1992/3	2002/3
Africa			
Cameroon	129.4	97.0	140
Cote d'Ivoire	848.9	800.0	1,320
Ghana	300.1	312.1	497
Nigeria	165.0	145.0	165
Rest of Africa	45.3	29.5	36
The Americas			
Brazil	324.1	308.6	163
Colombia	50.0	50.0	38
Dom Republic	43.0	52.0	45
Ecuador	86.7	67.4	85
Mexico	42.0	0.3	35
Peru	11.5	11.0	14
Venezuela	10.2	16.0	15
Rest of the Americas	20.3	21.8	21
Asia and Oceania			
Indonesia	93.0	240.0	425
Malaysia	225.0	225.0	40
Papua New Guinea	48.0	38.8	42
Rest Asia and Oceania	21.3	20.3	20

CONSUMPTION BY COUNTRY

	Kg per person
Switzerland	9.7
Norway	8.5
Germany	8.5
Ireland	8.5
UK	7.8
Denmark	7.5
Belgium	6.4
Austria	5.8
USA	5.3
Sweden	5.1
France	4.9
Holland	4.6
Finland	4.0
Italy	2.6
Greece	2.3
Japan	1.6
Brazil	1.1

CALORIE CONTENT OF CHOCOLATE

	calories per ounce
Bitter chocolate – ie approximately 60% cocoa solids and above	135
Sweet chocolate – ie commercial chocolate containing less than 35% cocoa solids	145
Milk chocolate	149
White chocolate	153
High fat cocoa powder	85
Low fat cocoa powder	55

Tasting Chocolate

I think, dear reader, that you will agree that nothing tastes as good nor stimulates and satisfies our tastes as chocolate. Nothing in the world has such a complexity of flavours and smells. The cocoa bean has over 400 distinct aromas - at least twice as many as any other gems of nature. The rose, a heavenly creation if ever there was one, has only fourteen and the gastronome's staple the onion, only half a dozen. The taste of chocolate is equally as complex as a result of the presence of over 300 different chemical compounds, including theobromine and methyl-xanthine - two mildly addictive caffeine-like substances - and phenylethylamine, a stimulant similar to the body's own dopamine and adrenaline. Phenylethylamine strikes the brain's mood centres and induces the emotion of falling in love, a matter of only partly understood brain chemistry. Then there is the actual physical pleasure of feeling the chocolate melt in the mouth - that certainly must be part of the legendary seduction.

Many of these chemical compounds are identical or similar to those found in fruits, vegetables, spices, herbs, and other substances. That's why we chocolate enthusiasts compare the aromas of different chocolates to those as various as melon, citrus, cherry, berry, raisin, honey, peach, vanilla, butterscotch, mint, bell pepper, grass, green olive, clove, liquorice, cedar, coffee and wine. We're not being fanciful; there's a chemical correlation underlying the comparison, and this fact explains the rich metaphorical language used to describe a chocolate's sensory characteristics.

The primary cocoa smells of chocolate, distinct by variety, make up its aroma, while secondary characteristics, caused by factors such as fermentation, drying, blending, roasting and the different manufacturers' production processes and recipes form the final tastes and bouquet.

Although taste is essentially a function of smell, tasting reveals aspects of a chocolate's personality that sniffing cannot. Humans can perceive many combinations of only four tastes: sweet, sour, bitter, and salt. These sensations are localized in taste buds on different parts of the tongue: sweetness on the tip, with acidity and bitterness on the sides and to the rear.

The food writer and intellectual Alan Davidson claims in his paper on *Taste, Aromas and Flavours* that smell and taste combine to create flavour (which is why we all taste things differently). He believes "that it is the flavour that is so exciting about chocolate. Often the chocolate eater will first get the aroma of the chocolate before it reaches the taste sensors of the mouth. This aroma sets off a stimulus that is further supported by the tastebuds. These two combine to create a flavour that is wonderful, to say the least".

But other foods can do the same. So what is it that is different about chocolate? Well, as I have pointed out before, chocolate is unique. It is the only food in the world to melt at body temperature, slowly flooding the mouth with all the complexities of its yielding nature.

But taste is more than just smell and tasting. It involves

three other senses - sight, sound and feel. Tasting of any kind is a science, but we all possess the natural instincts to distinguish the perplexities of good and bad, although it is true that some of us have more tastebuds and olfactory senses than others which is why (thank goodness) we have different likes and dislikes. However there are a number of consensual elements in tasting which I thought you might like to share.

Appearance: Chocolate should be a flawless, evenly coloured, deep, dark shade of mahogany or red. Black is not necessarily an indicator of a good chocolate. Cocoa beans are rarely jet black; if they are, it tends to indicate they have been over-roasted. No cracks or air pockets, streaks or sugar bloom caused by chocolate subjected to various temperature changes. Care in storage is needed.

Touch: It should feel silky and not sticky and should just begin to yield to the warmth of your finger.

Aroma: The chocolate should smell good as you unwrap it, with a complex fragrance. It should be sweetly fragrant but not overpowering. You could detect vanilla, berry, caramel-roasted nuts. It's bad to have no smell at all. If you can't smell you can't taste. Burnt, musty, chemically or medicine-y is not good.

Feel/Snap: Take a piece and break it - it should snap cleanly - if it splinters or crumbles it may not be good. Take a look inside; it should be solid all the way through with no blemishes or holes.

Mouthfeel or texture: Most tastebuds are on the front of the tongue which is where you should start tasting the chocolate. If it doesn't start to melt straight away this is probably a sign of poor quality. Here is the chocolate's biggest test - now should begin the taste explosion. It should be smooth and buttery, gently dissolving into a creamy liquid filling the mouth with its complexity of flavours. It must not be grainy or 'gluey'. If it's 'waxy' or 'clacky' it sometimes means the cocoa butter has been replaced with vegetable fat - and it's not true chocolate.

Flavour: The flavours from where most of the chocolate experience comes are located on different parts of the tongue:

Sweet (front); **Sour** (front/sides); **Bitter** (back); **Salt** (back/sides).

Everybody has his/her own body chemistry so you might taste any one or all of the flavours I have mentioned but essentially chocolate is going to be bitter-sweet, fruity and spicy with a good balance of acidity and should be subtle rather than overpowering.

Aftertaste: You want flavour to linger for several minutes with a clean aftertaste and no residue; and certainly not be overpoweringly sweet. Robert Linxe, the French champion of great chocolate, maintains that you should be able to taste a good chocolate some 45 minutes after you have eaten it.

Look out for these aromas and flavours:

DARK CHOCOLATE

Desirable: bitter-sweet, butter, acidity, fruit, toasted, caramel, almonds, hazelnuts, spice, citrus, orange peel, berries, leather, tannin, herbs, jute, smoky, tea, tobacco, freshly mown hay, clover, wild herbs, floral, earthy. Recently, I detected that glorious sweet smell of a horse's mane!

Undesirable: smoked, fatty, metallic, acid, medicinal, cardboard, astringent, musty.

MILK CHOCOLATE

Desirable: brown sugar, milky, creamy, cocoa, vanilla, honey, caramel, nutty, malt etc.

Undesirable: smoked, fatty, rancid, pungent, cardboard, acid, astringent.

WHITE CHOCOLATE

Desirable: sweet, vanilla, creamy, milky, honey, caramel, fruity.

Undesirable: alcohol, cooked, rancid, pungent.

I find it more difficult to detect as many flavours in both milk and white chocolate as in dark because of the low cocoa content, the milk and overpowering presence of sugar, which as I have already explained kills tastes and aromas. Having said this, a number of manufacturers have improved their milk chocolate recently using a higher proportion of cocoa solids, therefore less sugar. Worth hunting out.

One final point: just because a chocolate boasts a lot of cocoa solids does not guarantee its taste. A good chocolate depends on the quality of the cocoa beans - the better the beans the better the chocolate - as well as the chocolate makers' recipe.

Here are some chocolate manufacturers' own observations on the tastes and nuances of a selection of their confections:

VALRHONA

This was one of the first companies to launch a range of 'grand crus' on the basis of the wine grower's maxim that the better the fruit the better the end product. A grand cru is a single variety bean or bean from a single country.

Guanaja 70%: "named after the Caribbean Island of Guanaja where Christopher Columbus landed in 1502 and made from both the florally flavoured *criollo* beans and pungent *trinitario*. An exceptional bitter chocolate, its intense flavour, heightened by floral notes, has a powerful lingering intensity".

Caraïbe 64%: made from Caribbean *trinitario* beans; "discover its exceptional nose, with tobacco and wood notes. In the mouth, its fruit, barely sweet flavour recalls vanilla, almonds and roasted coffee".

Manjari 64%: "is a uniquely fruity chocolate made from the Madagascan *trinitario* "with notes of red berries and citrus fruits".

Jivara 40% milk: "combination of the finest Ecuadorean beans, whole milk, brown sugar and a hint of malt. Caramel and vanilla notes make it an exceptional milk chocolate".

CACAO BARRY

Santo Domingo 70%: "This is the result of a combination of *criollo* and *forastero* and is exceptionally long in the mouth.

Discover the wine flavour, with fruity, spicy, dense and powerful notes, which this cocoa has drawn from a naturally dark and chocolate-coloured mysterious soil".

Equateur 60%: "In the luxuriant shade of the plantations in Ecuador, *forasteros* of the Amelonado variety have produced a rare and aromatic and non-bitter cocoa: Nacional. It will only grow in this soil which, strangely, has given it a unique flavour of flowers and dried grasses, similar to an infusion".

Papouasie 36% milk: "A *criollo* and a Javanese *forastero* form the origins of this marvellous cocoa with a remarkable rosy-copper colour. Each plantation adds its typical flavour of cinnamon, caramel or walnut. Its aromatic tonality is accentuated by a pure Tahitian vanilla. Slightly spicy, a first impression of freshness on the palate is a prelude to a full harmony of flavours".

Indonesie 30% white: "Cocoa butter is like the memory of cocoa, as it retains the specific character. While it is original for being hard, well-constructed, spicy and flowery, it is long on the palate and recalls the gentle climate of its origins. Never has a white chocolate had so much personality!"

LA CHOCOLATERIE DE L'OPÉRA

Carupano 70%: (Venezuela) "From the Garden of Cocoas, a selected *criollo* cultivated in the northern area which enjoys ideal climatic conditions. The whole gamut of aromas of the Careno Superior slowly release themselves: firstly a classically typical taste, warm with character followed by an exceptional and very slightly bitter aftertaste".

Rio Guayas 70%: (Ecuador) "Only in Ecuador can one find the *forastero* type cocoa comparable to the *criollo* variety by its aroma. It is the Nacional cocoa of which we have selected the most delicate, the Arriba Summer Superior Selected. This connoisseurs' couverture provides subtle and unique sensation as it melts in the mouth. The initial taste is followed by the perception of wood, tobacco and tea mingling on the palate".

Manaus 70%: (Brazil) "The area of Bahia has always been the main area of production of the Brazilian *forastero*. Often under-estimated as it is usually for blending the Brazilian cocoa, it can now reveal its true personality. We have chosen the cocoa Bahia Superior to demonstrate perfectly the characteristics of the variety. Explosive and spirited are the adjectives that best describe this chocolate. An initial spicy roundness subdues itself progressively."

Madong 70%: (Papua New Guinea) "The discovery from the other side of the world. An island whose meticulous plantations extend on perfect volcanic soils. The cocoa tree of the *trinitario* variety is a Papua New Guinea Plantation - typical of the region. A truly original chocolate . . .a combination of fresh flavours, wild herbs, leather, earth . . . the revelation of our 1998/9 vintage".

Diva 40.5% milk: (Ivory Coast) "The Ivory Coast cultivates trees of the *forastero* variety . . . a light and classic taste. To harmonise cocoa and milk in a chocolate couverture has always proved to be a difficult art . . . the result is 'Diva'. The light aroma of the Ivory Coast cocoa is the foundation for the original fabric of flavours with a lingering aftertaste reminiscent of Danish pastries."

AMEDEI CHOCOLATE (TUSCANY)

Porcelana 70%: (Venezuela) This chocolate is one of "mankind's treasures". It is the heritage of the past, when the Maya prepared their traditional drinks using a distinct, aromatic cocoa… This is the 'Porcelana' (porcelain implying delicate), a pure cocoa from the Criollo bean. The Porcelana plantation, on the borders of Venezuela and Colombia to which Amedei holds exclusive rights, yields just 3,000 kilos of beans per year, producing 20,000 hand-numbered packs. It is not obviously fruity but tastes of roast almonds, olives and honey, overflowing with intensity and yet with a tantalising delicacy and buttery melting quality. At the end of 2003, the Oprah Winfrey Show declared Amedei's Porcelana "the best and most expensive chocolate in the world" - consequently there is very little available for sale!

Chuao 70%: (Venezuela) The cocoa from Chuao is considered to be the Petrus of the chocolate world. It is cultivated on a plantation of the same name, half an hour from the Caribbean Sea on Venezuela's northern coast. The plantation produces 15,000 kilos of Criollo beans per year. Chuao represents a myth that up until now was the exclusive

domain of the great French chocolate makers. In 2003, Amedei managed to break this long-standing tradition. A hard-fought victory, achieved after lengthy negotiations, substantial financial investments, and a good measure of risk. The chocolate is extremely easy to work with and at the same time has a flavour so rich and round but is balanced by a strong acidity. It is often reminiscent of ripe plum jam and rich red fruits.

Amedei also produces Toscano Black 70%, 66% and 63% and Milk 36% which is their skilfully blended chocolate from Trinitario beans grown mainly in the Caribbean and Venezuela. The company also produces Gianduja (milk chocolate with Italian hazelnuts) and Meditazione (pralines and truffles) as well as 'carres' made from single beans from different countries including Grenada, Madagascar, Jamaica, Ecuador, Trinidad, and Venezuela.

Important Note: The chocolates mentioned above are my personal favourites but by no means represent all the great and the good manufacturers - of which there are many from Europe including Germany, Switzerland, Holland Italy, Spain and of course Belgium. In addition, as you will have read in this book, some good chocolate is also being produced in the Americas and to a lesser extent even in parts of Africa.

Valrhona chocolate is widely available across the country and through The Chocolate Society, La Chocolaterie de l'Opéra is available through L'Artisan du Chocolat, and Cacao Barry, while more difficult to obtain in small amounts, minimum orders of not less than £50 can be ordered through Ritter Courivaud. See 'Suppliers' for addresses and contacts.

Stop Press: I have just been given some Dormori Chocolate from Italy by Suzanne Nuvelli, one of my best customers - so she obviously has taste. I had never heard of Domori before but I understand it will be available shortly in Britain. It is worth searching for. The beans used for the different varieties of chocolate all are all hybrids of the Venezuelan Criollo, for example Porcelana and Carenero Superior. Domori boast in their literature that they only use vintages from a single crop and "the process of refining and conching is realised in the ancient style. This is done while there is a needs to convert the wild force of Criollo cacao into the sensual taste of a mouthful of chocolate". I can vouch for this. The taste of their chocolate is powerful, a multitude of distinctive fruity and spicy flavours and elegantly creamy. Their Website is www.domori.com. Happy Tasting.

What to Drink with Chocolate

CHOCOLATE AND WINE?

A lot has been written and debated on the subject. It is so much down to individual tastes, likes and dislikes. What is heaven for some is purgatory for others - but there are a few partnerships worth trying.

A very French owner of a Bordeaux vineyard once enthused about the magic of drinking young claret with chocolate - which works if married to a straightforward 70% couverture. Once you introduce another ingredient, such as more sugar, cream or flavourings, then the result is tongue curdling. It is better to go for water, coffee or nothing at all. Having said this, if you are still keen to find a partner, I have had some modest success with some sweet wines like Banyuls, Marsala, a golden Rivesaltes and also a Sandeman's Ruby Port, or a fruity cognac make sound partnerships.

On a more detailed note, I made some pleasant discoveries on a recent trip to Madeira. On a week away, I met John Cossart, who lives in Funchal, the capital and is the owner of one of Madeira's oldest wineries, Henriques and Henriques. Upon hearing about this book, he proffered an opinion that chocolate works well with many of the legendary wines of the island. Sadly, Madeira may be known for its wines but not for its chocolate. Finding an appropriate chocolate partner proved more difficult that finding the wines. There seemed no alternative but to resort to the local supermarket where the confectionery shelves groaned under the weight of commercial chocolate-flavoured candy.

And so to the tasting: John Cossart had lined up some treasures ranging from dry Sercial, medium dry Verdelho, medium sweet Bual to sweet Malmsey with samples of blends of non-vintage to 3, 5, 10 and 15-year-old wines.

A 5-year-old Verdelho was a perfect foil for chocolate as it cut through the sweetness and brought our flavours in the chocolate that we never thought existed.

A 15-year-old Verdelho played a good game with a very ordinary 43% dark chocolate.

10-year-old Bual reached the heights of perfection with 70% chocolate and was also a winner with very sweet truffles giving a whole new perspective on mouthfeel!

Both 3 and 5-year-old Malmseys worked a treat with 'After Eights'.

An article appeared recently in the *Financial Times* by Giles MacDonagh on this very subject. Giles had invited many of the top London sommeliers to a tasting which included fortified wines and some spirits. This perfectly illustrated the whole concept of individuality. Remembering that there were some of the most finely tuned tastebuds and respected opinions in the business of wines, there was still hot debate and disagreement on whether some of the partnerships worked. The consensus, nevertheless, gave credit again to the fortified wines and Giles said that "if anything emerged it was this: port style wines, especially young port style wines, which still retain their blackberry-raspberry-fresh fig flavours, go best with dark and possibly bitter chocolate. The more butter you add the more acidity you need. Only Tokay or Madeira can cut through the richness".

Sadly, chocolate does not go with champagne - except, perhaps, an old vintage Krug.

Chocolate Clinic from A-Z

If there is one thing I have learnt over the years and learnt well, it is that working with chocolate requires patience, practice and perseverance. In my experience, one of the many joys of chocolate, even though as an ingredient it is difficult to manage, is that its unpredictability makes it such fun. As long as you make sure you are using the very best quality chocolate you can afford, then no matter how the recipe turns out, it will taste wonderful - as long as it's not burnt. We all have problems with our cooking from time to time. That's what makes cooking a constant challenge, and this is what inspires passion, without which it would be tedious.

We are at the mercy of so many different elements. Apart from our own moods and humours, our kitchens are influenced by the weather and the humidity, by the ingredients we are using, whether or not we have allowed ourselves enough time, fluctuating oven temperatures, quality of ingredients, new recipes, pressure of invited guests, and so on and so on.

I have read several books which describe the how and why of chocolate in pictures and they all look so clinically precise, and while they are mostly very helpful and informative, life with chocolate is just not like that.

Remember that, when you look at pretty pictures of faultless chocolate dishes, the pastry chef has been working at this for years. You don't get to be a pastry chef at this level without a long apprenticeship of basic training and practical experience of 5 or 6 years doing nothing but chocolate and other pastry desserts - day in day out. Similarly, the pictures you see in books are the painstaking work of home economists who, like the pastry chef, have years of work practice.

If you give the same recipe to 10 different chefs you will get 10 different results because each chef will use his own imagination - based on professional skill and experience. If you give the same recipe to 10 different home cooks, again you will get very different results, this time because of different levels of experience, domestic restrictions like ovens, equipment and availability of ingredients. The glorious selection of puds you are offered in an hotel or restaurant is not the result of a 'one off'. They have probably been prepared hundreds of times. Pastry chefs have considerable experience and practice and spent years as apprentices before becoming heads of the section. Many pastry chefs have the natural skills of painters, artists and architects and their knowledge and experience are easily comparable with a university degree - except that they are hands-on from day one of their careers.

Each time I cook a recipe it turns out differently, sometimes barely noticeable, sometimes recognisably.

I have included some milk chocolate in the recipes but it is not my personal preference and therefore I can only use my own taste as a pendulum. If you really do prefer milk chocolate then I suggest that you substitute it for some of the dark chocolate - but remember, this is not how I tested them and the results may be marginally disappointing but I will leave that to your judgement. I hope the following points prove useful. I have included a list of things to remember and to understand when cooking, and this applies to all recipes in general, but here we are dealing with chocolate.

First of all, as I have mentioned above, you must leave yourself enough time for the recipe - there are very few short cuts and most lead to misery.

Secondly, keep your sense of humour!

Here are some 'dos and don'ts' and a 'dictionary' of terms and ingredients which affect chocolate's performance and which you will find in this book.

* **Please read A-Z Clinic** (below) before you start trying the recipes. Also please read each recipe's instructions carefully. Every recipe in this book has been tested and sometimes re-tested. I know they work.

* **Have all your ingredients weighed and ready.** Don't find yourself half way through the recipe and discover that you have run out of the principal ingredient.

* **Do make sure you have all the appropriate equipment** before you start. Use the equipment described as these are the tins, moulds etc., which I have used when testing and upon which the success of certain recipes depends. The results might be affected if, say a tartlet tin is specified and you use a ceramic dariole mould, as the heat transference is different. It will still probably be fine just not as good.

* **Pre-heat the oven according to the recipe instructions.**

* **Please pay particular attention to hygiene** - it's pure common sense.

I always use free range organic ingredients - apart from enjoying the vastly improved taste, you are also contributing to a kinder world of farming and are less likely to poison yourself with salmonella. Sadly, the best chocolate is still 'conventionally' produced. However this is changing…

* **Make sure you have plenty of time - and patience…** and read the recipe first to gauge the length of time it will take. Some of them are involved but worthwhile and most of the time-consuming ones can be done in stages.

Everything is written on the assumption that the whisking will be done with an electric hand-whisk. If you have an electric Kenwood or Hobart you will need to adjust according to the manufacturer's instructions.

Finally, and vitally, only use the best quality chocolate you can find in the recipes, namely one that contains at least 55% cocoa solids, for dark chocolate; 35% for milk and 30% for white.

Arrowroot: Starchy powder, which comes from the rhizomes (roots) of the tropical arrowroot plant; it has no particular taste and it can be used in place of cornflour.

Bain marie: French for 'water-bath' essential for melting chocolate to prevent it from burning. You can make you own bain marie from a double boiler but I don't find it very successful as the chocolate burns easily. I prefer to use a large stainless steel bowl (into which the chopped chocolate has been placed) set in a roasting pan lined with foil and filled with an inch of water. The heat under the roasting pan must not exceed 50°C so keep the heat on the lowest setting - a 'pea-light' as my mother used to say! And on no account allow the flame or water to come anywhere near the chocolate. Move the bowl in the pan away from the direct heat. See also melting chocolate.

Bavarois: Light airy mixture of Crème Anglaise, gelatine and cream.

Blind baking: A baked unfilled pastry shell. There are various recommended methods. My preferred method is to line the inner rim of the pastry case with a sheet of baking foil, roughly pleated into three layers and moulded to fit inside the edge to protect the rim of pastry from slipping down while baking. (You can also try placing another tin one size smaller inside for the first 15 minutes of the cooking time). Many recipe books recommend beans or dry rice etc. to weight down the pastry as it cooks but I am too impatient. I somehow manage to lose the beans or spill the rice! Prick the centre all over with a fork. After about 5 minutes in the oven take it out and if the pastry has risen then gently force it down with the back of a fork. Return to the oven for the final baking time.

Butter: About 80% butterfat; although you can replace

butter with inferior margarine I would never recommend using anything but the best ingredients - it always pays in the long run as the end result will show.

Camouflage: This is for the 'dog's dinner' - when you have been in too much of a hurry or tried to alter the recipe or it just wouldn't work for you but you know its going to taste good - or it may just be that you want to cover a few 'seams'. You have no idea just how many recipes are born out of accidents. Cover the offending desserts/petits fours in cocoa powder, toasted, flaked almonds, and groundnuts, icing sugar or even caster sugar. Fruit can also have a stunning effect - just make sure that whatever you use does have an affinity with the ingredients of the dish.

Chocolate: (See pages 76 to 78).

Cornflour: Thickening agent - starch used to lighten a product and give it a 'short' texture. It doesn't go rubbery.

Cream: The word cream comes from the Greek word *chriein* which means to anoint, (the connection is the fat or oil contained in the cream).

Half and half cream is about 10.5% butterfat; Single is between 18-30%; Whipping is between 30-36%; and Double is between 36-40%; Clotted cream seems an essentially English tradition although there is a good trade in exports for the Japanese propensity for English cream teas; Clotted cream is at least 60-80% butterfat. UHT cream is heated to give it longer life. It is very stable but doesn't whip very well. I have tried to use it in truffle making to give them longevity but it doesn't work. After a few days they have a distinct sterilised flavour.

Custard: A cooked mixture of egg yolks, sugar and milk or cream. (See Sabayon).

Dariole Moulds: These are small pudding tins for cooking individual mousses, soufflés or timbales. Most of us use ramekins in their place (as we all seem to have gathered a selection at one time or another). This is fine but remember that metal moulds tend to be better because they conduct the heat very fast and very evenly. (see Ramekins).

Eggs: Please be careful about using raw eggs in any recipe. I always use free range organic; apart from enjoying the vastly improved taste, you are less likely to poison yourself with salmonella.

I egg yolk = I tbsp = 15 ml = $^1/_2$ fl oz

I egg white = I$^1/_2$ tbsp = 20 ml

Note: All the recipes in this book have been tested with large eggs, which I suggest you use unless otherwise specified.

Eggs, Whole: Used to form a soft creamy binding agent. Too many will produce a very firm but rubbery finish.

Egg Yolks: Are fragile and 'burn' on contact with sugar or salt so they must be beaten immediately. As with whole eggs, used to bind chocolate and other ingredients, usually cream and butter and will produce a firm but less rubbery finish. *To freeze:* Whisk lightly with half a teaspoon of sugar, freeze for no longer than four weeks.

Egg Yolks and Butter (or other types of fat or oil): easily split - how to redeem? Start again with an egg yolk and gradually add the split emulsion bit by bit, whisking all the time. This should sort out the problem.

Egg Whites: Used to make meringues and mousses (see recipes). Use glass or metal bowls - never plastic. Make sure that the whisk and bowl are scrupulously clean so never wipe with a cloth, which might be greasy. Also remember that the more you whip whites the more fragile they become - and once you go too far there is no saving them.

To freeze: Egg white can be kept in an airtight container for several weeks in the freezer.

Although many recommend a copper bowl for best results when whisking whites, mine now hangs on the kitchen wall as decoration. In my experience the minimal advantages are outweighed by the difficulty in keeping the bowl clean and glowing.

Flour: Gives a dense mix as the gluten makes a firm texture. Water mixes with the protein, which turns elastic.

Fondant: Perplexingly, this has many interpretations:

i: is a mixture of sugar, water and glucose cooked to 'soft ball' (235°-240°F also 'fudge') and is used in the production of 'creamy' textured confectionery, cakes and pastries. It is relatively complicated and time consuming for the amateur to make and easily available nowadays to buy from supermarkets and specialist suppliers.

ii: is covering paste, which is made with sugar icing.

iii: Couverture is often called fondant chocolate.

Ganache: How many discoveries are made by accident? In the nineteenth century, an apprentice in a Paris pastry shop accidentally knocked some boiling cream into a tub of chocolate. The boss called the poor boy "*un ganache*" (an imbecile) but attempted to redeem the disaster and hoped that the mixture might be usable. The result was a satin liquid, which turned to velvet when cool and has become the noblest base preparation in the chocolatier's repertoire. The modern ganache is a combination of chocolate and a liquid such as cream and/or butter or water. The liquid is usually boiled and twice its weight of finely chopped chocolate is gradually amalgamated like an emulsion with a whisk until a smooth, glossy, mixture results. Ganache has an infinite variety of uses: whilst warm to decorate and/or fill cakes and pastries and as a quality coating for tortes and gâteaux etc. Ganache is the essential foundation for truffles which can be mixed with alcohols, nuts (pistachio, almonds, hazelnuts, walnuts, etc), fruits (orange, lemon, cherry, blackcurrant, raspberries), spices and aromatics (tea, coffee, cinnamon, cardamom, cloves, mint, pepper, allspice, saffron, ginger, vanilla and even chilli etc). In fact the possible combinations are almost endless.

Gelatine: Setting agent derived from extreme reduction by boiling down the bones of beef - only occasionally called for with chocolate recipes as chocolate itself is brilliantly self setting. However, you will find a few recipes in the book which call for gelatine - to keep it light but firm enough to hold its shape without being heavy and damp. Agar is a substitute for vegetarians who don't care to use gelatine.

I use gelatine leaves because they don't taste as 'obvious' as the powdered form. You need to soak the leaves in a little cold water for about 5 - 10 minutes - the longer the better and then squeeze dry before using. 15 g of leaf gelatine soaked in water = 1½ sachets of powdered gelatine soaked in 4 tablespoons of water. If using in a recipe where all the ingredients are cold then heat gently until clear.

Génoise: A light 'all round' sponge with eggs, sugar, flour and possibly chocolate or cocoa powder. Génoise is often baked in a round shape and cut in two or three horizontally to provide 'sandwiches' or layers and is immensely versatile for all pastries, desserts, petits fours etc. Freezes well. Génoise comes from Genoa where it was invented in the fifteenth century.

Gianduja: (pronounced Jond-oo-ya). Invented by Caffarel (1817-67), originally a small triangular shaped bar of dark chocolate filled with the best hazelnuts from Piedmont (arguably the best in the world). The name is reputed to have come from Gian d'la Duja (John the Jug) a hero fighting for Italian independence. During carnival celebrations in 1865 he gave Caffarel's creations liberally to the crowds, declaring them 'giandujotti'.

Today Gianduja is usually a mixture of milk (sometimes dark) chocolate and hazelnuts. Has shelf life of only about 6 months because the nuts are likely to go rancid after that.

Gold Leaf: Real carat gold, extravagant decoration which is edible. Can be bought from art shops and ordered from Keylink and from Town & Country Chocolate supplies (see Chocolate Directory).

Glucose: Known as corn syrup in America, sometimes known as fructose or dextrose - has two meanings. First, it is a naturally occurring sugar in certain fruits and vegetables; it is also a colourless viscose liquid made from foods containing starch such as potatoes, maize and wheat. In simple terms, it is made by mixing together starch, water and small amount of acid. Liquid glucose is an important ingredient in the chocolatier's store cupboard as it prevents crystallisation and because it is hygroscopic - it absorbs moisture from the air - products stay moist and pliable. It also acts as a tasteless, inoffensive preservative.

Golden Syrup: An invert sugar which can be used in place of glucose etc. although Golden Syrup has a distinct flavour whereas glucose is tasteless.

Honey: A natural composition of fructose, glucose and water made from plant nectars collected by the honeybee; it also contains several enzymes and oils. The colour and flavour depend on the age and source of the honey, i.e. the bees and their food source. Light-coloured honeys are usually of higher quality than darker honeys; white honey is derived from the Californian white sage, Salvia Apiana. Bees make other high-grade honeys from orange blossoms, clover, and alfalfa. A well-known, poorer-grade honey is elaborated from buckwheat. Honey has a fuel value of about 3307 cal/kg (about 1520 cal/lb). It contains an average of about 75% invert sugar and is therefore noticeably hygroscopic, readily picking up moisture from the air and is consequently used as a moistening agent in baking. Glucose crystallizes out of honey on standing at room temperature, leaving an uncrystallized layer of dissolved fructose. Honey is usually heated by special processes to about 66°C (about 150°F) to dissolve the crystals and is transferred into containers that are then sealed to prevent crystallization. The fructose in crystallized honey ferments readily at about 16°C (about 60°F) or over. Fermented honey is used to make honey wine or mead. The earliest confectioners made good use of honey, mainly for its flavour, and many traditional sweets are based on honey such as nougat, truffles and marshmallows.

Ice Cream Machines: As a general rule, you should be able to make an ice cream using the lowest setting of your fridge freezer. However, you can't beat an ice cream or sorbet made in an electric machine. Apart from the noise, I couldn't recommend a Magimix more highly - especially for the chocolate sorbet (See recipe). If you want to really get into ice creams then read *Ices - The Definitive Guide* (See Bibliography). Apart from its ice cream history, it is full of fascinating information on ice creams, sherbet, sorbets etc and just about every recipe flavour and combination you can imagine.

A tip about ice cream making is that you need to be fastidious about hygiene; also ice creams are so much better when they are fresh - a week in the freezer is too long.

Lecithin: Derived from soya, it is used to maintain the homogenous fluidity of chocolate and chocolate products, which may be low in cocoa butter. Soya is also unfortunately one of the ingredients, which has currently fallen victim to the technology of genetic modification. Most chocolate manufacturers can produce chocolate using lecithin from another source so it's worth looking at the wrapper.

'Loosen': (sometimes known as 'Let down') when mixing two ingredients together, especially whisked egg whites, to add a little of the whites to the mixture first before folding it all together. (This can also apply to other mixtures). This just makes the process easier and sometimes more efficient. It also helps to keep the air in, therefore the lightness.

Marzipan: A pliable cooked paste made with sugar, finely ground almonds and egg whites or water. It is very similar to almond paste which is uncooked and made with the addition of liquid glucose and/or a little olive oil.

Melting: Always be gentle with chocolate and use heat sparingly. It hates high temperatures and when melting keep the bowl which contains the chocolate away from direct heat and always in a bain marie of some form or another. Don't let the temperature of the chocolate rise above 36°C, which is blood temperature, so you can gauge it by touch. Having established this rule, when you get used to chocolate's temperament, you can take a shortcut and try putting the chocolate in a saucepan (like a Circulon pan from Meyer, which I use and think is wonderful) on to a simmer-mat, over a low flame, and as long as you stir constantly to distribute the heat, you will find this perfectly suitable. (The ideal temperature at which to work, and which is kind to you and the chocolate, is around 65°F. Summertime is the chocolate makers' enemy and heat-waves are an absolute no-no!)

I cannot emphasise enough the importance of investing in a good battery operated digital probe thermometer. This applies to measuring the temperature of chocolate for melting chocolate 'by hand' as well as with the microwave. You can use it for other food uses so consider it an investment. Keylink stock good reliable professional varieties, which are not excessively extravagant and will save endless amounts of chocolate and tempers.(See also Tempering).

Meringue: Is a frothy emulsion of beaten egg whites and caster sugar not only to make sweet but to stabilise. Basis of many mousses, bavarois, etc.

American: Meringue made with egg whites and caster sugar with a pinch of cream of tartar and/or a teaspoon of vinegar which gives a very firm crust when cooked in the oven and a chewy texture.

French (*cuit*): Meringue made with egg whites and icing sugar in a bain marie to ribbon stage until it holds its own weight - good for petits fours when you need a dense base. This is the most stable of all the meringue types.

Italian: Is 'hot' meringue where the sugar is boiled first and very slowly poured onto whisked egg white while continuing to whisk until cold. This meringue is more stable than cold meringue and is used in mousses, creams, cold soufflés, sorbets and piped decoration.

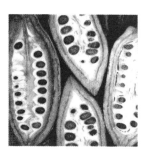

Swiss: (ordinary): Is cold meringue where the egg whites are loosely whisked and then the caster sugar is added while continuing to whisk until the required meringue is completed. This is good for meringues and toppings such as for Baked Alaska.

Microwave: Not something with which I am familiar. Most microwave ovens should come with instructions on melting chocolate. However, in the absence of these, I have it on good authority that this is the way the professionals use it for chocolate: 1 kilo for tempering is about the maximum amount for successful melting (although this depends on your microwave) otherwise it is brilliant for small amounts for all recipes. It is important to have the chocolate chopped into even pieces the size of buttons for homogeneous melting. Use a glass or microwavable bowl (not metal or it will 'short' the appliance). Melt it in short bursts of 10-20 seconds. Take it out after each burst and gently stir it making sure that you scrape down the sides to the centre. It may take about 2 minutes for 55g/2 oz to 6 minutes for 225g/8

oz. It is ready when it is uniformly and thoroughly melted and amalgamated and just warm to the touch - about 40°C.

Mixers, electric: All the recipes in this book have been tested using either a balloon whisk or an electric hand mixer. I have used the same model of a hand-held Kenwood very successfully which has regularly whisked immense quantities of ganache for my truffles for at least ten years - you couldn't have a better recommendation than that.

However, if you have your own preference for a large mixer, which is useful for a huge number of tasks, then I have no doubt that the recipes will work perfectly well.

Mousse: Is an essentially French creation, from the French word for froth. It is a light, creamy confection made from eggs, (sometimes using only the yolk and sometimes only the whites) and often cream and butter. Mousses can be cold and hot. Here, of course, I concentrate on chocolate variations, but mousses come in all shapes, sizes, densities, lightness and can be sweet or savoury; a mixture of fruit purées, gelatine, cream and eggs, sometimes semi-frozen lightened with egg whites.

Nuts: If overworked in the processor, which brings out volatile oils and added to chocolate at the wrong temperature, the mixture might split.

To skin: Toast the nuts in a roasting pan in the oven at 180°C/ 350°F/gas 4. Cool the nuts for about 15 minutes then rub the nuts between your hands or in a kitchen towel. The skins should flake off.

Pastry or pâte: There are a number of different types of pastry - mostly called by their French names, as the French are really master craftsmen at the art of *patisserie, chocolaterie* and *confiserie.* If you refrigerate a pastry tart when it is cooked and filled then it tends to soften so, if you haven't eaten it all, store it in an airtight tin in a cool place (rather than the fridge).

Choux: A cooked light and airy cream-puff pastry - see recipe for chocolate éclairs.

Brisée: A light and crumbly, mostly savoury, shortcrust - the foundation dough of pastry making used for tarts and flans.

Feuilletée: Another of the basic pastry doughs - also called puff pastry. Feuilletée means 'leaves' and the idea of this pastry is to fold and turn a number of times to build up the leaves. It is a very delicate and rich pastry where half of its weight to flour is butter. Please don't buy it until you have tried to make it yourself. None of the industrial puff pastries are made with butter - the fat that is used may be easier to handle but it sure alters the taste of the recipe. And there is nothing like the wonderful fresh taste of butter in a mille-feuille or a croissant.

If you really have trouble making puff pastry then you can cheat (I do often) by using filo pastry. Build up six (or so) layers by painting melted butter on each one before you cook it.

Sablée: Sometimes known as 'sand' pastry because it is very fragile, crumbly and delicate; also used for tarts and flans. When making it you have to work quickly as it is high in butter content and so softens very quickly.

Sucrée: Like a sweet Brisée. Used as Sablée but easier to handle and more robust - still delicious and used mainly for the recipes in this book.

Pâte à bombe: Sugar dissolved in water and cooked (boiled) to 121°F and dribbled on to whisked egg yolks.

Pâte à glacer: Chocolate covering usually with added fat to make it supple, easy to use and to keep its shine without tempering.

Paste, Chocolate: this is a pure chocolate block made from the whole cocoa bean, i.e. the solids with no added sugar. It is very powerful and used for adding to recipes to give that real chocolate kick.

'Plastic': Modelling chocolate made from a mixture of chocolate, cocoa, syrup and glucose which is used for moulding flowers, leaves and other decorations. Is also used for decorative plaques (See Basics).

Praline: a cooked mixture of nuts and sugar, then crushed. (See Basics).

Processors: Where would we be without a food processor nowadays? For the purpose of this book they are great for taking the chore out of pastry (but only if you are in a hurry because hand-made pastry is still the best), chopping nuts, making some custards etc. I have owned my Magimix for twenty years and it chops, purées, amalgamates, grates, shreds and makes orange juice as well as it ever did.

Ramekin: An individual straight-sided dish like a mini soufflé dish. They can be used for baking and chilling mousses and soufflés. While they range in size from 5 cm/2 in to 20 cm/8 in in width and 3 cm/1 in to 5 cm/2 in deep, the average, used in the recipes in this book are standard at about 8 cm/3 in. If you change the size of the ramekins in any of the recipes then you must be prepared to adjust to quantities of the recipe. This rule also applies to any mould especially Dariole moulds (See Dariole). The joy of a ramekin is that if you have any doubt about turning out the mousses (or whatever) you can simply leave in the ramekin and serve.

Run out: Means to dust with sugar or cocoa powder which helps to prevent the contents sticking to the sides.

Sabayon: A light frothy custard made by whisking egg yolks and sugar over a bain marie for about 5 minutes. Sometimes this forms part of another recipe and sometimes it is served as a sauce. In Italy with Masala, it is traditionally known as zabaglione.

Salt: Wonderful preservative, too much will kill the taste but just enough will bring out the flavour and give a bit of bite.

Scorch: Unless melted very carefully preferably in a bain marie, chocolate will burn very easily over direct heat. However, I used a good Circulon pan from Meyer (which you can buy at most good stores like the John Lewis Group) and a diffuser, which, with a little experience, produce faultless results.

'Seize': Chocolate seizes or separates and thickens when it comes into contact with small quantities of cold liquid especially water or steam (See below). It is possible to rescue by stirring in two or three teaspoons of cocoa butter (See Directory) or oil. However, this chocolate will only be good for recipes and NOT for tempering (See Tempering).

'Silpat': Is a recent innovation in baking which resembles a heavy duty, versatile non-stick mat which you can use to line baking trays. There are a number of sizes available (you cannot cut it) and it is washable and can be used over and over again. (see Directory). 'Silpat' is a trademark and there are other versions available.

Split: Is what happens when ingredients separate. This could happen when amalgamating chocolate and fats mainly cream, alcohol, nuts, etc. and can be avoided by warming and adding small amounts of the specified ingredient, i.e. cream to the melted chocolate and making an 'emulsion'. This state is sometimes known as 'short' which, like short pastry, is crumbly rather than smooth and creamy. Although this is generally not desirable neither is it disastrous - unless you are a renowned temperamental pastry chef with a reputation to protect.

Storing: Chocolate and chocolate products are susceptible to temperature, external odours and flavourings, air and light, moisture and time. Always keep chocolate in an airtight state and not in film as it tends to sweat. Foil is better. Raw chocolate should be kept in a cool dry place - and if you store chocolate or chocolates of any kind in the fridge you must keep it wrapped in an airtight tin or box. Milk and white chocolate should be stored for no longer than 12 months, while plain bitter chocolate will keep for up to 2 or 3 years - or best before date.

Sugar: Sugar has, over the years, become public enemy number one mainly because of its increasing overuse in manufactured goods. In moderation it is the most vital asset for *chocolatiers* and pastry chefs. In fact, man has been using sugar for centuries, along with salt, as one of the world's most natural and reliable preservatives, and it can make unpalatable foods exceedingly palatable - but in moderation. Sugar is a natural substance occurring in both cane and beet and in its refined form is vital to pastry chefs. It adds softness, sweetness and texture to desserts and confections as well as stabilising and preserving for a longer life. Occasionally recipes call for unrefined sugars which are used extensively in health products for their distinctive characteristics, and in manufactured confectionery and baked goods, for example; Barbados or Muscovado in boiled

sweets, rich fruit cakes and puddings; Demerara in fudges; Molasses in rum or other spirits; and Black Treacle in gingerbread products.

Granulated sugar is the most versatile type and the one most often used for fondants, boiled sugar work, jams and marmalades. It is also essential for biscuits as it provides the correct texture and uniformity of size.

Caster sugar (called superfine in America) is more finely ground than granulated therefore dissolves faster. It is good for confectionery, creaming, mixing, pastes, whisking and batters. It is particularly good for meringues because of its fineness, leaving no grainy traces.

Icing sugar (or confectioner's sugar, in US - or *glace de sucre* in France) is useful for icings, butter creams, fondants and pastes and also, of course, for dusting. It is just granulated sugar that has been ground to a powder. You can do this in the food processor if you find you don't have any in your store cupboard, although the home ground doesn't have the keeping qualities that the manufactured kind does as this will have an anti-caking agent added to stop it forming lumps. Always sift it before use.

Cube sugar is mainly used for boiled sweets, jam making, syrups and sauces. It is the most suitable for boiling because it needs a minimum amount of water.

Burying a split vanilla pod in a jar of granulated sugar for 24 hours and then grinding it to a fine powder can make vanilla sugar.

These are the main types of sugar which, apart from honey, will be specified in the recipes. If it does not then use whichever you have handy such as granulated or caster (which I prefer).

Always remember the rules of sugar are strict cleanliness - sugar will work better for you - and take extra care of your fingers when boiling sugar. It burns.

(See also Sugar Cooking in Basics).

Syllabub: Another version of custard without the eggs, which dates back to Elizabethan cookery. Whipping cream with sugar and wine or another sour agent like lemon juice makes a syllabub. You can also use it for fillings and toppings.

Taste: Not often mentioned in a book because it is assumed that as you are making the recipe you will, of course, taste it. However, there are too many cooks -and even some chefs - who take it for granted that the recipe will turn out well. Please don't take that chance. Tasting is an essential part of good cooking.

Tempering: (See page 98).

Thermometer: (See Melting).

Water or steam: Chocolate's real enemy, as when added or comes into contact with chocolate, water or steam will make it 'seize' or thicken and harden. This makes the chocolate almost impossible to use. If this happens during the tempering process, then the chocolate will only be good for cooking - and may have to be used in conjunction with a little butter or cream to help the melting process.

Basics

Basics: (clockwise from the top)
Dark Chocolate Shells (page 162);
Chocolate Tears (page 163);
Tuiles (page 106);
Chocolate Curls (page 103);
Leaves (page 106);
Caraque (page 103)

The tempering process is as follows:

Use at least 1-1½ kgs/2-3 lbs - it is difficult to work with less and the result is likely to suffer. At worst it will not set; at best you will not achieve that glossy snap which is the envy of *chocolatiers* and the vital characteristic of finely tempered chocolate

1 digital probe thermometer

1 large wooden/plastic spoon or spatula

1 large heavy gauge double boiler or bain marie - I use, with great success, a giant heavy bottom roasting pan which covers the top of my cooker - fill this with about 5 cm/2 in water which should be heated and maintain over a low flame - the temperature should never rise above 45°C

1 x 2 litre/4 pint stainless steel bowl (any bowl will do but s/s will control the heat better. China or porcelain tends to get hot more slowly and then suddenly the chocolate overheats without warning)

CHOCOLATE TEMPERING

Couverture (covering) chocolate is a suspension of sugar and cocoa particles in cocoa butter (fat from the cocoa beans). Cocoa butter is an expensive, hard setting fat with a low melting point and gives couverture a much better flavour and texture than its chocolate-flavoured inferiors.

It is, however, considerably more difficult to use, but well worth the effort. Remember, the philosophy is patience, perseverance and practice and ONLY the best quality ingredients. Couverture cannot be used for coating or enrobing unless it has been tempered. The purpose of tempering is to bring the material to a melted, amalgamated and crystalline state. The different fats it contains have different setting points. Tempering encourages and amalgamates those fats to form fat crystals which will ensure a high gloss. If the temperatures are too high or too low, the various fats will separate and the chocolate will not set or will set badly with a bloom or streaks.

Properly tempered couverture will set and form a hard protective surface with a good gloss and a brittle snap when fractured (ie bitten into) and provide a shelf life with minimum bloom.

Chop the chocolate into small pieces (about the size of a sugar lump). This helps to melt the chocolate quickly and evenly. Put three quarters of this into the stainless steel bowl and gently stir the couverture regularly to thoroughly amalgamate all the fats and sugar particles. In between gentle stirring NOT beating, cover with a large saucepan lid (which not only helps a more even melting but also reduces the opportunity for steam to come into contact with the melting couverture). Stir gently from time to time. This process cannot be hurried and will probably take at least one hour. Do not be tempted to turn up the heat.

When the couverture has completely melted to a temperature of between 45°-50°C remove from the heat. Use the probe thermometer to take the temperature in the middle of the chocolate and not just at the sides. The next stage is to reduce the temperature to 28°C. Grate or chop very, very finely the rest of the couverture and add to the chocolate, stirring frequently until 28°C has been reached - you will probably need to place the bottom of the bowl in cold water to achieve this. The chocolate around the sides of the bowl will start to set and stick to the sides. That is a good sign. Now return the bowl to the hot water and slowly bring the temperature up, again with gentle stirring all around the bowl - not just in the middle - to 31°C. Once again, take the temperature in the middle of the chocolate mass not at the sides or the bottom or you will get a false reading. Remove from the heat quickly as it is crucial not to overheat at this stage.

The couverture is now ready to use. Test it on a cold knife and let it set in the fridge for a few minutes. When it is hard, you can see how successful you have been.

If you are dipping chocolates you will need a dipping fork. Tap off the excess on the surface of the couverture and then any excess can be 'slid off' on the side of the bowl; Tip it off the fork onto a tray covered in cling film. When the temperature drops to below 27°C simply gently re-warm to 31°C.

The couverture sets quickly but should be left for a few hours to harden and develop its characteristic sheen.

Points to remember:

- *The entire process can be made significantly easier if you invest in a bain marie (a melting kettle). These kettles apply a gentle heat to melt chocolate and hold it at a set temperature. The cost may be a deterrent - the smallest which will melt 2¹/₂ kilos is likely to cost around £200 but well worth it. (You can use it also for keeping all sorts of things warm/hot). Both Vantage House's Chocolate World and Keylink sell good products. Of course, once you have understood the tempering process, if you feel extravagant, you can go fully automatic with the Chandré electronic machine (see Directory).*

- *At no time must you allow water in any form to come into contact with the chocolate. Chocolate just hates water and will 'seize' or, in other words, thicken and spoil and the couverture will then only be good for ganache and gâteaux. When removing bowls from water always remember to wipe the bottom with a sponge or cloth to prevent dips.*

- *Never overheat at any of the stages or you will blow all your good work and will have to start again with fresh chocolate. As long as the couverture has not been seriously overheated, i.e. not taken over about 55°C, then it can be used again for the tempering process once it has set.*

- *When you have gained some experience at the tempering process, to re-warm the chocolate, add a small amount of melted untempered couverture at around 38-42°C which you can keep ready melted in another bowl while you are tempering the main batch.*

- *Sometimes, when couverture has been used many times, it begins to thicken as it absorbs steam etc. from the atmosphere. This will still be good for truffles and other centres and gâteaux etc. So it is never wasted.*

- *Lastly, never give up - we all had to start somewhere and once mastered it is a truly satisfying achievement and one of the ironical joys of chocolate is that it is so unpredictable even for the master. This makes it a constant but rewarding challenge.*

- *If you can't face the tempering process then you can, of course, just melt the couverture to a temperature of not more than about 35°C and use it. However, it will take some time to set and may be streaky and brittle.*

SUGAR SYRUP - for fondants, parfaits, some ice creams etc

Made by melting equal quantities (until otherwise specified) of sugar and water. My standard sugar syrup is made from melting 375 g/12½ oz sugar with 375 ml/12½ fl oz water over a low flame which gives me 600 ml/1 pint simple sugar syrup. Keep in jar for 3-4 days at room temperature or for at least 2 weeks in the fridge.

Follow the table below for specific amount of syrup:

1,000 ml water	+	1,000 g sugar	=	1,600 ml syrup
625		625		1,200 ml
500		500		800 ml
375		375		600 ml
250		250		400 ml
125		125		200 ml

(with thanks to *Ices - the Definitive Guide* by Caroline Liddell and Robin Weir)

You need a sugar thermometer to determine accurately the correct temperatures and to make sure that the sugar syrup is cooked properly. It is possible to test for these stages without a thermometer (but I don't recommend it) which is to drop a teaspoonful of the syrup into a glass of cold water. When you press the syrup between your forefinger and thumb it should represent the characteristics described below.

Thread: 108-112°C: Dip a wooden spoon into the syrup and transfer a little to your finger and thumb. Join them together and when you pull them apart you should see a fine thread form between them. At this stage the sugar feels oily. Used also for jams etc.

Strong Thread: 112-115°C: (Also known as 'feather' as when it is blown it forms feather shapes). Similar to above except that the thread is thicker and the texture is more viscous. Used for fondants and marzipans.

Soft Ball: 116°C: Drop a little syrup into some cold water when it should form a tiny ball. However, when you take this out it collapses. Used for Italian meringue, butter creams and fudge.

Hard Ball: 120°C: As above except that when you take the ball out of the water it sets. Also used for Italian meringue, nougat and toffees.

Soft Crack: 138°C: The sugar sets like a sheet immediately when it is immersed in cold water. Used for rock sugar, butterscotch, and toffee.

Crack: 150-152°C: When cold the sugar will snap and crumble. Used for spun sugar, nougat rock sugar, piped sugar, and some sugar moulding.

Hard Crack: 155°C: As above except that the sugar is beginning to burn and will have a slight amber tinge. As cooking continues the colour darkens and turns to caramel. Used for glazed fruits, brittles, blown, poured, pulled and spun sugar.

Caramel: 160-182°C: Becomes transparent and quickly changes from golden to dark amber. Used for caramel, praline and nougatine.

COCOA GLAZE

100 ml/3½ fl oz water

100 g/3½ oz caster sugar

100 g/ 3½ oz cocoa

Boil the water and sugar together. Take off heat and add cocoa powder. Boil again and reduce to a simmer for 5 minutes. Strain and use.

You can use this glaze to decorate a cake and it will keep its gloss.

CHOCOLATE GLAZE

250 ml/8 fl oz sugar syrup
  (See page 100)

55 g/2 oz cocoa powder

115 g/4 oz plain chocolate, melted

Heat the syrup with the cocoa, whisking all the time. When it reaches 100°C (40°F) pour on to the chocolate. Whisk continuously until you have a smooth shiny glaze. Use immediately.

You can keep this in the fridge in a bowl covered in film for a few days. Reheat in a bain marie before use.

CHOCOLATE GLAZE (2)

115 g/4 oz plain chocolate, melted

115 g/4 oz sugar

6 tbsp water

Add the sugar and water to the melted chocolate and whisk briskly for a few seconds until the mixture is smooth. Use the glaze immediately while it is still warm - if it thickens just stir in a few drops of warm water.

175 g/6 oz unsalted butter,
  room temperature

175 g/6 oz caster sugar

5 tbsp water

3 egg yolks

150 g/5 oz couverture, melted

BUTTER CREAM

Not only can you use this for fillings but also you can cover a whole cake with this indulgent luxury. Vary the flavour by adding vanilla essence, rum, Armagnac, herbs, coffee.

Whisk the butter until it's creamy. Dissolve the sugar in the water then boil for 2-3 minutes to 107°C/235°F.

Whisk the egg yolks and pour in the syrup slowly, continuing to whisk all the time until the mixture becomes thick and very pale. Beat in the butter, a spoonful at a time.

Add the melted chocolate and whisk again for the final time.

Covers and fills a 23 cm/9 in cake

1 egg white

225 g/8 oz caster sugar

3 tbsp water

pinch salt

pinch cream tartar

$\frac{1}{2}$ tsp vanilla essence (optional) OR
  1 tbsp coffee essence

VANILLA OR COFFEE FROSTING

Lightly whisk all ingredients in a bain marie. Whisk continuously for about 7 minutes until mixture stands up by itself.

Pour frosting over the cake and spread with a palette knife.

CHOCOLATE FROSTING

Covers and fills a 23 cm/9 in cake

200 g/7 oz butter, at room
temperature

200 g/7 oz icing sugar, sifted

200 g/7 oz plain chocolate, melted

Cream together butter and icing sugar. Add the melted chocolate to the butter and sugar, whisking as you go.

Pour on to cake and spread with a spatula. Use this immediately as it sets quickly.

CHOCOLATE CURLS (about 8 cm/3 in) or CARAQUE (small curls about 4 cm/1½in)

**Makes about 20 large or
30-40 small curls**

225 g/8 oz chocolate melted,
preferably tempered

Spread chocolate on a marble slab or clean surface - the underside of a plastic or metal tray is ideal. Just before the chocolate is set hard using a scraper/ knife (like a decorators tool) push it away from you at an angle of about 30°. Remember the maxim perseverance, practice and patience and it couldn't apply any more emphatically here. If you have a problem, just scrape it all back into the bowl and melt again.

To make chocolate curls in plain and white (or milk), pipe alternate lines of different chocolate on to the surface. Smooth with a palette knife so that the lines spread into each other and follow above instructions.

You can also use biscuit or scone cutters to cut out shapes.

It's rewarding when it works and you can do it every time you melt chocolate and keep the curls in an airtight tin. You can also freeze them.

CHOCOLATE CURLS or SHAVINGS (2)

**Makes enough to decorate
20 cm/8 in cake**

225 g/8 oz bar of chocolate at
room temperature

Chocolate should be at just room temperature and in a block large enough to hold. Shave curls from the edge with a potato peeler. The curls are not as impressive as above but you can do this in a hurry and they do look good and professional.

**Makes enough to fill a
23 cm/9 in cake**

85 g/3 oz unsalted butter

125 g/4½ oz soft brown sugar

115 g/4 oz dark chocolate, in pieces

2 tbsp whipping cream

200 g/7 oz icing sugar, sifted

60 g/2 oz sugar

2 eggs

Heaped tbsp flour, sifted

Dtsp cornflour, sifted

Heaped tbsp cocoa powder, sifted

30 g/1 oz melted butter - you can
  leave this out if you feel nervous
  about adding it

FUDGE FROSTING

Gently melt the butter, brown sugar, chocolate and cream together in a pan until sugar is completely dissolved. Bring to the boil. Keep boiling for 2-3 minutes.

Remove from heat and carefully stir in icing sugar. Using a wooden spoon, beat for about 2 minutes until smooth and spreadable. Use straightaway, spreading on to cake with a wet palette knife.

CHOCOLATE GÉNOISE

Génoise is a light sponge with eggs, sugar, flour and possibly chocolate or cocoa powder which is named after the town of Genoa where it was invented in the Fifteenth century. It is often baked in a round tin and cut in two or three horizontally to provide sandwiches or layers and is immensely versatile for all pastries, desserts, petits fours etc.

When a plain génoise is needed omit the cocoa powder. This stores well in the fridge for a few days and for weeks in the freezer (in an airtight container, of course).

Butter and flour a 20 cm (8 in) springform flan or tart tin. Line the bottom with silicon paper - helpful but not vital. Heat the oven to 200°C/400°F/gas 6.

Whisk sugar and eggs in a bain marie (over hot water but off the heat) for about 7 minutes to a sabayon. Fold in the sieved flour and cocoa then melted butter if using. Bake for 30-45 minutes.

Allow to cool and then cut in half horizontally.

PRALINE

115 g/4 oz sugar

115 g/4 oz toasted and skinned almonds, walnuts, pine nuts, etc (if using seeds like sesame then reduce the quantity to about half)

Put the sugar into a medium-size heavy bottomed saucepan (about 15cm/6in diameter) over a low to moderate heat. Leave alone until sugar begins to melt and then stir to thoroughly amalgamate. When the sugar is a pale gold then add the nuts and continue to stir and cook for about 1 minute. Pour the mixture on to a lightly oiled baking sheet spread out and leave to cool for about 20 minutes at room temperature. When it's completely cold put it into a polythene bag and crush roughly with a rolling pin. Keep stored in an airtight jar until you need it. When you want to use it then weigh out the specified quantity and crush finely with a pestle and mortar. If you use a food processor you may end with a fine powder! So beware.

SWEET SHORT PASTRY OR PÂTE SUCRÉE

150 g/5½ oz flour

85 g/3 oz unsalted butter, diced and at room temperature

55 g/2 oz icing sugar

pinch salt

1 medium egg, lightly beaten

Sift the flour into a large mixing bowl and make a well in the centre. Place butter in the middle and then the sugar and salt. Amalgamate them all together and using your fingertips or a fork, mix in the flour. Add the egg and mix again gradually incorporating all the flour around the sides of the bowl.

Knead two or three times until smooth. Don't overwork. Wrap in a plastic bag or cling film and refrigerate for at least 30 minutes - or longer if possible before using.

To use for a 20 cm (8 in) flan ring. Preheat oven to 200°C/400°F/gas 6. Take pastry out of the fridge and flatten maliciously with a rolling pin. On a floured surface roll out to a circle about 3 mm/⅛ in thick. Transfer to the tin and if the pastry falls apart then just ease into place and around the sides with your fingers. Prick all over with a fork and bake blind: (see Chocolate Clinic).

After about 10-12 minutes in the oven take it out and if the pastry has risen then gently force it down with the back of a fork. Return to the oven for the final baking time - usually about 10 minutes.

Alternative method: It is possible to put the dry ingredients into a food processor with the butter and whizz until amalgamated. Take care not to over process. Now add the egg and when it leaves the side of the bowl immediately switch off.

Makes about 24

2 egg whites

75 g/2½ oz icing sugar and

30 g/1 oz cocoa powder and

45 g/1½ oz flour, sifted together

75 g/2½ oz butter, melted

TUILES

These use cocoa powder but if you want plain as an alternative then see the recipe for the Novelli plate of Liz McGrath chocolates (page 160).

Beat together egg whites, sugar, cocoa and flour. Stir in the melted butter.

Using no more than half the mixture (they cool so quickly after they have been baked and are then impossible to mould) spoon about 12 teaspoonfuls of the mixture on a baking sheet lined with parchment. Bake for 3-4 minutes or until golden.

Immediately and quickly remove from paper using a palette knife and fold them around a wooden rolling pin handle. Once set remove and allow to cool completely on a wire rack.

Repeat with the rest of the mixture.

Will keep in airtight tin interleaved with parchment for up to 4 weeks - after that they lose their crispness.

LEAVES

You will have to use the minimum amount of chocolate in order to temper it, i.e. 2 kilos, which of course you will not need unless you are thinking of starting a chocolate leaf factory, as 115 g/4 oz of chocolate will do at least 20 leaves. Just remember that you can re-use the chocolate after it's been tempered.

Make sure that the leaves you use are not poisonous! Use clean, dry and fairly stiff types like rose or bay with pretty shapes and pronounced veins (they look better). Using tempered (See page 98) chocolate apply a thin even coat with a brush on the underside of the leaves. Leave to set on a wire rack for 15 minutes and apply a second coat. Leave them in a cool place for about an hour and then **carefully** peel the leaf away from the chocolate. Once you have mastered this you can let your imagination and artistic talent run riot. Try using plain, milk and white chocolate for a marbled effect. To do this use the lighter coloured chocolate first and then the dark.

CHOCOLATE PLASTIC

225 g/9 oz dark chocolate, melted

4 tbsp liquid glucose

This is a very effective and professional looking covering for a cake or dessert. You can also make leaves or flowers with it (like plasticine but this is edible).

This recipe makes approximately 250 g/8¹/₂ oz which is enough to cover a 20-23 cm/8-9 in cake.

Stir the glucose into the melted chocolate until completely smooth. (You may need to reheat the mixture a tad if gets too difficult).

Using a rubber spatula, scrape the chocolate mixture up and transfer to a piece of plastic film. Gather into a ball and wrap tightly. Leave to settle at room temperature for about 4 hours or 2 hours in the fridge.

Knead the chocolate mixture on a wooden board (or smooth surface) until it is smooth and pliable. Roll out on a surface lightly dusted with cocoa powder. If you have a pasta machine you can use this for a really even finish.

Store in an airtight tin tightly wrapped in film - it should keep at least 6 months. If it gets too hard you can add half a teaspoon of liquid glucose.

CRYSTALLISED ROSE PETALS

rose petals

egg white

caster sugar

Take the most fragrant rose petals you can find - make sure that they have not been doused in chemicals or pesticides. Ensure that they are dry so don't gather them after a rain storm or first thing in the morning when they will be covered in dew.

Using a pastry brush and an egg white (not whisked) carefully paint both sides and then shower with caster sugar making sure they are well covered. Now leave them to dry on a tray covered in foil. They are better if left overnight but if you haven't got that amount of time then at least 3 hours. They will be gloriously crunchy and still smell of roses. They will last for months if kept in an airtight jar.

Sauces

Classic Dark Chocolate (page 110)

CHOCOLATE SAUCE

This is designed for Gordon Ramsay's Fondants - but goes equally well with the majority of the recipes in this book that call for a chocolate sauce.

Combine water, caster sugar and cocoa powder together in a saucepan and bring slowly to the boil. Add the cream and return to a simmer and cook for 3-5 minutes. Remove and cool and cover with cling film to prevent skin forming.

Serves 12

150 ml/¼ pint water

125 g/4½ oz caster sugar

3 tbsp cocoa powder

300 ml/½ pint whipping or
single cream

CLASSIC DARK CHOCOLATE

This is similar to the Chocolate Sauce above but uses chocolate rather than cocoa powder and is therefore richer.

Boil the cream and add the chopped chocolate. Over a low heat stir until melted and add the butter. Stir until the butter has melted and then whisk until completely smooth. Serve immediately.

Serves 4

115 g/4 oz dark chocolate

125 ml/4 fl oz whipping cream
(or water if you like a darker but
less rich result)

30 g/1 oz unsalted butter

CHOCOLATE AMARETTO

This will keep well in the fridge for up to 4 days. It will firm up so you will need to bring it to room temperature before using - or you can heat it gently - don't forget to stir all the time while you do this. Goes wonderfully with any dark chocolate desserts especially chocolate ice cream.

In a saucepan bring the cream to the boil and add the chocolate and butter. Remove from heat and stir until smooth. Add the Amaretto and stir until throughly incorporated. You can serve warm or when the sauce has cooled to room temperature.

Serves 4

100 ml/3½ fl oz single cream

170 g/6 oz bitter chocolate

55 g/2 oz unsalted butter, softened

2 tbsp Amaretto

HOT FUDGE SAUCE

Serves 4

115 g/4 oz bitter chocolate

115 g/4 oz butter

170 g/6 oz sugar

55 ml/2 fl oz water

1 tbsp liquid glucose or
  golden syrup

1 tsp pure vanilla essence or the
  seeds from a whole vanilla pod

Fabulous with vanilla or white chocolate ice cream.

Combine all the ingredients (except the vanilla) in a heavy saucepan and over a low heat stir until the sugar has dissolved. Turn up the heat and as soon as the sauce begins to boil, lower the heat and continue to boil gently for 10 minutes. Remove from the heat and stir in the vanilla. Keeps for several days in the fridge. Re-heat before use.

CUSTARD or CRÈME ANGLAISE

Serves 6-8

a vanilla pod

575 ml/1 pint milk (or single cream)

4 egg yolks

115 g/4 oz sugar

This is one of the classics of cuisine - and it's British! It hasn't changed for centuries.

While the method and ingredients have not changed much the eggs have - so make sure you use organically produced or at least free range.

Split the vanilla pod lengthways and scrape the seeds with the blunt side of a small knife - a teaspoon will also do the trick. Place the seeds and the skins together with the milk (or cream) into a medium-size heavy bottomed saucepan. Bring to the boil.

Meanwhile, whisk the egg yolks and the sugar together until creamy - about 2 minutes.

Remove the vanilla pods and pour the boiling milk over the egg yolks and sugar and whisk to amalgamate.

Transfer back to saucepan and over a very very low heat, simmer until the consistency coats the back of the spoon - about 7 minutes. Do not let boil or the mixture will curdle. However, you can always sieve out the lumps or blatantly cheat and whizz in the processor.

You can omit the vanilla and use any other flavouring or herb or spice that takes your fancy.

COULIS and PURÉES

The difference between a sauce and a coulis or purée is that a sauce is creamier as mostly they are made with butter or cream. A coulis is a lighter, purer fruit purée preferably made with a single fruit with a moderate proportion of sugar which should be to sweeten and not to overpower.

Many fruits work terrifically well with chocolate, especially blackcurrant, blackberry, raspberry, strawberry and orange. The sugars and acids in the fruits balance the bitter sweetness of the chocolate, likewise apricots, pears and sometimes apples. I have also tried prunes, raisins and sultanas with good effect but you have to soak these first, of course… Here are a few which I use often but you can choose your own fruits according to your taste - although don't be surprised if the odd one doesn't quite work and you end up with a mouth like a 'hedgehog'!

This will make about 450 ml/³/₄ pint of coulis which serves 4-6

450 g/1 lb fruit washed, dried, peeled and hulled

Juice of 1 lemon

150 ml/¹/₄ pint sugar syrup (See page 100)

Best done in a food processor. Whizz all ingredients until smooth. Sieve and keep in the fridge until you need it. This will also freeze well. When you de-frost you will need to re-whizz.

ORANGE SAUCE

From *Desserts - A Lifelong Passion* by Michel Roux. Will go wonderfully well with any of the dark chocolate tarts and warm chocolate cakes.

Serves 4

2 eggs

150 g/5¹/₂ oz caster sugar

250 ml/8 fl oz freshly squeezed orange juice

Break the eggs into a stainless steel bowl. (Don't use plastic or the boiling liquid - see below - might melt it.)

Add one third of the sugar and whisk to a ribbon consistency - about 5 minutes.

In a saucepan, boil the orange juice with the remaining sugar. Pour the boiling orange juice on to the eggs, whisking continuously. Pour the mixture back into the pan and cook over a medium heat for 2 minutes, again whisking continuously. Pass the sauce through a conical strainer into a bowl and leave to cool at room temperature, whisking from time to time.

This will keep for about 3 days in the fridge.

PISTACHIO SAUCE

Pistachios are a natural partner for chocolate - both dark and white.

Serves 8-10

575 ml/1 pint full cream milk

100 g/3^1/$_2$ oz finely ground skinned pistachio nuts (you can also use 50 g/2 oz pistachio paste if you can find this in small amounts - see suppliers - but you may need to cut down on the sugar as pistachio paste tends to have added sugar as a preservative)

5 large egg yolks

140 g/5 oz caster sugar

Bring the milk to the boil with the pistachio nuts. Meanwhile, whisk the egg yolks and the sugar together until creamy - about 2 minutes.

Pour the boiling milk over the egg yolks and sugar and whisk to amalgamate.

Transfer back to a saucepan and over a very very low heat, simmer until the consistency coats the back of the spoon - about 7 minutes. Do not let boil or the mixture will curdle. However, you can always sieve out the lumps or cheat and whizz in the processor.

Sieve and serve either hot or cold.

Small Pastries, Petits Fours and Breads

Profiteroles and Eclairs (page 118)

FLORENTINES

You can't beat home-made.

Preheat oven to 180°C/350°F/gas 4 and line 2 baking trays with silicon paper.

Over a low flame, melt butter with sugar and cream, stirring all the time. Boil and immediately remove from heat. Add nuts, fruit and flour and thoroughly amalgamate.

Drop generous teaspoonfuls of the mixture on to the baking sheets - they spread out during cooking so leave at least 5 cm /2 in between them.

Bake for 15-20 minutes until golden brown. Allow to cool for 15 minutes then you can trim the lacy bits around the edges - or leave them as they are.

Leave until completely cold and then spread the flat side of the Florentines with the melted chocolate. Using a fork, make wavy lines on it before it sets. Store in airtight container.

Makes 12-16

55 g/2 oz unsalted butter

55 g/2 oz caster sugar

2 tbsp whipping cream

85 g/3 oz mixture of nuts, e.g.
  almonds, pistachios, hazelnuts,
  walnuts, pecans, roughly chopped

30 g/1 oz glacé cherries, roughly
  chopped

30 g/1 oz glacé angelica, orange or
  lemon rinds, roughly chopped
  (in the absence of glacé lemons or
  oranges I have used the rind of fresh
  organic fruit - or fresh herb Angelica
  which I love - they make a delightful
  contrast)

55 g/2 oz plain flour, sifted

115 g/4 oz dark chocolate, melted
  (for the finish)

KRISPIES

An old time favourite for children and they are so quick and easy to make.

Melt the chocolate and butter together. Add the syrup and cocoa powder and stir until smooth.

Add the cornflakes and fold into the chocolate mixture until they are completely coated.

Spoon into paper cases and refrigerate for about 2 hours or until set.

Makes about 15

100 g/3½ oz dark chocolate,
  broken into pieces

55 g/2 oz unsalted butter

1 tbsp plus 1 tsp golden syrup

1 tbsp cocoa powder

125 g/4½ oz cornflakes

Makes about 36 biscuits

2 large eggs, room temperature

140 g/5 oz caster sugar

1 tsp vanilla extract

250 g/8½ oz dark chocolate and
55 g/2 oz unsalted butter,
  melted together

30 g/1 oz plain flour and
¼ tsp baking powder, sifted together

250 g/8½ oz chocolate chips
  (you can use dark or milk or
  half and half)

250 g/8½ oz whole macadamia or
  hazelnuts, or pecan or walnut
  halves

OTHELLOS

This recipe for delightful biscuits was given to me by a great friend Jennifer Allison, who tells me that it comes from an American cookbook. Her husband has to watch his cholesterol intake so Jennifer successfully substitutes the butter with Flora. I am a 'butter person' but her version also works perfectly well.

Preheat the oven to 180°C/350°F/gas 4. Line 2 baking sheets with foil, shiny side down or parchment paper.

In a bowl beat eggs, sugar and vanilla together until light and fluffy - about 5-7 minutes. Fold in the melted chocolate with a spatula. Now fold in the flour and baking powder.

Gently fold in the chocolate chips and nuts. Do not over mix. Using a tablespoon, scoop up the mixture and place spoonfuls 3 cm/1½ in apart on the baking sheets.

Bake one sheet at a time in the centre of the oven for 6 minutes. Turn sheet around and bake for another 3-4 minutes until tops appear dry. They will still be very soft.

Allow to cool completely on baking sheets. Repeat with the second tray. Store in an airtight container for up to 2 weeks - if they last that long! You can also freeze them for a couple of months. Defrost at room temperature in the container.

CHOCOLATE WALNUT CAKES

Nice and simple - almost like a cup cake without the paper cases. These cakes are light and airy but with the crunchy contrast of the nuts.

Preheat the oven to 180°C / 350°F / gas 4. Lightly butter a 12 hole bun tin.

Melt the chocolate with the water and set aside.

Cream the butter and sugar together until pale and fluffy. Gradually add the eggs and vanilla, beating well after each addition. Beat in the chocolate.

Sift together the flour, baking powder and salt and fold into the chocolate mixture until well incorporated. Fold in the nuts.

Spoon the mixture into the bun tin and bake for 15-20 minutes until well risen and springy.

Makes 12

55 g/2 oz chocolate, broken
  into pieces

2 tbsp water

85 g/3 oz butter, at room
  temperature

85 g/3 oz caster sugar

2 eggs, at room temperature and
  lightly beaten

1 tsp vanilla essence

85 g /3 oz plain flour

½ tsp baking powder

pinch salt

45 g/1½ oz walnuts, roasted and
  roughly chopped

Makes about 14-16

THE CHOUX

250 ml/8 fl oz boiling water

115 g/4 oz unsalted butter at room temperature, cut into pieces

225 g/8 oz plain flour

Pinch salt

4 eggs, must be large

THE FILLING

There are several alternatives for this. The easy one is:

450 ml/¾ pint whipped cream

1 tsp icing sugar

OR

CRÈME PÂTISSIÈRE, OR CONFECTIONERS' CUSTARD

575 ml/1 pint full cream milk

1 vanilla pod

4 egg yolks

85 g/3 oz caster sugar

30 g/1 oz cornflour, sifted

FOR THE CHOCOLATE GLAZE

85 g/3 oz dark chocolate

30 g/1 oz butter, unsalted

115 g/4 oz sugar

3 tbsp boiling water

CHOCOLATE ECLAIRS (Pâte à Choux) or PROFITEROLES

Also known as choux buns or chocolate puffs, these are really special little clouds of cream and chocolate and an all time classic. They are quite easy to make as long as you are happy to handle a pastry bag - otherwise you can use a teaspoon.

Preheat the oven to 200°C/400°F/gas 6. Line a heavy baking sheet with foil (the thicker the baking sheet the better. It will prevent the bottoms from browning too much).

To make the choux pastry: Put the boiling water and butter in a heavy based saucepan over a gentle heat. Bring slowly to just boiling - the idea is to have the butter melted just when the water is ready to boil. Don't boil for too long or the water will evaporate and the recipe will be altered.

Sift together the flour and salt and place in the bowl.

As soon as mixture boils, remove it from the heat and immediately sift in all the flour, beating hard with the wooden spoon until the mixture forms a ball and leaves the side of the pan. Transfer to a mixing bowl and using an electric whisk, whisk in the eggs, one at a time. Continue to whisk for about 1 minute scraping any that might be left on the sides. The mixture should be smooth and shiny.

Transfer to a pastry bag with a 2 cm (¾ in) nozzle and pipe out 14-16 finger shaped strips about 12 cm (4½ in) x 2 cm (¾ in) on to the baking sheet. Alternatively you can use a teaspoon and spoon out into little moulds. This turns them into profiteroles.

Bake for 30 minutes. Don't be tempted to open the oven door as this alters the 'puff' - they should be well risen and golden brown.

Remove from the oven, cut the eclairs or profiteroles in half horizontally and return to the oven for 5 minutes to dry out the centre. They should be dry and crisp. Cool on a rack.

For the whipped cream filling: Simply whip the cream with the sugar until thickened but still soft. Place in a piping bag and pipe down the centres of the eclairs or profiteroles.

For the crème pâtissière filling: Bring the milk and vanilla pod, to the boil. Split the pod and return the seeds to the milk. Discard the pod. Combine the yolks, sugar and cornflour and whisk until pale. Pour the milk over the egg mixture slowly and whisk until combined. Pour the mixture back into the saucepan and bring slowly to the boil, stirring continuously, until the mixture thickens. It will become alarmingly lumpy - but keep stirring and it will eventually turn smooth.

Allow the crème pâtissière to cool completely. When ready to use, whisk vigorously and pipe into the eclairs as above.

To make the glaze: Melt the chocolate and butter together. Dissolve the sugar in the boiling water. Allow to cool a little and add to the chocolate and butter and stir to combine. While still warm drizzle over the tops of the profiteroles - if the glaze thickens just stir in a few drops of warm water.

CHOCOLATE ORANGE STICKS

Makes 30-60 batons

3-6 oranges - depending on how many sticks you want. Each orange make about 10 batons

¹/₂ litre/16 fl oz water for syrup plus water for boiling sticks

300 g/10¹/₂ oz caster sugar

30 g/1 oz liquid glucose

450-550 g/1-1¹/₄ lb extra bitter chocolate for enrobing

It is infinitely preferable to use bitter marmalade oranges that you can find in the market in December and January. However, of course you can use sweet oranges anytime - they will not be quite as good. I also recommend organic and wax free fruits.

Wash the oranges and dry them thoroughly. Using a sharp knife follow the contours of the fruit from top to bottom shaving off slivers of peel about 5 cm x 5 cm (2 in x 2 in) long.

Remove all the pith and then cut into about four strips. Repeat with the other oranges. Place strips in a saucepan and cover with cold water. Bring to the boil and boil rapidly for about 7 minutes. Refresh under cold running water.

For the syrup: Put the sugar and glucose in the water and gently bring to the boil. Boil for about 2 minutes. Turn down the heat and transfer the orange peel to the bubbling sugar syrup and poach gently for about 1 - 1¹/₂ hours. Remove from the heat.

Leave for a few moments and then remove sticks from syrup and drain, and then transfer to a wire rack to cool completely. Leave for at least a day to dry out before dipping in chocolate. If you don't feel like going to the extent of tempering the couverture then you could try dusting them with cocoa powder as an alternative - not as good, so eat them au nature … they will keep for weeks in a dry place.

CHOCOLATE BANANA BREAD

Serves 8

85 g/3 oz butter, softened

225 g/8 oz sugar

2 eggs

³/₄ tbsp dark rum

2 large ripe bananas - mashed not processed as this will turn the banana to liquid

115 g/4 oz chocolate - grated or very finely and evenly chopped

175 g/6¹/₂ oz flour and

¹/₂ tsp cream of tartar and

¹/₄ tsp bicarbonate of soda and

1 tbsp cocoa, sifted together

115 g/4 oz hazelnuts, chopped

This is a light tea bread or can be served for a dinner party with a chocolate sauce. It is unexpectedly more-ish…! You can cover with a chocolate icing or leave as nature intended - delish…

Preheat oven to 180°C/350°F/gas 4. Lightly butter a 1 kg/2 lb loaf tin.

In a large bowl cream together the sugar and butter until fluffy, 5 minutes. Beat in the eggs, one at a time, mixing well after each. Add rum and mashed bananas, blending well. Stir in chocolate. Sift in the flour, cream of tartar, bicarbonate of soda and cocoa mixture.

Mix gently with an electric mixer on low or fold in by hand. Stir in the nuts.

Pour the batter into the prepared tin and bake for about 1 hour. It should be golden brown. Test with a skewer. Cool for about 15 minutes then turn out and leave until cold on a wire rack. You can cover with chocolate icing, sauce or leave it unadorned.

BROWNIES

There are Brownies… and there are Brownies… these are the 'business'! You can play around with the nuts and fruits as you wish.

Makes 15 squares

55 g/2 oz unsalted butter

115 g/4 oz bitter chocolate

2 eggs

115 g/4 oz granulated sugar

30 g/1 oz cocoa powder and
55 g/2 oz plain flour and
1 tsp baking powder, sifted together

pinch salt

55 g/2 oz ground almonds

115 g/4 oz mixed nuts, almonds,
    hazelnuts, walnuts, pecans,
    pistachios etc.

Preheat the oven to 180°C/350°F/gas 4. Line an 18 cm × 28 cm (7 in × 11 in) tin with parchment, buttered and floured.

Melt together butter and chocolate. Whisk the eggs with the sugar until pale and fluffy and add to the melted chocolate. Fold in the flour, cocoa powder, baking powder and salt. Fold in the ground almonds and mixed nuts.

Spread evenly in the tin and bake for 20-25 minutes. Leave to cool in the tin for about 20 minutes then cut into squares. Remove from the tin when cold. Store in an airtight tin or they lose their crispness very quickly.

CHOCOLATE FUDGE BROWNIES

This is also a terrific Brownie recipe. A rich and chewy mouthful from Claire Clark, Head Pastry Chef at Claridge's.

Makes about 20

400 g/14 oz dark chocolate

300 g/10½ oz unsalted butter

4 eggs

400 g/14 oz soft brown sugar

½ tsp vanilla essence

55 g/2 oz plain flour and
pinch salt and
2 tsp baking powder, sifted together

285 g/10 oz pecan nuts, chopped
    (these would benefit from toasting
    if you have the time)

Preheat the oven to 160°C/325°F/gas 3. Butter and flour a 20 cm × 29 cm × 5 cm (8 in × 11½ in × 2 in) baking tin.

Melt the chocolate and the butter together. Lightly whisk the eggs, sugar and vanilla and stir into the chocolate mixture. Fold in the flour, baking powder and salt. Fold in the pecans.

Pour into prepared tin and bake for 1 hour or until skewer comes out cleanly. Allow to cool and cut into squares.

Brownies, Chocolate Fudge Brownies (page 120);
Krispies (page 116) and Cup Cakes (page 123)

CHOCOLATE BISCUIT CAKE

Serves 8-10

115 g/ 4 oz unsalted butter

30 g/1 oz sugar

2 tbsp milk

170 g/6 oz bitter chocolate

30 g/1 oz cocoa powder

1 tsp ground ginger (optional)

225 g/8 oz crumbled biscuits, such as digestives

55 g /2 oz breadcrumbs

55 g/2 oz dried fruit (optional) like cherries or raisins (personally I think this is gilding the lily)

This is probably one of the most used and tested recipes in the world. It's so easy and you can vary the ingredients according to what you have in the store cupboard. My last dated copy is circa 1985 - source unknown. This is a great recipe for using any bits of leftover fruit, nuts, cocoa, chocolate, cake, all manner of bread/biscuit crumbs - if you use bread or even brioche crumbs they should be toasted.

Line a 20 cm (8 in) tart tin (or similar square or oblong) with parchment or grease-proof paper.

Melt the butter, sugar and milk in a large saucepan over gentle heat. Add the chocolate and cocoa (and ginger if using) plus half the biscuits. Stir throughly. Mix in rest of biscuits, breadcrumbs and fruit (if using). Turn out into tin and spread evenly. Allow to set in fridge for about 1 hour.

Alternatively, you can cover it with 115 g/4 oz chocolate and 30 g/1oz unsalted butter melted together and poured over. (Or even better cover it with tempered chocolate.)

CAPRICE DES DAMES

Makes 40 approximately

3 egg whites

115 g/4 oz caster sugar

115 g/4 oz ground almonds

Meringue petits fours which can be served alone or as an accompaniment to a pud or ice cream. Alternatively you can sandwich them together with ganache. Similar to almond macaroons but the tops will be crunchy and centres will be tantalisingly gooey.

Preheat oven to 160°C/325°F/gas 3.

Beat egg whites with teaspoon of sugar until stiff. Beat in the rest of the sugar. Fold in the almonds.

Using a pastry bag with a 1 cm-2.5 cm ($^1/_2$ in-1 in) nozzle, pipe out about 40 blobs on to a silicone baking sheet or baking sheet covered with parchment.

Bake for 20 - 30 minutes. When completely cold, eat or keep in an airtight tin.

ALMOND MACAROONS

Makes 20

1 egg white

55 g/2 oz caster sugar

55 g/2 oz ground almonds

1/4 tsp almond essence

These make a lovely contrasting accompaniment to many of the chocolate puddings in this book.

Preheat oven to 180°C/350°F/gas 4 and line a baking sheet with silicon paper.

Whisk the egg white with a pinch of salt for a couple of minutes until you have a soft peak. Whisk in the caster sugar. Fold in the ground almonds and the almond essence.

Spoon the mixture into a piping bag with a 1 cm-2.5 cm (1/2 in-1 in) nozzle. Pipe little mounds on to the baking sheet. (Alternatively you can use a teaspoon). They will spread out during the baking process.

Bake for 15-20 minutes. Leave to go cold and eat - or keep in airtight tin.

Variation: If you want to make these into Chocolate Macaroons replace 30 g/1 oz of ground almonds with 1 teaspoon of cocoa powder and decorate with toasted flaked almonds just before baking.

CUP CAKES

Makes 10-12

115 g/4 oz butter, room temperature

115 g/4 oz caster sugar

2 eggs, room temperature, lightly beaten

115 g/4 oz plain flour and
1/2 tsp cream of tartar and
1/4 tsp bicarbonate of soda and
30 g/1 oz cocoa powder, sifted together

ICING

55 g/2 oz unsalted butter

3 tbsp single cream

200 g/7 oz icing sugar

30 g/1 oz cocoa powder

I used to adore these as a child - still do, in fact. They stand the test of time as essential for a children's party.

Preheat the oven to 190°C / 375°F / gas 5.

Cream together the butter and sugar until pale and fluffy. Gradually add the beaten eggs, a little at a time and beating well between each addition.

Sift together the dry ingredients and fold into the egg mixture.

Fill a muffin or bun tin with paper cases and divide the mixture between them. Bake for 12-15 minutes and cool on a wire rack.

To make the icing, melt the butter and cream together. Sift in the icing sugar and cocoa powder and beat until smooth. Spread onto the cup cakes.

Cakes and Gâteaux

The Sacher Torte (page 144)

Serves 8

THE SPONGE

3 eggs, separated

55 g/2 oz sugar

3 tbsp cornflour and

1 tbsp cocoa power and

3 tbsp strong white flour and

1/2 tsp 4 spices (or mixed spice),
   sifted together

THE CHOCOLATE CREAM

5 tbsp milk

1 tsp cocoa powder

1 tsp custard powder

1 1/2 tsp sugar

1 egg yolk

15 g/1/2 oz unsalted butter

30g /1 oz plain chocolate, grated

2 small or 1 large gelatine leaf, soaked
   in cold water and squeezed dry

150 ml/1/4 pint whipped cream

55g/2oz praline grains (See page 105)

THE CARDAMOM MOUSSE

55 g/2 oz sugar

3 tbsp water

15 cardamom seeds, crushed

1 egg yolk

2 small or 1 large gelatine leaf, soaked
   in cold water and squeezed dry

100 ml/3 1/2 fl oz whipping or
   double cream

THE CHOCOLATE SYRUP

1 tbsp cocoa powder

55 g/2 oz caster sugar

4 tbsp water

chocolate curls for decoration

1492 - LA ROUTE DES ÉPICES

This recipe was created by Bagatelle, the heavenly French pâtisserie in South Kensington to celebrate the 500th anniversary of the discovery of cacao by Christopher Columbus in Central America. Columbus landed on the Caribbean island of Guanaja - after which Valrhona has named one of its precious dark couvertures. The gâteau consists of a spicy sponge laced with chocolate syrup supporting a layer of spicy sponge and finished with cardamom mousse. A new approach to chocolate, aimed at the adult, more sophisticated chocolate palate.

This is time consuming to make so allow yourself plenty of it - it's well worth the effort if you like something unusual and chocolatey and spicy.

Butter, line and flour a 20 cm (8 in) cake tin. Preheat the oven to 180°C/350°F/gas 4.
To make the sponge: Whisk the egg whites until stiff then add the sugar, 1 tablespoon at a time, continuing to whisk until stiff and shiny.

Lightly beat the egg yolks and add to the whites. Sift in the cornflour, cocoa powder, flour and spices. Fold in gently.

Pour into the cake tin and bake for 20-30 minutes. Test with a knife. The sponge should be light and springy. Cool on a rack.

To make the chocolate cream: In a pan, bring the milk and cocoa powder to the boil, stirring to remove any lumps.

In another bowl, mix together the custard powder, sugar and yolk. Pour over the hot cocoa milk, stir then return to the saucepan. Heat gently and stir until thickened. Do not allow mixture to boil.

Remove from the heat and add the butter, chocolate shavings and gelatine and stir well until blended. Allow to cool slightly - but not so much that the gelatine begins to set.

Whip the cream until it leaves a trail then fold it along with the praline grains, into the custard mixture. Set aside.

To make the cardamom mousse: First make the sugar syrup, with the sugar and the water. (See page 100) Add the crushed cardamom.

In a bowl, beat the egg yolk, add the warm cardamom syrup, strained. Add the gelatine and stir until dissolved. Lightly whip the cream until it leaves a trail, then fold it into the cardamom mixture. Set aside.

To make the chocolate syrup: Bring the cocoa powder, sugar and water to the boil and cook for 1 minute, stirring until smooth. Strain if necessary.

To assemble: Cut the sponge horizontally into 2. Place the bottom layer into a serving plate and drizzle with half the chocolate syrup. Spread with the chocolate cream. Turn the second layer over and drizzle the cut side with the rest of the syrup. Place it top-side up, on the chocolate cream layer. Spread the top with the cardamom mousse. Refrigerate. Decorate with the chocolate curls before serving.

BACCHUS

Serves 10-12

THE GÉNOISE

3 eggs

85 g/3 oz caster sugar

1 tbsp, heaped plain flour

1 tbsp, heaped cornflour

30 g / 1 oz cocoa powder

45 g/1½ oz unsalted butter, melted

THE MACAROON

6 egg whites

pinch salt

30 g/1 oz icing sugar

100 g/3½ oz icing sugar

100 g/3½ oz ground almonds

30 g/1 oz cocoa powder

THE GANACHE

75 g/3½ oz raisins

3 tbsp dark rum

300 g/10½ oz dark chocolate, grated

5 tbsp double cream

55 g/2 oz unsalted butter

THE SYRUP

75 ml/3½ fl oz water

75 g/3½ oz caster sugar

3 tbsp dark rum

Bacchus is one of the recipes from Robert Linxe, the fount of all knowledge concerning the finest French chocolates, which you can find in Paris (see Paris section). His talk of chocolate is lyrical and the sort of language that you might associate with the French. Bacchus is not terribly difficult to make but take some time as there are a number of steps. It is very rich and chocolatey, behaves well and is easy to slice.

To make the génoise: Butter and line a rectangular cake tin or roasting tray approximately 31 cm x 26 cm (12½ x 10½ in) with baking paper. Preheat the oven to 190°C/ 375°F/gas 5.

Bring about 5 cm / 2 in of water to boil in a medium sized saucepan. Remove from the heat, then place a large mixing bowl on top. Whisk together the eggs and sugar until thick and fluffy and the mixture leaves a trail. This will take about 8 minutes. Remove the bowl from the saucepan and continue to whisk until cool.

Sift the flour, cornflour and cocoa powder into the mixture, pour in the melted butter and fold in gently but thoroughly. Pour into the prepared tin and bake for 25-30 minutes until cooked through and springy in the middle.

Remove from the oven, leave in the tin for 15 minutes, then turn out on to a wire rack and allow to cool completely. When completely cold and with the long side facing you, cut vertically into 3 equal pieces. Cover and set aside. (It will also freeze well.)

To make the macaroon pastry: Use the same tin as for the génoise. Reduce the oven temperature to 180°C/ 350°F/gas 4.

Whisk the egg whites with a pinch of salt until they form medium peaks. Sift in the 30 g/ 1 oz of icing sugar, continuing to whisk until stiff and shiny. Sift together the icing sugar, ground almonds and cocoa powder and fold gently into the meringue mixture. Pour into the prepared tin and smooth the top. Bake for 15-20 minutes. Remove from the oven and cool, leaving the paper on. Place in the fridge until ready to assemble.

To make the ganache: Rinse the raisins in several changes of fresh water. Place in a small saucepan with the rum and heat through. Set alight and flambé the raisins. When the flames die down, cover the pan and leave to soak.

Bring 75 ml/3½ fl oz of water to the boil. Place the grated chocolate in a bowl. Pour the boiling water into the cream, then pour on to the chocolate. Stir gently until melted and smooth. Cut the butter into small cubes and add to the mixture, stirring until smooth. Add most of the rum-inflated raisins to the ganache, reserving some for garnish. Set aside to cool.

To make the syrup: Dissolve the sugar in the water and boil for about 5 minutes. Remove from the heat and add the rum. Allow to cool.

To assemble: Remove the macaroon from the fridge and cut it into three equal pieces as for the génoise. (You will only need 2 pieces of the macaroon.) Place a sheet of baking parchment on a baking sheet and lay one of the layers of génoise on it as the base. Drizzle with one third of the rum syrup. Spread with a thin layer of ganache. Place a piece of macaroon on top and spread with another thin layer of ganache. Lay a second piece of génoise on top and drizzle with half of the remaining syrup. Spread with ganache. Continue layering with a second macaroon, then the ganache, and top with the third piece of génoise soaked with the remaining syrup. Use the remaining ganache to ice the top and sides. Score the sides with a fork, if desired. Store in the fridge but remove one hour before serving.

CHOCOLATE BATTENBURG

Serves 8-10

125 g/4$^{1}/_{2}$ oz unsalted butter, room temperature

150 g/5$^{1}/_{2}$ oz caster sugar

1 tsp vanilla essence

3 eggs, lightly beaten

200 g/7 oz plain flour and 1 tsp cream of tartar, sifted together

30 g/1 oz cocoa powder

5 tbsp apricot, raspberry jam or orange marmalade

250 g/8$^{1}/_{2}$ oz white almond paste

Also called a chequerboard chocolate cake. It appears a tad complicated but follow the steps and you should not go wrong and it's effective to look at and delightfully light to eat. The combination of the chocolate and vanilla sponges is a real winner.

Preheat the oven to 180°C/350°F/gas 4. Butter the bottom of a 1 kilo/2 lb (23 cm x 11 cm/ 9 in x 4$^{1}/_{2}$ in) loaf tin with baking parchment or greaseproof paper. Cut another piece of parchment the same size as the one on the bottom. Butter both sides of the other piece.

Cream together the butter and sugar until pale and fluffy - about 5 minutes. Add the vanilla essence. Add the eggs, one at a time, beating well after each. Lightly fold in the flour. Turn half this mixture out into the tin and cover this with the piece of buttered parchment. Sift the cocoa powder into the other half - you may need to add a little milk to make it the same consistency as the first - and then turn this one out into the tin on top of the paper covering the vanilla sponge.

Bake for 40-45 minutes. Test the centre with a knife. Allow to cool for a few minutes then turn out on to a wire rack and leave to cool completely.

To assemble: Trim the edges and tops carefully to remove any crusts. Cut each cake in half lengthways so you have four equal lengths.

Roll out the almond paste on a flat surface dusted with icing sugar. Paint it with about half of the sieved jam or marmalade.

Place one of the chocolate sponges on to the coated almond paste and brush the three remaining sides with jam. Place a vanilla strip next to it, sandwiching it together. Brush its top with jam. Place the other two pieces on top, alternating colours and using the jam to sandwich them together. Bring up the ends of the almond paste and press together to form a join. Turn over so the seam is on the bottom and trim the edges of excess paste. (If you want an even prettier finish you can decorate the top using a sharp knife to make a criss-cross pattern.) Leave for about an hour to allow it to settle before cutting.

Chocolate Battenburg

BLACK FOREST GÂTEAU

A version of the famous masterpiece from Professor John Huber, who is to chocolate what Einstein is to the Theory of Relativity. When it is good - it's really good. And this is a good one. The secret is, of course, using the best ingredients and proper griottes. So many of the shop bought commercial imposters give this classic cake a bad reputation.

Butter and flour a 22 cm (9 in) cake tin, and line the base with greaseproof paper. Preheat oven to 190°C/375°F/gas 5.

Whisk the eggs and the sugar in a large bowl over a bain marie, until pale and creamy - about 5-7 minutes.

Gently fold in the sifted dry ingredients.

Add the melted butter.

Pour the mixture into the cake tin and bake for 25 minutes. Test with a skewer.

Allow to cool completely, on a wire rack. Cut into three horizontal layers.

Pour the reserved cherry liquid into a jug and make up with enough kirsch to measure 150 ml/¼ pint. Whip the cream until thick and soft.

Place the bottom layer of sponge on to a serving plate and sprinkle with one third of the syrup and kirsch mixture. Spread with one third of the jam, followed by one third of the whipped cream. Dot half of the cherries on top of the cream.

Place the second layer of sponge on top, soak with the syrup, spread with jam and cream, and finally the rest of the cherries.

Cover with the third layer of sponge, soak with the rest of the syrup and spread with the rest of the jam.

Use the rest of the cream to cover the top and sides, then dust with the chocolate shavings.

Serves 10-12

THE SPONGE

4 eggs

125 g/4½ oz sugar

55 g/2 oz flour and

30 g/1 oz ground almonds, just roast the almonds before grinding and

30 g/1 oz ground hazelnuts, roasted as with the almonds and

3 tbsp cocoa powder and

pinch cinnamon, sifted together

30 g/1 oz butter, melted

THE FILLING

1 tin x 400 ml griottes (must be griottes and not glacé cherries), drained with syrup reserved

450 ml/¾ pint whipping cream

55 g/2 oz vanilla sugar

5 tbsp kirsch

85 g/3 oz black cherry or raspberry jam (preferably home made)

200 g/7 oz plain chocolate couverture shavings

1 tbsp icing sugar

FLOURLESS BAKED CHOCOLATE CAKE

Serves 8-10 generous slices

200 g/7 oz caster sugar

4 eggs, separated

1 whole egg

225 g/8 oz plain chocolate, melted

125 g/4½ oz ground almonds and
1 tsp instant coffee and
1 tsp cocoa, sifted together

300 ml/10½ fl oz whipping
  cream to serve (or yoghurt or
  crème fraîche)

A dense chocolatey cake, which does not suffer from the omission of flour. This is a recipe from the multi-talented Claire Clark, Head Pastry Chef at Claridge's Hotel in London's Mayfair. The cake will have a firm but crisp crust and should be served cold dusted with icing sugar and lots of whipped cream.

Butter and flour a 18 cm x 6 cm (7 in x 2 ½ in) cake tin and line the base and sides with silicone, greaseproof or parchment. Preheat the oven to 190°C/375°F/gas 5.

Whisk half the sugar with the egg yolks and the whole egg until pale and creamy (about 5-7 minutes). Whisk the egg whites with remaining half caster sugar, in three stages, to soft peaks. Gently fold half the egg whites into the eggs and sugar. Gently fold melted chocolate into remaining whites and then fold in half the almonds, coffee and cocoa powder. Gently fold together the two egg mixtures and then fold in rest of almonds, coffee and cocoa powder. The last stages can be hard work but persevere.

Pour mixture into cake tin and bake in the middle of the oven for 40 minutes. Test with a knife and it should come out quite cleanly. It may need a little more cooking depending on your oven, so cook for further 15 minutes at about 150°C/300°F/gas 2. Do not be tempted to over cook. It is better a little undercooked or it will be dry. It will continue to cook as it cools.

Serves 8

ALMOND GÉNOISE

4 eggs

115 g/4 oz caster sugar

30 g/1 oz plain flour

30 g/1 oz cornflour

55 g/1 oz ground almonds

55 g/1 oz unsalted butter, melted

1/2 tsp vanilla essence

HAZELNUT PRALINE

100 g/3 1/2 oz caster sugar

100 g/3 1/2 oz hazelnuts, toasted
   and skinned (or almonds, pecans
   or pistachios)

IVORY ROSE GANACHE

125 ml/4 1/2 fl oz whipping or double
   cream, room temperature

4 tbsp rosewater

250 g/8 1/2 oz white chocolate,
   melted to no more than 38°C

CRYSTALLISED ROSE PETALS
   (See Basics page 107)

ALL BECAUSE CHARLIE LOVES WHITE CHOCOLATE

Charlie is the son of a great friend of mine and he adores white chocolate, and has asked me several times over the years for a recipe. The book concentrated my mind and we came up with this. It looks spectacular decorated with a rose - but this is purely optional and makes little difference to the taste. If you don't like roses then leave out the rosewater.

To make the almond génoise: Butter and flour a 20 cm (8 in) spring-form cake tin and line the bottom with greaseproof paper or baking parchment. Preheat the oven to 190°C/ 375°F/gas 5.

Bring about 5 cm (2 in) of water to boil in a medium sized saucepan. Remove from the heat, then place a large mixing bowl on top. Whisk together the eggs and sugar until thick and fluffy and the mixture leaves a trail. This will take about 8 minutes. Remove the bowl from the saucepan and continue to whisk until cool.

Sift the flours and ground almonds into the mixture and gently fold until smooth. Pour in the melted butter and vanilla and spoon into the prepared tin and bake for 25-30 minutes, until cooked through.

Leave in the tin for 15 minutes, then turn out on to a wire rack and allow to cool completely. When completely cold, use a long bread knife to cut in half horizontally.

To make the praline: Lightly oil a baking sheet. Place the sugar into a medium, heavy bottomed saucepan and heat gently until the sugar begins to melt. Swirl the pan to allow the sugar to melt evenly. Continue to cook until it begins to caramelise and is a pale-gold colour. Add the nuts and continue to caramelise for about 1 minute more or until it is a rich dark golden colour. Pour the mixture on to the baking sheet and leave to cool for about 20 minutes at room temperature. Place set block into a polythene bag and crush with a rolling pin to break up into pieces. Store in an airtight jar until needed.

To make the ivory rose ganache: Pour the cream and rosewater into a mixing bowl and whisk until the mixture thickens and just begins to leave a trail. Do not be tempted to over whip. Pour the melted white chocolate into the cream and fold in thoroughly and quickly.

To assemble: Carefully place one of the génoise layers on a serving plate. Sprinkle over 4-5 tablespoons of the praline. Spread over half of the white chocolate ganache. Place in the fridge and allow to set for 15-20 minutes. Place the second layer of génoise on top and cover entire cake with the remaining ganache. Decorate with crystallised rose petals for a really stunning finish.

DEATH BY CHOCOLATE

This is a famous name for a whole collection of recipes, some of which bear little resemblance to each other. Personally, I don't like any reference, be it recipe or not which indicates that chocolate is a sinner. It is not. On the other hand, it may have been called after the eponymous restaurant in Auckland, New Zealand. Naturally, the menu is all chocolate - save for the cheese and biscuits! It describes its 'Death' as "This is the one… a delicious assortment of chocolate delights, the chocolate lover's dream …" Well, this is my version. It has lots of chocolate…

Pre-heat oven to 180°C/350°F/gas 4. Using a 25.5 cm (10 in) loose-bottomed cake tin line the bottom with a greaseproof circle, butter and flour it and the sides.

Melt the chocolate, butter and water together over a low heat. Beat in the sugar and vanilla essence and leave to cool. Whisk in the egg yolks, fold in the soured cream.

Sift in the flour, bicarbonate of soda and cream of tartar.

Whisk the egg whites to soft peaks and fold into the chocolate mixture.

Pour into the tin and bake for about 1 hour until risen. Test with a skewer. Leave in the tin for 15 minutes and then turn out on to a wire rack to cool completely.

To make the filling: Melt the chocolate and butter together over a low heat. Add the vanilla essence and leave to cool.

When the cake is completely cool, place on a board and slice it horizontally into 3. (Don't worry if the middle layer has bits missing you can easily patch it up with the filling).

Remove the two top layers and set aside. At this stage it is easier to move the cake with the help of a 'pastry mover' (you can buy from Lakeland) to the thin base of a metal flan ring. (Or slide the base of the flan ring under the cake with the help of a spatula). Spread the bottom layer with half the filling mixture, coaxing it to the edges of the cake. Place the middle layer on top and spread it with the remaining filling. Sandwich the third layer on the top.

To make the icing: Bring the cream to the boil and pour over the chocolate broken into pieces. Stir until the chocolate has completely melted and the mixture is well combined, smooth and glossy.

Pour over the centre of the cake, letting it run to the edges and down the sides. You may need to spread it back up the sides to cover completely. It will set fairly quickly and leave marks it you try and touch it up, so try to get a good coverage the first time.

To make the chocolate curls: (See page 103) Melt the final portion of chocolate, pour into a marble slab or tough baking sheet and allow to set firmly. (You can put it in the fridge for 5 minutes or so to speed up the process.) Scrape the side of a palette knife along the chocolate to form curls or flakes. Decorate the cake with them.

Serves 8-10

THE CAKE

225 g/8 oz plain chocolate, chopped

115 g/4 oz unsalted butter

150 ml/¼ pint water

225 g/8 oz soft dark brown sugar - like Muscovado

1 tsp vanilla essence

2 eggs, separated

150 ml/¼ pint soured cream or crème fraîche

225 g/8 oz flour and
½ tsp bicarbonate of soda and
1 tsp cream of tartar, sifted together

THE FILLING

225 g/8 oz plain chocolate

225 g/8 oz unsalted butter

2 tsp vanilla essence

THE ICING

200 ml/7 fl oz whipping or double cream

200 g/7 oz dark chocolate

CHOCOLATE CURLS

200 g/7 oz dark chocolate

Serves 10-12

6 eggs, separated

350 g/12 oz sugar

350 g/12 oz whole blanched
    almonds, toasted lightly, then
    finely ground

225 g/8 oz semolina flour

2 tsp lemon rind, grated

2 tbsp fresh lemon juice

6 egg whites

CHOCOLATE GLAZE
115 g/4 oz plain chocolate, chopped

30 g/1 oz butter

flakes to decorate (optional)

PARROZZO DI PAPA - AN ITALIAN CAKE

This is a traditional Italian semolina and almond cake finished with a chocolate glaze. Truthfully, the glaze is the only thing about this cake which is chocolate - but the combination of lemon and chocolate, as you will know from reading this book, is one of my favourites.

Preheat the oven to 190°C/375°F/gas 5. Butter and line a 30 cm (12 in) loose bottomed cake tin. Beat the egg yolks and sugar together until pale and fluffy - at least 5 minutes. Fold in the almonds, semolina flour, lemon rind and juice. In another bowl, whisk the egg whites with a pinch of salt until they hold stiff peaks. 'Let down' the almond mixture with a large spoonful of the whites then gently but thoroughly fold in the rest. Spoon into the cake tin and bake for 45-50 minutes. Test with a skewer. Let the cake cool in the tin for 10 minutes then turn out on to a rack and allow to cool completely.

For the covering: Melt the chocolate and butter together. Drizzle the glaze over the cake allowing it to run casually down the sides. Let it set and, if using, decorate with the chocolate flakes. This is a dense cake and traditionally a mite dry. It is better after 24 hours and will keep for at least a week wrapped in foil and stored in an airtight tin.

CHOCOLATE CAKE HELENA

Serves 4-6

150 g/5½ oz plain chocolate

125 g/4½ oz butter

150 g/5½ oz caster sugar

3 eggs, lightly beaten

55 g/2 oz plain flour, sifted

COVER ICING

115 g/4 oz dark chocolate

2 tbsp milk

45 g/1½ oz butter

This recipe comes from Monica Patino, Chef Patron of the Taberna del Leon in Mexico City and one of the culinary stars of the Mexican food scene. It is part of the trio of chocolate desserts that I enjoyed so much when I was there. See also Chocolate Cake Micaela and Three Chocolate Mosaic with British Vanilla Cream.

Preheat the oven to 160°C/325°F/gas 3. Butter the sides and line the bottom of a 20 cm (8 in) cake tin with silicone, parchment or greaseproof paper.

Melt the chocolate and butter together, stirring until smooth. Mix in the sugar.

Gradually add the beaten eggs, stirring to incorporate. Fold in the flour.

Pour the mixture into the cake tin and bake for 15-20 minutes until the middle is just set. Allow to cool in the tin.

To make the covering: Melt all the ingredients together until smooth. Allow to cool a little.

Turn cake out on to a serving plate and cover with the icing.

MEXICAN CHOCOLATE CAKE

Serves 8-10

350 g/12 oz Mexican chocolate, or the strongest couverture you can find

115 g/4 oz unsalted butter

55 g/2 oz brown sugar

2 eggs

225 ml/7½ fl oz sour cream

115 ml/4 fl oz water

1 tsp vanilla extract

1 tsp baking powder and 175 g/7½ oz flour and 30 g/1 oz cocoa powder, sifted together

Another Mexican find from Glen Eastmann and the Four Seasons but this is created with Mexican chocolate. Mexican chocolate is pure ground cocoa straight from the bean with cinnamon and almonds and finally sugar added, so the texture is coarse and sugary and the flavour is much better defined than our chocolate. You should use the strongest couverture you can find.

Butter and flour a 30 cm (12 in) loose bottomed cake tin. Preheat the oven to 180°C/350°F/ gas 4.

Melt chocolate, butter and sugar until smooth. Gradually add the eggs, then the sour cream, water and vanilla. Blend well with a wooden spoon before folding in all the dry ingredients.

Pour into the prepared cake tin.

Bake for 30-40 minutes until springy. The finish is a little rustic so perhaps you should sprinkle with either icing sugar or cocoa powder. Also the centre is a little dense and chewy - this is how it is supposed to be.

Serve with Lavender or Angelica Ice Cream, Fruit Compote or Crème Anglaise or even a chocolate sorbet.

Serves 8

200g/7 oz bitter chocolate

2 tbsp water

140 g/5 oz caster sugar

150 g/5½ oz soft butter, plus extra for greasing

3 heaped tbsp self raising flour, sifted

5 medium eggs, separated

pinch salt

grated zest of small orange or Cointreau if liked or 30 g/1 oz shelled and chopped nuts

COATING (optional)

225 g/7 oz bitter chocolate

200ml/7 fl oz half-cream

4 walnuts or pecans

MARIE-PIERRE'S GÂTEAU AU CHOCOLAT

Marie-Pierre Moine claims that her idea of a home-made chocolate cake is dark, rich, solidly irresistible and definitely for feast days. Over the years she says that she has played with other ideas but always loyally comes back to this recipe. The cake always disappears pretty quickly, but will keep extremely well for several days in the refrigerator wrapped loosely in foil. It also travels well, and will make you a popular weekend or party guest. Perhaps you should leave the coating until you have arrived with your gift. The coating is 'over-the-top', optional but highly recommended.

Preheat oven to 160°C/ 325°F/gas 3 and generously butter a large loaf tin or loose bottomed deep round cake tin.

Over a very low heat, melt the chocolate and water together. Stir the sugar into the chocolate and water and take off the heat while you add the butter in pieces.

Return to a very low heat. Stir in flour lightly to combine, and cook for a couple of minutes.

Remove from the heat and let mixture cool a little. Work the egg yolks slowly into the chocolate mixture beating them in thoroughly. Add pinch salt to egg whites and beat until firm and stiff.

With large metal spoon, fold whisked egg whites into the chocolate mixture very thoroughly, but working lightly with upward movement.

Add the orange or Cointreau if liked at this stage and the nuts.

Tip the mixture into the greased tin and knock tin on working surface to ensure it is evenly settled.

Bake for about 45 minutes. Don't open oven door for first 25 minutes, then check, and turn the tin around if the cake is looking lopsided. Turn up the heat to the next setting for the last five minutes - test with a knife.

Leave to cool for a good 15 minutes and remove from tin and place on serving dish.

To coat the cake, wait until it is cold.

COATING

Melt chocolate with the half-cream in a saucepan stirring frequently with a wooden spoon.

Leave the mixture to cool a little then pour it over the centre of the cake.

Have a spatula at hand to smooth the coating evenly over the whole surface.

Arrange the nuts (if using) over the cake.

All Because Charlie Loves White Chocolate (page 132)

NEGUS

Serves 10

5 duck eggs (best with duck eggs but can use extra large hen's)

250 g/8½ oz caster sugar (bit less)

100 g/3½ oz flour and

75 g/2½ oz bitter cocoa, sifted together twice

TO COVER

4 eggs

200 g/7 oz sugar

150 g/5½ oz bitter chocolate

1 tsp concentrated black coffee

55 g/2 oz unsalted butter

flaked or grated chocolate

A contribution from Michael Raffael who says that he first came across this recipe - attributed to L'Auberge de Père Bise - at Annecy - in *Femmes d'Aujourd'hui* (c 1973). 'Père' Bise was one of the legendary 'godfathers' of modern French cuisine. This, as witness to its name, is an all 'black' chocolate cake.

Butter and flour a 20 cm (8 in) 'moule à manqué, /loose bottomed cake tin. Preheat oven to 190°C/375°F/gas 5.

Whisk yolks and sugar over a bain marie in tepid water, off the heat for about 7 minutes until ribbon stage. Continue to beat until cold. Rain in the twice-sifted flour and cocoa and gently fold in. Whisk whites until stiff and fold into mixture.

Bake for 30 minutes - or until knife tests clean.

Let cool and turn out.

For the covering: Whisk together eggs and sugar in a bain marie, as above.

Melt together the chocolate, coffee and butter. Fold into sabayon and cool.

To assemble: Cut the 'génoise' sponge horizontally into 3 discs and spread the filling on to layers. Decorate the final layer with chocolate flakes or grated chocolate.

GÂTEAU L'OPÉRA

Serves about 12 generously

THE ALMOND GÉNOISE

225 g/8 oz finely ground almonds

75 g/2½ oz plain flour

225 g/8 oz icing sugar, sifted

4 large eggs

4 large egg whites

2 tbsp granulated sugar

45 g/1½ oz unsalted butter, melted

SUGAR SYRUP

55 g/2 oz caster sugar

125 ml/4 fl oz water

This heavenly gâteau is the creation of the great Parisian pâtissier Gaston Lenôtre. The house of Lenôtre is a symbol of tradition for gourmands, as Gaston Lenôtre himself is one of the most celebrated pâtissiers in France and has spawned a whole new generation of pâtissiers, *confiseurs* and *chocolatiers*. Lenôtre even has his own brand of couvertures and other chocolate products.

The gâteau, created in honour of the Paris Opera House, has become a classic. Many have tried to copy the original but most have failed. The secret, according to M. Lenôtre, is to use the right chocolate! Traditionally it is made in a rectangle with three layers of almond génoise soaked in a sugar syrup and sandwiched together with butter cream and ganache. A generous decoration of gold leaf sets this cake apart from the ordinary, making a very rich and regal affair.

This is a lengthy exercise but you can do it in stages. So leave yourself plenty of time. Please read the recipe first to gauge the length of time this will take.

Line a 28 cm × 37.5 cm × 2 cm (11 in × 15 in × ¾ in) Swiss roll tin with buttered and floured parchment or greaseproof paper. Preheat the oven to 200°C/400°F/gas 6.

GANACHE

125 ml/4 fl oz whipping cream

170 g/6 oz dark chocolate,
  finely chopped

115 g/4 oz unsalted butter, softened

BUTTER CREAM

2 large eggs

2 large egg yolks

250 g/8½ oz caster sugar

125 ml/4 fl oz water

¼ tsp cream of tartar

400 g/14 oz unsalted butter,
  softened

1 tbsp coffee, made from freshly
  ground beans

COVERING

225 g/8 oz dark chocolate for
  covering

For the cake: Sift together in a large bowl the ground almonds, flour and icing sugar. Mix in two of the eggs and using a hand held mixer or a balloon whisk, blend together for about 3 minutes. Add the remaining 2 eggs and beat the mixture to ribbon stage - about 3 minutes. In another bowl whisk the egg whites to soft peaks. Gradually add the sugar until they hold stiff peaks but not too dry. Fold into the almond mixture a little at a time. Fold in the melted butter. Pour the mixture into the tin and tap on the sides to make sure that it spreads evenly. Bake for 8-10 minutes. The top should be springy. Transfer to a wire rack to cool.

For the sugar syrup: In a saucepan melt the sugar and the water together and then bring to the boil over a high heat. Allow to cool.

For the ganache: Bring the cream to the boil and pour over the chopped chocolate. Stir until melted and smooth. Allow to cool for about 2 hours. Whisk the butter until it is light and fluffy and add the ganache a bit at a time, blending slowly. Set aside in a cool place.

For the butter cream: Over a bain marie, whisk the eggs and the egg yolks until the mixture is thick and creamy, about 8 minutes. In a heavy-bottomed saucepan bring the sugar, water and cream of tartar to the boil over a high heat and cook to 117°C/242°F.

Now whisking slowly, pour the sugar syrup on to the egg mixture in a steady stream. Now increase the speed of the whisk and beat until the mixture is completely cold which will take about 6-8 minutes.

Beat in the softened butter, a tablespoon at a time until the mixture is light and fluffy which will take about 3 minutes. Now add the coffee. Set aside.

For the chocolate covering: Temper the chocolate or melt it very gently over a low heat. Using a rectangular board or tray about 30 cm x 15 cm (12 in x 6 in), line it with parchment and spread the chocolate evenly across it. Leave it to set in a cool place - about 30 minutes. Using a cardboard template cut out a 28 cm x 12 cm (11 in x 5 in) rectangle from the chocolate for the top of the cake. Set aside.

To make the gâteau: Cut the almond génoise horizontally into 3 layers. Place one layer on the cardboard rectangle template. Brush with some of the syrup and then spread half of the butter cream evenly over the top. Place another layer of the sponge on top of this and brush this with more syrup. Spread with chocolate ganache and smooth over. Place a third layer of the sponge on top of this and brush with the rest of the syrup. Spread the remaining butter cream over the top. Peel the parchment from the chocolate and trim if necessary and fit the chocolate rectangle over the top. Don't worry if it breaks, you can patch it up. Voila. You can use any leftover bits of chocolate to decorate. If you have some, then decorate with a sliver or two of gold leaf.

Refrigerate for about 2 hours and bring to room temperature before serving.

The original gâteau has l'Opéra piped in chocolate across the top - but you can leave this to the experts if you don't want to have a go yourself. If you do then use the chocolate as described in Sacher Torte. (page 144)

Serves 6-8

PUFF PASTRY LEAVES

225 g/8 oz strong flour

pinch salt

150 ml/¼ pint ice-cold water

225 g/8 oz unsalted butter

PRUNE CREAM

225 g/8 oz Agen prunes
  (or similar quality) weighed
  without stones

150 ml/¼ pint Calvados

200 ml/7 fl oz whipping cream

GANACHE

150 ml/¼ pint whipping cream

115 g/4 oz dark chocolate, broken
  into pieces

PRUNE, CALVADOS AND CHOCOLATE FLAKE

A delightful variation on puff pastry mille-feuille .

First make the puff pastry: Sift the flour with a pinch of salt. Add the ice water and mix with a fork to a doughy consistency. Turn on to a work surface and knead thoroughly for four or five minutes until smooth - almost like you would bread. Wrap in polythene or a cloth and leave in the refrigerator for 30 minutes to rest.

Lightly flour the work-top and roll the dough into a rectangle about 10 cm x 30 cm (4 in x 12 in). Place the butter between two sheets of greaseproof paper and bash with a rolling pin to get it into a flattened block about 9 cm x 8 cm (3½ in x 3 in). Place the butter in the middle of the pastry and now (to build up the leaves) fold the pastry over the butter like an envelope first by folding the third closest to you over the butter and then bring the top third down towards you. Press the sides together to prevent the butter escaping. Give a 90-degree anti-clockwise turn so that the folded, closed edge is on your left.

Now tap the pastry parcel with the rolling pin to flatten the butter a little, then roll out quickly and lightly, until the pastry is 3 times as long as it is wide. Fold it evenly in 3, by repeating the above, i.e. fold the third closest to you over the middle and then bring the top third down towards you. Give it a 90-degree anti-clockwise turn so that the folded, closed edge is on your left. Again press the edges firmly with the rolling pin. Then roll out again to form a rectangle as before.

Now the pastry has two rolls and folds, or turns as they are called. It should be put to rest in a cool place for 30 minutes or so. The rolling and folding must be repeated twice more, the pastry again rested, and then again giving 2 more turns. This makes a total of 6 turns. If the butter is still very streaky roll and fold it once more. Cut the pastry into three and roll each third out to approximately 15 cm x 10 cm (6 in x 4 in). Place on a large baking sheet (or 2 smaller ones) and bake for 5-6 minutes to until well-risen and golden brown.

Prune Cream: Place the prunes in a bowl and cover with Calvados and 75 ml/3½ fl oz water. Allow to soak for at least one hour. Preheat the oven to 230°C/450°F/gas 8.

Drain the Calvados and water into a small saucepan and boil to reduce to about 2 tablespoons. Set aside 10 whole prunes, for decoration, and chop the rest. Whisk the cream and reduced Calvados until it begins to hold its shape. Add the chopped prunes. Place in the fridge until ready to assemble.

To make the ganache: Bring the cream to the boil in a saucepan. Remove from the heat and add the chocolate, stirring until well blended. Allow to cool to room temperature. Whisk very lightly.

To assemble: Place one of the pastry leaves on a suitable serving dish. Spoon ⅓ of the ganache over the top. Spread with half of the prune cream. Lay a second pastry leaf on top, spread with ganache then the rest of the cream mixture. Top with the third pastry leaf and spread with ganache then the rest of the cream mixture. Top with the third pastry leaf and spread with the rest of the ganache on the top. Decorate with the reserved whole prunes and dust with icing sugar.

NO FLOUR CHOCOLATE ROULADE

Serves 6-8

5 eggs, separated

140 g/5 oz caster sugar

225 g/8 oz plain chocolate, chopped

5 tbsp water

1 tsp strong instant coffee

300 ml/½ pint whipping cream - lightly whipped (optional as you could choose any one of a number of other filling suggestions throughout this book - but this one is simplicity itself)

Along with Michel Roux's recipes for Roule this is definitely the best roulade recipe I have tried. It is also the hardest to manage but is worth the effort. You can also use this roulade as a base for other desserts.

Grease a baking sheet 30 cm x 38 cm (12 in x 15 in) well and line with parchment. Brush the paper with melted butter and flour and then sprinkle with caster sugar. Heat oven 200°C/400°F/gas 6.

Beat the egg yolks and sugar in a large bowl for about 5 minutes until pale and creamy.

Put the chocolate, water and coffee into a saucepan and melt over a gentle heat. Stir into the yolk mixture.

Whisk the whites until stiff. 'Let down' with a little of the chocolate mixture and fold in the rest of the whites into the mixture.

Spread evenly on the baking sheet and bake for 12 minutes or until it's firm to touch.

Slide cake and paper on to a wire rack and cover immediately with a damp tea towel and allow to cool. (The damp tea towel should help to stop the cake from cracking.)

Spread whipped cream on to roulade, or use whatever filling you wish. When filling, spread it evenly over the cake and roll up like a Swiss roll, removing the paper as you go. Don't worry if some of the roulade splits - you can patch it up and dust over any cracks with cocoa powder or icing sugar.

MICHEL ROUX'S ROULE MARQUIS

Serves 8-10

THE SPONGE

3 egg yolks

170 g/6 oz icing sugar

4 egg whites

55 g/2 oz cocoa powder

2 tsp cornflour

THE FILLING

250 ml/8 fl oz whipping cream

250 ml/8 fl oz red fruit coulis
  (See page 112)

2 tbsp framboise (optional)

170 g/6 oz fresh raspberries or
  strawberries

55 g/2 oz coffee liqueur beans
  (optional)

"A delightful, classic combination of chocolate 'Swiss roll' and raspberries". This recipe is generously given by Michel Roux, and was first published in *The Roux Brothers on Patisserie* which, although issued in 1986 is still one of the most extensive works on pastry and desserts for all. Not that it reveals the innermost secrets of just how Michel himself works miracles in pastry and sugar - that's a consummate talent that only he and a few others possess and the result of many years hard work, skill and a unique passion.

This dessert can be made in advance and refrigerated up to 24 hours. Use strawberries when raspberries are not available. The raspberry liqueur is not essential but does bring out the flavour of the fruit beautifully.

Coffee liqueur beans are available from specialist food shops and add a delicious crunch to the filling (see Directory).

Preheat oven to 220°C/425°F/gas 7. Line a baking sheet with parchment or lightly buttered and floured greaseproof paper.

To make the sponge: Beat together the egg yolks and 85 g/3 oz of the icing sugar, until they form a ribbon, about 5 minutes. Whisk the egg whites until half risen. Add 45 g/1½ oz icing sugar and beat at high speed for 1 minute until very stiff.

Using a flat slotted spoon, mix one third of the egg whites into the yolks and stir until completely blended. Very carefully tip in the rest of the whites all at once and fold in gently.

Before the mixture becomes too homogenous, sift in the cocoa and the cornflour, folding all the time. As soon as it is well blended stop or it will become heavy.

Using a palette knife, spread the roule mixture evenly on to the baking sheet making a rectangle of about 30 cm x 25 cm x 1 cm (12 in x 10 in x ½ in) thick.

Bake for 8-10 minutes. The top of the sponge should feel springy. If it is not sufficiently cooked it will stick to the cloth after baking. Remove from the oven and immediately invert the sponge on to a wire rack covered with a tea towel. Carefully peel off the paper, then leave in a cool place for 5-10 minutes.

To make the filling: Whip the cream with the remaining 40 g/1½ oz of icing sugar until it forms a ribbon. Mix together with the framboise and the fruit coulis. Brush the sponge with a quarter of the coulis and reserve the rest to serve separately.

Trim the edges of the sponge with a knife cutting off any slightly overcooked or dry parts. Using a palette knife, spread over the whipped cream to within 1 cm (½ in) of the edges of the sponge. Scatter over the raspberries and the coffee liqueur beans.

Use a tea towel to help you roll up the sponge from the short end like a Swiss Roll. Chill in the fridge for 2-3 hours before serving.

To serve: Cut into diagonal slices. Dredge with remaining icing sugar and serve on very cold plates. Serve the remaining fruit coulis separately in a sauce boat.

Prune, Calvados and Chocolate Flake (page 140)

THE SACHER TORTE

Serves 8

125 g/4 oz unsalted butter

125 g/4 oz caster sugar

6 eggs, separated

125 g/4 oz dark chocolate, melted

125 g/4 oz plain flour, sieved

pinch salt

125 g/4 oz apricot preserve - for the sandwich which is optional

5 tbsp apricot preserve for the glaze

THE ICING

200 g/7 oz dark chocolate

55 g/2 oz butter

100 g/3½ oz icing sugar

100 ml/3½ fl oz water

WHIPPED CREAM

300 ml/½ pint whipping cream

55 g/2 oz sifted icing sugar

½ tsp vanilla essence

The real Sacher Torte (pronounced Sacker) is considered to be the earliest recorded recipe to be based on chocolate, devised in Austria in 1778. Nearly two hundred years later it was the subject of a legal wrangle between the Sacher family, of the torte and hotel fame, and Demel's pâtisserie. Demel's pâtisserie, which had been making pastries for the Hapsburgs and the wealthy of Vienna for two hundred years, boasted 'the original Sacher Torte'. The situation reached a crescendo and eventually, in the 1950s, a furious Hotel Sacher initiated an inevitable lawsuit, which ended in Austria's supreme courts. The court decision granted Hotel Sacher the right to claim, by a chocolate plaque on the top of each torte, that theirs is 'genuine'. As a result there are now two versions; one sandwiched with apricot glaze and one coated under the icing.

This is a plain, dense un-sweet cake, which is how the cake is supposed to be, and must be served with mountains of whipped cream to balance the dryness.

There are no genuinely authentic versions left of this simple cake, with the all-important apricot jam and chocolate glaze, but this is my version which I love.

Butter and flour a 20 cm (8 in) deep cake tin. Set the oven to 180°C/350°F/ gas 4.

Cream the butter and three quarters of the sugar together until light and fluffy. Beat in the egg yolks one by one. Stir in the melted chocolate. Fold in the sifted flour.

Whisk the egg whites with the salt until they form a peak and whisk in the remaining sugar until stiff and shiny. Loosen the chocolate mixture with two tablespoons of egg white and then fold in the remaining whites and thoroughly but lightly amalgamate until there are no whites showing.

Turn the mixture into the tin and bake for about 50 minutes to one hour - or test with a skewer or knife.

Leave in the tin for 15 minutes until cool and then turn out on to a wire rack, upside down so that the bottom becomes the top which will give you a very flat smooth surface to decorate.

Leave for as long as you can - preferably several hours or overnight.

Gently heat the apricot preserve to the point when it is easy to spread.

Slice through the centre of the cake horizontally. Place on a wire rack and spread the strained preserve on the bottom slice and sandwich together.

Slowly bring the remaining apricot preserve to the boil and strain.

With the cake still on a wire rack, place a plate or board underneath so that you can catch the preserve, which may inevitably fall down the sides.

Pour the warmed strained apricot preserve over the cake and spread evenly across the top with a palette knife or long spatula. You may need to scoop up the excess, which drips down and around the sides.

To make the icing: Melt the chocolate and the butter together.

Dissolve the icing sugar in the water in a saucepan and bring slowly to the boil.

Add the melted chocolate and boil again. Immediately take off the heat and beat briskly until it's completely smooth. Set aside until it cools to room temperature and it begins to thicken slightly.

Reserve 3 tablespoons for piping 'Sacher' on top of the cake.

With the cake on a board or large plate, pour the rest of the icing very carefully on to the middle of the cake. Pick up whatever it is on and 'tilt and swirl' to help the icing run evenly across the apricot layer and down the sides. You don't want too much to run down the sides but if it does then just scoop up with the spatula and spread across the top. You may have to spread some icing up the sides for even coverage.

(If you have a problem with it and it runs all over the place don't worry, you have probably used it too hot. Wait a while and let it cool down gently tempting it on to the top of the cake again.)

The original Sacher Tortes have Sacher written across the centre so if you want to do the authentic thing, then use the reserved glaze and let the cake stand for a couple of hours until set. Then gently reheat the rest of the glaze and put into a small piping bag with a very small nozzle and away you go. This requires a certain amount of skill and patience with the piping but gives a great sense of achievement.

TRADITIONAL CHOCOLATE SANDWICH CAKE

Serves 6-8

170 g/6 oz butter, room temperature

125 g/4 oz caster sugar

3 large eggs

140 g/5 oz flour and
1/2 tsp baking powder and
30 g/1 oz cocoa powder,
 sieved together

This is a cake which I remember vividly from my childhood. It is one of those which should only be made by an aunt or grandmother and to which, as a child, you look forward on every rare visit. It has to be filled with a sugary vanilla filling to be absolutely genuine.

Lightly butter and flour two 18 cm (7 in) sandwich tins. Preheat oven to 190°C/ 375°F/ gas 5.

Cream together the butter and sugar until pale and fluffy. Add the eggs separately together with a teaspoon of flour/cocoa per egg. Mix together thoroughly, with a wooden spoon.

Mix in remaining flour and cocoa. It should be 'dropping' consistency (you might need to add a little milk). Divide the batter equally between the two tins.

Bake side by side for about 25 minutes - they should be springy to touch.

Allow to cool before turning out on to a cake tray. When absolutely cold spread with vanilla/butter icing, raspberry or apricot jam. Dust the top with caster or icing sugar.

CHOCOLATE DROP SPONGE

Serves 8-10

200 g/7 oz unsalted butter, softened and room temperature

200 g/7 oz raw caster sugar

4 eggs, lightly beaten

30 g/1 oz cocoa powder and 300 g/10½ oz plain flour and 1½ tsp baking powder, sifted together

125 g/4½ oz ground almonds, or pistachios

125 g/4½ oz flaked almonds, toasted

225 g/4 oz sultanas

255 g/9 oz chocolate drops

150 ml/¼ pint dark rum

Light fruit and nut sponge with the added treat of a chocolate drop or chip. This is a versatile cake, terrific for tea, dinner or a celebration. You can leave it plain for tea or serve it with a sauce or fruit compote for dinner.

Grease and line a 1 kilo/2 lb loaf tin or a 20 cm (8 in) cake tin with at least 10 cm (4 in) sides. Preheat oven to 150°C/300°F/gas 2.

Cream the butter and sugar until pale and fluffy. Beat in the eggs, one at a time, alternating with the sifted flour and baking powder and cocoa powder. Mix in the ground nuts, then the flaked almonds, sultanas, chocolate drops and the rum and blend thoroughly. It should be a soft consistency. Tip the mixture in. Bake for approximately 2 hours or until knife tests cleanly.

Leave to cool for 15 minutes then turn out on to a wire rack. Allow to go completely cold before serving. Keeps well for several weeks in an airtight tin, wrapped in grease-proof paper or foil.

VELOURS AU CHOCOLAT, GRIOTTES KIRCHÉES ET DACQUOISE PISTACHÉE

Serves 8

1 x 425g tin black cherries, stoned and drained

4 tbsp kirsch

THE MERINGUE FRANÇAIS
2 egg whites

100 g/3½ oz caster sugar

55 g/2 oz pistachio nuts, finely ground

From the irrepressible Raymond Blanc, Chef Patron of Le Manoir aux Quat' Saisons in Oxford. A must for good food lovers.

Place the cherries in a bowl, pour over the kirsch and allow to infuse while you prepare the rest of the components.

To make the meringue français: Preheat the oven to 100°C/200°F/gas ¼ . Place a piece of baking parchment on a baking sheet, draw a 20 cm (8 in) diameter circle with a pencil, turn the paper over and wipe it thinly with oil. Whisk the whites until they form soft peaks. Gradually add the sugar, continuing to whisk until the mixture is stiff and shiny. Fold in the ground pistachios. Spoon about three quarters of the meringue into the centre of the circle and spread carefully just inside the marks. (You should be able to see the pencil circle through the paper.) Place the meringue in the oven for 2 hours to dry out. Discard the remaining meringue or use it for another recipe. (This is because it is difficult to make smaller quantities of meringue.)

THE SPONGE

2 eggs, separated

55 g/2 oz caster sugar

55 g/2 oz plain flour

30 g/1 oz ground almonds

FOR THE PISTACHIO MOUSSE

1 gelatine leaf

100 ml/3½ fl oz milk

55 g/2 oz pistachio nuts, finely
  ground

2 egg yolks

2 tbsp caster sugar

5 tbsp whipping cream

THE CHOCOLATE MOUSSE

100 g/3½ oz good quality chocolate

85 g/3 oz unsalted butter

30 g/1 oz cocoa powder

1 tbsp dark rum

55 g/2 oz caster sugar

1 tbsp water

1 egg

To make the sponge: Preheat the oven to 200°C / 400°F / gas 6. Butter and flour the sides and line the base of a 20 cm (8 in) spring-form tin. Whisk the whites until they form soft peaks. Gradually add the sugar continuing to whisk until the mixture is stiff and shiny. Quickly whisk in the yolks. Sift in the flour and ground almonds and fold quickly and thoroughly. Spoon into the prepared tin and bake for 12 minutes. Allow to cool. When completely cold, remove from the tin and slice in half, horizontally. You will only need one of the layers. Use the other for another recipe (it also freezes well).

To make the pistachio mousse: Soak the gelatine leaf in a bowl of cold water. Place the milk and ground nuts in a saucepan and bring slowly to the boil. Remove from the heat. In a mixing bowl, cream together the yolks and sugar until thick and pale. Pour one third of the hot milk on to the egg mixture and whisk to combine. Return this to the saucepan with the rest of the milk, place over a medium heat and cook slowly, stirring continuously until the custard thickens. Take care not to boil it. Remove from the heat, squeeze any excess water from the gelatine and add it to the custard, stirring, until dissolved. Pour into a bowl and allow to cool but not to set. Whisk the cream until it thickens and just leaves a trail. Fold into the custard. Line a baking sheet with cling film, place a 20 cm (8 in) mould or spring-form tin (bottom removed) on to the film and pour in the mousse. Place in the freezer.

To make the chocolate mousse: Place the chocolate, butter, sifted cocoa powder and rum in a bowl and melt over a bain marie, stirring occasionally to combine until smooth. Make a sugar syrup with the sugar and water, heating to 116°C. Place the egg in a mixing bowl and whisk while slowly pouring on the syrup. Continue whisking until the mixture is cool. Fold the melted chocolate mixture into the egg and syrup mixture.

To assemble: Remove the pistachio mousse from the freezer and spread half the chocolate mousse on top, smoothing evenly.

Drain the cherries, reserving the kirsch soaking liquor. Dot the cherries over the chocolate mousse. Lay the sponge on top of the cherries. Sprinkle with the reserved kirsch. Spoon the remaining chocolate mousse on top of the sponge. Finally, place the dried out meringue on top and press gently to stick to the mousse. Now place back in the freezer for 1 hour.

Remove from the freezer and carefully turn upside down on to a board or serving plate. Remove the tray and cling film. Warm a thin bladed knife and run it around the sides of the mould or tin to loosen. Carefully remove the mould.

Professionals decorate with a chocolate spray using a special gun. However, having tried this wonderful creation, it is terrific without any other embellishment.

FRANCES BISSELL'S VIENNESE CHRISTMAS CAKE

A Christmas cake with a difference. It is lighter than our traditional fruit cake but delicious nonetheless.

Serves 10-12
  (or fewer if you are greedy)

250 g/8½ oz unsalted butter

275 g/9½ oz dark muscovado sugar

4 free range eggs, lightly beaten

325 g/11 oz self raising flour

pinch salt

125 g/4½ oz ground almond

125 g/4½ oz chopped almonds

125 g/4½ oz raisins

125 g/4½ oz dried cherries

1 tsp pure vanilla essence

milk

6 tbsp aged rum

400 g/14 oz white marzipan

3 tbsp sieved apricot jam

200-300 g/7-10½ oz dark chocolate (at least 70 per cent cocoa solids)

Grease and line a 1 kilo/2 lb loaf tin. Preheat oven at 150°C/300°F/gas 2.

Cream the butter and sugar until light and fluffy. Beat in the eggs and flour alternately.

Stir in the rest of the ingredients except 3 tablespoons of rum, marzipan, jam and chocolate and add enough milk to give a soft dripping consistency. Spoon mixture into tin and smooth the top. Bake for two hours. Allow to cool in the tin.

Pour the remaining rum over the cake having poked holes in it with a skewer. Cover with foil and allow to stand in a cool place until the rum is absorbed. Then wrap the cake in greaseproof paper and foil. It will keep for several weeks.

A week before you want to serve it, spread the cake with the apricot jam; roll out the marzipan and cover the cake with it. The day before you serve it, melt the chocolate and set the cake over a wire rack and pour the melted chocolate all over, taking care to give it an even coating. Leave the chocolate to set for a day before serving the cake, which can also be decorated with the usual Christmas bits and pieces.

LE SUCCES DE BERNACHON

Serves about 10

THE CHOCOLATE GANACHE

500 ml/16 fl oz crème fraîche or whipping cream

300 g/10½ oz dark chocolate, chopped into tiny pieces .

THE MERINGUE

175 g/6 oz unblanched almonds

175 g/6 oz caster sugar

6 large egg whites

2 tbsp cocoa powder

Today fewer than a dozen French artisan manufacturers still begin with the raw cacao beans to make their chocolate. One such firm is Bernachon chocolates, based in Lyon - the acknowledged gastronomic capital of the world - and run by Maurice and his son Jean-Jacques. Worried that the industry was heading toward an undesirable uniformity of tastes, the recipes were perfected by Maurice Bernachon during the 1970s. The company roasts its own carefully selected beans from the Indian Ocean, South America and Indonesia. Different varieties of beans are combined in different proportions to create a dozen crus, which are kept a closely guarded secret. These distinctive flavours have become one of the principal elements that make Bernachon's chocolate a venerated model chocolate.

Here is my much thumbed copy of the recipe for Bernachon's Almond Meringue Gâteau with Chocolate Cream. It has the advantage of a light meringue in contrast to the richer chocolate ganache and is relatively simple to make.

For the chocolate ganache: Bring the crème fraîche or whipping cream to the boil in a medium sized saucepan. As soon as it begins to boil remove from the heat and add the chocolate, stirring until it is completely melted and smooth. Set aside to cool and then cover with cling film and refrigerate for about 3 hours.

For the cake: Preheat the oven to 180°C/350°F/gas 4. Butter and flour 2 baking sheets, marking a 20 cm (8 in) circle on each.

Whizz the almonds and all but 2 tablespoons of sugar in a food processor to a medium fine powder. Beat the egg whites in a large bowl until stiff but not dry. Slowly add the remaining sugar as the whites begin to stiffen. The mixture should be very stiff.

Fold in the powdered almonds.

Using a pastry bag fitted with a large plain tube, pipe the meringue on to the prepared baking sheets into 18 cm (7 in) circles, starting in the centre and spiralling outwards.

Bake for 15 minutes, or just until the meringue begins to turn golden. Remove the ganache from the fridge to bring to room temperature.

Remove the meringues from the oven and loosen them from the trays. Allow them to cool completely before transferring them to a work surface.

To assemble the gâteau: If the ganache is not soft enough you may need to very very gently begin to reheat. As it starts to soften (but don't let it melt) you can take it off the heat and amalgamate the mixture to evenly distribute again. Place one layer of the meringue on a serving plate, smooth side up. Spread it with half the chocolate cream. Place the second layer on top and spread the remaining half of the ganache on to it and spread some around the sides. Refrigerate for about 3-6 hours or overnight. Dust with cocoa powder before serving.

Puddings - Cold and Hot

Steamed Chocolate Sussex Pond Pudding
(page 154)

CHOCOLATE BRÛLÉE SURPRISE

Serves 6

4 large egg yolks

85 g/3 oz sugar

575 ml/1 pint whipping cream

1 vanilla pod

115 g/4 oz chocolate, melted

225 g/8 oz caster sugar, for caramelising

This is a cocoa-y version of the old fashioned Cambridge Burnt Cream. The surprise is the discovery of the chocolate under the conventional vanilla cream.

Beat the yolks and sugar together until creamy - about 5 minutes. Bring cream to the boil with the split vanilla pod and pour on to the eggs and sugar and beat until thoroughly amalgamated.

Return mixture to pan, over a very low heat, stirring all the time until it thickens. Pour one third into another bowl and add melted chocolate.

Divide this chocolate mixture between 8 buttered ramekins and top with the remaining custard.

Refrigerate for about 2 hours and then cover each with a good layer of the caster sugar and place under a very hot grill, until caramelised - about 2-3 minutes.

Return them to the fridge and allow to set firm overnight - or at least 2 hours. This tends to be a little runny - all the better! If you want a firmer set then add another egg yolk. Fresh Scottish raspberries, English strawberries or wild blackberries go wonderfully well with these brûlées.

CHOCOLATE CREAM CUPS

Serves 4

175 g/6½ oz double cream

2 tsp instant coffee (optional)

175 g/6½ oz chocolate, dark or milk or white

Called cups because this is how the cream is served, although you can use small bowls or ramekins. This can also be used as a filling or spread for cakes, sandwiches, scones etc.

Bring the cream to the boil and take off the heat. Add the coffee powder (if using). Add the chocolate and allow to melt gently in the hot cream. Cool for 15 minutes, but when still warm beat with an electric whisk until cold.

To serve, fill 4 small coffee cups or *demitasse*.

Serve with almond or hazelnut macaroons. (See page 123)

JUNKET

Serves 4

55 g/2 oz chocolate

2 tbsp cold water

30 g/1 oz sugar

1/2 tsp vanilla essence

450 ml/3/4 pint milk

1 tablet rennet

A blast from the past.

Melt together chocolate and water. Add sugar, vanilla and milk. Keep warm.

Dissolve rennet in 1 teaspoon of cold water and stir into chocolate mixture. Pour into a 575 ml/1 pint dish and leave undisturbed for 2 hours.

Serve with cream.

CHOCOLATE SNUFF BOX

For 6 people

1 1/2 sheets gelatine

500 ml/16 fl oz double cream

1/2 tsp vanilla essence

125 ml/4 fl oz brandy or rum
  (or other alcohol)

225 g/8 oz plain chocolate, grated

THE SAUCE

225 g/8 oz chocolate, chopped

125 ml/4 fl oz whipping cream

125 ml/4 fl oz water

5 tbsp brandy

This is dedicated to a lovely and brave lady, Leine Watson. Her husband Simon gave me the recipe saying that *"my grandmother's cook, Miss Jeannie Robertson (but called Mrs. Robertson as was customary in a household with several servants to show her seniority) had been General Haig's cook before joining my grandmother. Chocolate snuff box was said to be his favourite pudding"*.

This is a quick, simple pudding to make and particularly interesting to look at - the hardest part is grating the chocolate, because it should be done by hand. The processor tends to get too hot and the chocolate goes lumpy.

One square or round cake tin, about 15 cm (6-7 in) in diameter and 15 cm (6 in) high lined with cling film leaving a generous amont hanging over the top, to lift out later. (Or use three rings stocked on top of each other.)

Soak gelatine in warm water until soft. Squeeze dry. Whip the cream to soft peaks. Add the gelatine to the cream and the vanilla and brandy and continue to beat until the cream just begins to hold its shape but is still floppy. Pour two thirds of the cream into the bottom of the cake tin. Keep at least a third back to cover the top.

Fill the centre with grated chocolate to within about 2.5 cm (1 in) around the sides around which the cream should fill to form the sides of the 'box'. Cover with the remaining cream making sure that it covers the grated chocolate around the sides.

Chill for at least 4 hours or overnight if possible. Run a knife dipped in hot water around the insides of the tin and gently lift out the cake with the cling film. It will be completely covered by the cream and look like a box.

Make a hot chocolate sauce with the rest of the chocolate, whipping cream and water. Bring to the boil and add more brandy or vanilla etc. This also goes wonderfully well with a raspberry coulis.

Serves 6-8

THE STEAMED SPONGE

85 g/3 oz butter

55 g/2 oz dark chocolate, broken
into tiny pieces

170 g/6 oz strong white flour and
1 tsp baking powder and
55 g/2 oz cocoa powder,
sifted together

170 g/6 oz caster sugar

2 eggs, lightly beaten

2 tbsp milk

THE FILLING

1 lemon, thoroughly and deeply
pricked all over with a fork or
a skewer

100 g/3½ oz unsalted cold butter,
diced

100 g/3½ oz caster sugar

STEAMED CHOCOLATE SUSSEX POND PUDDING

I adore the combination of chocolate and lemon especially with this pudding. The lemon makes a refreshing contrast to the dense chocolate; when you cut into this one you will see why. It is not for the faint hearted.

To make the steamed sponge: Butter and flour a 1.2 litre/ 2 pint pudding basin. Boil the kettle.

Melt the butter and chocolate together. Sift flour, baking powder and cocoa into a mixing bowl. Stir in the chocolate and butter. Add the sugar. Add the eggs and mix until combined.

Add the milk. If the mixture seems a little thick and dry, add a little more milk. Spoon two thirds of the mixture into the pudding basin teasing some of it up the sides, so you have a well in the middle.

Place the lemon in the middle and dot the diced butter around the sides and on top. Cover with the sugar. Cover with the rest of the pudding mixture. Cover with buttered greaseproof paper and foil and tie with string around the sides of the top. Place into a large lidded saucepan and pour in the boiling water so that it reaches half way up the sides of the basin. Cover and steam gently for about 2 hours. You may need to replenish the water.

When ready, remove bowl from the pan and allow to cool a little before removing paper and inverting it on to a serving plate.

Serve, so that each portion has a section of soft lemon in the centre, with an orange sauce - or just as it is.

Serves 4-6

CHOCOLATE CRÊPES

2 eggs

125 ml/4 fl oz single cream

125 ml/4 fl oz water

2 tbsp caster sugar

pinch salt

55 g/2 oz melted butter

85 g/3 oz plain flour

2 tbsp cocoa powder

THE SAUCE

200 g/7 oz chocolate, chopped

125 ml/4 fl oz espresso coffee
    sweetened with 55 g/2 oz sugar

30 g/1 oz unsalted butter

2 tbsp rum

WHIPPED CREAM

300 ml/10$\frac{1}{2}$ oz whipping cream

1 tbsp tasteless salad oil

1 tbsp icing sugar

1 tsp vanilla extract

CHOCOLATE FETTUCINI

This is an original concept and quite simple to make, also relatively light and effective to eat. The fettucini can be made in advance and then re-heated with care before serving.

To make the crêpes: Combine all ingredients in a food processor and whizz until smooth. Sieve mixture into a bowl or jug and allow to rest for 30 minutes.

Smear an 18 cm-21 cm(7in-8in) frying pan, preferably non-stick, with a thin layer of oil or butter and heat over a medium flame (test with a teaspoon of the mixture - it should sizzle).

Pour 2-3 tablespoons of the mixture into the pan to cover the bottom and swirl the batter until it evenly coats the pan. Immediately pour any excess batter back into the jug. Cook the crêpe for about 20 seconds until dry on the top. Carefully turn over to cook the other side for another 20 seconds or so. (This is where any previous 'tossing the pancake skills' can be useful). Set aside on a plate and keep warm.

Repeat until all the crêpes are cooked, stacking them on the plate.

To make the sauce: Melt all the ingredients together in a bain marie or microwave. Stir until the sauce is smooth.

For the whipped cream: Blend all the ingredients together and whip lightly. (The oil should stop the cream congealing on the fettucini when it is re-heated.)

To assemble: With a very sharp knife, cut each crêpe into a long thin strip about 1 cm/$^3/_8$ in wide. Separate so each strip looks like fettucini pasta.

To serve: Warm a large shallow serving bowl and place chocolate fettucini inside. Gently make a well in the centre and spoon in whipped cream. Toss fettucini with the cream so all the strips are well coated. Serve in individual bowls with warm chocolate sauce.

ICKY STICKY TOFFEE CHOCOLATE PUDDING

Serves 6-8

170 g/6 oz dates, chopped

350 ml/12 fl oz boiling water

1 tsp bicarbonate of soda

55 g/2 oz butter, softened

170 g/6 oz dark brown sugar

2 eggs, lightly beaten

55 g/1 oz dark chocolate, melted

170 g/6 oz flour and
1 tsp baking powder, sifted together

TOFFEE SAUCE
115 g/4 oz butter

55 g/2 oz light muscovado sugar

2 tbsp double cream

2 tbsp brandy (optional)

This is based on the fine old English pudding that is so popular with schoolboys - and grown-up schoolboys - but for chocolate lovers this is just that little bit more special. And so simple to make.

To make the pudding: Pre-heat the oven to 180°C/350°F/gas 4. Grease a 20 cm (8 in) cake tin and line the bottom with greaseproof paper.

Pour the boiling water over chopped dates and stir in the soda. Set aside.

Cream the butter and sugar with an electric whisk. Add the eggs slowly, beating after each addition. Stir in the melted chocolate. Fold in the flour and baking powder followed by the dates and the water. Blend quickly and thoroughly. Pour into the prepared tin and bake for 25-30 minutes or until a skewer inserted in the centre comes out clean.

The finished pudding will freeze well and can be reheated and also portions can be microwaved for a minute.

The toffee sauce is not part of the original recipe but you may want to use it. It does make the whole experience very luxurious.

Place all the ingredients in a saucepan and heat until melted. Bring to the boil and allow to thicken slightly. Serve with the pudding.

STEAMED CHOCOLATE AND PRUNE PUDDINGS

Serves 6

115 g/4 oz prunes, stoned and
roughly chopped

2 tbsp brandy

55 g/1 oz unsalted butter

55 g/1 oz self raising flour

300 ml/½ pint milk

115 g/4 oz dark chocolate, broken
in pieces

2 eggs

55 g/1 oz caster sugar

This is a recipe from food and wine writer, Hugo Arnold.

Soak the prunes in the brandy for at least 20 minutes. (You can speed up this process by heating gently in a microwave and leave to stand for 5 minutes.)

Preheat the oven to 200°C /400°F/gas 6. Boil the kettle for a bain marie. Butter 6 dariole moulds or ramekins.

Melt the butter over a medium heat and stir in the flour until you have a smooth paste. Cook out the flour for 1 minute. Remove from the heat and set aside.

Heat the milk gently and add the chopped chocolate. Stir until melted and smooth. Pour this into the flour mixture and stir until smooth. It will become quite thick. Add the prunes and any remaining brandy.

Whisk the eggs and sugar together until pale and thick enough to leave a trail. Fold this into the chocolate mixture. Divide between the moulds and place in a roasting tin. Fill with boiling water and bake in the centre of the oven for 25-30 minutes until set. Turn out of the moulds and place on individual plates. Serve with plenty of lightly whipped cream.

Icky Sticky Toffee Chocolate Pudding

PUDDING AND SPICE

A fine 'fleshy', gooey steamed chocolate pudding, with an after-kick of chilli - contrasting with soft ginger and milk chocolate centre.

To make the steamed sponge: Butter a 1.2 litre/2 pint pudding basin. Boil the kettle.

Melt the chocolate and butter together. Remove from the heat. Beat in the eggs, sugar and water until smooth. Fold in the flour, chilli and cocoa.

Spoon two thirds of the mixture into the pudding basin, making sure that some of it is tempted up the sides so you have a well in the centre.

Combine all the filling ingredients and spoon into the well. (The milk chocolate will melt together with the other ingredients whilst cooking and make an almost immoral sauce.)

Cover with the rest of the 'batter'. Cover the basin with one layer of greaseproof paper and one layer of foil and tie firmly around the top of the bowl with string. Place into a large lidded saucepan and pour in the boiling water so that it reaches half way up the sides of the basin. Cover and steam gently for about 2 hours.

Allow to cool slightly (so you don't burn yourself) before inverting on to a serving plate. Serve with whipped cream.

Serves 6

THE STEAMED SPONGE

115 g/4 oz plain chocolate, chopped

55 g/2 oz unsalted butter

2 eggs, lightly beaten

175 g/6 oz caster sugar

3 tbsp water

225 g/8 oz plain flour and
1 tsp chilli powder and
30 g/1 oz cocoa powder,
  sifted together

THE FILLING

85 g/3 oz milk chocolate, chopped
  into pieces the size of $\frac{1}{2}$ a walnut

150 g/5$\frac{1}{2}$ oz unsalted butter

55 g/2 oz finely chopped stem ginger

3 tbsp rum

ZABAGLIONE

This is a light airy pudding for the time when you must have some chocolate but really you have had enough to eat. Zabaglione is Italian for sabayon or custard.

This is traditionally served in glasses but you could also use small tea or coffee cups or even ramekins.

Whisk sugar and eggs with an electric whisk over a bain marie, until light and fluffy, about 5 -7 minutes.

Remove from heat and continue to whisk until cold, when it should hold its own shape, another 5 minutes. Gradually whisk in the sifted cocoa powder and lemon juice.

Serve in glasses with sponge fingers (*Langue de Chat*) or amaretti biscuits.

Serves 6

2 tbsp caster sugar

3 free range eggs

2 tbsp cocoa powder, sifted

1 tsp lemon juice

CHOCOLATE PUDDLE PUDDING

Serves 6

100 g/3 ½ oz soft butter

100 g/3 ½ oz caster sugar

3 large eggs, lightly beaten

125 g/4 ½ oz self-raising flour and
2 tsp heaped, cocoa and
pinch salt, sifted together

100 ml/3 ½ fl oz milk

THE SAUCE

100 g/3 ½ oz soft dark brown sugar,
like muscovado

4 heaped tbsp Green & Black's
drinking chocolate OR
4 tbsp cocoa powder

3 tbsp dark rum or whisky, optional

300 ml/½ pint boiling water

A recipe from Lindsey Bareham, written at the time of London's first International Festival of Chocolate. She says "you don't have to be a chocolate freak to love the intriguingly named chocolate puddle pudding. Its exact origin is vague although it has been around for years. But whoever invented it is a genius. It reminds me of a lemon surprise pudding - both are light sponges which generate their own sauces - and the recipe is foolproof (I like it!). It is also one of those puddings that you can more or less prepare in advance, then pop in the oven before you tuck into the main course. Its divine cooking smell will gradually pervade the room".

Preheat the oven to 180°C/350°F/gas 4. Butter a 575 ml/1 pint soufflé dish.

Cream together the butter and sugar until light and fluffy. Beat in the eggs. Fold in the flour, cocoa and salt and finally the milk. Spoon the mixture into the buttered dish.

Cover it with the ingredients for the sauce in the order given, finishing with the boiling water.

Bake in the centre of the oven for about 40 minutes. The pudding swells through the sauce to make a juicy sponge covered with a thin crust. Bubbling around the edges is the puddle, or surprise - a luscious chocolate sauce.

If you use a food processor you can whizz all the ingredients together.

Serves 6

5 egg whites

250 g/8½ oz caster sugar

250 g/ 8½ oz butter

250 g/ 8½ oz dark chocolate,
   melted

8 egg yolks

30 g/1 oz plain flour and
100 g/3½ oz ground almonds,
   sifted together

SWISS SACHA TARTE

There is a fine restaurant with rooms on the east coast of England not a million miles south of York on Humberside. Not the most exciting place in the world you might think and as you are driving across the flatland of the area the thought crosses your mind that you must be lost. But lo! Around the corner looms this oasis of gastronomic bliss and welcome, at odds with its surroundings. That's Winteringham Fields, where Annie and Germaine Schwab are among the most captivating hosts you could wish for. Annie has recently been awarded an MBE for her monumental services to the industry. Go and try the place for yourself. In the meantime here is one of their chocolate offerings.

Butter and line a 23 cm (9 in) loose bottomed cake tin. Preheat the oven to 150°C/ 300°F/ gas 2.

   Whisk the egg whites with half of the sugar and set aside. In a separate bowl over a bain marie, whisk the butter with the rest of the sugar - about 5 minutes. Mix in the melted chocolate, and blend well. Add the egg yolks, one at a time and milk until smooth. Gently fold in the flour and almonds.

   Gently fold in the egg whites until completely blended.

   Pour into the prepared tin and bake for 1½ - 1¾ hours. Serve warm with a scoop of vanilla ice cream.

Serves 6

WHITE CHOCOLATE ICE CREAM
675 ml/1 pint milk

300 ml/½ pint whipping cream

5 tbsp liquid glucose

200 g/7 oz caster sugar

4 egg yolks, lightly beaten

225 g/8 oz white chocolate, broken
   into small pieces

HOT AND COLD DARK AND WHITE CHOCOLATE PLATE - LIZ McGRATH

From the skilled hand of Jean-Christophe Novelli, that smoulderingly handsome Frenchman who owns the Novelli restaurants in London and also Novelli at the Cellars in Cape Town, South Africa. Jean-Christophe dedicated this dish to Liz McGrath who owns The Hohenort Cellars on the edge of the vineyards at Peltenburg in Cape Town.

   The ice cream must be made 24 hours in advance of serving. All the other components of this Plate can be made in advance, except the Hot Chocolates which must be served hot.

To make the white chocolate ice cream: Bring the milk, cream and glucose to the boil. Remove from the heat and immediately add the sugar, yolks and white chocolate. Stir gently until the sugar is dissolved and the chocolate is melted. Churn in an ice cream maker. Alternatively, allow to cool completely, place in a covered plastic container, and

Makes 24

TUILE MIX

125 g/4 oz unsalted butter, softened

125 g/4 oz icing sugar, sifted

4 egg whites

125 g/4 oz plain flour, sifted

DARK CHOCOLATE SAUCE

150 ml/1/4 pint water

3 tbsp cocoa powder

3 1/2 tbsp double cream

100 g/3 1/2 dark chocolate, broken into pieces

WHITE CHOCOLATE SAUCE

250 ml/8 fl oz milk

3 egg yolks

30 g/1 oz caster sugar

30 g/1 oz white chocolate, melted

THE HOT CHOCOLATES

150 g/5 1/2 oz dark chocolate, broken into small pieces

150 g/5 1/2 oz unsalted butter

4 eggs

4 egg yolks

85 g/3 oz caster sugar

1 tbsp plain flour, sifted

freeze for two hours. As the mixture begins to freeze, whisk with an electric whisk to incorporate ice crystals. Continue to freeze until solid, at least eight hours or overnight.

To make the tuiles: Preheat oven to 180°C/350°F/gas 4. Line a baking sheet with greaseproof or silicone paper.

Cream together the butter and icing sugar with an electric whisk until it becomes white and quite stiff. Gradually beat in the egg whites. As soon as the whites are incorporated, fold in the flour, taking care not to over mix. Spread about one teaspoonful of mix on to the paper and flatten into a thin round.

Repeat with as many as you can fit on to a baking sheet and bake 3 to 4 minutes until just beginning to go golden at the edges.

While the tuiles are still warm, mould them around a rolling pin to form a boat shape. Allow to cool completely. They should hold their shape. Store until needed in an airtight tin.

To make the dark chocolate sauce: Use a little of the water to make the cocoa powder into a paste. Bring the cream and the rest of the water to a boil. Reduce heat to low and add the cocoa and chocolate. Simmer and stir until the chocolate is melted and sauce is smooth. Strain and allow to cool. Keep covered until needed.

To make the white chocolate sauce: Bring the milk to the boil. Remove from heat. Whisk the yolks and sugar until light and fluffy about 5 minutes. Add the scalded milk, and cook over a bain marie until slightly thickened. Add the melted chocolate and stir to combine thoroughly. Keep covered until needed.

To make the hot chocolates: Preheat the oven to 180°C/350°F/gas 4. Butter six dariole moulds. Melt the chocolate and butter together. Beat together the eggs, yolks and sugar.

Whisk the egg mixture into the chocolate until incorporated. Fold in the flour and divide evenly among the moulds. Place on a baking sheet and bake for 8 minutes.

Serve immediately as follows:

To serve: Turn out the Hot Chocolates on to a 28 cm (11 in) plate. Spoon or drizzle the white chocolate sauce around it. Place a scoop of the White Chocolate Ice Cream opposite. Spoon or drizzle the dark chocolate sauce around this and decorate with a tuile biscuit.

MICHEL TRAMA'S 'TRUFFLE HUNT' CHOCOLATE PLATE

Serves 6-8

CHOCOLATE SORBET

425 ml/³/₄ pint sugar syrup
   (made with 350 g/12 oz caster
   sugar and 350 ml/12 fl oz water)

300 ml/¹/₂ pint water

100 g/3¹/₂ oz cocoa, sifted

griottes to decorate

THE PASTRY

85 g/3 oz butter, softened

25 g/³/₄ oz caster sugar

25 g/³/₄ oz icing sugar

1 tbsp ground almonds

pinch salt

few drops vanilla essence

1 egg, lightly beaten

175 g/6 oz plain flour, sifted

CHOCOLATE FILLING

2 tbsp water

25 g/³/₄ oz cornflour

250 ml/8 fl oz single cream

225 g/8 oz bitter chocolate

85 g/3 oz butter

Gold leaf to decorate (optional)

WHITE AND DARK
CHOCOLATE SHELLS

100 g/3¹/₂ oz white chocolate,
   melted and preferably tempered

Michel Trama owns and runs l'Aubergade, a 2 star Michelin restaurant in the heart of the Dordogne truffle country, at Puymirol. Its external wall is unremarkable but inside is a baronial hall, all timber and plaster some 500 years old. His chocolate puds are also remarkable.

I have called this Truffle Hunt because this is what Michel Trama served to a party of intrepid truffle hunters (as in the fungi variety), of which I was one, in the truffle hunting season of 1998. One of my fellow truffle hunters described it as "an out of body experience!"

Of course, you can take some of the components and serve as one dish rather than make them all in one go - which is a lengthy process.

To make the chocolate sorbet: Bring the sugar syrup and water to the boil and stir in the sifted cocoa. Adjust the density of the sorbet to 22% of the refractometer (this is a specialist sugar syrup gauge, which is very useful but not essential).

Strain through a fine sieve and churn in an ice cream maker. Alternatively, allow mixture to go completely cool and place in a plastic container and put in the freezer. Check it after 2 hours and break up any ice crystals that have formed. Continue to freeze until completely set. Set aside the griottes. (See assembly below)

To make the pastry for the mini tarts: Preheat the oven to 180°C/350°F/gas 4. With an electric whisk cream together the butter, caster sugar, icing sugar, ground almonds, salt and vanilla. Mix in the egg followed by the flour. Whisk on medium speed until just incorporated. Bring together into a ball, wrap in cling film and leave to rest in the fridge for 30 minutes.

You will need 12-14 (2¹/₂ cm/1 in) round or oval fluted tartlet tins. Roll out the pastry and line the tartlet cases. Place on a baking sheet and bake blind for 15 to 20 minutes, until pale golden.

To make the chocolate filling: Dissolve the cornflour in the water and add to the single cream.

Bring to the boil, take off the heat and then add the chocolate, broken into pieces.

Mix well and when thoroughly melted add the butter. Spoon the mixture into the tartlet cases and leave to cool.

If using, decorate with a tiny gold leaf.

This is a cunning way of making tiny chocolate 'shells': Take an ice cube and wrap it in cling film. Twist the ends so that you have something to hold on to when you dip the ice cube into the chocolate. The chocolate will cling to the outside of the film as it shrinks on touching the freezing surface.

Sprinkle on the grated chocolate or coffee beans quickly before the chocolate sets.

100 g/3½ oz dark chocolate,
  melted and preferably tempered

30 g/1 oz white chocolate, grated
  or coffee beans, ground

30 g/1 oz dark chocolate, grated, or
  coffee beans, ground

CHOCOLATE CREAM
WITH ANGELICA FILLING
(for the chocolate shells)
100 ml/3½ fl oz milk

2 egg yolks

55 g/2 oz caster sugar

1 tbsp cocoa

30 g/1 oz confit of angelica
  (crystallised), diced

CHOCOLATE TEARS
115 g/4 oz dark chocolate, melted
  and preferably tempered

CHOCOLATE SUPREME FILLING
45 g/1½ oz dark chocolate

85 g/3 oz butter

45 g/1½ oz sifted cocoa

2 egg yolks

55 g/2 oz caster sugar

55 ml/2 fl oz strong coffee
  (can be made with granules)

125 ml/4 fl oz double cream,
  lightly whipped to soft peaks

cherries to decorate

To make the chocolate cream with angelica filling: Bring the milk slowly to the boil. In a bowl, whisk the egg yolks and sugar until pale and fluffy, about 5 minutes. Add the cocoa and then pour on the scalded milk. Place the bowl in a bain marie or over a saucepan of simmering water. Stir until the mixture thickens slightly. Remove and allow to cool.

When cool stir in the angelica. To serve, spoon in the chocolate shells.

Make the tears: By using strips of acetate film 4 cm x 20 cm (1½ in x 8 in) which you can get from artist shops and stationers.

Brush two layers of tempered/melted chocolate on to the acetate strips and bring the two short ends together with the chocolate inside, forming a tear shape.

Seal the ends with a paper clip and allow to set.

To make the chocolate supreme filling: Melt the chocolate, butter and cocoa together in a bowl over a saucepan of simmering water.

In a separate bowl whisk together the egg yolks and sugar until pale and fluffy.

Add the chocolate mixture and the coffee and stir through.

Reserve about 3 tablespoons of the whipped cream for the decoration and gently fold the rest into the chocolate mixture.

When ready to serve Truffle Hunt Plate, gently remove the acetate from the chocolate tears. Lay them sideways on a serving plate and using a piping bag, pipe the chocolate supreme into the tears. Top with a blob of the reserved whipped cream and a griotte.

Arrange two chocolate tartlets, two to three chocolate shells filled with angelica chocolate cream and sorbet. Dust the plate with cocoa.

DEMOULDED CHOCOLATE SOUFFLÉ

Although not a very glamorous title for a glamorous pudding, this was nevertheless inspired by John Burton Race from l'Ortolan just outside Reading, in Berkshire.

Melt the chocolate and fill 4 cubes of an ice-cube tray. Place in the freezer to set. Preheat the oven to 180°C / 350°F / gas 4.

To make the pastry cream: Place the milk and vanilla pod in a saucepan and bring gently to the boil. Split the pod and scrape out the seeds, adding them to the milk.

In a medium sized bowl, whisk the yolks and sugar until thick and pale. Whisk in the flours.

Pour about one third of the boiling milk over the yolk mixture and stir until blended. Return to the saucepan with the rest of the milk and place back on the heat. Bring to the boil, stirring continuously until thickened. Simmer for about 1 minute. Remove from the heat and use as directed. To store, allow to cool and refrigerate. It will become quite thick and set and will need to be whisked or put in a food processor before using.

To make the soufflés: Use the melted butter to brush the insides of 4 dariole moulds, 7.5 cm tall × 5 cm diameter (3 in tall × 2 in diameter). Dust with the grated chocolate, completely covering the insides of the mould and gently tap out any excess. Put the moulds on a tray and refrigerate to set.

In a large mixing bowl place 50 g (about 3 tablespoons) of the pastry cream and whisk until smooth. Beat in the cocoa powder and when smooth add the egg yolk. Set aside. Remove the chocolate cubes from the freezer and tap them out of their moulds.

In another large mixing bowl whisk the whites until they reach medium peak. Add the sugar gradually, continuing to whisk until all the sugar is added and the mixture is stiff and shiny.

Loosen the chocolate pastry cream mixture with a spoonful of whites, then gently but thoroughly fold in the rest. Fill each dariole mould about two-thirds full with the soufflé mixture. Place a frozen chocolate cube in the centre of each and cover with the remaining soufflé mixture. Take care not to over fill the moulds and ensure that no soufflé mixture is overlapping the edge of the moulds or it will stick and prevent the soufflé rising.

Place the soufflés in the oven on the baking tray and bake for about 12 minutes.

Remove from the oven and, using a cloth, quickly release the sides and turn them upside down on individual serving plates. Dust with icing sugar and serve immediately.

Serves 4

115 g/4 oz plain chocolate

THE PASTRY CREAM (CRÈME PÂTISSERIE)

200 ml/7 fl oz milk

1 vanilla pod

2 egg yolks

30 g/1 oz caster sugar

2 tsp cornflour

2 tsp plain flour

SOUFFLÉ MIXTURE

30 g/1 oz unsalted butter, melted

20 g/3/4 oz plain chocolate, grated

1 tbsp cocoa powder

1 large egg yolk

3 large egg whites

55 g/2 oz caster sugar

icing sugar for dusting

Chocolate Brûlée Surprise (page 152)

MARBLED CHOCOLATE AND GRAND MARNIER SOUFFLÉ

Serves 8-10

CHOCOLATE ORANGE TRUFFLES

100 ml/3¹/₂ fl oz orange juice

100 ml/3¹/₂ fl oz whipping cream

300 g/10¹/₂ oz dark chocolate, chopped into small pieces

You can use 'bought' truffles, of course

THE CHOCOLATE SOUFFLÉ

250 ml/8 fl oz milk

1 egg yolk

1 egg

85 g/3 oz caster sugar

55 g/2 oz flour and 20 g/³/₄ oz cocoa powder, sifted together

5 eggs yolks

THE GRAND MARNIER SOUFFLÉ

250 ml/8 fl oz milk

1 egg yolk

1 egg

85 g/3 oz caster sugar

85 g/3 oz flour

5 egg yolks

zest one orange

2 tbsp Grand Marnier

5 egg whites (for both soufflés)

This is a recipe from the delightful Peter Kromberg whose restaurant at London's Inter-Continental Hotel, Le Soufflé has been named after his legendary signature sweet and savoury soufflé dishes. Peter is one of the only chefs who is able to cope with 700 soufflés all served at the same time for a banquet. However this recipe is only for 8-10. Halve the mixture if you want it for only 4-6.

You need to make the chocolate truffles at least six hours in advance - a day is even better. However, if you have some truffles handy you can use them - or you can (but I don't advise it) leave them out altogether if you are short of time.

You can either serve it in individual soufflé dishes (ramekins) or in a large 2 litre/3¹/₂ pint soufflé dish.

For the chocolate orange truffles: Boil the cream with the orange juice and pour onto the chopped chocolate and mix until smooth.

Leave to set (about 2 hours in a cool place). Cover a tray (or similar) with parchment and using a pastry bag with a large nozzle pipe into batons. Set in the fridge. Cut into 2 cm/³/₄ in pieces and leave in the fridge.

For both the soufflés, the method is the same. Prepare the chocolate first followed by the Grand Marnier adjusting the ingredients accordingly. Prepare the 12 large ramekins or one large soufflé dish by buttering sides with softened butter and 'run out' with sugar.

Boil the milk. Mix the single yolk, whole egg, sugar, flour and cocoa and a little of the milk together. Slowly add the rest of the milk and beat well.

Return to the heat and 'cook out' until the paste thickens. Remove from the heat.

Gradually add the yolks one at a time, whisking as you do this until it forms a smooth thick paste. Leave to rest on one side but keep warm as the egg whites fold in more easily.

Repeat now for the Grand Marnier, adding the Grand Marnier and orange zest after the egg yolks.

In a large bowl whisk the egg whites to soft peaks for both soufflé mixtures - it is a bit of an effort. Now divide the whites between the chocolate and the Grand Marnier batters and fold in carefully.

Place one spoonful of each soufflé mix at a time to layer up the mould/moulds. When full place one truffle in each mixture (or 12 truffles spaced evenly if using the large mould).

If cooking the individual soufflés then cook on a baking sheet in the centre of a preheated oven at 230°C/450°F/gas 8 for approximately 12 minutes. If cooking a single large soufflé then again set on a baking sheet in the centre of the oven at 190°C/375°F/gas 5 for 20-25 minutes. Once cooked, remove from the oven and dust with icing sugar and serve immediately.

Chocolate Snuff Box (page 153)

MEXICAN CHOCOLATE SOUFFLÉS

Serves 6

225 g/8 oz dark chocolate, broken into tiny pieces

85 g/3 oz unsalted butter

1½ tsp instant espresso powder (or rich coffee granules)

pinch salt

6 egg yolks

85 g/3 oz caster sugar

1 tsp vanilla extract

1 tsp ground cinnamon

2 egg whites

TO SERVE

125 ml/4 fl oz whipping cream, whipped

fresh raspberries and/or mint sprigs (optional)

"This is one of America's most popular desserts" says a great friend of mine, Carole Bloom (we met over the Net through our mutual love for chocolate). Carole is a European-trained pastry chef and an authority on chocolate in America. She has also written a chocolate book, which is mentioned in the Bibliography. Carole goes on to describe these little cakes as "*a chocolate soufflé cake with a rich molten center. Cinnamon, espresso and vanilla give the cakes a Mexican accent*". Carole uses tartlet tins but I have tried ramekins with equal success.

Butter six, 11 cm (4½ in) tartlet tins (or ramekins) with 2 cm (¾ in) sides and removable bottoms. Preheat the oven to 200°C/400°F/gas 6.

Melt the chocolate and butter in a heavy medium saucepan over a low heat. Stir until melted and smooth. Remove from the heat. Blend in the espresso powder or coffee granules and salt. Allow mixture to cool, stirring occasionally.

Using an electric whisk, beat the yolks and all but 1 tablespoon of the sugar, with the vanilla and cinnamon in a large bowl until thick and pale - about 5 minutes. Fold in a quarter of the egg mixture into the chocolate. Fold the chocolate mixture into the remaining egg mixture.

In a separate large bowl whisk the whites until soft peaks form. Add the remaining 1 tablespoon of sugar and continue to whisk until firm. Fold into the chocolate mixture.

Divide the batter among the prepared tins, cover and place in the fridge for at least 1 hour and up to 4 hours.

Bake the soufflés in the middle of the oven for about 11 minutes until the edges are set and the centres are soft. Cool on a wire rack for 2 minutes. Run a knife around the sides to loosen the cakes then remove the sides and bottoms.

Place soufflés on individual serving plates and top each cake with a dollop of the whipped cream.

Garnish with raspberries and mint. Serve warm.

HOT CHOCOLATE SOUFFLÉ

Serves 8

115 g/4 oz sugar (plus 2 tbsp)

1 tbsp flour

4 tbsp whipping cream

4 eggs, separated

170 g/6 oz dark chocolate, melted

1/2 tsp pure vanilla essence

pinch salt (optional)

pinch cream tartar

2 tsp icing sugar, to dust

This is a simple, almost fool-proof, soufflé which generally has a more than agreeable effect on the guests. You can make it in advance and freeze it. If you do this you must give it at least another 10-15 minutes. A treat is to add 8 crushed cardamom seeds to the basic roux.

Butter a 1 1/2 litre/2 1/2 pint ceramic soufflé dish and 'run out' with the extra 2 tablespoons of the sugar. Preheat oven to 190°C/375°F/gas 5.

Sift the sugar and flour into a medium heavy saucepan (off the heat).

Add the whipping cream, a spoonful at a time, mixing well after each addition and mix well again. Try to get rid of any lumps so you get a smooth paste. Cook over low to medium heat until sugar melts. Add the egg yolks one at a time to the sugar/flour, stirring continuously until thoroughly mixed. Remove saucepan from heat and stir in the melted chocolate, vanilla and salt. Set aside to cool.

In a large bowl, beat the egg whites with the cream of tartar to form soft peaks not too stiff or it won't incorporate into the mixture.

Gently and thoroughly fold in the melted and cooled chocolate into the egg whites - a little at a time. Spoon the soufflé mixture into the prepared dish. Put the dish on to a baking tray - it conducts the heat more evenly - and bake on the middle shelf for 30-35 minutes until well risen. Dust with icing sugar and serve immediately.

You can serve with a raspberry sauce made from 225 g/8 oz fresh or frozen raspberries and 115 g/4 oz sugar melted together and cooked gently until it forms a thick purée. You can use it as it is or pass through a sieve. Or try a coffee sauce.

Warm Cakes

Glenn Eastman's Warm Chocolate Cakes
(page 174)

CHOCOLATE BISCUIT - "RUNNING WITH THE AROMAS OF COCOA"

Serves 12

THE GANACHE

250 g/8¹/₂ oz chocolate
(Michel Bras uses Valrhona
Guanaja - 70% cocoa)

100 g/3¹/₂ oz unsalted butter

400 ml/³/₄ pint double cream

125 ml/4 fl oz water

100 g/3¹/₂ oz clarified butter
to grease the hoops

THE SPONGE (but not sponge in
the conventional sense)

225 g/8 oz bitter chocolate

100 g/3¹/₂ oz butter

4 medium eggs, separated

75 g/2¹/₂ oz ground almonds and
85 g/3 oz ground rice,
sifted together

175 g/6¹/₂ oz caster sugar

A recipe created by famous French chef, Michel Bras, which took 18 months for him to develop properly. It's a dish to practise but as I have said so many times before, don't worry if it doesn't turn out with precision the first time, it will still taste absolutely wonderful. This recipe comes courtesy of Michael Raffael from a series of articles he wrote so evocatively in *Chef Magazine*, featuring the cooking of the brightest culinary lights of France.

METHOD - DAY ONE

Make the ganache: Melt the chocolate and butter together. Heat the cream and water to simmering point and pour on to the chocolate and butter. Beat together until throughly mixed.

Lay a sheet of silicone paper or film in a 12 cm x 20 cm (5 in x 8 in) rectangular dish.

Pour in the ganache. It should reach the height of about 3.5 cm (1¹/₄ in). Chill overnight in the freezer.

DAY TWO

Brush twelve, 5 cm wide x 4 cm high (2 in x 1¹/₂ in) hoops with clarified butter and line them with silicone paper which comes about 2.5 cm (1 in) above the rim. Put the hoops on a baking sheet.

Preheat the oven to 190°C/375°F/gas 5.

Cut out 12 cylinders of ganache with a 5 cm (2 in) scone cutter and place in fridge or freezer till needed.

To make the sponge: Melt together the chocolate and butter. Lightly mix together the egg yolks and fold into the chocolate and butter. Rain in the sifted almonds and ground rice and mix well.

Whisk the egg whites to medium peak, add sugar a little at a time then whisk until shiny and then fold into the chocolate.

Fill a piping bag (plain tube) with the chocolate mixture and pipe enough of the mixture to come half way up the silicone paper. Using a skewer, spike the centre of the ganache cylinders and place them dead centre (essential) in the hoops.

Pipe the rest of the mixture into the hoops. It must cover the cylinder, but leave enough room to rise to the top of the silicone paper like a soufflé. Bake for 20 minutes.

To serve: transfer the hoops directly to the serving plates and lift off the hoop and peel off the paper. Michel Bras often changes the accompanying sauce. One of his favourites is an infusion of wild mint, into a traditional Crème Anglaise - without the vanilla pod. (See recipes for sauces page 111.)

HOT CHOCOLATE FONDANT

Serves 12 or 6

ITALIAN MERINGUE

350 g/12 oz (175 g/6 oz)
   caster sugar

2 tsp (1 tsp) liquid glucose

100 ml/3½ fl oz water

6 (3) egg whites, stiffly beaten

FONDANT

350 g/12 oz (175 g/6 oz) dark
   chocolate, broken into tiny pieces,
   plus extra for dusting

150 g/5½ oz (85 g/3 oz) unsalted
   butter, plus 25 g/1 oz for greasing

6 (3) egg yolks, lightly beaten

30 g/1 oz (1 tbsp) flour

30 g/1 oz (1 tbsp) cocoa powder

1 tbsp (1 tsp) instant coffee
   granules (optional)

These are wonderful chocolate soufflé look-alikes with a difference. I am grateful to Roz Denny, food writer, television personality and Gordon Ramsay's recipe 'mum'. If you are lucky enough to eat at Gordon Ramsay's restaurant in Royal Hospital Road, Chelsea, you might find this fondant on the menu. The second time I tried this recipe I slightly overcooked the syrup for the meringue and, rather than the disastrous consequences I anticipated, it provided flecks of caramelised sugar which contrasted well with the chocolate and gave an interesting texture to the finished fondant.

You can cook half and freeze half (or whatever you wish) which is the beauty of this recipe. I have given the amounts for 6 in case this suits you better.

To make the Italian meringue: Make a caramel syrup with the sugar, glucose and water. Melt all three together over a low heat and then bring to the boil until it begins to turn golden brown. As soon as the sugar syrup begins to caramelise take it off the heat and trickle it on to the egg whites, whisking all the time. Set aside. The meringue will hold well.

To make the fondants: Grease 12 dariole moulds with butter and dust with cocoa powder or grated chocolate. Chill.

If you are preparing ahead you can freeze them after the next stage - or cook half and freeze half. To bake preheat oven to 190°C/375°F/gas 5.

Melt the chocolate and butter together slowly in a bowl over barely simmering water.

Remove from the heat and gradually add the egg yolks.

Sift together flour and cocoa (and coffee if using) and fold into chocolate mixture. Fold in the Italian meringue. Spoon the mixture into the moulds, tapping the bases to ensure that there are no gaps.

Bake for 15 minutes or 20 minutes if frozen. (This depends on the variety of moulds you use and the type of oven).

Shake the fondants out of the moulds on to plates and serve with a chocolate sauce (see page 110) or ice cream (vanilla, cardamom, blackcurrant for example).

GLENN EASTMAN'S WARM CHOCOLATE CAKES

Glenn Eastman is the Executive Chef at the Four Seasons in Mexico City and is a man committed to quality and flavours. When I ate there worms, ants eggs and grasshopper were the starters followed by local fish Pompano and Red Snapper Veracruz style (spicy) followed by a delicate portion of Warm Chocolate Cake and some vanilla ice cream. Sheer, unadulterated bliss. Glenn gave me the recipe which is simplicity itself. Don't be tempted to overbake. The recipe says 12 minutes and it means 12 minutes and not a minute more… When you cut into the cake the centre should be warm and liquid silk.

Serves 8

200 g/7 oz dark chocolate, broken into tiny pieces

200 g/7 oz unsalted butter

200 g/7 oz icing sugar, sieved

4 eggs

4 egg yolks

55 g/2 oz plain flour

55 g/2 oz cocoa powder

Butter 8 ramekins. Preheat the oven to 200°C/400°F/gas 6.

Place the chocolate and butter in a bain marie and melt together, stirring occasionally.

Add the icing sugar and whisk until blended. Add the eggs and yolks and continue to whisk until blended. Sift together the flour and the cocoa powder and fold into the chocolate mixture. Spoon into the ramekins and bake for 12 minutes.

Allow to cool on a wire rack for 2 minutes, then loosen the edges with a thin knife and turn them out on to individual serving plates and serve with ice cream or a fruit sauce - or just alone.

SHAUN HILL'S WARM CHOCOLATE CAKE WITH COMPOTE

THE CAKE

225 g/8 oz dark chocolate

100 g/3 ½ oz unsalted butter

4 eggs, separated

225 g/8 oz icing sugar

few drops vanilla essence

2 tbsp cornflour

THE COMPOTE

300 ml/½ pint water

100 g/3 ½ oz sugar

few drops lemon juice

225 cherries or apricots, dried
  (If using fresh fruit, reduce the
  water by a half)

Shaun Hill owns and cooks at the Merchant House in Ludlow. He is one of the best, most imaginative cooks in the country… and one of the funniest with a wry sense of intellectual humour - the sort which is prerequisite to writing a thesis on Greek tragedy - another of his fortes! Shaun says of this recipe *"Cakes made with little or no flour suffer if overcooked. Underdone, this will sag a touch in the middle in the same way as many otherwise splendid people. It will still be soft and chocolatey rather than raw, however."*

To make the cake: Preheat the oven to 180°C/350°F/gas 4. Line a 17.5 cm (7 in) cake tin with baking parchment.

Melt the chocolate and the butter together. Whisk whites until stiff.

Whisk yolks, icing sugar and vanilla together. Fold in the cornflour and continue to whisk for a few seconds as the mixture creams and whitens. Add butter and chocolate, and mix thoroughly. Fold in the egg whites, a third at a time.

Pour the batter into the cake tin and bake for 40 - 45 minutes. Use the knife test.

To make the compote: Place all the ingredients in a saucepan and boil together. Simmer until tender. If using dried fruit then purée before using.

Serve with slices of the warm chocolate cake.

Ices

Guy tucking into a pot of Chocolate Ice Cream (page 179)

CHOCOLATE AND CARAMEL ALASKA

Serves 8-10

CARAMEL ICE CREAM

100 g/3¹/₂ oz caster sugar and

30 g/1 oz butter and

3 tbsp hot water, for the caramel

575 ml/1 pint full cream milk

5 egg yolks

55 g/2 oz caster sugar

CHOCOLATE ICE CREAM

300 ml/¹/₂ pint full cream milk

75 ml/2¹/₂ fl oz whipping or
   double cream

85 g/3 oz dark chocolate, chopped

3 tbsp cocoa powder

3 eggs

85 g/3 oz caster sugar

CHOCOLATE SPONGE

9 eggs, separated

255 g/8 oz caster sugar

75 g/2¹/₂ oz cocoa powder

BLACK CHERRY SAUCE

1 x 400 g tin black cherries

1 tbsp cornflour

2 tbsp kirsch

MERINGUE

6 egg whites

225 g/8 oz caster sugar

Black and white magic - well, not quite black! This is a chocolatey version of the traditional Baked Alaska and is made with a flourless chocolate sponge, which is wrapped around a very intense bitter chocolate ice cream and a bittersweet caramel ice cream, sandwiched together and enveloped in French meringue. This insulates the ice creams to keep them frozen as the meringue cooks and caramelises in its short life in the oven. A yummy optional addition is black cherries and kirsch.

However, this is an ambitious project and should be made when you are guaranteed to have 8-10 guests around to eat it. Having said that, it looks and tastes spectacular and can be made well in advance and finished off at the last minute. Begin two days in advance.

First, make the ice creams. Line two, 1 kilo/2 lb loaf tins with cling film.

For the caramel ice cream: Combine the sugar and butter in a saucepan and melt over a low heat until well caramelised. When a nice brown colour, carefully pour in the hot water. It will splutter and spit. Stir to amalgamate.

Bring the milk to the boil. Add the caramel and mix thoroughly.

Whisk the egg yolks and sugar together until pale and add to the pan with the milk and caramel mixture.

Cook over a low heat until thickened slightly. Do not boil.

Strain, leave to cool, pour into one of the lined loaf tins (it should come about half way up the side) and freeze overnight or until firm.

To make the chocolate ice cream: Place the milk, cream, chocolate, and cocoa powder in a saucepan and bring to the boil. Stir to combine thoroughly and remove from the heat. Meanwhile whisk the whole eggs and sugar together until pale and creamy, about 5 minutes. Add the eggs and sugar to the chocolate mixture and cook gently over a low heat until thickened, like a custard. Do not let boil.

Strain and leave to cool, pour into the other lined loaf tin and freeze overnight or until firm.

To make the sponge: Line a 30 cm x 25 cm (12 in x 10 in) roasting tin with lightly greased baking parchment or greaseproof paper. Preheat the oven to 200°C/400°F/gas 6.

Whisk together the yolks and 200 g/7 oz of the sugar until pale and creamy. Whisk the whites to medium peaks then gradually add the remaining sugar. Continue to whisk until stiff.

Loosen the egg and sugar mixture with one quarter of the whites, sift in the cocoa powder then gently fold in the rest of the whites until they and the cocoa powder are well incorporated. Spread on to the greaseproof paper and bake for 15-20 minutes until well risen and springy. Allow to cool.

To make the cherry sauce: Drain and pit the cherries. Chop into quarters. Place the juice in a saucepan, reserving about 1 tablespoon of the liquid in a small bowl. Mix the cornflour into the reserved juice. Heat the juice and add the slaked cornflour mixture. Boil gently until thickened. Add the chopped cherries and the kirsch, remove from the heat, cool and refrigerate until needed.

To assemble the Alaska: Dip the loaf tins of ice creams into hot water to loosen. Remove and peel off the cling film. Lay the sponge with the shortest side towards you and spread some of the cherry sauce over a strip in the middle; about one third of the sponge. Lay the caramel ice cream lengthways across the middle. Spread more of the sauce on top. Lay the chocolate ice cream on the caramel and cherry layer and spread with a little more sauce. Now trim the sides of the sponge even with the ends of the ice creams. (You should have about 3-4 cm/1½ in on either side.) Set aside. Now fold up the front and back of the sponge to cover the sides of the ice creams. Use the cut-off edges of the sponge to lay on top and cover the exposed layer of ice cream. This eventually forms the base.

Lay a sheet of greaseproof paper on a baking sheet and turn the Alaska upside down on to it. You should have a rounded top. Now place in the freezer for at least several hours or overnight. (It must be well frozen to withstand the heat of the oven.)

When ready to serve: Preheat the oven to 230°C/450°F/gas 8. Whisk the egg whites to medium peak. Gradually whisk in the sugar, a little at a time, until the mixture is stiff and shiny.

Take the Alaska out of the freezer and cover with the meringue. Bake in the hot oven for 6-8 minutes until the meringue turns golden brown.

Remove and transfer to a rectangular serving plate and serve immediately.

Note: you could substitute good quality bought ice creams. Allow them to soften sufficiently to spread in the loaf tins and refreeze. This way you could vary the flavours.

CHOCOLATE ICE CREAM

I adore ice cream - the home-made sort, that is. It is a real weakness and I have made 'tons' of the stuff. This is the best and easiest chocolate ice cream that I have used. It freezes equally well with or without a machine.

Bring milk, cream, chocolate and cocoa powder to the boil. Whisk eggs and sugar together till pale and creamy, about 5 minutes. Amalgamate both together and cook out on top of stove over low heat until custard consistency (80°C). Strain, cool and freeze.

Serves 6

575 ml/1 pint full cream milk

150 ml/¼ pint whipping cream

140 g/5 oz dark chocolate, at least 70%

85 g/3 oz cocoa powder

5 whole eggs

170 g/6 oz caster sugar

VANILLA ICE CREAM

Serves 6

575 ml/1 pint milk

1 split vanilla pod, scrape out seeds

5 egg yolks

115-140 g/4-5 oz caster sugar (or more depending upon your sweet tooth)

300 ml/½ pint whipping cream or yoghurt

Here's another of my favourites and the combination of chocolate pudding and vanilla ice cream was definitely made in heaven.

Bring milk and vanilla pod and seeds to boil. Leave to infuse for 10 minutes. Whisk egg yolks and sugar until white and fluffy. Strain the milk and bring back to boil. Pour on yolks whisking at the same time. Return to clean pan and over a very low heat, cook until mixture thickens and coats the back of a spoon. Strain, cool and add whipping cream or yoghurt and freeze.

Lots of recipes specify more egg yolks (up to 12) and sugar (up to 350 g/12 oz) and 2 or more vanilla pods. The more fat you use (i.e. cream, eggs) the better it will keep. If you use yoghurt then you have to eat it quite quickly as the water content turns the ice cream very hard because the water crystals freeze like ice. However being moderately conscious of calories I use the one above. Remember the unfrozen custard will always taste stronger than the finished ice because flavour depreciates with freezing.

HERE ARE SOME ALTERNATIVES YOU CAN MAKE TO THIS BASIC VANILLA ICE CREAM:

ANGELICA: Angelica and vanilla work wonderfully well together. Don't use the leaves of the plant (I'm no fan of the candied stuff but you could try). Use the stems. At the beginning of the season in April/May they are at their youngest and tenderest but you can use them all season until September. When the stems are old they are stringy but if you treat them like celery and snap them the string peels back. Chop finely, about a good 2 tablespoons. Add the milk at boiling stage and infuse with the vanilla. After you have strained the custard tip the angelica back and freeze together. You can happily omit the vanilla and go for neat angelica.

LAVENDER: Omit vanilla and infuse 4-6 heads lavender flowers according to taste.

LAVENDER and **HONEY:** Omit vanilla and infuse 4-6 heads etc. and replace sugar with honey.

ROSE PETALS: Omit vanilla and use generous fistful, depending upon strength of perfume.

PISTACHIO: Omit vanilla. Add at least 2 dessertspoonfuls pistachio paste (not liquid green flavouring as, however natural, it always tastes like marzipan). You can either buy pistachio paste (difficult) or pulverise 85 g/3 oz nuts.

CARDAMOM: Omit vanilla and use the seeds of 10 cardamom pods.

FLAMED CHOCOLATE BOMBE LUCIFER

This flaming ice cream creates a spectacular effect and it is relatively easy to make; it is great instead of Christmas pudding. From the delightful Ernst Bachmann (see Directory).

Serves 8-10

8 egg yolks

200 g/7 oz caster sugar

575 ml/1 pint full cream milk

1 vanilla pod

pinch salt

225 g/8 oz dark chocolate, grated

55 g/2 oz cocoa powder

575 ml/1 pint double cream

55 g/2 oz finely chopped kumquats
  OR 150 g/5$^1/_2$ oz chopped prunes

150 g/5$^1/_2$ oz dark chocolate
  1 tbsp Grand Marnier and
  brandy mixed

Whisk together the yolks and sugar until pale.

Bring the milk, vanilla pod and salt to the boil. Pour over the yolk and sugar mixture and mix thoroughly. Add half the grated chocolate, the cocoa powder and the cream. Stir until well combined. Strain through a fine sieve, pour in a suitable container and place in the freezer for 1-2 hours or until beginning to freeze but not yet solid. Remove and fold in the reserved grated chocolate and chopped fruit.

Spoon into individual dariole moulds or one large ice cream bombe and place plastic lolly sticks in the middle (wood doesn't work so well though you could also use a chopstick or short wooden spoon). Freeze until solid. Melt and have ready the 150g/5$^1/_2$ oz of dark chocolate. Dip the mould into warm water and pull out the stick (you may need to trickle a few drops of boiling water around the stick to get it out). Now invert the bombe on to a plate - you should still have the centre hole into which you will pour the Grand Marnier and brandy. Place the stick back into this hole while you pour the melted chocolate over the top of the bombe - it should set immediately as it comes into contact with the frozen ice cream. Now remove the stick again and return to the freezer until ready to serve. Heat the Grand Marnier and brandy and pour over the bombe - it should fill the hole that the stick has left - and set alight. The chocolate will melt again and form a lovely Gran Marnier and brandy rich sauce - please don't set your house on fire with this one!

FROZEN MISSISSIPPI MUD PIE

This is a frozen version of the cold tart, which is as close to the authentic American as I can find - with a few personal twists, like using caramel ice cream. You can of course use any ice cream you fancy making - or buying.

Butter a 23 cm (9 in) loose bottomed cake tin.

Mix the biscuits with the melted butter. Fill the cake tin with the biscuits and press over the bottom easing about 4 cm (1½ in) up the sides. Freeze for 3-4 hours.

Transfer the softened ice cream to the biscuit base and freeze while you make the topping.

For the topping: Whisk together the egg yolks and cream until thoroughly blended. Add to the melted chocolate and blend until smooth. Over a very low flame, stir constantly until mixture coats the back of a spoon, about 8-10 minutes. Remove from the heat and allow to cool completely.

When completely cold, whisk the egg whites and fold into the custard.

Pour the chocolate custard over the caramel ice cream and return to the freezer for another 2-3 hours.

To serve: Remove from the tin and serve alone or with Hot Fudge Sauce. (See Sauces)

Serves 6-8

BASE

225 g/8 oz crushed biscuits, such as Duchy Originals organic ginger, orange, or any digestives or ginger nuts

170 g/6 oz unsalted butter, melted

FILLING

1 litre/1¾ pints caramel ice cream, slightly softened (see Ices) - you can use coffee etc or anything you prefer with a variety of added flavours such as liqueurs and alcohols

CHOCOLATE CUSTARD TOPPING

2 eggs, separated

115ml/¼ pint whipping cream

115 g/4 oz plain chocolate, melted

CHOCOLATE SORBET

This is more an ice cream as the cocoa butter makes up for the dairy creams. It is best made in an ice cream machine at home. Not really suitable for home freezing as the mixture turns rock hard, it also melts quickly once you have served it.

Melt water, sugar and glucose together over a gentle heat and then boil for about 2 minutes.

Pour on to broken chocolate. Stir until all melted and then cool and then chill in fridge.

Sorbet is now ready to freeze. It will take 25 minutes to churn or in the freezer occasionally mix until frozen, a few hours.

Serves 4

500 ml/16 fl oz water

150 g/5½ oz caster sugar

30 g/1 oz liquid glucose

150 g/5½ oz chocolate, broken into tiny equal pieces

THREE CHOC MOSAIC WITH BRITISH VANILLA CREAM

Serves 8-10 very generous slices - or 10-12 for less hungry people depending upon garnishes

THE WHITE CHOCOLATE

4 egg yolks

55 g/2 oz sugar

125 ml/4 fl oz single cream

125 ml/4 fl oz double cream

1 vanilla pod

1 tsp instant coffee

85 g/3 oz white chocolate, chopped into tiny equal pieces

250 ml/8 fl oz whipping cream

THE MILK CHOCOLATE

4 egg yolks

55 g/2 oz sugar

125 ml/4 fl oz single cream

125 ml/4 fl oz double cream

1 tsp malt

1 vanilla pod

85 g/3 oz milk chocolate, in pieces

250 ml/8 fl oz whipping cream

THE DARK CHOCOLATE

4 egg yolks

55 g/2 oz sugar

125 ml/4 fl oz single cream

125 ml/4 fl oz double cream

1 tsp instant coffee

1 vanilla pod

85 g/3 oz dark chocolate, in pieces

250 ml/8 fl oz whipping cream

If you ever go to Mexico City you must not miss the Taberna del Leon. My experience of the menu was to enjoy some outstanding local ingredients including calamares and artichokes; black bean soup with cheese and nopal (great cactus); salmon spinach and a mild chile sauce; then three superb chocolate puddings: Chocolate Cake Helena; Chocolate Micaela; and a Three Choc Mosaic with British Vanilla Cream (very patriotic). All of which are included in this book.

Line a rectangular terrine or mould, 30 cm x 7.5 cm x 7.5 cm (12 in x 3 in x 3 in) with cling film. Set the freezer on the lowest setting.

White Chocolate Layer: In a bain marie beat egg yolks and sugar to a ribbon, about 5 minutes. Boil together single and double creams, vanilla and coffee. As soon as it boils take it off the heat. Add the white chocolate, stir until melted. Remove vanilla pod and scrape out seeds. Return seeds to chocolate mixture.

Pour on to egg mixture and transfer to a mixing bowl and beat until it gets cold like a mousse. Takes about 6-8 minutes. Refrigerate until completely cold.

Whip whipping cream to soft peaks and fold into the chocolate mixture. Spoon into the bottom of the rectangular mould and freeze.

Milk Chocolate Layer: Beat egg yolks and sugar to the ribbon stage. Combine single cream with double cream, malt and vanilla. As soon as it boils, take it off the heat and add milk chocolate. Stir until melted.

Remove vanilla pod and scrape out the seeds. Return the seeds to the chocolate mixture.

Pour on to egg mixture and transfer to a mixing bowl and beat until it gets cold like a mousse. Takes about 6-8 minutes. Refrigerate until it gets cold.

Whip the whipping cream to soft peaks and fold into the chocolate mixture. Spoon on top of the white chocolate layer and return to the freezer.

Dark Chocolate Layer: Beat egg yolks and sugar to the ribbon stage. Combine single cream with double cream, coffee and vanilla pod. As soon as it boils, take it off the heat and add dark chocolate. Stir until melted. Remove vanilla pod and scrape out the seeds. Return the seeds to the chocolate mixture.

Pour on to egg mixture and transfer to a mixing bowl and beat until it gets cold like a mousse. Takes about 6-8 minutes. Refrigerate until it gets cold.

Whip the whipping cream to soft peaks and fold into the chocolate mixture. Spoon on top of the milk chocolate layer and freeze all night.

Presentation: Take the mosaic out of the mould, cut slices with a hot knife and put in the centre of the plate. Decorate with mint leaves and/or strawberries and serve with British Vanilla Cream (Crème Anglais or Custard. See page 111).

Mousses

Sara Jayne's Truffe Gâteau (page 194)

PHILIPPA'S CHOCOLATE APRICOT PUDDING

Serves 6-8

250 g/8 oz dried apricots or prunes
(or half and half)

2 cinnamon sticks

300 ml/½ pint double cream
(or 284 ml tub plus 2 tbsp milk)

4 large eggs, separated

125 g/4½ oz dark chocolate,
melted

85 g/3 oz caster sugar

This is a recipe by Philippa Davenport, the prize-winning recipe writer in the *Financial Times* (and other publications) as well as author of many books. Philippa claims not to be particularly fond of chocolate so I thought that this must be a little special - and it is. It sounds rather modest but is a joy to eat. Philippa describes it as "a happy combination of tart apricot purée and softly set chocolate soufflé topping which can be served warm or cold". I have tried it with prunes and I think it is even better than with apricots - but it's a personal preference, as in most things. You could use any dried fruits and it would work.

One buttered ceramic or Pyrex soufflé dish, 26 cm (10 in) and about 9 cm (3 in) high. Preheat the oven to 180°C/350°F/gas 4.

Cover the dried fruit and the cinnamon sticks with water or china tea and bring slowly to the boil. Cover and simmer until tender. Discard the cinnamon, reserve the liquid and purée the fruit to a smooth pulp. Return some of the liquid (or all of it) and make a thick purée. Pour into the soufflé dish.

Whip the cream to soft peaks. Add the egg yolks, one by one, to the chocolate, stirring in thoroughly. Fold the chocolate and eggs into the cream. Whisk the egg whites gradually incorporating the sugar. Slacken the chocolate cream with a spoonful of meringue then fold in the rest.

Spread the mixture over the fruit purée.

Bake for 40 minutes. It is ready when gently puffed up and set - perhaps cracked around the edges but still a mite wobbly in the centre. Remember the pudding will continue to cook after it has left the oven. It is advisable but not imperative to keep it in a warm place as it cools, out of any mischievous draughts or sudden cold spots as it is likely to sink - but it will still be absolutely top notch.

MR TURNER'S BLACKCURRANT AND CHOCOLATE MOUSSE

Serves 8-10

THE CHOCOLATE GÉNOISE

55 g/2 oz sugar

2 eggs

25 g/³/₄ oz flour and
1 dtsp cornflour and
25 g/³/₄ oz cocoa powder,
 sifted together

4-6 tbsp cassis

THE MOUSSE

85 g/ 3 oz caster sugar

5 tbsp water

2 egg yolks

1 large egg

1 leaf gelatine, dissolved in cold
 water and squeezed dry

200 g/7 oz bitter chocolate, melted

250 ml/8 fl oz whipping cream

200 ml/7 fl oz blackcurrant purée -
 made with blackcurrants, a little
 water and sugar to taste

THE GLAZE

115 g/4 oz blackcurrant purée

100 ml/3¹/₂ fl oz cassis

115 g/4 oz apricot jam

2 gelatine leaves, dissolved in cold
 water and squeezed dry

Brian Turner is the television personality and owner of Turner's in London's Walton Street. This recipe is a divine, airy chocolate mousse with fresh blackcurrants and cassis. I had this once for supper in Turner's as part of their exceptional set menus. The balance of the meal was immensely satisfying but I would go there just for this one alone! I have tried it with raspberries and blackberries and also tried it with home-made jam instead of making a purée - and it works.

Butter and flour a 23 cm (9 in) springform flan or tart tin. Line the bottom with silicon paper, helpful but not vital. Pre-heat the oven to 200°C/400°F/gas 6.

Whisk sugar and eggs in a bain marie for about 7 minutes to a sabayon. Fold in the sieved flour and cocoa. Pour into prepared tin and bake for 8-10 minutes.

Allow to cool, and then cut in half horizontally. Soak one half with cassis for the mousse and reserve the other half for another day - it freezes well and keeps for days. Line a 23 cm (9 in) flan ring with acetate or clingfilm, place the cassis soaked génoise on the bottom.

To make the mousse: In a medium size pan slowly melt the sugar with water and when it's completely dissolved and clear bring to boil to 121°C/250°F.

Whisk together the egg yolks and the whole egg and then dribble on the hot syrup while whisking with small electric hand whisk.

Slowly add the dissolved gelatine leaf and keep whisking until cold.

Add this sabayon of eggs and sugar to melted chocolate.

In another bowl whisk the cream and blackcurrant purée.

Fold into the chocolate mixture.

Pour into ring which has chocolate sponge, soaked with cassis, in the base.

Refrigerate for at least 2 hours.

To make the glaze: Boil purée, cassis, and the jam together. Add the soaked gelatine, pass through a sieve.

When cool, put a thin layer on top of the mousse. Level with spatula and chill again.

Serve with a Crème Anglaise or an ice cream or sorbet.

CHOCOLATE CREOLES

This is very light and mousse-like. The rum adds a nice kick and blends wonderfully with the chocolate.

Serves 4

55 g /2 oz plain chocolate, broken into pieces

11.7 g/1 level tbsp powdered gelatine

3 egg whites

2 tbsp caster sugar

75 ml/2½ fl oz whipping cream

2 tbsp rum

icing sugar to dust

Lightly oil four dariole moulds.

Melt the chocolate with 2 tablespoons of water and allow to cool.

Place 2 tablespoons of water in a very small saucepan and sprinkle the gelatine evenly over the top. Allow to 'sponge' into the water. Place over a very low heat and dissolve. Take care not to over heat the gelatine.

Whisk the whites until stiff and add the melted gelatine, followed by the sugar.

Continue whisking until stiff and shiny. Whip the cream and rum together until thickened but still soft. It should just leave a trail. Fold the chocolate mixture into the whisked whites, then fold in the whipped cream. Spoon mixture into the prepared dariole moulds. Place in the fridge and allow to set.

To serve, dip the moulds quickly into hot water, invert on to serving plates and sprinkle with icing sugar if desired.

CHOCOLATE TRUFFE WITH FIGS AND MÛRE

The combination of figs, mûre (blackberry liqueur) and chocolate is heavenly.

Serves 10-12

10 ripe figs

300 ml/½ pint mûre (you could use cassis)

55 g/2 oz caster sugar

TRUFFLE

450 g/1 lb dark chocolate

575 ml/1 pint whipping cream, at room temperature

Line a 23 cm x 11 cm x 6.5 cm tall (9 x 4 x 2½ in) loaf tin or terrine, with cling film.

First poach the figs: Trim any rough stems from the tops of the figs. Pour the mûre into a saucepan large enough to hold the figs in one layer, add the sugar and swirl to dissolve. Add the figs, right side up and if necessary add enough water to just cover the fruit. Poach gently for about 5-7 minutes, depending upon the ripeness of the figs.

Remove the figs carefully with a slotted spoon and set aside. Boil the poaching liquid until reduced to about 3-4 tablespoons. Remove from the heat to cool.

To make the truffe: Melt the chocolate over a bain marie until just melted. Allow to cool to blood temperature (if using a thermometer about 38°C).

Add the fig syrup to the cream and whip until just slightly thickened. **Note:** It is important that the cream is at room temperature and that you do not overwhip (which is tempting). It should begin to thicken but not to leave a trail.

Gently fold the cream into the melted chocolate, just until it is evenly blended. Spoon half the mixture into the loaf tin. Place the figs upside down in the chocolate layer. Carefully spoon the remaining chocolate mixture over the upturned figs, taking care not to dislodge them. Refrigerate the truffe for at least 4 hours.

To Serve: Turn out on to a serving dish and carve into slices with a sharp knife.

IMPERIAL CHOCOLATE INDULGENCE

This brings back a romantic memory of many moons ago, too long ago to recall with any comfort, except that this pudding was one of the first of my encounters with real chocolate and is memorable for that too.

Line two moulds, approximately 7½ cm (3 in) diameter with cling film. Ramekins will work.

Combine the nuts and zests. Dissolve the sugar in water over a medium heat. Add the cocoa powder and butter and beaten egg. Mix until smooth and fold in the nuts. Add Grand Marnier and melted chocolate.

Pour into the moulds and tap on the table to expel any air. Refrigerate for 6 hours. Turn out and peel off the cling film.

Make the sauce by boiling together cream, milk and sugar. Add the chocolate and cook for a couple of minutes. Remove from the heat and add the butter a little bit at a time and finally flavour with the Grand Marnier.

Pour the sauce on to a plate, add a thread of fresh cream and use the point of a knife to make a zigzag pattern. Carefully place the Chocolate Indulgence on top of the sauce. Have a great evening!

FOR DINNER 'A DEUX'

1 tbsp chopped Brazil nuts, (about 3)

1 tbsp chopped pistachio nuts

pinch lemon zest

pinch orange zest

2 tbsp water

2 tbsp sugar

2 tbsp cocoa powder

100 g/3½ oz butter, diced

1 small organic or free range egg - note this is uncooked

1 tbsp Grand Marnier

100 g/3½ oz dark chocolate, melted

THE SAUCE

2 tbsp double cream

4 tbsp milk

1 dtsp sugar

100 g/3½ oz dark chocolate, melted

1 dtsp butter

1 tbsp Grand Marnier

CHOCOLATE MARQUISE

Serves 10-12

20 langue de chat (sponge fingers),
  optional but preferable

100 g/3$^1/_2$ oz unsalted butter,
  room temperature

85 g/3 oz caster sugar

2 tbsp cocoa powder

$^1/_2$ tsp instant coffee powder

3 egg yolks

2 tbsp rum or brandy

300 ml/$^1/_2$ pint whipping cream

3 egg whites (optional)

200 g/7 oz dark chocolate, melted

2 tbsp very strong black coffee
  (if using biscuits)

cocoa powder for dusting

This is from a recipe I have cherished since the early Eighties. It's very rich and filling. I made twelve of these for 100 guests at a friend's wedding once - every scrap was consumed, even after a copious lunch of other goodies.

If you use the egg whites, it softens it up a bit and makes it less dense - but it is the denseness which makes this pudding so luscious. It's perfect for a dinner party as you can make well in advance.

Line a terrine mould or 1 kilo/2 lb loaf tin with cling film or if using the langue de chat then butter the base of the mould and line the sides with the biscuits after dipping them into the coffee.

Cream together the butter with half the sugar until pale and fluffy - two or three minutes. Beat in cocoa and coffee. In another bowl whisk egg yolks with remaining sugar until pale and creamy - about five minutes. Whisk in rum or brandy.

In another bowl lightly whip the cream until the whisk leaves a trail. If using, whip the egg whites with a pinch of cream of tartar, bulky but still soft.

To assemble: Beat melted chocolate into butter and sugar until smooth. Pour into egg mixture and lightly mix together. Fold in cream. If using, now fold in the egg whites.

Pour the marquise mixture into the terrine or loaf tin carefully if you have lined it with the biscuits so as not to dislodge them from the sides. Smooth across the top.

Refrigerate for 2 -3 hours before serving. Turn mould/tin upside down on to a plate and dust top with cocoa powder. The sides will look impressive if you have used the biscuits but just as good, plain and simple if you have not. Cut into slices. Serve on its own or with a fruit purée or coulis.

Do take care with the melted chocolate because the other ingredients take a little while to prepare and the chocolate can start to set before you use it.

A SIMPLE ECONOMICAL CHOCOLATE MOUSSE

Serves 4 (if you use the whipping cream then it will easily serve 6)

4 large eggs, separated

115 g/4 oz plain chocolate, melted

125 ml/4 fl oz whipping cream (optional)

I have had this recipe for more years than I care to remember. This is foolproof and economical to make - it is a dark rich mousse which you can make in minutes and takes about 2 hours to set in the fridge. It does use raw eggs so be warned. It is also very chocolatey so you may want to add some cream to lighten it up. You can also use this for fillings and toppings. This is one of those divine recipes that, with a little imagination, you can tart up in any way you wish. You can add brandy or any other alcohol or nuts, raisins etc. which you should add after the egg yolks. Don't be too liberal until you know this recipe or you will alter the balance and it might not set.

Lightly beat the egg yolks and add one at a time to the chocolate.

Whisk the whites until fairly stiff. If using the cream then whip until you see the trail and fold into the chocolate and egg mixture at this stage.

Fold into the chocolate.

Divide between 4 or 6 ramekins and leave to set in the fridge for 2-3 hours - the longer the better.

MICHAEL NADELL'S MOCHA CHOCOLATE SABAYON

Serves 4

115 g/4 oz caster sugar

2 eggs

2 egg yolks

1 tsp very strong black coffee

30 g/1 oz dark chocolate, broken into tiny pieces

Michael Nadell is one of the country's most successful and talented pastry chefs. He has a large 'pastry lab' in North London and, as well as serving London's top establishments with wonderful croissants, Danish, and pastries seven days a week, Michael is also very keen on training. Some of the country's best-trained pastry chefs have 'done their time' at Nadell's.

This is a relatively simple dessert, which you can make in advance. It is velvety and rich and very effective.

Place about 5 cm (2 in) water in a medium sized saucepan and bring to the boil. Reduce the heat to simmering, then place large mixing bowl on top, the bottom of the bowl should NOT touch the water.

Add all the ingredients to the bowl and whisk for about 12-15 minutes until it quadruples in volume. The chocolate pieces will melt as you whisk.

Divide between 4 small coffee cups or *demitasse* and serve with a biscuit of some kind.

CHOCOLATE NEMESIS

**Serves about 10 people
depending on the greed and
wisdom of the eater**

6 whole eggs

300 g/10½ oz caster sugar

350 g/12 oz bitter chocolate

225 g/8 oz unsalted butter, softened

This recipe is an adaptation of one of the River Cafe's most famous recipes - if not sometimes infamous! The River Cafe (for those who don't know) is one of London's most fabled eateries run by Ruth Rogers and Rose Gray. I tried the original at the restaurant and it is divine. I suspect this is the pudding that gave birth to the often used expression 'to die for'. It is very, very rich and all the better for it, deserving its reputation as one of the world's greatest chocolate puddings.

The River Cafe original uses a great deal of chocolate and the 30 cm/12 in cake tin in a bain marie takes up more than most normal domestic ovens can spare; it also serves about 20 people, so I have adjusted the recipe.

Preheat oven to 160°C/325°F/ gas 3. Line 20 cm x 5 cm (8 in x 2 in) cake tin (not with a loose bottom) with greaseproof paper, grease and flour it. Before you start make sure that you have a large roasting tin that will take the cake tin and enough water to reach the top of the sides. Boil the kettle.

Beat the eggs with a third of the sugar for at least 6 minutes, with an electric mixer until the volume quadruples.

Slowly melt the remaining sugar in a small pan with 115 ml (4 fl oz) water which will take a few minutes. Bring to the boil to about 121°C. This will give you a sugar syrup.

Put the chocolate and butter in a relatively large pan (large enough to hold all the recipe's ingredients which have to be mixed in at the next stage) and add the sugar syrup. Over a low heat melt all together and stir to thoroughly amalgamate. Leave to cool a little. Add the eggs to the chocolate and butter and beat gently until all combined, about 20 seconds no more.

Pour into the cake tin and place in hot bain marie; it is essential if the cake is to cook evenly, that the water in the bain marie (a large roasting tin) comes up to the rim of the tin. The safest way to do this is to place the filled cake tin in an empty roasting tin, set it on the oven shelf and then pour in the boiling water. Slide the roasting tin gently into place in the oven. Bake for 1 - 1¼ hours. Test with a skewer. It should still be creamy, as the cake will continue to firm up and cook as it cools.

Allow to cool **completely** before turning out. Serve dusted with cocoa powder and a dollop of crème fraîche or just a simple almond biscuit.

Note: If you have problems with the bain marie you can try cooking without. The difference is that it will form a thin crunchy crust and cook firmly on the outside, will be soft towards the middle and the centre will be creamy - almost liquid. Delicious. My husband said that this was, at the time of testing, one of the best recipes so far - but then he thrives on richness at which others' knees would buckle.

Michael Nadell's Mocha Chocolate Sabayon (page 191)

SARA JAYNE'S TRUFFE GÂTEAU

Serves about 15 people

450 g/1 lb dark chocolate, the better quality the better the result

500 ml/16 fl oz whipping cream, use at room temperature

3 tbsp rum (optional)

Chocolate curls, icing sugar or cocoa powder or cinnamon to dust

This is to die for, and once mastered it is relatively simple and quick to make. However, you need a bit of practice and to follow a few basic rules. See below. Using smaller quantities doesn't really work but it keeps for at least 7 days in the fridge - some people like it even more 'mature' - and if you have any over, it freezes like a dream.

It is great with all sorts of fruit, custards and ice creams.

Using cling film line a 25.5 cm (10 in) flan ring or an oblong container about 21 cm × 7.5 cm × 10 cm (81/2 in × 3 in × 4 in) deep.

Melt the chocolate in a bain marie - do not let the water temperature rise above 40°C.

While you are waiting for the chocolate to melt, lightly whip the cream and rum (if using) in a large bowl. Stop when the whisk leaves a trail.

Pour about half the chocolate into the cream and fold in. Then fold in the rest of the chocolate until completely amalgamated.

Pour the mixture into the container, smoothing the top. Refrigerate for at least three hours or longer for a really firm finish. Turn out and dust with cocoa powder or icing sugar or a touch of cinnamon (go easy on this or it will overpower - you can use a mixture of cinnamon and cocoa or icing sugar).

Vital Points to remember:

• *The cream must be at room temperature. If it is too cold the mixture sets the chocolate as soon as they make contact and it goes grainy. If too hot it doesn't set properly.*

• *The chocolate must be about 35°C (within a margin of a degree or two). Again if it is too cold it won't amalgamate with the cream properly - and if it is too hot, it won't set.*

• *DO NOT OVERWHIP the cream - however tempting this may seem. It does not make a good truffe. Conversely it does not work to under-whip either. The correct consistency is gauged the moment the whisk leaves a soft trail.*

TURINOIS

This is another recipe from the lovely Michael Raffael, once a chef now a thoughtful food writer. This is such a fabulously simple recipe around which you can create all sorts of magic with other favourite ingredients.

Line a 25.5 cm (10 in) flan ring or an oblong container about 21 cm x 7.5 cm x 10 cm (8 1/2 in x 3 in x 4 in deep) with cling film.

Add sugar to sweeten chestnuts. Melt chocolate, butter and rum together. Combine with chestnuts. Pour into terrine and leave to set in cool place or fridge.

You can add 300 ml/1/2 pint whipped cream to the base - it gives more volume. You can also add chopped marrons glacés.

Another version which I invented on one occasion when I had no marrons was to replace them with 425 g/1 lb of prunes - de-stoned, of course and soaked in Armagnac then puréed. Absolutely fantastic.

Serves 10

1 x 425 g tin unsweetened purée de marrons

2-3 tbsp sugar to sweeten chestnuts

200 g/7 oz bitter chocolate

100 g/3 1/2 oz unsalted butter

rum, to taste

sugar or honey, to taste

ST EMILION AU CHOCOLAT

Not sure why it's called St Emilion - perhaps this is where it originated. Perhaps someone can tell me? Whatever the provenance, this is an old, very quick to make, favourite variation on a terribly rich chocolate mousse.

Crush 4 of the macaroons and cover with cognac. Set aside.

Whizz the crème fraîche and the melted chocolate in a food processor. Add the coffee and remaining macaroons. Process for 6 seconds until all ingredients are evenly mixed together. Transfer to a large bowl.

Whisk the egg whites to soft peaks. 'Let down' the chocolate mixture with 1/4 of the whites then fold in the rest.

Divide the crushed macaroons and cognac between the glasses or ramekins and then top with the chocolate mixture. Chill thoroughly for about 4 hours. Dust with cocoa powder or flaked chocolate and serve each with one of the remaining macaroons.

Serves 6 in stemmed glasses or ramekins

16 amaretti biscuits or macaroons (see recipe for Caprice des Dames)

2 tbsp brandy or cognac

300 ml/1/2 pint crème fraîche

170 g/6 oz dark chocolate, melted

5 tbsp strong coffee, freshly made and cooled

4 large egg whites

Tarts – Cold and Hot

*Rowley Leigh's Special
Chocolate Tart (page 204)*

CHOCOLATE TART WITH CARDAMOM

Serves 10-12

85 g/3 oz plain flour, sifted together with 45 g/1½ oz cocoa powder

75 g/2½ oz unsalted butter

30 g/1 oz ground almonds

55 g/2 oz caster sugar

1 large egg, lightly beaten

8 cardamom seeds, peeled and crushed (see method in recipe for Pistachio and Cardamom truffles, page 215)

THE FILLING

225 g/8 oz bitter chocolate

55 g/2 oz unsalted butter

3 large eggs, separated

85 g/2 oz caster sugar

6 tbsp double cream

1 tsp concentrated coffee

Cardamom has been part of the English food scene since Richard the First's Crusades brought it back with them. It was popular in Medieval cooking here and seems to have made a comeback. Cardamom, also known as Grains of Paradise, adds subtle depth to this chocolate tart.

Butter and flour a 23 cm x 2.5 cm (9 in x 1 in) flan tin.

Pre-heat the oven to 200°C/ 400°F/ gas 6.

Put all the ingredients into a food processor and whizz for about 15 seconds - not more or it becomes greasy and will be tough. Make a ball with the mixture with your hands.

Cover and refrigerate for about 30 minutes. Beat out with a rolling pin and roll out thinly.

Transfer to the tin and leave in the fridge for another 30 minutes. Line with foil and bake blind (see Chocolate Clinic) for 15 minutes. Remove from oven. Take out the foil and bake for another 15 minutes.

To make the filling melt together the chocolate and butter. Cool slightly. Whisk the egg whites to soft peaks - don't overbeat. Lightly whisk the eggs yolks and sugar to a frothy stage. Stir in double cream and coffee. Add the chocolate and butter and stir gently. Fold in the beaten egg whites.

Tip the mixture into the tart case and spread with a spatula.

Bake for 20 - 25 minutes, the tart should be very soft in the centre. It will firm up as it cools.

Serve cold with a dollop of soured cream or ice cream etc.

GRASSHOPPER PIE

So called because, apparently, the name implies lightness of a grasshopper while the mint adds coolness. Believe that if you like but I have no other explanation - except that it is a fabulous classic American pie.

Melt together the butter and chocolate and thoroughly mix with the biscuits. (You can do all this in a food processor.) Spoon into a 25 cm (10 in) loose bottomed flan tin and press along the bottom and up the sides.

To make the filling, gently melt the gelatine in a small bowl over a bain marie.

Stir into the sour cream. Whisk the egg whites to stiff peaks, then add the sugar, a tablespoon at a time, and continue to whisk until stiff and shiny. Lightly whisk the cream until it just holds a ribbon, then fold in the mint.

Fold the cream into the soured cream and gelatine mixture, followed by the whisked whites.

Pour into the biscuit case and place in the fridge for several hours until set.

For the icing: combine all the ingredients together in a pan over a low heat, stirring occasionally until completely smooth. Cool. Pour over the pie - leave to set before removing from tin.

You can omit the icing and cover with a veil of cocoa powder or other chocolate decoration.

Serves 8

THE BASE

225 g/8 oz Duchy biscuits or similar, crushed

115 g/4 oz unsalted butter

85 g/3 oz dark chocolate, broken into pieces

THE FILLING

2 leaves gelatine, soaked in cold water and squeezed dry

225 ml/7½ fl oz sour cream

2 egg whites

55 g/2 oz caster sugar

150 ml/¼ pint whipping cream or double cream

3 tbsp fresh mint leaves, finely chopped

THE ICING

115 g/4 oz dark chocolate

55 g/2 oz cocoa powder

55 g/2 oz caster sugar

6 tbsp water

Serves 8

THE PASTRY

170 g/6 oz flour

55 g/2 oz icing sugar

115 g/4 oz unsalted butter

1 egg

few seeds from a vanilla pod

THE CHOCOLATE FILLING

2 eggs

85 g/3 oz caster sugar

170 g/6 oz plain chocolate, melted

3 tbsp cocoa powder, sifted

300 ml/½ pint whipping cream

THE LEMON FILLING

2 egg yolks

2 whole eggs

140 g/5 oz caster sugar

3 lemons, zest of 2 and juice of all 3

150 ml/3½ fl oz double cream

LEMON AND CHOCOLATE TART

Now, I love the combination of chocolate and lemon and this recipe has taken many attempts to get the lemon and chocolate custards to the same ethereal texture. Not many of my chef friends believed in the idea of this recipe but the results have proved my imagination right. The lemon and chocolate custards create the most unexpected and wonderful contrasts on the tongue. I hope you enjoy it.

To make the pastry: Preheat the oven to 180°C/350°F/gas 4. Put the first three ingredients in a food processor and whizz for a few seconds until everything amalgamates. Then add the egg and the vanilla seeds. Whizz again and when the dough leaves the sides of the bowl and clings to the middle, it is ready. Lightly mould into a ball, put in a polythene bag and leave to rest in the fridge for 30 minutes. Roll out to a thickness of 3 mm (⅛ in) and line a 23 cm (9 in) flan tin. Place the tin in the fridge or freezer for 30 minutes to rest. Bake blind for 15-20 minutes. Reduce the oven temperature to 140°C/275°F/ gas 1.

For the chocolate filling: Whisk the eggs and sugar over a bain marie for at least 5 minutes to ribbon stage. Fold in the melted chocolate, then the cocoa and then the cream. Pour on to the tart case.

For the lemon filling: Whisk egg yolks, eggs, sugar, lemon juice and zest until pale and creamy over a bain marie as above for about 5 minutes. Fold in the cream.

Pour the lemon custard directly into the centre of the chocolate - the chocolate custard should rise above the lemon but sometimes (for reasons of its own) it doesn't. Don't worry just gently swirl the two together for a marbled effect. Bake for 50-55 minutes. Test with a knife.

Allow to cool and refrigerate for about 1 hour. Serve at room temperature.

I love this 'undressed' but you may want to serve an orange (or other) sauce (see page 112) with it.

Grasshopper Pie (page 199)

Serves 6-8

THE CHOCOLATE GÉNOISE

55 g/2 oz sugar

2 eggs

25 g/^{3}/$_4$ oz flour and
1 dtsp cornflour and
25 g/^{3}/$_4$ oz cocoa powder,
 sifted together

LINZER PASTE

115 g/4 oz unsalted butter

55 g/2 oz caster sugar

pinch salt

2 egg yolks

1 tbsp whipping cream

115 g/4 oz plain flour

55 g/2 oz ground almonds

^{1}/$_2$ tsp cinnamon

4 tbsp good sharp raspberry jam

3 tbsp framboise liqueur

GANACHE

200 ml/7 fl oz double cream

3 tbsp milk

300 g/10^1/$_2$ oz dark chocolate,
 broken into tiny pieces

NADELL'S TARTE AU CHOCOLAT

Michael Nadell is one of this country's most brilliant sugar technicians. His sugarwork is like finely wrought gossamer. Unfortunately, the general public cannot buy his products directly but see Directory for more information. This tarte is very dense and chocolatey. Once it's set it serves and slices beautifully.

Start by making the chocolate Génoise: Butter and flour a 23 cm (9 in) springform flan or tart tin. Line the bottom with silicon paper, helpful but not vital. Preheat the oven to 200°C/400°F/gas 6.

Whisk sugar and eggs in a bain marie for about 7 minutes. Fold in sieved flours and cocoa. Pour into prepared tin and bake for 8-10 minutes.

To make the Linzer paste: Cream together the butter, sugar and salt until pale. Add the yolks and cream and combine. Sift together the flour, ground almonds and cinnamon and blend into the butter mixture. This can be done in the food processor but take care not to over-process once you have added the dry ingredients.

Place in a bowl, cover and allow to rest in the fridge for at least 1 hour or overnight.

Roll out the paste between two pieces of cling film - this is the best way to do it as the pastry is very sticky. Peel the top layer of cling film off. Using the bottom layer of cling film, lift the pastry into a 23 cm (9 in) loose bottomed flan ring, turning it over so the film is on top. Press the pastry into the ring and up the sides. Peel off the film and patch any holes with the extra pastry. Allow to rest in the fridge for 1 hour.

Meanwhile, make the ganache: Bring the cream and milk to the boil. Remove from the heat and add the chocolate. Stir to combine, then leave to cool to room temperature. (Do not cool in the fridge.) Preheat the oven to 190°C/375°F/gas 5. Prick the pastry base with a fork and bake for 25 minutes or until golden brown. The pastry will fall a little on the sides. This is normal. Cool on a wire rack then remove the ring and the base. You will need to loosen the pastry from the ring.

To assemble: Spread the base of the flan with the raspberry jam. Cut the Génoise sponge in half horizontally. (You only need one half for this recipe.) Place the chocolate sponge Génoise disc on to the jam and sprinkle with the framboise.

When the ganache is cool, pour over the sponge layer until it reaches the top of the flan. At this point it can be chilled or allowed to cool further at room temperature. It takes an hour or two to set.

To serve, dust with cocoa powder.

CHOCOLATE CAKE MICAELA

This recipe is served in the Taberna del Leon, by Chef Patron Monica Patino, one of Mexico's celebrity chefs. The Taberna del Leon is one of Mexico City's most innovative and popular restaurants serving very imaginatively prepared Mexican food with an international influence. Monica's recipes use lots of good, dark cocoa-y chocolate. 'Micaela' is served as part of a chocolate trio including Three Choc Mosaic with British Vanilla Cream and Chocolate Cake Helena (See pages 183 and 135).

To make the pastry: Preheat the oven to 190°C/375°F/gas 5.

Place butter, egg yolk, vanilla and icing sugar in a food processor and whizz to make a paste. Add the flour and process until it comes together. Allow to rest in the fridge for at least 30 minutes. Roll out and line a 20 cm (8 in) tart case and blind bake for 12 to 15 minutes until golden. Lower the oven temperature to 160°C/325°F/gas 3.

To make the filling: Melt the chocolate and butter together. Whisk the egg, egg yolk and sugar together. Add the chocolate and the butter and whisk until incorporated. Fold in the almonds. Pour into the pastry case and bake for 9 to 10 minutes until just set. Leave to cool. Serve dusted with icing sugar and whipped cream or ice cream if desired.

Serves 4-6

PASTRY

100 g/3½ oz unsalted butter, softened

1 egg yolk

drop vanilla essence

55 g/2 oz icing sugar

150 g/5½ oz plain flour

FILLING

100 g/3½ oz dark chocolate

55 g/2 oz softened butter

1 egg plus 1 egg yolk

1 tbsp caster sugar

150 g/5½ oz blanched almonds, roasted and chopped

MISSISSIPPI MUD PIE

This is a dense, rich-tasting version of the famous pie which originated from the banks of the Mississippi. The pie is the colour and texture of Mississippi mud.

To make the base: Butter a 20 cm (8 in) loose bottomed cake tin. Mix the biscuits with the melted butter. Fill the cake tin with the biscuits and press over the bottom easing about 4 cm (1½ in) up the sides. Chill.

To make the filling: Preheat the oven to 190°C/375°F/gas 5.

Melt the chocolate and butter together. Cool slightly. Whisk in the eggs, sugar and coffee powder until well blended. Whisk in the cream. Fold in the pecans, pour into the biscuit base and bake for 30-40 minutes. Cool before removing from the tin and serve with whipped cream or ice cream.

Serves 8-10

THE BASE

225 g/8 oz ginger Duchy biscuits, crushed

100 g/3½ oz unsalted butter, melted

THE FILLING

170 g/6 oz plain chocolate, chopped

170 g/6 oz unsalted butter

4 eggs, lightly beaten

170 g/6 oz dark Muscovado sugar

2 tsp coffee powder or granules

150 ml/¼ pint whipping cream

100 g/3½ oz pecan nuts, roasted and chopped

ROWLEY LEIGH'S SPECIAL CHOCOLATE TART

Serves 8-10

THE PASTRY

200 g/7 oz flour

100 g/3 ½ oz unsalted butter

85 g/3 oz caster sugar

1 egg

THE FILLING

2 whole eggs

4 egg yolks

55 g/2 oz sugar

300 g/10½ oz plain chocolate, melted

This is a simple, but adult chocolate treat, which works wonderfully every time. Rowley Leigh is the Chef/Partner of Kensington Place and also the relaxed food writer for the *Sunday Telegraph*. Many people will have become addicted to his witty, charming style of recipe writing. A man to be taken seriously.

To make the pastry: Preheat the oven to 180°C/350°F/gas 4. Have ready a 23 cm (9 in) flan or tart tin.

Put the first three ingredients in a food processor and whizz for a few seconds until everything amalgamates and then add the egg. When the dough leaves the sides of the bowl and clings on to the middle it's done. Take it out and lightly mould into a ball and put it into a polythene bag. Leave it in the fridge for at least 30 minutes.

This is Rowley's method: Cream the butter and sugar in a food processor, or in a bowl with a wooden spoon. When they are smooth, incorporate the beaten egg to form a wet paste. Sieve the flour and add it to the mixture, folding it in gently without working the dough. Roll the dough into a thick log about 12 cm (4¾ in) diameter and refrigerate until you need it.

Soften the pastry by beating it with a wooden rolling pin and then roll it out to a thickness of about 3 mm (⅛ in). Roll it around the pin and lift it off the table and drop it into the tart tin. Make sure there are no gaps in the corners and let 1 cm (½ in) overhang at the edge. Crimp the border gently, slide the tart on to a metal baking sheet and put it in the freezer for about 30 minutes.

Prick the base of the pastry case with a fork and bake blind for 15-20 minutes. Check after about seven minutes and if it has risen up gently push it down again with the back of a fork.

To make the filling: Whisk the eggs, egg yolks and the sugar until they form a thick, white, frothy cream, about 5-7 minutes. Fold in the melted chocolate and blend to a rich dark cream.

Pour into the baked tart case and cook for 12-15 minutes in the oven at 180°C/350°F/gas 4. The mixture will be just set.

This tart is best served lukewarm with a little cream or crème fraîche. However it is also great when cold.

HOT BITTER CHOCOLATE AND ORANGE TART WITH HAZELNUT PASTRY

Serves 8-10

THE FILLING

juice of 2 oranges

zest of 1 orange, grated

5 eggs

25 g/³/₄ oz cocoa powder

150 ml/¹/₄ pint double cream

PASTRY

225 g/8 oz flour

100 g/3¹/₂ oz unsalted butter, cold and diced

100 g/3¹/₂ oz caster sugar

pinch salt

25 g/³/₄ oz ground hazelnuts

1 egg, lightly beaten

Here's one from the irrepressible Herbert Berger, Head Chef of 1 Lombard Street, in the City of London. Makes a tart with deliciously light pastry. Oranges go really well with chocolate. The orange filling needs to rest for 24 hours, so start this the day before you want to serve it.

To make the filling: Whisk together by hand the orange juice, orange zest, eggs and cocoa powder. Whisk in the cream. Pour into a glass bowl in the fridge and allow to stand for 24 hours.

To make the pastry case: Preheat the oven to 190°C/375°F/gas 5. Have ready a 25 cm (10 in) flan or tart tin. Combine the flour, butter, sugar, salt and hazelnuts in a food processor. Add the egg and process until just beginning to come together. Shape into a ball and allow to rest in the fridge covered in film for at least 30 minutes. Roll out to 3 mm (¹/₈ in) and line the tart case or flan ring. Bake blind for 20 - 25 minutes until golden brown.

When ready to bake, reduce the oven temperature to 140°C/275°F/gas 1. Pass the filling through a fine sieve into the baked tart case. Bake for 1 to 1¹/₄ hours until just set. Allow to cool slightly and serve dusted with icing sugar or cocoa powder. Serve with vanilla sauce barely flavoured with chillies. See recipe for Crème Anglaise (page 111) and add a dried chilli to the cream at the same time as adding the vanilla pod, before bringing to the boil, then continue to follow the instructions.

HOT CHOCOLATE AND MARMALADE TARTS

For 8 Individual Tarts

THE PASTRY

55 g/2 oz icing sugar

100 g/3½ oz unsalted butter, softened

55 g/2 oz dark chocolate, grated

2 egg yolks

few drops vanilla essence

175 g/6 oz flour, sifted

pinch salt

8 tbsp marmalade

FILLING

250 g/8 oz plain chocolate

100 g/3½ oz unsalted butter, softened

4 egg yolks

8 egg whites

100 g/3½ oz caster sugar

This is a delicious recipe from Ernst Bachmann who owns the Bachmann Pâtisserie in Thames Ditton, Surrey (see Directory). Marmalade adds denseness to the chocolate without making it too 'jammy'.

To make the pastry: Sift the icing sugar into a mixing bowl and cream lightly with the butter and grated chocolate. Add the egg yolks, one at a time, and then the vanilla. Gently fold in the flour and salt. Bring together, wrap in cling film and allow to rest in fridge for at least 30 minutes.

Roll out the pastry and line eight 10 cm (4 in) tartlet tins. Spread each lined tin with 1 tablespoon of marmalade. Place back in the fridge while you make the filling.

Pre-heat the oven to 180°C/350°F/gas 4.

To make the filling: Melt the chocolate and butter together and add the egg yolks. Amalgamate thoroughly. Whisk the egg whites to a medium peak. Gradually add the sugar, one tablespoon at a time and continue to whisk until stiff and shiny. Fold the meringue into the chocolate mixture and spoon into the tartlets. Place them all on a baking sheet and bake for 20-25 minutes.

Serve hot with a hot chocolate sauce; or hot Sauce Anglaise with Crème de Cacao or an Orange Sauce. (see Sauces page 112)

Note: You can freeze these once assembled (before cooking) and cook from frozen for 5-10 minutes longer.

Tarte Au Chocolat Aux Poires (page 208)

Serves 8

PASTRY

170 g/6 oz plain flour

55 g/2 oz butter, finely diced

55 g/2 oz caster sugar

55 g/2 oz ground pistachios

1 egg, lightly beaten

THE CHOCOLATE CREAM FILLING

85 g/3 oz butter, softened

85 g/3 oz caster sugar

1 egg, lightly beaten

30 g/1 oz flour, sifted

85 g/3 oz dark chocolate, melted

2 large ripe pears, peeled and
quartered, preferably Comice,
but Williams or Conference will
work well too

TARTE AU CHOCOLAT AUX POIRES

The juiciest sponge of deeply rich and dark chocolate supports two soft pears in a buttery pistachio pastry case.

To make the pastry: Preheat the oven to 180°C/350°F/gas 4.

Place the flour and butter in a food processor and whizz until the mixture begins to resemble breadcrumbs.

Add the sugar and nuts and whizz again briefly to incorporate.

Add the egg and whizz again lightly until the mixture just comes together. (This can also be done by hand by rubbing in the butter first.) Form into a ball and leave to rest in the fridge for at least 2 hours or overnight.

Roll out the pastry to about 3 mm ($\frac{1}{8}$ in) on a floured surface and line a 23 cm (9 in) flan tin. Trim any excess pastry.

To make the chocolate and pear filling: Whisk butter and sugar till pale and fluffy.

Beat in the egg, mix well, then the flour, then the melted chocolate.

Spread mixture evenly in the pastry case.

Cut the quartered pears lengthways into 4 slices and arrange the slices into 4 'fans' over the chocolate cream. Cook in the middle of the oven for 40-50 minutes until centre is firm.

Serve with whipped cream. This is also good cold.

HOT CHOCOLATE AND APRICOT FILO TARTS

This is a delightful recipe of crispy layers of filo pastry full of bubbling creamy chocolate, from Professor John Huber.

Serves 8

450 g/1 lb (2 tins × 400 g) apricot halves, drained weight, juice reserved from one of the tins

5 tbsp water

115 g/4 oz caster sugar

5 tbsp apricot brandy or ordinary brandy or Armagnac

THE PASTRY CASES

6 sheets filo pastry, thawed if frozen, approximately 30 cm/12 in square

100 g/3¹/₂ oz melted butter

THE CUSTARD

450 ml/³/₄ pint milk

150 ml/¹/₄ pint whipping cream

2 egg yolks

85 g/3 oz caster sugar

2 tbsp cocoa powder

3 tbsp cornflour

140 g/5 oz chocolate, broken into bits

Make a syrup with the reserved apricot syrup, water and sugar. Bring to the boil, simmer for 2-3 minutes then remove from the heat. Add the brandy and pour the syrup over the apricots to infuse. Set aside while you make the pastry cases.

To make the pastry cases: Preheat oven to 190°C/375°F/gas 5.

Brush 3 sheets of filo with melted butter and lay them one on top of the other. Cut into nine 10 cm (4 in) squares. Repeat with the other sheets of filo.

Lay a square inside a 10 cm (4 in) tartlet tin (or a similar sized Yorkshire pudding tin) with corners pointing up. Lay another square on top of the first at an angle so you make a star shape, again with the corners pointing up. Carefully line with a piece of crumpled baking foil or crumpled greaseproof paper and baking beans and bake blind for 5 minutes until golden on the edges. Remove the foil or paper and beans and bake for another 2 minutes to cook the inside.

Carefully remove the pastry cases from the tin and place on a baking sheet.

To make the custard: Heat the milk and whipping cream to boiling point. Whisk the yolks and sugar until well blended. Sift together the cocoa powder and cornflour and mix in the yolk mixture. Add the hot milk and cream.

Place mixture in a saucepan over a medium heat and bring slowly back to the boil, stirring continuously. The mixture will go alarmingly lumpy but keep stirring and it will become smooth. Simmer gently for about 1 minute.

Remove from the heat and add the chocolate pieces, stirring until melted and incorporated into the custard.

To serve: Slice the apricot halves into 3 slivers and heat gently (can be done in a microwave or in a saucepan with extra syrup). Reheat the filo cases in a low oven. Place cases on warmed serving plates. Fill with custard and top with the apricots.

Truffles

Sara Jayne's Truffles

212 Chocolate: the definitive guide

CHOCOLATE TRUFFLES are rich, infatuating little follies, so named because when dusted with cocoa powder they resemble those rare earthy little gems of fungus, and similarly precious to all lovers of exciting food. The chocolate truffle is believed to be an invention of about 80 years.

A good truffle is my idea of the perfect chocolate confection. It's got to be hand-made - I know all about economies of scale but I don't think a machine has yet been invented or perfected that can touch a man's passion or skilled and practised hand. The basic nature of a truffle is the ganache, the chocolate and cream (and sometimes butter) which is the vital component of the centre, which should be enrobed with a thin coating of 60%-70% couverture. I am attracted to the chocolate by the sight of a glossy finish. Instinct tells me if I should be tempted any further. The smell is important. It should be 'lush', full and fruity with intense cocoa-y overtones and a balance of spicy acidity. The bite should be crisp and clean through its chocolate coat, which after all is only the means to hold its 'soul' - yielding to the charms of the ganache centre, which should be light and creamy in texture and intensely chocolatey in flavour. Robert Linxe, the great French chocolate guru of modern times, is horrified by the thought of whisking the ganache and says that "the amalgamated chocolate and cream confection should be moved like a mayonnaise". However, I am a fan of the very lightly whisked variety and the resulting lightness, which gives it ethereal qualities that aid its complete melt-in-the mouth experience while the flavours burst around the palate. The combination of flavours should be clean and distinct with a long, clearly defined aftertaste.

I know that some swear by chocolates straight from the fridge while others believe that this is sacrilege and chocolate must be enjoyed at room temperature. I'm one of the former. Holding a bite of cool chocolate on the tongue soon brings it to a contrasting body heat - the temperature in the mouth at which it gently explodes into a warm sensual liquid and which develops chocolate's unique characters.

I have made literally thousands of truffles - of every different flavour and filling you can imagine - some have proved absolutely fabulous and some have stayed with me. Others have not withstood the test of time and hundreds of different mouths. Here are a few basics and some ideas of the other flavourings and fillings you can try.

PLAIN DARK CHOCOLATE TRUFFLES

Makes about 85

225 g/8 oz BEST dark chocolate - evenly broken into tiny pieces, the size of buttons

300 ml/½ pint double or whipping cream

1 kg/2.2 lb couverture chocolate for tempering (see under TEMPERING for method) or cocoa, icing sugar, nuts, 'vermicelli' etc for rolling

Plain merely indicates the natural, unflavoured element of these truffles - because there is nothing at all plain about them…

Take a large, heavy chopping board or a baking tray and cover it tightly and completely with cling film or waxed paper. (You may need to fix it with Sellotape underneath to make sure it is taut - if you don't wrap the film tightly enough it lifts up when you try to remove the truffles, when they are set.) You can use the inside of a supermarket carrier bag too. Wash and dry it first.

Place the chocolate in a large mixing bowl - at least 1.75 litre/3 pint size. In a saucepan, bring the cream to a rolling boil and immediately pour over the chocolate.

Blend thoroughly until all the chocolate is melted. Leave to cool at room temperature, which will take **at least one to one and a half hours**. (You can hurry the process by placing the bowl in a sinkful of cold water - but don't allow any of the water to 'plunder' the ganache).

YOU CAN NOW EITHER:

Proceed to making the truffles. This is my favourite method and I think by far the most satisfactory for a light airy truffle.

Using an electric hand whisk (you can use a balloon whisk but you need muscles of iron!) gently whisk the mixture to the point where it just begins to stop 'running'. The whisk should barely begin to leave its trail. NO MORE or it might split (separate) and becomes unmanageable and sets before you have a chance to continue. It is better to stop whisking when it is still soft - as it soon sets.

Transfer the mixture into a 35 cm (14 in) piping bag with a 1 cm (½ in) nozzle and pipe little 3.5 cm (1½ in) truffle spheres or 'tits' on to the film covered baking sheet.

Refrigerate for about one hour.

OR:

When the mixture has set in the bowl, use a teaspoon to spoon-out little bite-size portions.

Roll them into balls in the palms of your hands, dusted with icing sugar to prevent sticking. This is very messy but is just as good as the first method.

At this stage you can enrobe the truffles in chocolate - but if ambition deserts you, just roll the truffles in cocoa powder, icing sugar, chopped nuts, or chocolate vermicelli - but they won't stick as efficiently as they do to tempered or melted chocolate. The truffles will keep for at least a week. You can always sprinkle with cocoa powder from a sieve or tea strainer at the last minute if they need 'tarting up'.

The glory of using the best possible chocolate is that it doesn't really matter what they look like - they will taste absolutely wonderful.

Variations: You can vary the truffles by adding numerous other flavours of your choice.

Liqueur: 5 tablespoons of rum, brandy, calvados (or any other alcohol you may fancy) and the rougher the better as the 'fine' alcohols get lost in the depth of flavour of the chocolate. Add to the truffle mixture immediately after the chocolate and cream have been amalgamated.

Rosemary/Angelica: Someone once called me the Queen of Angelica as I use it in so many different ways such as ice creams, cakes, pastries, breads, scones, jams etc. I love it - but only the fresh herb straight from the garden and not the candied stuff found amongst hundreds and thousands on the cakes of our childhoods.

Increase the quantity of cream by 55 ml/3-4 tablespoons and add 30 g/1 oz fresh rosemary leaves/angelica stems and bring to the boil. Take the cream off the heat and leave with rosemary infused for 10 minutes to bring out most of the flavour. Bring to the boil again and strain immediately on to the chopped chocolate. Proceed as above.

Tequila and Chilli: Now here's a combination that I would never have dreamt of before I went to Mexico. The chilli comes through as the truffle leaves the mouth perpetuating a warmth on the palate with a long chocolate finish. Yum. Bring the cream to the boil with 2-3 dried chillies and proceed as for rosemary, adding the Tequila after the chocolate has completely melted.

Nuts: Add 85 g/3 oz finely chopped nuts after chocolate has melted.

Lapsang Souchong/Earl Grey/Rose Pouchong: Add two teaspoons of tea to the cream and proceed as for Rosemary/Angelica.

Ginger and Saffron: 6 balls of stem ginger - finely chopped plus 5 g (a pinch) of saffron stamens - pounded to a powder. Bring 175 ml/6 fl oz of cream to the boil with the saffron and leave to infuse. Boil again and strain on to the chocolate. As soon as the chocolate has melted add the ginger. Proceed as above.

Venus Nipples: Sorry have to keep something a secret!

Maldon Sea Salt: This is a revelation for balancing the sweetness of a milk chocolate truffle. Add 1 level teaspoon per 200 grams of milk chocolate and 175 ml double or whipping cream for the ganache at the point where the cream and chocolate are just amalgamated.

MILK RUM TRUFFLES

Boil the cream and pour over the chopped chocolate. Stir until all the chocolate has melted

Stir in the rum. Allow to cool and follow basic truffle instructions.

You can cover these in either dark or milk couverture. I prefer the contrast of milk and bittersweet. These work well with cocoa powder.

Makes about 60

200 ml/7 fl oz whipping cream

225 g/8 oz milk chocolate,
  finely chopped

5 tbsp dark rum

IVORY WITH PISTACHIO AND CARDAMOM

In a mortar, lightly bash the cardamom pods and they will come away from the seeds. Discard the pods and give the seeds a good pounding.

Bring the cream to the boil with the cardamom seeds and pour over the chopped chocolate. Mix well until all the chocolate has melted. Stir in the pistachio nuts.

Leave to cool for about 1 hour. Follow the instructions for basic truffles. Either dip in tempered ivory couverture or cover with suggested finishes.

**Makes between 40-60
(depending on the size)**

The seeds of 4 large pods
  of cardamom

200 ml/7 fl oz whipping cream
  (you can use double cream for
  a richer texture)

225 g/8 oz ivory couverture,
  finely chopped

55 g/2 oz pistachio nuts, ground
  quite finely in the food processor,
  but not too finely that they turn
  to a paste or this will affect the
  natural oils which quickly go
  rancid and might have a tendency
  to 'split' the ganache

Savoury Dishes

Still Life with Chillies and Chocolate

SAVOURY USES FOR CHOCOLATE

The idea of using chocolate in cooked food would have been alien to the Aztecs - not a single reference can be found in the extensive writings on the Aztec period that suggests they used chocolate for anything but drinking. However, the Mexican dish Pavo in Mole Poblano is often credited as typical of traditional Mexican cuisine - traditional now perhaps but its place in Mexican cuisine is but a few hundred years old.

This dish emanates from Hispanic influences. *Pavo* in Mexican-Spanish means Turkey, *mole* is a sauce; and poblano refers to the place of origin of the dish and the sauce; probably the creation of nuns in the Sixteenth century, living in the very beautiful central colonial Mexican city of Puebla de los Angeles, whose origins are Spanish with little or no Aztec connections. There are a number of stories which relate to the origins of this dish and just like other culinary creations it may well have been the result of an accident in the kitchen; with a container of chocolate falling into the sauce while the nuns were preparing a meal for the visit of their bishop.

However there is a European tradition of using chocolate in savoury dishes. Recipes in Italy dating from 1680 onwards list cacao in the ingredients for pastas and meat dishes. There is a recipe for lasagne from 1786 with a sauce containing almonds, anchovies, walnuts and chocolate. Other recipes from Eighteenth century Italy include black polenta with chocolate and sliced liver dipped in chocolate and fried. Clearly its use was widespread, for the poet Francesco Arisi in his work *Il Cioccolato* complains bitterly of those who misuse cacao in cooking.

Chocolate used in moderation in any savoury meat dish brings out a certain richness which other ingredients cannot. But judicious use is the key. The purpose of the chocolate is to enhance not overpower. Chocolate and chilli, which I discovered in Mexico, is a perfect combination. In addition you can add a 15 g/½ oz piece of chocolate or a level teaspoon of cocoa powder to a dish for 6 people such as duck, Chilli Mince (especially good), Steak and Kidney Pudding and Spaghetti Bolognaise. Yes, chocolate even transforms a humble Spag Bol. Sprinkle a little bitter cocoa powder on to the skins of trout before you grill it. The combinations are endless.

MOLE POBLANO DE GUAJOLOTE

Serves 6-8

1 x 3 kg/6½ lb turkey

55 g/2 oz lard

2 large onions, chopped

3 carrots, diced

2 sticks celery

1 bouquet garni (including parsley, thyme, and a bayleaf)

THE MOLE SAUCE

6 dried mixed peppers

2 fresh or dried hot chillies like mulato, ancho, pasilla, etc. (or more if you like really hot stuff)

4 cloves garlic, crushed

3 tomatoes, skinned, de-seeded, chopped

55 g/2 oz raisins

55 g/2 oz almonds, flaked

4 star anis

2 cloves

1 tsp cinnamon

100 g/3½ oz bitter chocolate

pepper, salt

70 g/2½ oz sesame seeds

Mole is the black, often fiery, sauce which is traditionally made with chocolate and cocoa as well as some 30 other ingredients including chillies, coriander and cornflour. The mole sauce here, although less complicated, is nevertheless excellent.

Cut away turkey flesh and dice into large pieces and put to one side. Brown the carcass in the oven and put into a stock pot (or similar). Make a stock from it, covering it with water and adding herbs (but no salt). Bring to the boil and immediately turn down to simmer for at least one hour. Strain through a fine sieve, return to pan and reduce to about 1 litre/1¾ pints. Reserve liquid.

Brown the turkey pieces in a large casserole dish with the lard. Add the chopped onions and the diced carrot, then the celery. Half cover with stock (about a litre/1¾ pints) and leave to simmer with the bouquet garni for about 45 minutes.

To make the mole sauce: Using a food processor, grind the chillies and peppers to a powder (or paste if using fresh) and add the crushed garlic, tomatoes, raisins and almonds. When the turkey is cooked, bring to the boil with the star anis, cloves and cinnamon and simmer for 5 minutes, strain, reserving stock in the pan, and place turkey on a serving dish and keep hot.

Remove any fat from the stock in the casserole dish and pour in the sauce. Add the chocolate and when it is thoroughly melted and blended in, strain and add salt and pepper to taste.

To serve: Cover the turkey pieces with the sauce and sprinkle with the sesame seeds.

Serves 4

350 g/12 oz onions

115 g/4 oz butter

1 tbsp plain flour

scant 1/2 glass fruity white wine

scant 1/2 glass water

salt and pepper

30 g/1 oz extra bitter chocolate

dozen or so sliced button
     mushrooms

450 g/1 lb (approximately) fish of
     the strong variety like cod

GLYNN CHRISTIAN'S SAVOURY FISH RECIPE FROM NORTHERN SPAIN

Glynn Christian was one of the finest food journalists and chef imports, from New Zealand. Sadly he has gone home and left a void. However, here is something to remember him by. He says that "such chocolate-flavoured onions will make a wonderful partner to chicken or to turkey (for example). What brave new worlds there remain to discover…!"

Finely slice onions and fry in shallow pan with the butter until very soft and sweet but largely uncoloured - about 40 minutes. Stir in flour and then the wine and water. Season with salt and pepper and grate in the chocolate. Stir in the mushrooms and then ease in the fish either whole or in slices. Cover and simmer until cooked.

Remove the fish and keep it warm. Stir the sauce adding extra wine if necessary. Serve with the fish.

Serves 4-6 (depends on size of fish)

1 live lamprey, (weight about
     400-500 g/1 lb)

1 onion, diced

3 carrots, diced

1 clove garlic, crushed

1 bouquet garni (small bunch
     dried parsley, thyme, bayleaf)

1 bottle red Bordeaux

150 g/5 1/2 oz butter

4 leeks, white part only

2 slices Bayonne ham, cut into cubes

30 g/1 oz flour

55 g/2 oz bitter chocolate

salt, pepper

LAMPROIE À LA BORDELAISE

Here's an interesting dish from Christian Constant (See Paris). Don't squirm at the idea of live eel. You can perfectly well use a dead one. You can also use eel and omit the blood. If you do then halve the amount of chocolate used. I have tried it and it works.

Take a live lamprey, bleed it and reserve the blood for the sauce. Place the fish in hot water and carefully scrape off the skin. Cut off the head and the tail, removing the spinal cord, which runs between the two. Cut into pieces.

In a high-sided frying pan or shallow casserole dish, brown the diced vegetables in a little butter and add the pieces of fish, the garlic and the herbs. Cover with the wine and cook for about ten minutes.

Meanwhile, put half the butter into a saucepan and brown the leeks and the diced ham over a medium heat.

Strain the fish and set aside.

Make a roux from the remaining butter and the flour in a saucepan, using the fish stock (made with the wine). Reduce a little. Turn off the heat and now add the fish and leave for 5 minutes. Remove the fish and place on a serving dish.

Strain the sauce and then mix with the chocolate and then the blood, taking care not to heat above 60°C or the blood will curdle. Pour over the fish and serve with croutons fried in butter.

Paris - A Chocolate Lover's Guide

I have a deep, abiding love affair with the French. It's no secret. Ergo you will not be surprised to know that this passion extends to their chocolate. I think the very best, the purest and the most elegant chocolate is made by the French. The French are indeed gastronomically inspired. So, I believe that every serious chocolate lover owes it to him or herself to take a trip to Paris to get a real feel of what's happening in the chocolate world. It's quite remarkable and very inspiring.

Parisian chocolate shops can offer you just about every chocolate combination that you have ever dreamed of - and probably many more beyond your wildest imagination! What's more your choice of filling might be enrobed in any one of a number of couvertures from around the cocoa-growing world such as Brazil, Venezuela, Ecuador, Papua New Guinea and so on. It is immensely exciting and it's this concentration of effort that makes this experience so unique.

Also, I have never seen cocoa pods on sale anywhere else but you can buy them in the streetmarkets and some of the shops here. Crack them open and scoff the beans. They are delicious.

But what is surprising is that French enthusiasm for the exceptional, sophisticated and complex chocolate goes back only some twenty years. Events of World War II took precedence over the quality and choice of the food chain. Just like the rest of Europe, the French had to accept whatever food was available. There was no opportunity to be fussy and so the customs of the artisan chocolate makers, or at least those left after the War, and their expertise were stifled and overtaken by industrial production. According to chocolate guru, Robert Linxe, until two decades ago the French were content with what they might now describe as mediocre chocolate made from an amalgam of anonymous beans from any number of plantations anywhere in the chocolate-growing world. Cocoa content was of little importance. But now that has changed.

When you get to France arm yourself with a copy of *Guide des Croqueurs de Chocolat* which lists over 150 of the best *chocolateries* across France - 35 of which are in Paris alone. (Any of the good chocolate shops will sell you a copy.) *Le Club des Croqueurs de Chocolat* (formerly *Club de cinglés du chocolat* - chocolate nuts) was started in 1981 by the journalist and gastronome, Claude Lebey, Nicolas de Rabaudy and Jean Paul Aron with 7 members. Now it is strictly limited to 150, including Sonia Rykiel, Irène Frain, Jean Bourin and Lionel Poilane … and a long waiting list. The club holds six blind tastings a year when the merits of the chocolates are discussed and dissected and marks awarded.

I visited barely a handful of the best chocolate shops which had been recommended - and noted only a small selection of the varieties to be enjoyed in each case because it is so much a matter of personal taste. I sampled so many wonderful chocolates that it would take another whole book to record them all. I urge you to go and enjoy for yourself. In the meantime, here is my guide, though it is by no means the definitive list. I brought back a giant sack of samples which I had purchased (or in some cases been given, by Michel Chaudun and Christian Constant) and I invited over two of Britain's top food writers Frances Bissell, the *Times Cook* and Marie-Pierre Moine, the food guru for *House and Garden* - both blessed with sensitive tastebuds. We tried these after a very copious dinner, based on the theory that this is probably when most chocolates are eaten. Debating about other apposite times to eat chocolates, we concluded that for a serious chocolate-lover it is any time the cocoa fancy takes you. We each awarded marks out of 10 - although Frances was so excited about Maison du Chocolat that she gave the chocolates 11!

For those *chocolatiers* and shops I visited, as well as our own tasting results, I have included the Guide's own scores which are denoted by 'bites' ❤. Top score is 5 (which means chocolate madness):

La Maison du Chocolat ❤❤❤❤❤: 225 rue du Faubourg Saint-Honoré 75008. ☎ 01 42 27 39 44. Open Monday-Saturday 9.30-19.30 (19.00 in winter) also 4 other shops in Paris. Staff a joy.

Robert Linxe is one of the first of the modern *chocolatiers* who, over the last two decades, has changed the perception of serious chocolate. In doing so he has become a legend - not only in France but also throughout the chocolate world, recognised for his pioneering chocolate touch. Always, always passionate about chocolate, he opted, in spite of his father's protestations, for a professional life in chocolate. Most of the French chocolate then was made on a semi-industrial basis in Bayonne, the historical home of the Portuguese Jews where the first couverture was invented about 70 years ago. No-one was making artisan chocolates in France except at Easter and Christmas.

Linxe's first shop flourished in the avenue de Wagram from 1965-1974 as *Traiteur/Pâtissier/Chocolatier* - and was the ONLY one in Paris at the time making fine hand-made chocolate confections (called bonbons in France) daily to guarantee absolute freshness. For the last three years he worked in partnership with Gaston Lenôtre - another *pâtisserie* legend - and eventually, longing for his artistic and autonomous freedom again, sold the shop to him.

He broke new ground as the first person to set up a business devoted exclusively to chocolate, founding 225 rue du Faubourg, Saint-Honoré, the first of his five shops. Linxe liked number 225, a former wine shop, because it had a large cellar, "a cellar good for wine is also good for chocolate". He also liked it for its location near la Salle Pleyel, one of the finest music rooms in Paris. "Music and wine and chocolate - the most attractive and appealing combination" - a concept which has since been reflected in many of La Maison du Chocolat's creations, such as the *bonbons* Rigoletto, Figaro, Traviata. Within the first week of making his chocolates, Le Maison du Chocolat was so successful that he was overwhelmed with orders. He found no time to work with milk chocolate but only with unsweetened dark chocolate, and his persistence has paid off.

Linxe used Cacao Barry for a long time but twenty years ago swapped allegiance to Valrhona. The great Linxe/Valrhona partnership began and Linxe has been its guiding light ever since. At that time, the characteristics of Valrhona chocolate tended towards excess acidity, so he set about working with the company to remedy this. The result has been an overwhelming success for the fortunes of both Linxe and Valrhona. The majority of the best French *chocolatiers*, and Linxe in particular, favour Central and South American beans dismissing the 70% that come from Africa as industrial bulk.

Linxe has often been called the wizard of the ganache. His inspiration comes from the heart. He stresses that "ganache should never be whipped but only moved like a mayonnaise". (I personally prefer a lighter ganache and all my truffles are whipped - although recently I have inclined to do this less with the same airy effect). I asked him for his definition of a perfect chocolate. He said "it should never be sugary, nor greasy, nor acid, nor astringent, nor sour. *Beau chocolat* is when you eat a chocolate and you want a second one. You should still be able to taste the chocolate 45 minutes later. More than about 65% chocolate should never be used to make a *bonbon* or it will be overpowering".

The interior of La Maison du Chocolat is certainly one of 'sobriety, quality, refinement'. It is a traditional chocolate shop with no frills, where the chocolate does all the talking. The chocolate-brown boxes incline towards the masculine in style, relieved by the Hermès designer touch. All his chocolates are still made by hand with the help of the Rolls-Royce of enrobers made by the German manufacturer Sollische. He has 130 staff, including 7 *chocolatiers*, at his chocolate 'laboratory' in Colombes, who produce 14 tons at Christmas alone.

The range includes pure natural ganache truffles made with the Guayaquil bean - a relation of the *criollo* family; Linxe claims that "of all the fillings available, ganache is certainly the finest"; Liselotte: praliné of crushed roasted almonds and hazelnuts; and dark chocolate truffles with 'melon' … surprising until you remember that when the cocoa pods are first split open the fresh bean tastes of melon/lychees - so the flavour of melon really does bring out the fruity taste of chocolate. The other flavour I loved - well, I loved them all - was citron. I think lemon is absolutely terrific with chocolate. We also liked fresh mint and Linxe has 'conspired' two notable natural ganaches one called 'Quito', made from Ecuadorean cacao and the other 'Caracas' from Venezuelan *criollo*. So delicious were the orange peel sticks that we ate them all before we got home … so none for the London tasting!

The Bissell/Moine/Stanes tasting: 54¹/₂/60. 'serious'; 'traditional'; 'long finish'; 'harmonious'; 'clean'; 'a heavenly symphony'…

La Fontaine au Chocolat ❤ 201 rue Saint Honoré, 75001. ☎ 01 42 44 11 66 (Monday-Saturday 10.00 - 19.00). Staff very helpful- some tasting.

The company, Michel Cluizel, was started in 1946 by grand-père Cluizel and is now run by his four grandchildren who separate their responsibilities into the Paris shops, marketing, finance and production. The *laboratoire* with its 120 staff is in Normandy and produces mostly industrialised products and supplies over 6,000 shops in France as well as Japan and the United States. It is very good chocolate nonetheless. In the window of the shop a great 'fountain' of chocolate cascades down a wall in the window - an unusual and effective expression of chocolate… and mouth-watering. Michel Cluizel chocolate is available in some shops in London.

The Bissell/Moine/Stanes tasting: Selection of Grand Cru chocolate tablets from single countries: 35/60. Ranging from 'Not impressed' and 'rough' to 'balanced acidity'; 'good chocolate'; 'clean' and 'beautifully boxed'.

Jean Paul Hevin ❤❤❤❤ 231 rue Saint-Honoré 75001. ☎ 01 55 3535 96 (Tuesday-Saturday 10.00-19.00). Not very friendly (also at 3 rue Vavin, 75006 where they were charming). Absolutely no tasting.

As a *chocolatier* and *pâtissier* Hevin's skills evolved from time spent in Japan watching and understanding Japanese tastes. He has worked with such names as Robuchon. Uses lots of ginger and smoked teas. Hand makes all chocolates at 16 avenue de la Motte-Picquet. Won many prizes for his chocolates and is sometimes compared to Robert Linxe. A fan of Valrhona.

Bissell/Moine/Stanes tasting: 38¹/₂/60 surprising given his status and approval among other *chocolatiers* of France: 'no comment'; 'interesting and unusual'; 'fragrant'; 'industrial textures';' patchy flavours';' overpowering smoky tea flavours'.

Debauve et Gallais 30 rue des Saints Pères 75007. ☎ 01 45 48 54 67 (Tuesday-Saturday 9.00-19.00). Contemptuous, positively rude staff. Slap wrists for even thinking about tasting.

The shop is a stunning historical museum of two centuries of French chocolate, and worth seeing for the historic value alone, however the chocolates while good are nothing special in French terms. They no longer produce 'medicinal' chocolates which I have described earlier, although they still sell a range of 'historical' varieties such as *les pistoles de Marie Antoinette*, as well as their famous unsweetened health chocolate. No longer are they made exclusively by hand but are semi-industrial and manufactured by Michel Cluizel.

Bissell/Moine/Stanes: 27/60. 'fillings too sweet and indistinctive';'dry and uninspiring'.

Fauchon ❤ ❤ 26-30 Place de la Madeleine 75008. ☎ 01 47 62 60 11. Charming staff.

August Fauchon was a barrow boy at the end of the Nineteenth century and moved to a shop on the corner of the Place de la Madeleine in about 1890. His range of products was always unique and extensive and by the 1920s

Fauchon had expanded to own a delicatessen, *pâtisserie*, wine shop and restaurant. The origins and philosophy of Fauchon have remained true to August Fauchon's principles and the name Fauchon is known around the world of good food for its exclusive and exotic products and for its striking black and white packaging. One of Fauchon's three shops (all on Place de la Madeleine) is dedicated to chocolate and includes an extensive range of more-ish chocolates as well as chocolate cakes and pastries. One particularly worth noting is an innovative gâteau designed in the shape of a jigsaw puzzle. Each 3 pointed star puzzle piece is full of a lightly made intensely flavoured filling such as cherry, tea, natural chocolate ganache, nuts etc. You can buy an individual piece for about two people or a whole puzzle cake with pieces of your choice that all fit together in a higgledy piggledy arrangement. It's delicious.

Bissell/Moine/Stanes: 41/60. I stress that this was only for one product and that was Fauchon's *Chocolat Noir aux Incrustations de Fèves de Cacao* which is 70% cocoa solids stuffed with fragments of cocoa beans. Comments: 'lingering finish'; 'like it'; 'light crunch'.

Richart Design et chocolat ❤❤ 258 boulevard Saint-Germain 75007. ☎ 01 45 55 66 00 (Tuesday-Friday 10.00-19.00 and Monday and Saturday 11.00-19.00). Staff hard work but malleable. Strictly no tasting.

My eyes were like saucers as I looked through the shop window at the collection of Richart's designer chocolates. The delicate but striking designs seem leagues apart from traditional chocolate confectionery. The Richart family *chocolatiers* go back to 1925. Today the family business is still one of constant innovation through Michel Richart, who was a designer before he took over the company. In his view "design and aesthetic perfection are inextricably linked with epicurean pleasure". Tiny Japanese inspired chocolates, pyramids and *trompe-l'oeil* are only a few examples of this modern chocolate art. It would be grossly unjust to say that these are the most elegant chocolates in Paris but they do carry a distinctive trade mark of pure bewitching ingenuity - and no stinting on the gold leaf. They are made with a wide variety of couvertures from around the world, and are sold around the globe from Barcelona to Hong Kong and beyond. Exceptional range of plain chocolate tasting squares from around the cocoa growing world to ganaches, alcohols, fillings, nuts etc. Be charmed with varieties such as praliné of hazelnuts from Piedmont and Arabica coffee; ganache with wild raspberries; coulis of caramel with fresh salted butter; coulis of apricot with lemon peel; bergamot; thyme; nutmeg and even curry … and so on and so on …

Bissell/Moine/Stanes: 48½/60. 'harmonious'; 'perfect size'; 'dinky'; 'intense'; 'quality matches marketing'; 'boxes flimsy and inconsistent with the designer chocolates inside'.

Michel Chaudun ❤❤❤ 149 rue de l'Université, 75007. ☎ 01 47 53 74 40 (Tuesday-Saturday 9.30 - 19.30) Atmosphere and staff (family) charming and enthusiastic.

Michel Chaudun appeared with a huge ear-to-ear smile from the back of the shop - where I discovered he still makes all his chocolates by hand, after 30 years at the top of his profession. Despite our language barrier, he couldn't speak a word of English, which matched my practically non-existent French - we got along just fine. His unrelenting passion for chocolate dazzles with warmth and displayed itself as paramount to life. His shop is a chocolate paradise with its exotic and pervasive aromas willing you to enter his orderly cavern of cocoa. He was keen for me to know that he was the first, 5 years ago, to create chocolate for Weiss with slivers of crushed roasted cacao beans. "*Voila, voila*" he exclaims as he opens a spacious drawer full of copycat bars from every well-known manufacturer around the world.

He gently plied us with sample after sample of his lip-smacking creations and wouldn't let us leave without giving us a box of his choice and seemed almost insulted at any offer to pay for them. Among his specialities are pepper and green cardamom. We left dazzled by cocoa. Michel Chaudun is another of the greatest *chocolatiers* of France and is immensely popular with his peers, press and public alike. He welcomes you whomever you are. All you need is to share a little of his love for chocolate. Pure liquid chocolate passion.

Bissell/Moine/Stanes: 55/60. 'got to get a case of this one!'; 'happy memories';' lingering joy'; 'honeyed'; 'very clean and fresh'; 'lovely light ganache'; 'delish'; 'exquisite finish'; 'more…';

Christian Constant ❤❤❤❤ 37 rue d'Assas, 75006. ☎ 01 5363 1515 (8.00-20.30 daily). Staff are a joy.

Christian Constant is my sort of far-away chocolate hero whom I had always wanted to meet. Some years ago he sent me a copy of his book *Le Chocolat* which I muddled through (it's in French) but enough to fall in love with his philosophy. I was not disappointed. He is a model of French charm and passion and oozes chocolate generosity, which I suspect is the norm for all his customers. In his early days of chocolate, Constant worked for both the great Lenôtre and Linxe. He opened his first shop in the rue du Bac at the beginning of the Seventies and has since moved to rue d'Assas. He seems to have achieved star status in the chocolate world, working with some of the great designers like Sonia Rykiel to create some classy, elegant packaging. He has made a point of visiting practically every cocoa-growing region in Central and South America and has worked with the IRCC (the *Institut Recherché Cafe et Chocolate* in Montpellier - Research Institute of Cocoa and Coffee) researching the origins of cocoa and its future breeding.

He has a penchant for cocoa from Trinidad and the rest of Central and South America such as Venezuela, Ecuador, Colombia and Guatemala. He is not a fan of African cocoa as, like Robert Linxe, he considers it as "bulk for the industry and not flavoured enough". The Constant eyebrows shot up at the mention of organically produced chocolate about which he was positively unflattering.

Christian Constant now has two shops in Geneva and is just about to take Santiago, Chile, by storm where he says there are many Europeans who know about chocolate.

Constant creates a combination of daring and exotic flavours like ylang-ylang; green tea; jasmine; and sensational crystallised mandarin sticks. He also produces such gems as rose and Corinthian raisins, orange blossom, Tahitian vanilla, sesame crunch. His literature is pure seduction. Here is a an example: "Along the past through the islands of the Indian Ocean, the Chocolate Road continues through Arabia and Yemen where the jasmine and orange trees blossom… At Mayotte, the golden flowers of the Ylang-Ylang plants surround the plantations of pure *criollo* and impart a sweet perfume over the largest atoll in the world.

"On the slopes of the Fournaise volcano of Réunion, *petits blancs* cultivate vetiver and geraniums rosa in order to distill an extract from their leaves of the most precious rose essence ever searched out."

Bissell/Moine/Stanes: 49/60. 'elegant packing and elegant chocolates'; 'perfect size'; 'delicate flavours'; 'magic'; 'wow'; 'a taste sensation'; 'some perhaps a little too sweet'; 'chocolate not as well defined as some of the others'.

Here are 3 more that I did not have time to visit but come highly recommend:

Lenôtre: ❤❤❤ 121 avenue de Wagram, 75017. ☎ 01 45 02 2121 (open daily from 9.00-20.00).

The house of Lenôtre is a symbol of tradition for gourmands, as Gaston Lenôtre himself is one of the most celebrated *pâtissiers* in France and has spawned a whole new generation of *pâtissiers*, *confiseurs* and *chocolatiers*. Every *pâtissier* and *chocolatier* worth his salt knows of Lenôtre. Now less involved in the business himself, preferring to tend his vines in the Loire, his products still bear the great man's influence of quality and the height of good taste. Lenôtre even has his own brand of couvertures and other chocolate products.

Dalloyau: ❤❤❤ 101 rue du Faubourg-Saint Honoré, 75008. ☎ 01 42 99 90 00.

Gérard Mulot: ❤❤❤ 76 rue de Seine, 75006. ☎ 01 43 26 85 77.

With apologies to the rest of France especially Lyon where so much great chocolate work goes on… another time, another book, perhaps. But see recipe for Bernachon's Meringue, page 149.

CHOCOLATE DIRECTORY

Please note, dear readers, that this list of chocolate producers and suppliers is by no means exhaustive nor do I necessarily endorse every product represented. We are all different with different likes and dislikes. Sourcing 'real' chocolate and selecting a favourite is a peculiarly personal experience. Nevertheless, among the following you will undoubtedly find the best chocolates in the world.

Artisan Chocolate Confectionery and Truffle Makers

L'ARTISAN DU CHOCOLAT
89 Lower Sloane Street
London SW1 8DA
☎ 0207 824 8365 (and mail order).
www.artisanduchocolat.com
L'Artisan du Chocolat is a small, young and dynamic business started in 2000 by its two founders Gerard Coleman and Anne-Francoise Weyns. Today it still employs only a handful of people in its production laboratory near London and at the shop in Lower Sloane Street.

Irish born Gerard is a chef and pastry chef by training. After several years in kitchens in London and New York, he sharpened his knowledge and experience of chocolate in Belgium. His partner, Anne-Francoise is the business brain, ensuring that L'Artisan du Chocolat remains viable, family run and independent.

Gerard Coleman is probably one of, if not the best, chocolate makers in the UK at the moment. His chocolates are devoured by a faithful following and many of the UK's top restaurants. He makes very serious 'mind-meets-mouth' chocolates including his range of lovingly blended sensual ganaches using the best French chocolate and brilliantly sourced fresh ingredients for the flavours. At any one time there are over 50 from which to choose including lavender, red wine, fresh

Moroccan mint, tobacco, or Bramley Apple (they are seasonal and must be tasted). Gerard's sea-salted caramels are a mouth popping combination of sweet and savoury.

AUDREY'S CHOCOLATES
28 Holland Road
Hove
East Sussex BN3 1JJ
☎ 01273 735561
Audrey's 'griottes' are amongst the best liqueur chocolates you will find - anywhere. They were started at London's famous Fortnum and Mason in 1929 and are still made to same recipe, which survived World War 11. The Morello cherries from Kent (not many are grown in England and Audrey's nearly always buys the whole orchard) are soaked in French brandy for two years before being transformed into the perfect chocolate liqueur. Using only enough cherries for one-days production, the cherries are stoned and dipped in brandy fondant. Each one is partly dipped in chocolate to strengthen its bottom and then fully dipped in dark, bitter chocolate. Ideally they should stand for at least three weeks to allow the fondant to be dissolved by the spirit, leaving the cherry floating in the brandy. Divine, like their rose and violet creams. See also Fortnum's where the founder of Audrey's, Mr. Pain, spent many

of his early years as their master chocolate maker. Sadly the great Mr Pain died a few years ago but the traditions of this great chocolate maker are safe with his successor David Burns.

BACHMANN'S PATISSERIE
6 Criterion Buildings
Portsmouth Road
Thames Ditton
Surrey KT7 OSS
☎ 0208 398 1988
Best hand-made patisserie and chocolates you will find in south west London.

CHARBONNEL AND WALKER
1 The Royal Arcade
28 Old Bond Street
London W1X 4BT
☎ 0207 491 0939 fax 0207 495 6279
www.charbonneletwalker.com
Charbonnel et Walker has been established since 1875 when Edward VII - then Prince of Wales, persuaded Madame Charbonnel to leave the chocolate house of Maison Boissier in Paris to join Mrs. Walker in London to establish a fine *chocolaterie* and confectionery house. Legend has it that Madame Charbonnel was one of the Prince's mistresses ... on the other hand it could have been Mrs. Walker! The legacy of their enterprise continues today and many of the recipes of Charbonnel et Walker's English chocolates come from Madame Charbonnel's own recipe book and include truffles, noisettes, marzipans, caramels, fudges and creams and are good value for their quality and variety. Charbonnel and Walker's Rose and Violet Creams remain a firm classic. Madame Charbonnel will be content to know that *'plus ça change, plus c'est la même chose'*!

CHOCOCO

Commercial Road
Swanage
Dorset BH19 1DF
☎ 01929 421777
www.chococo.co.uk
Cocoa Central, their shop and factory is open 6 days a week.

Claire and Andy Burnet set up Chococo, the Purbeck Chocolate Co. in 2002. They decided to turn Claire's love of proper chocolate into an opportunity to change direction, re-train and escape their London corporate lives to live in Dorset with their young daughter Lily.

Claire and Andy are purists who refuse to compromise – they work with El Rey's Criollo bean Venezuelan chocolate, make all their ganaches with local fresh whipping cream, natural ingredients, no preservatives or chemical additives and only a modest amount of sugar. They are also passionate about using fresh Dorset produce and the finest ethically produced ingredients wherever they can. Coming to the world of chocolate with fresh eyes, they have created an original and distinctive selection of chocolates and truffles with such flavours as chilli, honey, lemon curd, fresh mint, cardamom and pistachio, nutmeg, vanilla, raspberry, ginger and coffee as well as classic plain chocolate truffles.

Claire and Andy's passion is reflected not just in their pure, fresh chocolates but also in their modern, vibrant packaging.

SALLY CLARKE

Kensington High Street
London W8
☎ 0207 221 9225
www.sallyclarke.com
Sally Clarke is a well-known perfectionist - that goes for her restaurant as well as her adjoining bakery where the breads and the hand-made chocolates are among the most popular in town.

THE CHOCOLATE GOURMET

16 Castle Street
Ludlow SY8 1AT
☎ 01584 879332
69 Wyle Cop
Shrewsbury SY1 1UX
☎ 01743 343477
www.chocmail.co.uk
Janette Rowlatt stocks an expertly chosen range of some of the most sophisticated chocolates - including over 30 single origin bars - in the UK. The Chocolate Gourmet is another jewel in Ludlow's crown which is now accepted as the gastronomic capital of the west where 'stars' of the kitchen include Shaun Hill of the Merchant House. Janette has recently opened her second shop in Shrewsbury.

THE CHOCOLATE SOCIETY

Clay Pit Lane
Roecliffe, Boroughbridge
N. Yorkshire YO51 9LS
☎ 01423 322230 fax 01423 322253
e-mail: info@chocolate.co.uk
www.chocolate.co.uk
Alan Porter
London shop: 36 Elizabeth Street
Belgravia, London SW1W 9NZ.
☎ 0207 259 9222 fax: 0207 259 9666
Everything the enthusiastic chocolate lover and maker needs. The Chocolate Society is committed to elevating chocolate to its rightful status as one of the world's gourmet treasures. The Chocolate Society was born over a glass of wine at the 1990 Harrogate Gift Fair out of a frustration at the mediocre chocolates available in Britain. Its founders Alan and Nicola Porter nurtured their chrysalis of a campaign for better chocolate and a desire for the public to know what 'real' chocolate really is and what is happening in the chocolate world. Not quite realising what they had started, the Porters were surprised at the speed with which they had caught people's imagination and were soon flooded with enquiries. And the rest is history. Fifteen years on the Chocolate Society distributes a newsletter to its members twice a year which contains news about chocolate and the cocoa industry, who's who in chocolate, chocolate recipes and of course a comprehensive list of ingredients and products.

All the Chocolate Society's goodies are hand made and they have an extensive range of chocolates and truffles. I am particularly keen on the Organic Dark (67%) which won the Organic Food Award 2003. It is made from the Criollo bean from a single cocoa plantation in Madagascar, in association with Valrhona. It has an unusual and fabulous melting quality like the richest double cream with hints of tobacco and citrus. CS has also a new range of organic truffles and pralines with an eclectic range of flavours – loved the coffee and cardamom. Plus for a very serious treat, try the truffles, skilfully created with textures and flavours that are worth going back for including deep and dark, raspberry and raisins. Their products, including ice cream, can be ordered via mail order or can be bought from the Chocolate Society shop in Elizabeth Street in Belgravia and now the new shop in Shepherd Market. Can also be found in selected supermarkets and 'real food' shops.

WILLIAM CURLEY

10 Paved Court
Richmond
Surrey TW9 1CZ
☎ 0208 332 3002
William is a rising star. His career has included some of the country's best restaurants including Le Manoir aux Quat'Saisons, La Tante Claire, The Savoy etc., and has developed products for Waitrose and Marks and Spencer. William has also won numerous chocolate and

pastry awards and successes at the Culinary Olympics. As a passionate perfectionist, his skills, tastes and single minded pursuit of the best raw ingredients shine through in every chocolate and pastry he produces.

DUCHY ORIGINALS

The Old Ryde House
393 Richmond Road
East Twickenham TW1 2EF
☎ 0208 831 6800
www.duchyoriginals.com
Hardly a chocolate maker you may think but Duchy Originals produce some excellent chocolate products and the philosophy of the company is very dear to my heart. Duchy Originals is the company established by His Royal Highness the Prince of Wales in 1990 to encourage more sustainable methods of farming and food production and to raise funds for the Prince of Wales' Trust, a charitable foundation. Duchy produce a number of products nearly all of which are made from natural ingredients sourced from organic production systems. Duchy's Applemint Thins are made with 70% organic chocolate and flavoured with natural oils, these thin chocolate wafers are also made with ginger, tangerine and plain. Featuring ginger again, (a personal weakness) I loved the Chocolate Coated Stem Ginger Sticks and also the Mediterranean Orange Peel. Duchy Originals' chocolate is one of the few luxury organic chocolates with packaging to match. Currently stocked by most good supermarkets and delicatessens across the country.

FORTNUM AND MASON

Piccadilly
London W1A 1ER
☎ 0207 734 8040 fax 0207 437 3278
The history of Fortnum's dates back to 1707 when William Fortnum, footman in the Royal Household of Queen Anne, persuaded Hugh Mason to join him as a partner in setting up a grocery shop. Connected from the beginning with service to the Royal Family, Fortnum and Mason has served twelve successive monarchs and has been involved in most events of historical significance, from supplying troops in the Napoleonic Wars to providing provisions for the first successful Everest ascent in 1953, and more recently during the Falkland and Bosnian conflicts.

From the mid 19th century, chocolate became a delicacy to be eaten as well as a popular drink. Early records are incomplete but in the late 1920's, when Mr. Pain, Fortnum's *chocolatier* first trained there, the Chocolate Department was fully established. A 1927 Fortnum's catalogue lists a variety of 50 chocolates and, nearly 70 years later, the majority of them are still available and made with the same care. The story of Mr. Pain and Fortnum and Mason are entwined. Mr William Pain, late of Audrey's Chocolates in Hove, had been making chocolates for over 75 years. He started work in De Panny, New Oxford Street, soon after the Great War and moved to Fortnum's in the late 1920s when Fortnum's was still importing is own cocoa beans from Trinidad, Java, Maracaiba and Venezuela. Mr. Pain found himself making chocolate fondants, hand dipped nuts, caramels, creams, nougats and marzipans that were already part of the chocolate tradition. It is the variety that reflects the marriage between the *chocolatier* and confectioner that is now regarded as typically British and is increasingly difficult to obtain as traditional craftsmanship is deposed by mechanisation. During the War, Fortnum's introduced its 'service chocolate' in a distinctive pink wrapper, which was ordered by the Ministry of Food for the officers' survival kit. It was this bitter chocolate that became the coating for the famous Fortnum's slimline peppermint and soft green fondant.

By the start of the Second World War, the Fortnum and Mason Chocolate Factory had been moved from Piccadilly to Brewer Street, and, under Mr Floris, a talented Hungarian refugee, and with Mr. Pain as the General Manager, it was formed into a separate company wholly supplying the shop. However, in 1948, the new Canadian owner of Fortnum's decided to restore the theatre of chocolate to the fifth floor and, employed Mr. Pain's number 2, Chris Wolf, leaving Mr. Floris and his general manager to fend for themselves. As a result, Floris' Chocolatier was conceived and successfully found its own market for exquisite chocolates. The two factories and shop co-existed with the occasional exchange of temperamental chocolate dippers until 1961. After Mr. Floris' death, Mr. Pain and his wife retired to buy a small chocolate factory 'Audrey's' where the traditions learnt in Piccadilly are still practised today by Mr. Pain's successors. Chris Wolf stayed on at Fortnum and Mason until the 1980s when manufacture finally ceased in Piccadilly. In 1983, contact with Audrey's was made and the old partnership renewed.

Today, Fortnum and Mason's chocolate department is blessed with the talents of Chloe Doutre Roussel. Chloe is considered supreme among chocolate tasters with super sensitive, analytical taste buds and a keen knowledge of all things chocolate. You will find some of the world's best chocolates including Amedei, Valrhona, Michel Cluizel and if you have ever felt like eating your tool-kit or pair of scissors, you can buy them fashioned by the multi-award winning Italian chocolate 'sculptor' Andrea Slitti.

SARA JAYNE'S TRUFFLES

53 Cavendish Road
London SW12 0BL
☎ 020 8673 6300 fax 020 8673 6543
mobile 07889 874808
sarajaynestanes@aoca.org.uk

Now you wouldn't expect me to leave out my own chocolates, would you? They are among the finest hand made chocolate truffles, made with one of the world's best couvertures: Amedei and ingredients including fresh green pistachios, cardamom, chilli, Szechuan Pepper, Earl Grey tea, Maldon Sea Salt and a variety of Eau de Vies, nuts, spices and alcohols by mail order. Made for people who simply adore chocolate and are designed to fit an expectant mouth ... as smooth as a kiss ... and veritably hand-made - not a machine in sight! I tend to produce truffles these days for pleasure rather than for the bank!

KSCHOCOLAT

Merchant Square
Candleriggs
Glasgow
☎ 0141 553 1978
www.kschocolat.com

At Kscholat you can sit and drink or eat any one or more of your favourite continental chocolates – they stock over 120 varieties – at this popular Glasgow chocolate-café-cum-boutique.

JAMES CHOCOLATES

Leighton Lane
Evercreech
Shepton Mallett
Somerset BA4 6LQ
www.bar-chocolat.com

James Hutchins has a penchant for the best quality ingredients. He uses Cacao Barry couvertures, 'Fleur de cao' for his range of handmade chocolates including chocolate boxes actually made from chocolate full of different varieties; and paper thin wafers of orange and cardamom, mocha Java etc.

James is an entirely self-taught chocolate maker who produces some unusual varieties in his own unique recipes including real raspberries, rhubarb and cream, peaches, sun-dried bananas, Aztec spice, vanilla pod. All ingredients are natural products. No artificial additives, preservatives or sweeteners are used. Everything bursts with fresh, natural flavours. James Hutchins James now owns three specialist chocolate café bars in Clifton Village Bristol, Bath and Selfridges in Birmingham called 'bar chocolat'. An environment dedicated to the enjoyment of all things made from proper chocolate, 'bar chocolate' serves 'The Ultimate Hot Chocolate' full of real chocolate and cream, cakes, coffee and handmade ice cream while acting as a permanent shop window for the James Chocolate range. Shops are open Monday to Saturday 9am-6pm and 11am-5pm Sunday. The Mall, Clifton Village, Bristol 0117 9747000

LA MAISON DU CHOCOLAT

45-46 Piccadilly
London W1J 0DS
☎ 0207 287 8500
www.lamaisonduchocolat.com

At last. Us chocolate evangelists have been waiting with bated chocolate-breath for the opening of La Maison du Chocolat in London's Piccadilly. And the wait's been worth it. The shop is a hushed, subdued house of worship. Robert Linxe is the champion of the chocolate world and has led the fashion for chocolate in Paris for nearly 30 years. He once described to me the perfect method of mixing a ganache (chocolate and cream) 'you must do absolutely no more then gently move it around, like a mayonnaise...' His ganaches are so light and sublime – and the chocolate is still allowed to 'speak for itself'. Try Caracas – just plain and decidedly dark ... an emulsion of truly divine proportions or flavours such as basil and jasmine. They glow in the mouth!

MARASU

79 Boileau Road
Ealing W5 3AP
☎ 0208 998 2222 fax 0208 998 4555

Marasu is a derivative of the names of Rolf Kern's three children: Martin, Rainer and Susanna. As one of the most experienced German pâtissiers, Rolf Kern now runs a chocolate-confectionery manufacturing unit in a 400 square metre purpose built block in Park Royal, London. He supplies nearly all the top London hotels and many of the capital's restaurants and specialist chocolate outlets and a number of airlines. If it is a petit four, Rolf probably makes it. Marasu's portfolio of petits fours and truffles runs into more than a 100 varieties - too many to 'road test' here but Rolf Kern's chocolate enrobed saffron and ginger 'fudge' is a sensation. The result is clean and sweet but perfectly balanced with a gentle sour finish leaving the mouth tingling and begging for more. A lingering memory. Stocked by Fortnum and Mason.

PIERRE MARCOLINI

6 Lancer Square
London W8 4EH
☎ 0207 935 6611
www.pierremarcolini.co.uk
Pierre Marcolini is another small producer who makes a range of his own chocolate from bean to bar and then lets his imagination run riot with his vast collection. Using white, milk and of course dark it extends from a ganache with jasmine tea filling to a lemon and lime fondant to a champagne truffle. The outcome can be exciting, surprising, stunning or simply luscious, but in all cases, pleasurable and memorable. I love his single bean bars from Madagascan plantations with cocoa 'feves' (beans) to give an exciting crunch. Also his Pistachio 'Marzipans' are a must for marzipan freaks (and that's me). Another addition to the range is his single bean chocolate pastries. (Pierre has won numerous awards as a pâtissier). The Venezuelan (pastry) is with a cinnamon ganache and caramelised pecans; the Madagascan is with a saffron cream and the Ecuador with a raspberry compote. £4.75 each. The shop is a haven for chocolate lovers and David Colic and Deborah O'Neil make chocolate shopping a real pleasure.

PLAISIR DU CHOCOLAT

251 Canongate
Edinburgh EH8 8BQ
☎ 0131 556 9524
www.plaisirduchocolat.com
Considered by those 'in the know' in Edinburgh to be among the best source of chocolate and chocolate products in the city. Its extensive collection changes twice a year and has no less than 15 varieties of hot chocolate. Customers are encouraged to learn about and enjoy their chocolate as they would a fine wine. Stockists of Amedei.

THE NADELL PATISSERIE

9 White Lion Street
London N1 9HJ
☎ 0207 833 2461 fax 0207 713 5036
The Nadell Patisserie makes the most sensational three tier chocolate wedding cake with extraordinary sugar work decoration at which Michel is considered by his peers to be best in the country. To order only. Also top of the range chocolates, patisserie and Danish but for the Trade only. All private orders considered.

ROCOCO

321 King's Road
London SW3 5EP
☎ 0207 352 5857 fax 0207 352 7360
also 45 Marylebone High Street
London W1U 5HG
www.rococochocolates.com
Near the 'S' bend in the King's Road a mile and a bit from Sloane Square you will find this perfectly formed artisan's shop, designed by the irrepressible Chantal Coady. Chantal comes from an art school background and is blessed with a flair and good taste for chocolate. Between them as independent retailers, Chantal Coady together with Nicola and Alan Porter of the Chocolate Society contributed more for the profile of 'real' chocolate in this country in the 90s than anyone else achieved in twice that time in the latter part of the twentieth century. Since 1983 when it was opened, as well as some of the world's finest chocolates, Rococo has continually provided a delightful theatre of colours and shapes which change with the seasons and the 'festivals' of the year. The windows are piled high with a flourish of ribbons, bags and boxes, and appears more lavish and extravagant than many of the shops you will find on the chocolate-versed continent. Rococo specialises in handmade bars made exclusively for the

shop with many 'original' ingredients with surprising affinities to chocolate. The Grand Cru bars are made from the world's finest cocoa beans and include Valrhona's Manjari, which is a uniquely fruity chocolate made from a single bean - the Trinitario "with notes of red berries and citrus fruits". A second shop opened in 2004.

GERARD RONAY

gerard.ronay@lineone.net
Gerard is one of Britain's most artistically talented *chocolatiers*. He is among the few who have been honoured by Paris' famous Club des Croqueurs (See Paris Guide). He now practises on a small scale producing the most amazing 'one-off' chocolate sculptures and paintings. He will consider any private order however large or small. He also teaches and give demonstrations and workshops and spends as much time as possible (as he says) 'out on the road spreading the gospel - trying to get more people to appreciate the potential of chocolate.'

Other Chocolate Suppliers and Shops

AMEDEI

29 Via San Gervasio
56020 (La Rotta) Pisa
Italy

☎ 00 39 (0) 587 484849
www.amedei.it
Chocolate in another league! Also available in the UK through Laura King at King's Caviar 0208 894 1111

BARRY CALLEBAUT UK

Wildmere Industrial Estate
Banbury Oxon OX16 3UU
☎ 01295 224700
www.barry-callebaut.com
(For trade callers only - but you can buy this world famous chocolate from Ritter Courivaud - See further on in list of suppliers).

BETTYS and TAYLORS

1 Parliament Street
Harrogate
North Yorkshire HG1 2QU
☎ 01423 50746
www.bettysandtaylors.co.uk
Also at Ilkley, Northallerton and York. Famous family run tearooms offering very English chocolates.

CARLUCCIO'S

28a Neal Street
London WC2H 9PS
☎ 0207 240 1487 fax 0207 497 1361
Carluccio's, in fact, specialises in all sorts of Italian foods of which chocolate plays a big part. Especially worth the trip are the *Cioccolato Artiganale Fondente* (handmade Italian chocolates) and a fabulous traditional chocolate drink.

CHOCOLATERIE DE L'OPERA IN THE UK

Grivan Products Company Limited
Unit 5, Deptford Trading Estate
Blackhorse Road
London SE8 5HY
☎ 0208 692 6993 fax 0208 691 2053
You can buy Chocolaterie de l'Opera from L'Artisan du Chocolat.

DAYLESFORD ORGANIC FARM SHOP

Daylesford
Near Kingham, GL55 0YG
☎ 01608 731700 fax 01608 731701
www.daylesfordorganic.com

DIVINE CHOCOLATE

The Day Chocolate Company
4 Gainsford Street
London SE1 2NE
☎ 020 7378 6550
www.divinechocolate.com
Divine and Dubble carry the Fairtrade Mark. This is an independent guarantee from the Fairtrade Foundation that the chocolate is made with cocoa beans bought under internationally agreed Fairtrade terms and conditions. These include a guaranteed, secure price above the world market price for cocoa, an extra social premium payment, long term trading contracts, decent health and safety conditions and a commitment to support for community programmes aimed at empowering farmers to increase their abilities to be self sufficient.

For the UK consumer Fairtrade is about being able to make the choice to take part in a dignified trading relationship. Buying Fairtrade is a very simple choice, as Mr Ohemeng, Managing Director of Kuapa Kokoo, a co-operative of over 30,000 Ghanaian cocoa farmers, points out 'We all have to go shopping, and Fairtrade is just going shopping with a bit of respect.' Divine chocolate is widely available and in most supermarkets.

EL REY

Esquina calles 5 y 7, Parcela B3-01
Urbanizacion La Urbina, Caracas
Venezuela
☎ 58 (2) 242 6874 fax 58 (2) 241 1250
elrey@bg.net
Available in the UK from HB Ingredients
01435 812808

KEYLINK LIMITED

Green Lane
Ecclesfield
Sheffield S35 9WY
☎ 0114 245 5400 fax 0114 245 5600
www.keylink.co.uk
Everything for the professional and amateur chocolate maker, from equipment and accessories, to a variety of couvertures and cocoa products to boxes and packaging. I use them all the time and they are without equal. They don't stock the very best superior couvertures like Cacao Barry or Valrhona but what they do offer is very close in quality and half the price, and they are terribly nice people. All orders under £100 are charged postage and packing. Over £100 are free.

MORTIMER AND BENNETT

33 Turnham Green Terrace
Chiswick
London W4 1RG
☎ 0208 995 4145 fax 0208 742 3088
www.mortimer-bennett.co.uk
Full range of single cocoa bean chocolate varieties from Bonnat and the infamous Kama Sutra, don't need any begging to be bought from this eclectic super food shop.

RITTER COURIVAUD

17 Northfield Estate
Beresford Avenue
Wembley
Middlesex HA0 1GJ
☎ 0208 903 7177 fax 0208 900 1215
www.rittercourivaud.co.uk
Marvellous selection of ingredients for the chocolate and pastry chef. Importers and distributors of fine foods including specialist products such as: nuts, dried fruits, spices, 'arômes', compounds, oils, chocolate products and couverture including Cacao Barry and Callebaut.

TOWN and COUNTRY CHOCOLATES

52 Oxford Road
Uxbridge
Middlesex UB9 4DH
☎ 01895 256166 fax 01895 257700
www.tcfinefoods.co.uk
Various couvertures including the stunning Swiss Karma, pre-moulded shells, chocolate ingredients, marzipans, gold leaf, compounds and flavourings etc.

VALRHONA FACTORY SHOP

14, Avenue de Président Roosevelt
Tain l'Hermitage, France
☎ 00 33 75 07 90 62
www.valrhona.fr

VALVONA and CROLLA

19 Elm Row
Edinburgh EH7 4AA
☎ 0131 556 6066 fax: 0131 556 1668
www.valvonacrolla.co.uk
Aladdin's cave with genuinely agreeable and thoroughly knowledgable food lovers who stock Amedei and Valrhona; Café Tasse; Spanish Chocovic and Belgian Delfin, with unusual range of flavours including red pepper and pink peppercorns.

Department Stores

HARRODS

Brompton Road
London SW3
☎ 0207 730 1234
This world famous Knightsbridge store boasts the largest selection of chocolate available anywhere in the country offering Belgian, German, Swiss, French, Swiss and English varieties. Harrods also has chocolate kitchen paraphernalia.

HARVEY NICHOLS

Sloane Street
(corner of Knightsbridge)
London SW1
☎ 0207 235 5000
Also Manchetser, Leeds and Edinburgh
The Food Hall is world famous and also has a much-vaunted restaurant The Fifth Floor. It opened in 1992 along with the rest of the Fifth Floor at Harvey Nichols. The idea was to create an all-encompassing contemporary environment for specialist food retailing, fine dining, casual café, serious cocktail bar all within a unique fashion retail business. As well as its own label range of chocolate, Harvey Nichols also stocks Amedei, The Chocolate Society, Valrhona and Enric Rovira among other world famous brands.

SELFRIDGES

Oxford Street (near Marble Arch)
London W1
☎ 0207 629 1234
Another top department store, which makes a point of carrying a diverse range of premium products from across the world - some exclusive to Selfridges for example, Ghiradelli from the United States.

SUPERMARKETS like Safeway, Sainsbury, Tesco and Waitrose have moved on from the 'old days' when the only chocolate available was 'cake covering' (an invention of the Devil and to be avoided) and currently sell many different types of good plain bitter, milk and white. For example, Sainsbury has its own 72% but also stocks The Chocolate Society and Valrhona which is well worth paying the (lot) extra for; and Waitrose also stocks its own delicious brands as well as organic and some of the better known and loved.

CHOCOLATE AT TEATIME

You can find some great chocolate pastries and desserts among the afternoon teas - and menus - at the Dorchester, the Connaught, Claridge's, The Ritz, Harrods, The Wolseley in Piccadilly, Le Manoir aux Quat' Saisons in Oxfordshire, Winteringham Fields in Humberside and Betty's in York.

Chocolate Courses

BALLYMALOE COOKERY SCHOOL

Shanagarry
Midleton
Co. Cork, Ireland
☎ 00 353 21 646785
fax 00 353 21 646909

CONFIDENT COOKING

PO Box 841 Devizes
Wiltshire SN10 3ST
☎ 01380 840396

LE CORDON BLEU CULINARY ACADEMY

114 Marylebone Lane
London W1M 6HH
☎ 0207 935 3503
www.cordonbleu.edu

LEITH'S SCHOOL OF FOOD AND WINE
21 St Albans Grove, London W8 5BP
☎ 0207 229 0177 fax 0207 937 5257
www.leiths.com

THE TANTE MARIE SCHOOL OF COOKERY
Woodham House
Carlton Road, Woking
Surrey GU21 4HF
☎ 01483 726957 fax 01483 724173
www.tantemarie.co.uk
Also check out your local a colleges for example Thames Valley University in Ealing runs the best pâtisserie (including chocolate) courses for professionals.

Chocolate Exhibitions and Festivals

CHOCOLATE WEEK
The Studio
3 Thorney Hedge Road, Chiswick
London W4 5SB
☎ 020 8630 9214
enquiries@chocolateweek.co.uk
www.chocolateweek.co.uk
Annually across Britain in October/November.

CADBURY WORLD
Linden Road, Bournville
Birmingham B30 2LD
☎ 0121 433 4334
www.cadbury.co.uk

EUROCHOCOLATE FESTIVAL
Perugia, Italy
www.chocolate.perugia.it
Annually in October

MUSEUM OF COCOA AND CHOCOLATE
13 Grand Place, 1000 Brussels
☎ 02 514 20 48 fax: 02 514 52 05
Open: 10am - 5pm - closed Monday

SALON DU CHOCOLAT
Espace Eiffel-Branley, Paris
Enquiries: 70 Rue de la Tour
75116 Paris
☎ 00 33 145 03 21 26
fax 00 33 1 45 03 40 04
www.chocoland.tm.fr
October/November

Other Useful Addresses

CHOCOLATIER MAGAZINE
Subscriptions: PO Box 33
Mt. Morris, Il. 61054
Tel: (815) 734 1109
Editorial: 45 West Street 34th Street
New York NY 10001
(212) 239 0855

THE FAIRTRADE FOUNDATION
16, Baldwin Gardens
London EC1N 7RJ
☎ 0207 405 5942 fax 0207 405 5943
www.fairtrade.org.uk
The Fairtrade Foundation which started in Britain in 1992 is a charity and independent certification body, supported by Christian Aid, Oxfam, Cafod, the National Federation of Women's Institutes, Traidcraft Exchange and the World Development Movement. It also gets help from the European Union. It aims to tackle poverty in the Third World by offering British consumers the opportunity to buy products that offer a fair deal for the producers - so when you see a packet of tea, coffee, chocolate (like Green and Black, Divine Milk Chocolate, Equal Exchange chocolate-covered Brazil Nuts and Organic Cocoa) with the stamp of the Fairtrade Foundation you know that this is a guarantee that a better price has been paid to the growers and that you are helping to prevent thousands of farmers and producers throughout the Third World from exploitation by large unscrupulous companies. You are supporting minimum wages, adequate housing, minimum health, safety and environmental standards. The products which qualify for the Fairtrade mark are strictly and constantly monitored.

THE INTERNATIONAL COCOA ORGANIZATION (ICCO)
22 Berners Street
London W1P 3DB
☎ 0207 637 3211 fax 0207 631 0114
www.icco.org
In 1973 the (ICCO) was set up to manage the Buffer Stock (a specified tonnage of cocoa beans) mechanism which was designed to stabilise world cocoa prices and protect cocoa farmers. The Buffer stock was actually liquidated in 1994 but the ICCO still exists as the main world forum for the gathering and dissemination of information on cocoa, for the promotion of cocoa research and studies of the economics of cocoa production, consumption and distribution and for the encouragement of development projects concerning cocoa.

THE INTERNATIONAL COCOA GENE BANK
The Cocoa Research Unit
The University of the West Indies
St. Augustine
Trinidad
001 868 662 2002
www.dcms.uwi.tt/cru/cra.asp

THE COCOA RESEARCH UNIT
SCHOOL OF PLANT SCIENCES
THE UNIVERSITY OF READING
Whitenights
Reading RG6 6AS
☎ 0118 931 6467
www.plantsci.rdg.ac.uk

ROYAL BOTANIC GARDENS
Kew, Richmond
Surrey TW9 3AB
☎ 020 8332 5000
www.rbgkew. org.
Among many other special and rare plants you can see a living cocoa tree.

THE EDEN PROJECT
Bodelva
St. Austell
Cornwall PL 24 2SG
☎ 01726 811932
www.edenproject.com
Small cocoa plantation growing in one of its tropical 'pods'.

Chocolate in Mexico

MEXICAN MINISTRY OF TOURISM
41 Trinity Square
London EC3 4VJ
☎ 020 7488 9392
www.visitmexico.com

Advice on chocolate tours in Mexico

LA HACIENDA DE LOS MORALES
Vazquez de Mella 525
Polanco C.P
11510 Mexico, DF
☎ 52 (5) 281 4554

LA TABERNA DEL LEON
Plaza Loreto San Angel
52 (5) 616 3951
Modern Mexican food and the chef loves chocolate.

CATHY MATOS MEXICAN TOURS
75 St. Margaret's Avenue
Whetstone
London N20 9LD
☎ 020 8492 0000
Specialises in tours to Mexico.

Chocolate in Venezuela

BILLY ESSER
Hacienda Bucare
Chacaracual
Rio Caribe 6164
Estado Sucre
Venezuela
☎ 58 96 465 2003 fax 58 96 456 2004
This stunning part of the world is where you can stay amongst the cocoa trees and learn to make chocolate the 'local' way. This 'Hacienda with rooms' is extensively civilised for tourists and the perfect place to enjoy a constant supply of chocolate from the source. UK Travel arrangements through Geodyssey 0207 281 7788
www.geodyssey.co.uk

Suppliers of Equipment

CREEDS (Southern)
New Street
Waddesdon
Aylesbury
Bucks HP18 OLR
☎ 01296 658849 fax 01296 658443
www.creeds.uk.com
Equipment and disposables to the baking trade including pastry bags, dipping forks, moulds, etc.

CONTINENTAL CHEF SUPPLIES
Unit 4c, South Hetton Industrial Estate
South Hetton
Co. Durham DH6 2UZ
☎ 0191 526 4107 fax 0191 526 8399
Professional and specialist equipment (moulds, knives, cutters, stencils, bakeware, patisserie products) etc. Will source one-offs and 'made-to-measure' cake frames etc.

DIVERTIMENTI
33 Marylebone High Street
London W1H 9LE
☎ 020 7935 0689

139-141 Fulham Road
South Kensington
London SW3 6SD
☎ 020 7581 8065
www.divertimenti.co.uk
Hotch potch of good kitchen equipment - not particularly choc specialist but often have interesting chocolate items. Also run workshops and demonstrations.

FALCON CATERING EQUIPMENT
PO Box 37, Foundry Loan, Larbert
Stirlingshire, Scotland FK5 4PL
☎ 01324 554221 fax 01324552211
(Trade Enquiries only)
Great cookers. Available through the John Lewis Partnership stores.

M. FISH LIMITED
7 Faraday Close
Oakwood Business Park
Clacton on Sea
Essex CO15 4TR
☎ 01255 475964 fax 01255 221125
Wonderful boxes in stock and made to order.

LAKELAND LIMITED
Alexandra Building
Windermere
Cumbria LA23 1SQ
☎ 015394 88100 fax 015394 88300
www.lakelandlimited.com
Lots of goodies including baking equipment, chocolate essence (exclusive to Lakeland), 'real' vanilla essence, aprons etc. etc. Telephone for catalogue.

PETER JONES/THE JOHN LEWIS GROUP - all over the country but I use:
Sloane Square
London SW1
☎ 0207 730 3434
Good range of baking equipment, baking parchment, etc. limited but useful range of

chocolate tools and mould at Christmas, Valentine and Easter. Fantastic range of knives at best prices.

B.R. MATHEWS & SONS
12 Gypsy Hill
Upper Norwood
London SE10 1NN
☎ 0208 670 0788
Extensive range of cake tins, boards, cake decorating equipment, chocolate, moulds, etc.

KENWOOD
New Lane
Havant
Hants PO9 2NH
☎ 01705 476000
'Longlife' Hand whisks and other top class electrical products including Kenwood 'Chef', etc. Available through all good deparment stores and electrical shops nationwide.

MEYER PRESTIGE (UK)
Wirral International Business Park
Riverview Road
Bromborough
Wirral CH62 3RH
☎ 0151 482 8000
Makes of terrific cookware. Circulon saucepans which are brilliant for using (carefully) when melting chocolate. You can find them in most good department stores.

MAGIMIX/GELATO
19 Bridge Street
Godalming
Surrey GU7 1HY
☎ 01483 427411
Best ice cream machines and also one of the original and best food processors. Available through all good department stores and electrical shops nationwide.

DAVID MELLOR
4, Sloane Square
London SW1W 8EE
☎ 0207 730 4259
The Round Building
Hathersage, Sheffield
S32 1BA
☎ 01433 650220
Variety of good desirable kitchen equipment - with useful selection of chocolate tools.

VANTAGE HOUSE
72 High Street, Brighton
East Sussex BN2 1RP
☎ 01273 645000 fax 01273 645009
www.vantagehouse.org
Chocolate course, equipment and machinery i.e. melting kettles (bain maries), tempering and enrobing machines.

VICTORINOX KNIVES
Burton McCall
163 Parker Drive
Leicester LE4 0JP
☎ 0116 235 1111 fax 0116 235 0069
Make marvellous knives which I find indispensible for chopping chocolate. Widely available.

Chocolate Sites – The best on the web for online chocolate lovers
www.chocs.com
Lots about good chocolate and its origins.
www.chocexpress.com
Interesting and varied selection of chocolate to buy.
www.chocoholic.com
Chocolate shopping from all corners of America and Europe
www.chocolate.com
Large links page to many other chocolate sites from Cadbury to 'Chocolate Perfume'
www.chocolatetradingco.com
Good site to navigate. Offers wide

selection of quality chocolate.
www.choco.com/faq.html
Answers to questions such as 'Can I give chocolate to my dog?'
www.payoung.net
Currently Paul Young, one of the ones to watch on the London chocolate scene, devotes himself to running 'live' demonstrations and workshops for beginners and experts alike.
www.seventypercent.com
Martin Christy is a real enthusiast and has put together a fun and informative way to learn about chocolate on line. Seventypercent.com stocks some of the very best including Amedei, Michel Cluizel, Valrhona. etc. Also has news and views and lists 'what's going on' including shows and exhibitions and Chocolate Week.
www.chocophile.com
US Clay Gordon's on-line chocolate discussions, news, views and sources.
www.thecocoatree.co.uk
Small Devon based company using organic chocolate made from Fair Trade Venezuelan and Guyanan beans. Also using local seasonal ingredients including wild elderflowers and wild blackberries.
www.scharffenberger.com
Scharffen Berger, the home of one of America's first and best 'artisan' chocolate manufacturer.
www.greenandblacks.com
The home of Green and Black's organic chocolate.

BIBLIOGRAPHY

Barry Callebaut, *Chocolate from A - Z*, Flammarion, Paris, 1997; Dr. Basil Bartley, Various papers on cacao genetics and origins 1999; Carole Bloom, *The International Dictionary of Desserts, Pastries and Confections*, Hearst Books, New York 1995; Carole Bloom, *The Art of Chocolate Tasting*, Paper Oxford Food Symposium 1998; Carole Bloom, *All About Chocolate*, Macmillan USA 1998; Shirley Bond, *Home Measures*, Grub Street 1996; W.A. Cadbury, *Labour in Portuguese W.Africa 1910*; Chantal Coady, *The Chocolate Companion*, Apple Press 1995; Christian Constant, *Le Chocolat: du Nectar à la Ambroisie*, Nathan, Paris 1988; Sophie D Coe and Michael D Coe, *The True History of Chocolate*, Thames and Hudson 1996;

Bernal Diaz del Castillo, *The True History of the Conquest of Mexico* 1568, translated by Maurice Keating, George G. Harrap Company, London;

Cat Cox, *Chocolate Unwrapped*, The Women's Environmental Network 1993;

L. Russell Cook, *Chocolate Production and Use*, Rv'sd Dr E.H. Meursing, Harcourt Brace Jovanovich, New York, 1988; Eileen M. Chat, *Cocoa: Cultivation Processing Analysis*, Interscience Publishers, London / NY 1953; Robin Dand, *The International Cocoa Trade*, Woodhead Publishing, 1993; Ivan Day, Paper Oxford Food Symposium 1998; Robert Fitzgerald, *Rowntree and the Marketing Revolution 1862-1969*, Cambridge University Press 1996; Thomas Gage, *The English American, His Travail 1648 Sea and Land, or New Survey of the West Indies*; AG Gardiner, George Cadbury 1923; Sylvie Girard et Jacques Pessis, *Souvenirs En Chocolat*, Editions Mille et Une Nuits, 1997; Hannah Glasse, *The Art of Cookery Made Plain and Easy - By A Lady*, 1747; Martin Gonzalez de la Varra, *Historia del chocolate en Mexico*, Nestlé Mexico, 1990; RS Hammond, *The Growth of Food Policy vol 1*, HMSO and Longmans

and Green & Co. 1951; Brandon Head, *The Food of the Gods*, George Routledge & Sons 1903; Historicus, (Cadbury), *Cocoa: All About It*, Sampson Low Marston 1892; Hammond Innes, *The Conquistadors*, Collins, 1969; Cath Kerry, *The Haigh's Book of Chocolate*, Wakefield Press, South Australia 1998; Ron Lees, *A History of Sweet and Chocolate Manufacture*, Specialised Publications 1988;

Prue Leith and Caroline Waldegrave *Leith's Cookery Bible*, Bloomsbury 1991; Anthony Lejeune, *White's - The First Three Hundred Years*, A&C Black, 1993; Caroline Liddell and Robin Weir, *Ices - The Definitive Guide*, Grub Street, 1995; Robert Linxe, *La Maison de Chocolat*, Robert Laffont, 1992; Elisabeth Luard, *The Princess and the Pheasant*, Bantam Press 1987; Laura Mason, *Sugar-Plums and Sherbert*, Prospect Books 1998; Menon, *La Science de Maitre d'Hotel and Confiseur* - circa 1700; Ministry of Defence Admiralty Library Collection of Notes on Health of the Navy *'How Seamen Are Fed'* 1867; Marie-Pierre Moine, *Cuisine Grand Mère*, Barrie & Jenkins 1991; Rémy Montavon, *Nestlé and cocoa*, Nestec Limited, 1992; Marcia & Frederic Morton, *Chocolate An Illustrated History*, Crown NY 1988; Adrianne Marcus, *The Chocolate Bible*, Longman, Toronto, 1978; Harold McGee, *On Food & Cooking*, Charles Scribner & Sons NY, 1984; D.J. Mela and P.J. Rogers, *Food, Eating and Obesity, The Psychobiological Basis of Appetite and Weight Control*, Chapman and Hall, London 1998; Nestlé, *Henri Nestlé*; Jill Norman, *The Chocolate Lovers Guide to Complete Indulgence*, Dorling Kindersley, 1990; Robert Opie, *Museum Of Advertising*, Pavilion 1988; Beryl Peters, *Etiquette for Chocolate Lovers*, Copper Beech Publishing, 1997; William Hickling Prescott, *The History of the Conquest of Mexico*, Gibbings, London 1843; Elizabeth Raffald, *The Experienced Englifh Houfkeeper, for the Use*

And Ease Of Ladies, Houfkeepers, Cooks etc. 1778; Michel and Albert Roux, *The Roux Brothers on Patisserie*, Macdonald 1986; Michel Roux, *Desserts a Lifelong Passion*, Conran Octopus 1994; Helge Rubinstein, *The Chocolate Book*, 1980; William Salmon, *Family Dictionary or 'Houfhold Companion for ufe of Ladies, Gentlewomen and fuch other Perfons, Whofe Station requires their taking Care of the Houfe'* (sic) 1692;

Skuse's Complete Confectioner, Twelfth Edition W.J. Bush, London 1928; Henry Stubbes, *The Indian Nectar* 1662; Hugh Thomas, *The Conquest of Mexico*, Pimlico 1993; Various, *The Book of Chocolate*; VD Wickizer, *Coffee, Tea, & Cocoa: The Food Research Institute of Economic and Political Analysis*, Stamford University, 1951; C. Anne Wilson, *Food and Drink In Britain*, Constable circa 1970; Wood & Lass, *Cocoa* 4th Edition, Longman; Allen M Young, *The Chocolate Tree*, Smithsonian Institute, 1994; Various articles in *The New Scientist*, *The Guardian*, *The Times*, *The Telegraph*.

FURTHER SOURCES OF INFORMATION: Anthropological Museum, Mexico City; Biscuit, Chocolate, Cake and Confectionery Alliance (BCCCO); British Library, Euston, London NW1; Cadbury's Library, Bournville; International Cocoa Organisation (ICCO); Imperial War Museum, London SE1; Guildhall Library EC4; Latin American Centre, London, SW1; Ministry of Defence Admiralty Library; Mexican Ministry of Tourism, London SW1; Wandsworth Library SW11.

GENERAL INDEX

RECIPE INDEX